FROM THE BABE TO THE BEARDS

FROM THE BABE TO THE BEARDS

The Boston Red Sox in the World Series

BILL NOWLIN & JIM PRIME

SPORTS PUBLISHING

Much of the content in this book was originally published in *The Boston Red Sox World Series Encyclopedia* by Bill Nowlin and Jim Prime (Rounder Books, 2008). This book has been updated and dozens more photographs have been added.

Sports Publishing books may be purchased in bulk at special discounts for sales promotion, corporate gifts, fund-raising, or educational purposes. Special editions can also be created to specifications. For details, contact the Special Sales Department, Sports Publishing, 307 West 36th Street, 11th Floor, New York, NY 10018 or sportspubbooks@skyhorsepublishing.com.

Sports Publishing® is a registered trademark of Skyhorse Publishing, Inc.®, a Delaware corporation.

Visit our website at www.sportspubbooks.com.

10 9 8 7 6 5 4 3 2 1

Library of Congress Cataloging-in-Publication Data is available on file.

Cover design by Owen Corrigan
Cover photo credit: Library of Congress/Bain News Service and Boston Public Library (top) and Associated Press (bottom)

All player profile photographs are supplied by the Boston Public Library, Boston Red Sox, Library of Congress, and Bill Nowlin.

ISBN: 978-1-61321-727-6
Ebook ISBN: 978-1-61321-732-0

Printed in China

CONTENTS

INTRODUCTION

Wе hope that this book rapidly becomes outdated. We would enjoy nothing better than to update it every year.

We're hoping, first of all, that the Red Sox win the World Series again in 2014. And then keep piling up championships like cordwood, though perhaps pausing—with gracious generosity—so that Cubs fans might enjoy that taste of victory that we've savored since 2004. And then back to the winning, until we pass 27 and leave the Yankees in the dust.

The Red Sox are trying to be the team of the twenty-first century. Yankees fans can wallow in the glories of the past. In this century, the Red Sox hold a 3-1 edge. That's not a bad start. Kids born in 2001 are already more than twelve years old. They might not even know what it's all about. A curse? 1918?

The older among us, grizzled souls that we are, can remember some of the calamitous defeats of days gone by.

Four times in a row, the Red Sox took World Series to a Game Seven, and lost every time. That builds character, in teams and in fans. The Red Sox have won their last three World Series with relative ease, without one of them requiring a Game Seven. Will today's Sox kids grow up with a feeling of entitlement? Let's hope to Heaven they carry themselves with more humility than Yankees fans from the Olden Days. After all, those who don't learn from the past are condemned to relive it.

Not only did Boston lose every World Series after 1918 through 1986, there were plenty of times the Sox fell just short of reaching the Fall Classic—just one win short in 1948, 1949, 1972, 1978, and 2003. There was a great deal of agony, and very little ecstasy in those finishes. Those who say that anticipation is better than realization are fooling themselves.

It is true that recalling the years the Red Sox made the Series, but ultimately lost out, just doesn't seem as painful anymore. A few short years ago, no one wanted to hear about 1918 ever again. The sarcastic chants—"1918! 1918!"—from Yankee fans cut like a knife and the date became a profanity of sorts. The scars have healed now, and there really do exist sentient human beings who can't exactly remember the details of 2003. Grady Little? Who was that?

In this book we are able to offer a deeper context, and look at past disappointments with less angst and more perspective. Suddenly, somehow, it's OK to talk about 1918. And why not? After all we won that year too. And even 1986. We can now *look* back at that year instead of *flashing* back to it. Sort of. For those of you who lived through it, try reading the 1986 entry without closing the book at Game Six. It can be done. In fact we've done it without the benefit of intoxicants of any kind. It doesn't feel as bad now that we have tasted sweet victory. It made the recent victories all the sweeter, in fact.

We now take nothing for granted and savor every success. Let's just make sure that we wear our victory mantle with dignity, so that the phrase "obnoxious Red Sox fan" is oxymoronic. Because there are already enough morons around.

Yes, the history of the Red Sox and the World Series is more than a little unusual—the first two Series they played both ran eight games long (not seven), and the first two of the twenty-first century were four-game sweeps. A remnant of humility should be prompted by the realization that the 2013 world championship win was the first one won and celebrated at Fenway Park in ninety-five years. Both 2004 and 2007 were clinched on the road.

There was one Fall Classic that was over before autumn began, played to completion on September 11. In 1915, Babe Ruth himself was given but one brief pinch-hitting appearance in the first game and was never called on again. And in 1916 and 1918, Ruth contributed but as a starting pitcher with a 3-0 record and an earned run average of 0.87. Babe the hitter had but a single hit in the three World Series combined.

There are the visual moments that stick with us—Fisk's home run in Game Six of the 1975 World Series, the ball that got through Buckner's legs in Game Six, 1986, Papelbon leaping into the air after the final out in '07. There have been well over 100 World Series played to date, and some dramatic ones, but somehow the ones involving the Red Sox seem to stand out—and not just in New England or Red Sox Nation.

Since '86, the Sox have been in the postseason twelve times. The first four times they were swept, or virtually swept, in the first round, for a record of 1-14. In 1999, they made it to the second round but lost there, 1-4. In 2008, they beat the Angels in the first round and then took the LCS into the seventh game, before losing to Tampa Bay.

Four times they've won at least one series with three consecutive backs-to-the-wall elimination game victories—in 1999, 2004, 2007, and 2008. That didn't happen in 2013. They were never even down a game in the Division Series, winning it in four games. They were never down a game in the ALCS. And though they were down two games to one to the Cardinals at one point in 2013, they never faced an elimination game.

And things felt different this time around. It used to be that Red Sox fans lived in fear. You knew better than to get your hopes up too high. Watching a game or listening on radio, there was an ominous cloud hanging low overhead: if something could go wrong, it would. It was just a matter of time. An endless waiting for the other cleat to drop. In 2013, there was some of that, especially in the first half or maybe the first three-quarters of the season. As they got to the playoffs, the cloud seemed to lighten and lift. A ray of sunshine appeared. You know, they could actually win this! Anyone over thirty knew not to get too hopeful, but the familiar foreboding that something *would* go wrong may not have burdened us as badly. Looking ahead to the next game, or the next inning, Sox fans could watch the game unfold without such a heavy history weighing us down.

It was a season that was unexpected. They'd suffered a horrific collapse in 2011 and finished in last place in 2012. Only the 1991 Twins had ever gone from last place one year to world champions the next. Unflappable general manager Ben Cherington made the moves over the winter to solidify what was already a solid, if dysfunctional core, bringing in gamers of good character to help rebuild the sense of team. He brought in—alphabetically—Ryan Dempster, Johnny Gomes, Mike Napoli, David Ross, Koji Uehara, and Shane Victorino. Some of the other additions, such as Joel Hanrahan, tabbed as closer, didn't pan out. But all in all, it worked.

With the Red Sox, it's not just been about the World Series that were, but also the ones that almost were. It's worth remembering this arc that took us from Cy Young in 1903 through the 1912–18 dynasty (the Harry Hooper years) and then up to the present. It was Cy Young to The Babe to the Idiots to the Beards.

2007 was the first time ever that the Sox won the division, the pennant, and the World Series all in the same year. They did it again in 2013.

This new lightness of spirit made for a more enjoyable playoff run. Baseball in Boston can once again be fun. It doesn't have to be agony. For more than a couple of decades, when Doris Kearns Goodwin watched a game at home, she only watched half the game. When the other team was up, she'd leave the room. She didn't want to see it when the opposition rallied. Let's hope she, too, now finds the games easier to take. When the playing field seems more evenly balanced on the scales of history, and fans no longer anticipate defeat, when one can just watch the games and truly feel hopeful, it's a lot more fun.

As for that entitlement issue … we wouldn't want to get to the point where we as fans felt *entitled.* We saw enough of that in another city to the south of Boston. So let's go for the titles and lose the entitlement.

Maybe the Red Sox won't win every year. But we do hope that we'll need to update this edition yet again. And soon!

———————————————

Let's start from the beginning, and it was the beginning. The 1903 World Series was the first of the modern era. The very first World Series was a best-of-nine competition.

1903 WORLD SERIES
BOSTON AMERICANS 5, PITTSBURGH PIRATES 3

Though the 1903 Series began on October 1, it was by no means foreordained. The first public mention of a possible series between the two league leaders hit the newspapers on September 1, 1903. As August ended, the Pittsburgh Pirates held a solid 8 ½ game lead in the NL and the Boston Americans were 9 ½ games ahead of second-place Cleveland. [Before the 1908 season, the Red Sox were known as the Boston Americans.] The *Boston Globe* reported that Americans owner Henry Killilea would be meeting with Pirates owner Barney Dreyfuss to discuss staging a series "between the winning teams

Scorecard from the first World Series, produced by Nuf Ced McGreevey. (Boston Public Library)

of the two major leagues, and play for the championship of the United States." It was not yet called the World Series.

But as late as its September 25 edition, the *Chicago Tribune* headlined "Big Games Will Not Be Played."

Dreyfuss had signed the Pittsburgh ballplayers to contracts that ran through October 15, and therefore would cover any postseason play. All the Boston player contracts expired on September 30, two days after the season ended. Naturally, the Boston players wanted a couple of weeks' extra pay but they also wanted a share in the proceeds. Killilea didn't want to pay either, which predictably pushed the players to discuss other plans, including the possibility of barnstorming New England on their own. After all, they would no longer be legally bound to the Americans. In the end, and at nearly the last minute, a compromise was worked out. Despite their eventual loss in the series, the Pittsburgh players had a more generous owner and actually fared better financially than the champions.

It was on September 26 that the official announcement was made. The *Globe* headline read "World's Series On Again." The games to decide the championship of the United States had, during the course of September, become a more grandiose World's Series. Such was the public interest in the games that the Boston players felt forced to compromise their stance on sharing the revenue, and the games were on.

Five days later, the Series was to begin. Tickets were set at $1.00 apiece, half that for bleachers seats or standing room.

THE GAMES

Game One: Huntington Avenue Grounds, Boston / October 1, 1903

Pittsburgh 7, Boston 3

Pittsburgh	401	100	100	—	7	1	2
Boston	000	000	201	—	3	6	4

WP: Phillippe (1-0)   LP: Young (0-1)   HR: Sebring (1)

The first World Series game ever played took place in Boston, but the Pittsburgh Pirates proved inconsiderate guests, beating the home team, 7-3. A well-rested Cy Young (with a league-leading 28 wins to his credit) started the 3 p.m. game for the Americans and retired the first two batters he faced. During the regular season, Young's record was 28-9, with a 2.08 ERA.

Then the roof fell in, starting with a Tommy Leach ground-rule triple into the roped-off crowd that packed out the outfield. Honus Wagner's single drove in Leach. What followed were three stolen bases, a walk, and a run-producing error by Lou Criger. Jimmy Sebring singled to drive in two more. It was a tough inning— Young struck out the eighth batter, but Criger dropped the ball and Ed Phelps reached first on the misplay. Finally, the Pirates pitcher, Charles "Deacon" Phillippe, struck out for the fourth and final out, but four runs had scored and Boston never recovered.

Hopeful fans milling around the main entrance to the Huntington Avenue Grounds before the third game in Boston. (Boston Public Library)

Phillippe struck out two batters in the first and when he struck out the side in the bottom of the second, the Huntington Avenue Grounds fans expressed appreciation of great pitching with polite applause.

The Pirates added a run in the third and another in the fourth. Sebring's inside-the-park homer in the top of the seventh staked the Pirates to a 7-0 lead before Boston finally put a run on the board. Buck Freeman tripled to the right-field fence and Freddie Parent tripled into the crowd in left. Candy LaChance then drove home Parent with a sacrifice fly. This time applause erupted "like the roll of thunder" (*Boston Globe*). It was 7-2. A Pittsburgh error, a single, and another LaChance sacrifice fly brought home the third Boston run in the bottom of the ninth.

Phillippe (25-9, 2.43 ERA in the regular season) struck out ten and walked none. Young walked three and struck out five, and surrendered 12 hits to Phillippe's six. Boston committed four errors, and four of the seven Pittsburgh runs were unearned. Boston had been 10-8 favorites, but Young may not have been in the best of shape. The *Globe* said he "looked several pounds too heavy." Pittsburgh captain Fred Clarke made several spectacular plays in the field. Leach was 4-for-5, but Sebring's 3-for-5 drove in four runs.

The game took less than two hours to play and was officiated by umpires Hank O'Day and Tommy Connolly.

An interesting note: with the ball hit into the crowd deemed a triple under the ground rules for the day, the game saw five triples and no doubles.

Gambling on ballgames was common at the time. The Boston newspapers devoted coverage to the wagers at play, not hesitating to name names and amounts from time to time. Given the disgruntlement of the Boston players over the question of compensation for Series play, and the way the Pirates seemed to so easily score those first four runs, suggestions have been made that the game may not have entirely been on the up-and-up. Glenn Stout and Richard Johnson, writing in *Red Sox Century*, boldly state, "The very first game of the very first 'world's series' was, in all likelihood, thrown by Boston. … One may be tempted to blame Boston's poor play on nerves or chance, but Boston made at least eight questionable plays in the field during the game. …" The *Boston Post* questioned it at the time: "Many around town last evening asked if Boston lost on purpose."

PLAYER PROFILE: CANDY LACHANCE

George Joseph "Candy" LaChance broke into the majors with the National League Brooklyn ballclub in 1893. When the AL as we know it was formed, LaChance became a member of the Cleveland Blues and played first base for Cleveland in 1901, hitting .303 (his fifth season hitting over .300). He was traded to Boston (for Osee Schrecongost) in November 1901. In each of his years in Boston, his average declined (.279, .257, and .227), and he was released before the end of April in 1905, batting just .146 at the time.

In 1903, LaChance didn't miss a game, and contributed a middle-of-the-pack 53 runs batted in. He was slightly below the team average in batting, on-base percentage, and slugging (he hit just one home run, but had 22 doubles and six triples). In the 1903 World Series, Patsy Dougherty and Hobe Ferris each drove in five runs, but Candy drove in four. Two of his RBIs came in Game One, accounting for two of Boston's three runs. He managed this without benefit of a base hit, on sacrifice flies in the seventh and the ninth. LaChance hit .240 in the Series, and scored five runs.

Game Two: Huntington Avenue Grounds, Boston / October 2, 1903

Boston 3, Pittsburgh 0

Pittsburgh	000	000	000	—	0	3	2
Boston	200	001	00x	—	3	9	0

WP: Dinneen (1-0)   LP: Leever (0-1)   HR: Dougherty 2 (2)

Big Bill Dinneen shut out the Pirates to even the first World Series at one game apiece. With 32 complete games, Big Bill had posted a 21-13 record (2.26 ERA) during the 1903 season, and faced off against Pittsburgh's statistically superior pitcher, Sam Leever, who brought a league-best 25-7 record (with a 2.06 ERA) into the postseason.

Boston fielded the same lineup, but Pittsburgh had Harry Smith catching in place of Ed Phelps; the two had split duties during the season but Phelps had been the more productive hitter.

Dinneen struck out leadoff hitter Ginger Beaumont, walked captain Fred Clarke (but then caught him off first base), and struck out Tommy Leach. Boston's first batter, Patsy Dougherty (.331), hit an inside-the-park home run to kick off the game—though with the capacious center field at the Huntington Avenue Grounds, the ball may have traveled as far as 500 feet. He slid in headfirst and beat the relay. After Collins flied out, Chick Stahl doubled and Buck Freeman singled in Stahl. Boston had a 2-0 lead, more than enough as it turned out. Leever didn't even start the

It was a surprise that Boston lost the first game. The odds were in Boston's favor. We have seen that Glenn Stout and Richard Johnson didn't mince words in *Red Sox Century*. "As with the rampant betting which took place during the Temple Cup series in the 1890s, some players may have felt the new 'world's series' to be merely glorified exhibition games and have harbored little guilt over their play in games which did not 'count.'"

In this same regard, it's interesting that Tom Hughes only pitched two innings for Boston, starting Game Three and giving up three runs (two earned) before being removed. In 1903, Hughes won 20 games (five of them shutouts) while only losing seven, with a 2.57 earned run average. There is no question but that he was, with Young and Dinneen, a key part of the pitching rotation. After he was pulled from the game, manager Jimmy Collins never let him pitch another inning—ever. (He was traded to New York in December). Cy Young's biographer Reed Browning asks, "Could the gamblers have gotten to Hughes, and might Collins have suspected as much?"

second inning; Bucky Veil was brought in for his one and only appearance in the Series, never used again despite giving up just one run in seven innings—a hard-hit solo homer by Dougherty in the sixth over the left-field fence. It was Dougherty's second four-bagger of the game, and only the second ball ever hit over the left-field fence at the Huntington Avenue Grounds.

Veil otherwise pitched very well indeed, despite having only thrown 70 innings of major league ball prior to being placed at center stage in the battle for baseball's world championship. In seven full innings of work, he gave up just four other hits—though he did walk five.

Dinneen allowed just three scattered singles, in the fourth, fifth, and eighth. The outfielders had a bit of an off-day; only four balls ever made it out of the infield. Second baseman Hobe Ferris prevented a run in the fourth. With runners on second and third, he speared Honus Wagner's hard-hit liner and converted it into an unassisted double play, doubling Clarke off the bag at second. The two runners were the only two to reach as far as the second-base bag. Big Bill walked two batters, but struck out 11. He had himself a postseason shutout to go with the six he'd recorded earlier in the campaign.

PLAYER PROFILE: PATSY DOUGHERTY

Dougherty broke into baseball with Boston in 1902, leading the ballclub by batting .342 in his first big league season. The 6'2" outfielder didn't hit even one homer that first year, but drove in 34 runs and scored 77 (his .407 on-base percentage led the team). Not the best of fielders, though, his .898 fielding percentage in 1902 was the worst ever by a Boston franchise position player. In 1903, he led the team in hits (195 in a 141-game season) and in runs scored (107). He hit an even .333 and was apparently a big hit with the fans as well. He hit four homers and drove in 59, and set a record on September 5 that still stands with three triples in the same game.

During the World Series, he went 3-for-4 in Game Two, remarkably hitting not only the first postseason home run for Boston, but the second as well. Leading off the game in the bottom of the first, he gave Boston a quick lead with an inside-the-park home run to the deep center field at the Huntington Avenue Grounds, tagging Pittsburgh's Sam Leever. He hit a solo home run off reliever Bucky Veil in the sixth inning, thus responsible for two of the three Boston runs in the 3-0 win. In Game Five, Dougherty hit two triples and drove in three runs.

The following year, in a June trade almost certainly orchestrated by AL czar Ban Johnson to attempt to create a more competitive league, Boston traded the massively popular Patsy Dougherty for New York's Bob Unglaub. It almost came back to bite Boston, who only took the pennant from New York on the final day of the season.

Traded to the White Sox in June 1906, he saw World Series action once more but only managed two singles in 20 at-bats.

Game Three: Huntington Avenue Grounds, Boston / October 3, 1903

Pittsburgh 4, Boston 2

Pittsburgh	012	000	010	—	4	7	0
Boston	000	100	010	—	2	4	2

WP: Phillippe (2-0)   LP: Hughes (0-1)

Working on just one day's rest, Pittsburgh's Phillippe pitched another complete game and recorded another win, a masterful four-hitter. Clarke would normally have started 16-game winner Ed Doheny, but just two weeks earlier Doheny had had to leave the ballclub due to severe mental illness—so severe that he was institutionalized on October 10 in the Danvers Asylum for the Criminally Insane.

The Saturday afternoon contest drew the largest crowd of the Series, and saw Boston start Long Tom Hughes (20-7, 2.57). The park was packed out to more than twice its listed capacity (estimates run as high as 25,000 in the park built for 9,000—with another 10,000 or so turned away). As many as 1,000 fans scaled the fence in left after tickets had sold out. The iconic Cy Young himself did double duty, helping take tickets from the incoming masses. The crowd in the outfield had to be driven back several times by over-matched police working with baseball bats and a 30-foot length of rubber hose; the masses encroached as close as 30 yards to the infield. Ironically, the enthusiastic Boston fans may well have cost Boston the ballgame.

Changing the ground rule that obtained in Game One, balls hit into the crowd were deemed to be doubles rather than triples. Hughes got the first five Pirates to ground out, but he didn't last long. Second baseman Claude Ritchey doubled with two outs in the second, and after a walk to Sebring,

Phelps's two-bagger drove in Ritchey. 1-0, Pirates. Both doubles landed just feet away from outfielders Dougherty and Stahl, who camped under them to no avail; both fell into the pressing crowd. Phillippe grounded out to end the threat. In the third inning, Beaumont walked to lead off and Clarke doubled him to third. Tommy Leach's single to left field brought in Beaumont; Clarke pulled up at third. Collins had seen enough and called on Cy Young to take over for Hughes.

Young hit the first batter, Wagner, then got two outs before Parent's error let Sebring reach and allowed Leach to score. Wagner was retired in a rundown after he wheeled around third base "going blindly for home." The score stood at 3-0.

Freddie Parent's sacrifice fly scored Collins in the bottom of the fourth. The police finally managed to push the crowd back farther, creating some real room in the outfield, and as Boston began to find their bats, the balls were hauled in for outs. Boston only tallied one more run, in the bottom of the eighth, when Collins doubled and Chick Stahl singled him home. But the Pirates had scored again in the top of the inning on Wagner's double, Young's error handling a sacrifice bunt, and Ritchey's infield single to third base. Four of Pittsburgh's five doubles were said to be "fungos" that landed in the crowd for ground-rule doubles, and resulted in three of Pittsburgh's four runs. LaChance's long drive in

Game Three was sold out, so some fans found their own way to see the game, climbing one of the exterior walls outside the park. (Boston Public Library)

the second inning should have tied up the game at one apiece; it shot over the heads of the fans in left-center field and almost certainly would have been an inside-the-park home run—but under the ground rules of the day it was counted as a double and Ferris grounded out to strand him on base.

The final score was 4-2 in favor of the Pirates, who took a 2-1 lead in the Series. Both teams prepared to travel to Pittsburgh, as did 100 or more of Boston's fervent fan club, the Royal Rooters.

PLAYER PROFILE: LONG TOM HUGHES

Right-hander Hughes had an 11-24 record in the National League, before he jumped leagues in 1902. No one expected the year he put together in 1903: a 20-game winner (with five shutouts) against seven losses. His start in Game Three didn't go well; he lasted just two full innings, and put on the first three batters in the third before being pulled. It was enough to cost Boston the game, and manager Jimmy Collins never used him again. In fact, he saw to it that Boston traded him to New York in December for Jesse Tannehill.

Hughes was a 23-game loser in 1904 and a 20-game loser in 1905. He pitched for the Senators through 1911, with one good season (1908, when he was 18-15, 2.21 ERA) amongst a number of mediocre ones. His younger brother Ed played briefly for Boston in 1905 and 1906, but only had 17 total at-bats and the two brothers never faced each other on the field of play. After leaving the game, Long Tom ran a saloon in Chicago.

Game Four: Exposition Park, Pittsburgh / October 6, 1903

Pittsburgh 5, Boston 4

Boston	000	010	003	—	4	9	1
Pittsburgh	100	010	300	—	5	12	1

WP: Phillippe (3-0)   LP: Dinneen (1-1)

After a travel day and a day off due to rain, the two teams squared off in Pittsburgh for four games in the best-of-nine competition. The Pirates started Deacon Phillippe for the third time in four games, this time allowing him the two rest days in between starts. Meanwhile, Boston asked Bill Dinneen to even up the Series at two games each. Both pitchers performed well through six innings.

The Pirates drew first blood in the bottom of the first with three singles, Kitty Bransfield driving in the run. Boston tied it in the top of the fifth, with a single by LaChance, a grounder that moved him to second, and Criger's single to right field. But Pittsburgh re-established their one-run lead in the bottom of the fifth when Beaumont tripled and Leach singled him in. They then blew the game open in the bottom of the seventh. Phillippe helped his own cause with a single down the left-field line, and reached second when Dougherty misplayed the ball. Beaumont bunted to advance Phillippe and reached safely when Dinneen failed to cover first—he took second base on a throw to the plate to hold Phillippe at third. Clarke flied to left but not deep enough to score a run. Boston pulled the infielders in to try to cut off a possible run at the plate, but both base runners scored when Leach tripled past the drawn-in LaChance. Wagner followed with a single that plated Leach. A strike-'em-out, throw-'em-out double play spared Dinneen from further damage, but the Pirates held a 5-1 lead. The *Globe* termed Dinneen's pitching "a little erratic."

It was enough—barely enough—to deliver a 5-4 Pittsburgh win as Boston scored three times in the top of the ninth. Jimmy Collins singled, Stahl singled, and Freeman singled to score Collins. Parent hit into a force play which brought in Stahl. LaChance singled to put runners on first and second, and Ferris singled to load the bases. Parent played too conservatively and held up at third, when he could well have scored. Backup catcher Duke Farrell, injured for most of the season but hitting .404 in the 52 at-bats he assembled, batted for Lou Criger (.192 during the season) and hit a high fly ball to left, which brought in Parent. But when Jack O'Brien pinch-hit for Dinneen, rather than the superior batter Jake Stahl—who never saw duty in the Series—he popped up to second base and Phillippe had three wins after four games had been played.

Boston was counting on Cy Young to try to cut the deficit in Game Five.

Game Four was notable for one other thing: the three-run rally in the top of the ninth that fell just one run short of tying the game was accompanied by raucous rooting for the Bostons by the coterie of Royal Rooters who had traveled to Pittsburgh to cheer their team. After the loss in Game Three, Tom Burton of the Rooters found some sheet music at a Pittsburgh music store and the Rooters wrote parodied lyrics to the popular Broadway song of the day, "Tessie." They hired a band and felt the music had spurred on their players. Starting the following day, they had the band play "Tessie" over and over, and over again, with particular power in the ninth. "They played it so often and delivered it with such vigor—incessantly, relentlessly, *ad nauseam*—that it began to take its toll on the opposition. Even decades later, Pittsburgh's third baseman Tommy Leach said, "I think those Boston fans won the Series … We beat them three out of four games, and then they started singing that damn Tessie song … Sort of got on your nerves after a while. And before we knew what happened, we'd lost the Series.'" [*Love That Dirty Water*]

The Pittsburgh papers were impressed by the fervor of the fans from Boston. Roger Abrams

quotes the *Dispatch* as reporting the Rooters as "howling maniacs, overjoyed to a delirious stage" as the rally progressed. "The Boston rooters had simply lost control of themselves, war dances, cheers, yells and songs resounding clear across the Allegheny River."

PLAYER PROFILE: JIMMY COLLINS

Boston manager Jimmy Collins started in the majors with Boston's NL entry, the 1895 Boston Beaneaters. The third baseman is considered by many to have revolutionized fielding at the hot corner with his aggressive play to cut down bunt attempts. A star player for the 1897 Beaneaters, he hit .346 with 132 RBIs, and led the NL with 15 homers the next year, with a .328 average and 111 RBIs. When the American League decided to place a team in Boston, the first move they made was to entice Collins to jump leagues. It was a wise move; he brought a number of teammates with him and was player-manager from the beginning.

His .332 average and 94 RBIs helped him remain a star in Boston and helped solidly establish the new franchise.

In 1903, Collins helped lead his team to the first World Series, with a .296 average. With his team down 5-1 in the top of the ninth during Game Four in Pittsburgh, Collins singled and started a three-run rally that fell just short of tying the score. In Game Six, he singled to drive in the first run of the game, scoring a couple of batters later. Collins led Boston to yet another pennant in 1904. In 1906, Collins was replaced as skipper by Chick Stahl and was traded to Philadelphia in 1907.

Game Five: Exposition Park, Pittsburgh / October 7, 1903

Boston 11, Pittsburgh 2

| Boston | 000 | 006 | 410 | — | 11 | 14 | 2 |
| Pittsburgh | 000 | 000 | 020 | — | 2 | 6 | 4 |

WP: Young (1-1)   LP: Kennedy (0-1)

For five innings, Cy Young and 12-year veteran pitcher Brickyard Kennedy traded zeroes. Kennedy had 187 wins to his credit, but was just 9-6 with a 3.45 ERA in what proved to be his final year. Collins's first-inning triple proved fruitless when Honus Wagner threw home on Chick Stahl's grounder and cut him down at the plate. Even Stahl's stolen base, a walk, and Parent's single to third base failed to produce a run. Off the hook, Kennedy settled down, allowing just one more single over the next four frames.

Young allowed a leadoff double by Kennedy and two singles in the third, but none to any effect.

Boston broke the game open in the sixth inning, playing with "dash and determination." It started quietly enough with Stahl reaching safely when Clarke dropped the ball in shallow left field. Freeman singled, and there were runners on first and second. Parent bunted to move up the two runners, but Wagner couldn't hold on to the ball at third and the bases were loaded. A seemingly unnerved Kennedy walked LaChance and forced in a run. The third error of the inning—again Wagner's, a throwing error—let both Freeman and Parent score. Criger sacrificed and advanced the runners to second and third. Cy Young struck the big blow, tripling down Exposition Park's left-field line and driving in two. Dougherty hit a carbon-copy triple and Young scored. Finally, Kennedy got Collins and Stahl, stranding Dougherty on third base. The fact that five of Boston's six runs were unearned was likely of little solace to the Pirates' pitcher. The *Pittsburgh Gazette* concluded, "Clarke's crew went to pieces."

The *Globe* expressed appreciation of the work of the band hired by Boston's Royal Rooters. "While the home team has 12,000 voices to howl for it, this army of supporters had nothing on the band of 'royal rooters' and their brass band, located back of the Boston bench."

After three quick outs, Boston resumed their assault on Brickyard in the seventh. Freeman and Parent both singled. A force play cut down Parent. Freeman scored from third on Ferris's single to center field. Criger walked to load the bases. Young's grounder was productive, bringing in a runner from third. Dougherty's triple into the overflow crowd in right field scored both base runners. Collins grounded out. This time, all the runs were earned, and the Americans were enjoying a 10-0 lead.

Gus Thompson took over for Kennedy and was greeted with a triple by Stahl, the fifth of the game for Boston. Buck Freeman grounded out, but Stahl scored, 11-0. Pittsburgh scored twice in the bottom of the eighth; after two outs, Beaumont singled—though it appeared that he was out by at least a step, Clarke reached on an error, and Leach tripled to drive both in. A single in the ninth was the sixth hit off Young but nothing came of it. Boston won easily, 11-2. And the Series stood at three games to two in Pittsburgh's favor.

Hughes was apparently in the doghouse; observers noted that he didn't dress for the game. The *Globe* wrote, "Hughes had the chance of his life to make good, but lost his opportunity in Boston, being too sporty."

PLAYER PROFILE: CHICK STAHL

Best known as the manager who committed suicide during spring training, Stahl began his major league career with Boston's NL team in 1897 and came over to the Americans with Jimmy Collins in time to launch the new team in 1901. Stahl hit .303 and .323 his first two seasons with the Americans. He missed time in 1903 but was healthy again by the postseason and led the team in batting, hitting .303 in the World Series. Game Five was an 11-2 rout, with Stahl one of four Americans who scored two runs. Only Freddy Parent's eight runs scored topped Stahl and Buck Freeman's six runs scored in the eight Series games. Stahl, Parent, and Freeman each tied for the team lead with three triples apiece. In 1904, Chick's 19 triples led the league and the left-handed outfielder helped lead the team to a second consecutive pennant.

Stahl hit a healthy .286 in 1906 and took over the managerial reins after Jimmy Collins went AWOL in midseason. Things were looking up for 1907 when Stahl—apparently a ladies man who'd become involved in compromising circumstances—ingested carbolic acid and took his own life.

Stahl's career had lasted ten seasons and he left with a .305 average—having hit a home run in what would prove to be his very last at-bat.

Game Six: Exposition Park, Pittsburgh / October 7, 1903

Boston 6, Pittsburgh 3

Boston	003	020	100	—	6	10	1
Pittsburgh	000	000	300	—	3	10	3

WP: Dinneen (2-1)   LP: Leever (0-2)

The third of the four games scheduled in Pittsburgh resulted in another win for the Americans, evening the Series at three games apiece. It was a matchup of Game Two starters, Sam Leever for Pittsburgh and Bill Dinneen for Boston. Leever, suffering from an injury he'd incurred before the Series, had lasted just one inning in the earlier game, while Dinneen not only threw a shutout but pitched a second time—the loss in Game Four. Now he was back on the mound after just one day off.

Neither team scored in the first two frames, but Boston got to the still-subpar Leever early enough, scoring three times in the top of the third. The inning started with Sam looking strong—he fielded Ferris's grounder deftly and threw him out at first, then induced Criger to pop up in foul territory to his Pirates counterpart. It was Dinneen who started it with a single to left field. Dougherty walked. Collins singled to center field, scoring Dinneen but Dougherty held at second. Stahl's single, also to center, scored Dougherty but left runners on first and third. Second base was open; Stahl stole it. Leach failed to get a handle on Freeman's slow groundball, and Collins came in to score the third run on the error. The eighth man up, Parent, ended the inning as it began with a grounder to the pitcher, 1-3.

It was a 3-0 lead for Boston, they added two more in the top of the fifth. Leever remained shaky, surrendering three singles in the fourth but miraculously none of the three base runners scored. Stahl kicked off the fifth with a triple and trotted home on Freeman's sacrifice fly to center field. Parent was hit by a pitch and scored when a hit-and-run play resulted in a two-out error by Wagner that allowed him to come all the way around on Ferris's single to center.

Boston added a sixth run in the seventh on Parent's triple and LaChance's double to the very same spot.

With a 6-0 lead heading into the bottom of the seventh, three singles by Sebring, Phelps, and Beaumont, and the two-run double by Clarke cut the lead in half. Leever retired the side in order in both the eighth and the ninth. Dinneen gave up just a leadoff ninth-inning single to Beaumont (his fourth of the game) but Clarke lined into a double play to clear the bases and Leach fouled out to catcher Criger who took the ball close to the seats.

As it happened, Game Seven—the final game in Pittsburgh—would pit Cy Young against the undefeated (3-0) Deacon Phillippe. Even should the Pirates win, though, it would not end the Series as this was a best-of-nine championship. Understandably, Pirates owner Barney Dreyfuss and player-manager Fred Clarke held great faith in Phillippe.

PLAYER PROFILE: BUCK FREEMAN

Back in 1901, Buck Freeman drove in the first run ever put across by the team that became the Red Sox, on the April 26 Opening Day, singling Jimmy Collins in to score. He also hit the first home run in franchise history, four days later. Freeman also hit the first homer recorded in Boston, on May 8. His 12 home runs in 1901 were twice as many as anyone else on the team. In 1902 and 1903, he led the American League in RBIs and in 1903 led the league with 13 home runs.

He'd started with Washington as a pitcher way back in 1891, had played in 1900 for the Beaneaters primarily in the outfield, and was part of the group that came over to the AL to start 1901; Freeman played first base that inaugural year. For most of his time, Buck was—like Chick Stahl—a left-handed outfielder but he continued to see stretches of work at first base.

He batted .290 with four RBIs in the World Series. In Game Six, he collected one of those RBIs but—like LaChance in Game One—did so without a hit. Chick Stahl tripled to lead off the fifth inning and Freeman hit a deep fly ball to bring him home. He'd played a part in scoring two of Boston's six runs. It was the third game in a row Freeman had driven in a run.

Game Seven: Exposition Park, Pittsburgh / October 10, 1903

Boston 7, Pittsburgh 3

| Boston | 200 | 202 | 010 | — | 7 | 11 | 4 |
| Pittsburgh | 000 | 101 | 001 | — | 3 | 10 | 3 |

WP: Young (2-1)   LP: Phillippe (3-1)

The seventh and not-deciding game of the first World Series saw Boston—for the third game in a row—jump out to a solid start, scoring two runs in the top of the first and two more in the fourth. The game had been postponed a day due to cold weather and high wind, affording Phillippe the luxury of the opportunity to pitch on three days' rest. Cy Young started again after just two days off. How cold the weather really was is open to debate; Pittsburgh papers put temperatures in the middle 50s, but both by league rules and agreement between the two teams for the Series, it was the home team's call and the call gave the Deacon an extra day. Of course, Cy got an extra day, too.

Outfielder Chick Stahl in front of the team's dugout during one of the games at Pittsburgh's Exposition Park. Note the boisterous Royal Rooters in the stands behind and even on the edge of the field. One can see a beanpot sharing a pole with the American flag. (Boston Public Library)

The teams were fairly evenly matched in the contest, with Boston hitting safely 11 times and Pittsburgh ten, while Boston made four errors and Pittsburgh three. In the most significant statistic, runs scored, Boston held a decisive edge however, winning handily, 7-3. The game could hardly have been livelier, what with dueling bands each attempting to out-do the other, and the "chorus of cowbells" that often erupted either in celebration or when the Pittsburghers hoped to rattle the Boston players.

This was another game of triples—five by Boston and two by the Pirates. The Series as a whole saw 25 triples, 11 doubles, and three home runs. After Dougherty grounded out to lead off the game, Jimmy Collins tripled over the crowd in left field and Chick Stahl followed with another three-bagger, this one over the crowd in right. A fielder's choice let Freeman reach first, and allowed Stahl to score when the catcher, Phelps, dropped the ball on the throw to the plate. 2-0.

It was Freeman's triple over the center fielder's head in the fourth that set up the first of two more runs. He came in on Parent's grounder to deep short. LaChance fanned for the second out, but then Ferris tripled deep to the flagpole—normally a home run, but under the day's ground rules yet another three-bagger. Criger singled him in. 4-0.

Worcester's Kitty Bransfield tripled in the bottom half of the fourth and came in on Ritchey's grounder to third base. The 4-1 score stood until the Americans hit for two more in the sixth. A single, an error on a bunt, and a successful sacrifice bunt set things up for Criger's single to right field to score both Parent and LaChance. Americans 6, Pirates 1.

Clarke's leadoff triple and Wagner's bunt brought Pittsburgh a second run, but Parent's eighth-inning triple into the right-field crowd led to yet another Boston run when Phillippe uncorked a wild pitch to the next batter. Three successive singles by Pirates batters saw Phill-lippe drive in the third Pirates run, but it was the last one of the game. Americans 7, Pirates 3.

It was deemed a "most dashing and brilliant game" and the Royal Rooters were exuberant, and the two teams took the 11 p.m. train back to Boston for Game Eight. It was a 25-hour excursion by rail. They arrived in Boston in time to find Monday's game rained out, affording each team the chance to start their best pitchers: Dinneen and, yet again, Phillippe.

Dreyfuss had even offered an unprecedented incentive to his players prior to Game Seven. Bring home the championship, he said, and he would give them 100 percent of the net proceeds from the Series.

After seeing their team win three consecutive games in Pittsburgh, Boston's Royal Rooters were jubilant and weary after they arrived by train back in Boston. (Boston Public Library)

PLAYER PROFILE: CY YOUNG

With the best-of-nine World Series tied at three games apiece, it was on Young's watch that Boston took a four-games-to-three lead, beating Pittsburgh 7-3. Young was 0-for-4 at the plate but held the Pirates to just three runs in the complete game win and let his teammates supply the offense. He'd lost the first game, but won Game Five. He never played in another World Series, but wound up with a 2-1 record in the first one ever played.

Cy Young, of course, was one of the main reasons that Boston had won the pennant. He'd won 28 regular-season games himself, every one of them a complete game victory. His 1903 record was 28-9, with an ERA of 2.08. It was the third year in a row he'd led the league in wins, though a bit of a comedown after winning 33 in 1901 and 32 in 1902! This was the man they named the Award after. He still leads the Red Sox in wins, with 192, and leads all of baseball with an untouchable 511 victories. No one has 30-win seasons anymore; Cy Young had five of them. Fifteen times, he won 20 or more games in a given year. Six seasons, he finished the year with an ERA under 2.00. He was, quite obviously, the gold standard among pitchers.

Game Eight: Huntington Avenue Grounds, Boston / October 13, 1903

Boston 3, Pittsburgh 0

Pittsburgh	000	000	000	—	0	4	3
Boston	000	201	000	—	3	8	0

WP: Dinneen (3-1)   LP: Phillippe (3-2)

Since a win would give Boston the championship, no one was surprised that manager Jimmy Collins selected Dinneen to throw Game Eight. Big Bill and Cy Young both had 2-1 records in Series play, but Dinneen had enjoyed four days' rest and was ready to go. Fred Clarke had little faith in his other pitchers; it was an elimination game and Phillippe (3-1) was the only Pirates pitcher who'd won a game. It was risky, in that he was being asked to start his fifth game in 13 days, this one on just two days' rest—granted the second day because it had rained on Monday. Phillippe didn't pitch poorly. He didn't walk a Boston batter, and gave up eight hits in eight innings with one of Boston's three runs being unearned, thanks to the three errors in the Pittsburgh defense.

The problem was that Dinneen pitched a better ballgame. The crowd was less than half that of several earlier games, the smallest turnout of any during the Series in part because large blocks of tickets had been snapped up by speculators—and "the public would not submit to the extortion." (*Chicago Tribune*)

Dinneen retired the side on seven pitches in the first. For three innings, neither team scored a run. Neither Boston's two singles nor Pittsburgh's first error resulted in a score. Dinneen's pitching hand was hit by a stinging shot off Sebring's bat in the third inning, and it split his finger but despite the bleeding that continued to stain the balls he threw throughout the game, the gritty right-hander continued to pitch well.

It was another triple that started the scoring, in the bottom of the fourth, deep to left-center field—Buck Freeman's third triple of the games. Buck stayed on the bag through an error on a bunt that permitted Parent to reach first, and again on a sacrifice bunt that moved Parent to second. With two outs, Hobe Ferris shot a single to center that brought in both Freeman and Parent. After Dinneen singled, Ferris was thrown out trying to score and the inning was over.

Boston added a third run, in the sixth, on Candy LaChance's two-out triple to right field and Ferris's single to center—his third RBI of the game. There were no other runs scored.

The fielding was superb, with nothing but superlatives accorded the Bostons. The *Post* in particular noted several plays, and praised Collins who "covered acres of ground and threw as only he can throw." The infield work in general made the Pirates "look amateurish by comparison."

Dinneen shut out the Pirates, again by a 3-0 score as in Game Two, on just four hits, striking out the great Honus Wagner in the ninth to end the game. There was no need for a Game Nine. Boston had won its fifth game—four in a row—and the first World Championship was theirs.

Wagner, the particular target of the Royal Rooters, hit .222 with six hits (only one double) and made six errors. Third baseman Leach made four errors, though he drove in seven runs to lead the team. Sebring's .333 was the best average and his four RBIs (all in the first game) ranked him second in that category. Boston's Dougherty and Ferris each drove in five, while Criger, Freeman, LaChance, and Parent each drove in four. Parent's eight runs scored led the team. Stahl's .303 was the leading average; he scored six times, as did Freeman. Only Ginger Beamont, with six, scored more than three runs for the Pirates.

Boston mounted a better offense, but in the end it came down to pitching. Phillippe was terrific, but Pittsburgh captain Fred Clarke conceded to the *Boston Journal*, "Boston won on its merits. We were weak in pitchers."

Boston manager Jimmy Collins credited the support shown the team by the fans. "The support given the team by the 'Royal Rooters' will never be forgotten … no little portion of our success is due to this selfsame band of enthusiasts. Noise—why they astonished Pittsburgh by their enthusiasm." [Ryan, p. 157]

Phillippe wound up with five decisions in a World Series, all complete games, something we will never expect to see again. He posted a 2.86 ERA for the Series, but lost twice. Leever was 0-2, and Kennedy bore the loss in Game Five.

Dinneen was 3-1 (2.06), throwing two 3-0 shutouts in the same World Series. Young was 2-1 (1.85). Between the two men, they'd pitched all but two innings of the eight games. Tom Hughes threw those two innings. He was 0-1. Despite being a 20-game winner in 1903, Hughes was banished to New York after the season, traded in December for Jesse Tannehill.

The rewards were plentiful, but surely among the best was simply reading a headline like that in the *Journal* the morning after the final game: "Boston Americans Are Now the Champions of the World."

Dinneen had an even better year in 1904 than he did in 1903, winning 23 games. Cy Young saw his 1904 win total drop for the fourth year in a row—but it dropped to "only" 26 wins, with a 1.97 ERA. (There's a reason baseball's top pitching award bears his name). Boston as a whole did pretty well in 1904, too, winning the pennant and playing well enough that John McGraw and the New York Giants refused to play them in the World Series.

PLAYER PROFILE: BILL DINNEEN

Bill Dinneen beat the Pirates in the final game of the World Series, throwing a four-hit 3-0 shutout. He struck out seven and walked only two. He improved his Series mark to 3-1 with the win, finishing with a 2.06 ERA. Needless to say, very few pitchers have ever won three games in a given World Series. The only time the Pirates ever got a man into scoring position was in the fourth, and an attempted double steal saw Leach cut down at home plate.

A 20-game winner in 1900, Dinneen was one who Jimmy Collins brought with him to the American League. For the next four years, Big Bill kept his ERA under 3.00, winning 15, 21, 21, and 23 games. Pitching on the same staff as Cy Young, his 21-13 (2.26) mark in 1903 and 23-14 (2.20) totals in '04 were big parts of what enabled Boston to win the pennant both years.

He began to lose his effectiveness after '04, and ultimately left player ranks to become an American League umpire from the latter part of 1909 all the way through the 1937 season. He umpired in eight World Series, and in the first All-Star Game ever staged (1933).

1912 WORLD SERIES BOSTON RED SOX 4, NEW YORK GIANTS 3 (WITH ONE TIE GAME)

The 1912 team was as different as night and day from the fifth-place 1911 Red Sox, who finished those 24 games behind Philadelphia.

Now Smoky Joe Wood was pretty good in 1911—who's going to complain about a 23-17 (2.02 ERA) pitcher on a breakeven (78-75) ballclub? But in 1912, he put up colossal numbers: 34-5 with a 1.19 earned run average. In 1911, Eddie Cicotte (11), Ray Collins (11), and Larry Pape (10) each reached double digits in the wins column, but both Cicotte and Collins had more losses than wins. The 1911

outfield had three .300 hitters in Duffy Lewis (.307 with 86 RBIs), Tris Speaker (.334 with 70 RBIs), and Harry Hooper (.311 with 45 RBIs). Not one starting position player hit below .257. The Red Sox scored 680 runs while only allowing 643, but still only won 51 percent of their games.

In 1912, Speaker batted .383. Lewis drove in 109 runs. Third baseman Larry Gardner jumped from 44 to 86 runs batted in. Jake Stahl came back to baseball after a year off running a bank in Chicago to deposit a .301 average and cash in 60 RBIs. Heinie Wagner went from 38 RBIs to 68. Almost everyone blossomed on offense.

The real change was on the mound. In 1912, the team boasted two 20-game winners (as well as the 34-game–winning Wood), both of them rookies: Buck O'Brien (20-13, 2.58 ERA), who'd gotten his feet wet in 1911, and the 22-year-old Hugh Bedient (20-9, 2.92 ERA). Collins was 13-8 and Charlie Hall was 15-8. The pitchers and defense allowed 544 runs while the offense scored 799, and they won what still remains a franchise-high 105 games against just 47 losses.

The Red Sox were also playing in a new home ballpark, Fenway Park, and apparently felt right at home; they won 74 percent of their decisions at Fenway. The Sox were under new ownership—former ballplayer and manager James McAleer—and he'd installed Jake Stahl as manager (and first baseman) of the 1912 team. Stahl was, interestingly, a player on the 1903 championship team—the only man to play for both the 1903 and 1912 World Champions.

Needless to say, it all made a big difference. The Red Sox finished a full 14 games ahead of second-place Washington, a 27-game swing for the Sox from the year before. They were ready to take on the New York Giants, at the Polo Grounds, on October 8. The Giants had won handily, too, an even ten games ahead of the Pirates.

On September 25, McAleer called "heads" but lost the coin toss to determine where the Series would open. The Red Sox wanted to begin the very day after the regular season ended, which would be October 7. New York wanted to start on October 8. McAleer called "heads" again, but tails came up a second time. The two clubs agreed on a system used in both 1906 and 1911, whereby they would alternate home fields until the Series was won. This meant that after the game on October 8, both teams had to travel to Boston for Game Two, then would board trains back to New York for Game Three, and so forth and so on. The same shifting from city to city was used again in 1913 between New York and Philadelphia.

THE GAMES

Game One: Polo Grounds, New York / October 8, 1912

Boston 4, New York 3

Boston	000	001	300	—	4	6	1
New York	002	000	001	—	3	8	1

WP: Wood (1-0)   LP: Tesreau (0-1)

Though the Red Sox had won 105 games, the Giants weren't going to be pushovers. They'd won 103 games. They'd driven in more runs, hit for a higher average, scored more runs, and in Christy Mathewson and Rube Marquard had a couple of 20-game winners of their own. McGraw was still manager for the New Yorkers, as he had been back in 1904. Joshua Pahigian writes, "Red Sox fans still remembered how McGraw had dodged the Boston Americans in 1904 and they believed the Giants manager had deprived them of a world championship that had been rightfully theirs." At least among the fans, there was a bit of a reckoning at stake.

Game One featured their stingiest pitcher, Jeff Tesreau—his 1.96 earned run average led the National League and helped him post a 17-7 record, though the rookie spitballer was "the algebraic X" in the words of the *Los Angeles Times*, an unknown quantity. The Red Sox started Smoky Joe. If Tesreau was stingy, Joe Wood was equally miserly with, as noted above, an ERA of 1.91 and in 38 starts he'd won an astonishing 34 games, with—perhaps not surprisingly, in light of the ERA—ten shutouts among them.

Facing the best the National League had to offer, he didn't shut down the Giants' offense for long. They put the first two runs on the board after two outs in the bottom of the third, when right-fielder Red Murray, New York's leading RBI man (92 on the season) singled in both Josh Devore and Larry Doyle with a shot into center field. Murray was cut down trying to make it to second base on the play. Tesreau, who'd been a trifle shaky the first three frames, seemed to settle down after going up 2-0.

For 5 ⅓ innings, the Red Sox only hit two balls out of the infield—both easy fly balls. Tesreau had a no-hitter going until Speaker tripled in the top of the sixth. The ball "shot through the racing [Fred] Snodgrass's outstretched hands and rolled to the fence." (*New York Times*) Duffy Lewis grounded out to second base; Doyle's only play was to first base and Speaker scored.

In the top of the seventh, the Red Sox struck—and maybe got a break. After Jake Stahl grounded out, Heinie Wagner singled to center, and so did Hick Cady. With runners on first and second,

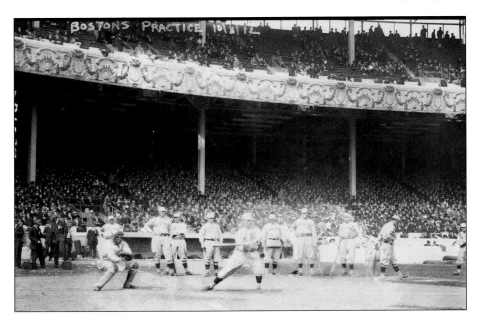

BOSTONS PRACTICE 10/8/12

The Red Sox taking batting practice, prior to Game One at the Polo Grounds. (Library of Congress/Bain News Service)

Wood grounded out to second base but only the middle runner was retired. And therein lay the break. Christy Mathewson, in a ghostwritten syndicated column, said it was a ready-made double play ball to Doyle at second, but "it took a jump away from him and to his right. He was lucky to knock it down and very lucky to get Cady." The Giants narrowly missed getting out of the inning without a run coming across. Behind in the count 0-2, Harry Hooper hit a "fierce smash" (Hugh Fullerton, writing in the *New York Times*) of a double over the first base bag and easily drove in Wagner; Wood held up at third base. With two men in scoring position, Sox second baseman Steve Yerkes brought them both home with a single to left field. Speaker struck out, but the Sox had added three runs and taken a 4-2 lead.

The *New York Times* termed Snodgrass's sixth-inning play a "blunder" in that Devore was closer to the ball but Snodgrass called him off. Giants manager McGraw agreed, ripping Snodgrass in print in his own newspaper column. He wrote that Snodgrass "turned what should have been a sure out into a three-base hit." McGraw couldn't have been angling for friends among his men. He also took Meyers to task for failing to catch a foul pop-up and giving Hooper fresh life in the seventh.

With one on and two outs in the bottom of the seventh, Tesreau was taken out for pinch-hitter Moose McCormick, who got a hold of one but flied out to left field. Doc Crandall relieved Tesreau and retired the Red Sox in the eighth and ninth with only a double to Wagner.

Wood kept the ball in the infield in the eighth with two 6-3 grounders and a pop-up to Gardner at third, but faltered in the ninth. Fred Merkle swung at the first pitch and hit a one-out single to left, and Buck Herzog singled the other way—to right. Hooper may have failed to fully track it in the late afternoon shadows. The third single in a row, by catcher Chief Meyers, scored Merkle. Herzog took third and Meyers took second on the futile throw to Cady at home plate. Herzog might well have scored, save for Hooper fielding the ball bare-handed and firing it home in time to head off Herzog and hold him on third base. With runners on second and third, and just one out, the game hung in the balance. Joe Wood had been smoked for three consecutive singles, but now Wood buckled down and struck out both shortstop Art Fletcher and the pitcher Crandall (a good-hitting pitcher, he'd batted .313 during the 1912 regular season and had 19 runs batted in).

Like McGraw and Mathewson, Wood, Speaker, and Tesreau all had bylined newspaper columns. Wood admitted he'd feared Fletcher would try to squeeze home Herzog from third in the ninth. He called Crandall a "hitting pitcher" and said "no one can safely take chances with him." Crandall worked the count to 3-2. Then, Wood wrote, "I saw that Crandall was standing well away from the plate, and so I put one over the outside corner, which he missed." Strike three. Game over. Red Sox 4, Giants 3. Wood had struck out 11, eight of them looking.

Wood, Mathewson wrote, showed he was under considerable strain in the ninth and "pitching on nerve alone." Mathewson said the Giants were not discouraged. He felt the Sox had showed a certain lack of aggressiveness and "I don't think that we will have so much to fear from now on." He didn't anticipate that this best-of-seven Series was going to go eight games.

PLAYER PROFILE: SMOKY JOE WOOD

It's a fair guess that Joe Wood's astonishing 34-5 won-loss record helped ensure that the Red Sox reached the World Series. Ten regular-season shutouts and an earned run average of 1.91 were part of the equation as well. He won three of the four games that decided the Series, with a 3-1 record and a 4.50 ERA. He started Games One, Four, and Seven, and came on to relieve—and win—Game Eight, but almost blew that one, rescued when the Red Sox scored two runs in the bottom of the 11th.

Wood had joined the Red Sox late in 1908, and ran up a record of 116-56 through the 1915 season. That final season was one of his best, 15-5 (1.49), but accumulated injuries caught up with him and destroyed his effectiveness as a pitcher. He saw no action in the 1915 World Series. After not playing at all in 1916, the Sox sold him to Cleveland in February 1917. He only ever appeared in seven games for the Indians, as a pitcher, but had always been a good batter and played parts of six seasons with the Indians, leaving major league ball after the 1922 season with a lifetime .283 average.

Game Two: Fenway Park, Boston / October 9, 1912

Boston 6, New York 6 (tie, 11 innings)

New York	010	100	030	10	—	6	11	5
Boston	300	010	010	10	—	6	10	1

No winning pitcher and no losing pitcher.

There was strong suspicion that by starting Tesreau against Boston's best pitcher, Wood, Giants manager John McGraw may have partially conceded Game One so that he could throw his two big guns—Christy Mathewson and Rube Marquard—against two supposedly lesser Red Sox pitchers (Ray Collins and Buck O'Brien) and thus gain a two-games-to-one edge. The Series had, after just one game, reverted to Boston without a day off in accord with the questionable plan of alternating cities until the Series was completed.

Collins, in the fourth of seven seasons he pitched for the Red Sox, was ready to go. He was the only left-hander on the Sox staff. It was his only Series start, despite a good 13-8 (2.53 ERA) regular-season record.

Though Snodgrass doubled into the temporary stands in left to lead off the game, Collins retired the next three men, leaving Snodgrass on third. Boston benefited from three quick runs in the bottom of the first. Hooper singled, the ball glancing off Mathewson's glove, then stole second off him. Shortstop Fletcher's error saw Hooper reach third with Yerkes on first. Speaker bunted for a base hit and loaded the bases, as Hooper held. Duffy Lewis hit the ball to Herzog at third, who threw home to cut down Hooper; the two runners moved up. Gardner grounded out back to the mound, but again the ball ticked off Matty's outstretched glove. It caromed to Doyle at second, whose only play was at first, and Yerkes came in the back door with the first run. Jake Stahl singled past third base and drove in two more before Wagner popped out to end the inning. 3-0, Red Sox.

Herzog tripled to the right-field barrier and Meyers singled when the ball bounced up freakishly and glanced off Gardner's face, and the Giants put a run on the board in the top of the second. They added another in the fourth on Red Murray's leadoff triple and, two batters later, Herzog's sacrifice fly to Speaker in center. The Red Sox scored once more in the bottom of the fifth. After the pitcher struck out, Hooper singled to center field (already his third hit of the game). The sun was giving Murray trouble in right field so McGraw had Murray and Snodgrass change defensive positions, Murray moving from right to left and Snodgrass moving left to right. Meyers threw out Hooper stealing second—but Fletcher dropped the ball, and Harry was safe. Yerkes tripled to center field, scoring Hooper, but Speaker failed to cash in, hitting into a 6-5 double play.

In the top of the eighth, the Giants edged the Sox to take a 5-4 lead. Duffy Lewis made the only error of the game for Boston, and Snodgrass reached first. When Doyle singled to Speaker, Snodgrass moved up one base. He took third when center-fielder Beals Becker grounded out forcing Doyle at second. With runners on first and third, Murray doubled and drove in Snodgrass. Manager Stahl reacted quickly and brought in "Sea Lion" Hall to pitch to Merkle. Merkle fouled out to Bill Carrigan, catching for the Red Sox. Herzog doubled and drove in both Becker and Murray, before Hall got Meyers to ground out.

The slim New York lead didn't last long, though at first it looked like Mathewson would escape without trouble as both Yerkes and Speaker were retired. Lewis hit one off the right-field bleacher fence for two bases, though, and scored from second when Fletcher fumbled Gardner's ball. Then Stahl reached on Doyle's error and stole second, but Wagner whiffed. The errors were the third and fourth miscues committed by Giants fielders. Fletcher had three all by himself. The game was tied, 5-5.

Though Hall walked the side with two outs in the top of the ninth, Murray hit into a force play. Mathewson set down the Red Sox 1-2-3 without letting the ball leave the infield.

Leadoff triples are never good for the team in the field, and when Merkle hit a three-bagger to start the 10th, Boston fans held their breath. Herzog grounded out, Wagner looking Merkle back to third base before throwing to first for the initial out. Meyers was walked intentionally, and McGraw inserted the speedier Tillie Shafer to run for the Chief. He then brought in Moose McCormick to bat for Fletcher. As in the first game, Moose flied out to left—but this time it was a successful sacrifice fly that scored Merkle. Mathewson, still in the game, popped up to second.

Yerkes grounded out. But then Tris Speaker tripled to the fence in center field and scored on the play as the relay was momentarily fumbled by substitute shortstop Shafer. As Speaker ran for the plate, Shafer recovered and threw in time to catcher Art Wilson, who'd just entered the game. But Wilson dropped the ball. The score was retied, on yet another New York error. Mathewson hadn't walked a batter; he had given up six runs, but not one of them was an earned run. Nonetheless, it was a whole new ballgame. Though Duffy Lewis doubled, Mathewson bore down and got two ground balls to close out the 10th. Had Speaker not scored, as Hugh Fullerton pointed out, it might well have led to scandal since he was interfered with three times while running the bases—incredibly, not one of them called by an umpire.

Hugh Bedient came on in relief of Hall—and hit the first batter, Snodgrass. But Carrigan promptly cut him down on an attempted steal. After Doyle was called out on strikes, Becker walked, and Carrigan did it once again—threw out the man trying to steal. Carrigan had thrown out three men in the game, a tight contest the *Globe* described as "desperately fought."

Matty induced three ground balls, fielding the third of them himself. It was 6-6 after 11, but at that juncture the game was called on account of darkness. The Giants had used their marquee moundsman, but the five Giants errors had deprived him of a win. That encouraged the Red Sox, as did the poor fielding (five errors) by the Giants.

This was one of only three World Series games to end in a tie (the others were Game One of the 1907 Series and Game Two in 1922, Giants against the Yankees). Because the game ended in a tie, and the hour was late, both teams stayed in Boston to play Game Three before resuming the back-and-forth travel between cities.

PLAYER PROFILE: TRIS SPEAKER

One of the greatest hitters in baseball history, Speaker holds a lifetime .345 average, placing him fifth among ballplayers since 1900. He had some power, too, and his ten homers led the American League in 1912. Speaker reached base 310 times that year as well, leading the league in doubles, base hits, and on-base percentage. He was that year's Chalmers Award winner, the MVP Award of the day. He hit .383 in 1912, and drove in 90 runs.

He played with Boston through the 1915 season, but a salary dispute in the wake of the collapse of the Federal League and the depressing effect that had on player compensation led to him being traded to Cleveland just before the 1916 season began. With the Indians, Speaker continued to shine, hitting .386 in 1917 and five times in all batting .370 or better.

A brilliant center fielder, he set records that will likely never be topped, including participation in 119 double plays.

He hit .300 for the Red Sox in the 1912 Series (and .294 in the 1915 Fall Classic). In Game Two, his bunt single loaded the bases with nobody out in the first inning and he scored the second of three runs in that frame. With the game tied 5-5 after nine innings, the Giants took a 6-5 lead in to the top of the 10th, but—with one out—Speaker tripled to center field and scored the tying run on an error at the plate on the relay home. The game wound up as a tie.

Game Three: Fenway Park, Boston / October 10, 1912

New York 2, Boston 1

New York	010	010	000	—	2	7	1
Boston	000	000	001	—	1	7	0

WP: Marquard (1-0)   LP: O'Brien (0-1)

Rube Marquard (26-11) faced Buck O'Brien (20-13) in Game Three. Both pitched exceptionally well. Marquard had started off the 1912 season like gangbusters. He won every single one of his first 19 decisions from Opening Day on April 11 through July 3. And he truly should have been credited with a 20th win, on April 20. He entered the game in relief and, after putting out the fire in the top of the ninth, the Giants scored three times to win the game in the bottom of the ninth. Joe Wood had run off a string of 16 straight victories in 1912, too, but today he'd be matched against O'Brien for Boston.

Josh Devore hit a leadoff single just over O'Brien's glove, was almost picked off first, and was shortly cut down stealing. Marquard kept the ball in the infield and retired the first three Boston batters.

O'Brien was touched for another leadoff hit in the second, this time a double to center by Red Murray. Merkle sacrificed Murray to third, and Herzog hit a fly ball to Hooper that sacrificed him home. Meyers grounded out 5-3 and it was one run for the Giants.

Duffy Lewis singled in the second and Tris Speaker managed another base hit in the fourth, but that was all the Sox could get off Marquard through the first four. The Giants added one more run in the top of the fifth. It was another leadoff hit, another double, that set up the run when Buck Herzog hit the ball over the third-base bag. Meyers tried to hit away, but produced an inadvertent sacrifice, bouncing back to O'Brien—who had to throw to first as Herzog took third. Art Fletcher slammed a single—his first hit of the Series—and Herzog came home. There was considerably more action, but just the one run came in. O'Brien was fortunate to have only given up two runs in the game, though the three walks and seven hits don't look that bad in the boxscore.

Stahl singled in the fifth, Yerkes singled in the sixth, and Stahl doubled in the seventh—only the second Red Sox runner to reach second base—but the Red Sox were held scoreless through eight. Stahl's ball had nearly gone out; it hit off the top of the wall and bounced back into play.

Hugh Bedient pitched the top of the ninth for Boston, O'Brien having been pinch-hit for by Neal Ball in the eighth (Ball struck out). Bedient hit the first batter, Herzog, but he was thrown out trying to steal second a minute or two later. Meyers singled, but then Fletcher flied into a double play, Meyers being doubled off the first-base bag. The score still stood 2-0, Giants.

Speaker popped out in the bottom of the ninth, but then Lewis singled to Merkle at first base (Marquard failed to cover the bag in time) and Larry Gardner doubled down the first-base line, scoring Lewis. On the play, a coaching mixup hurt the Sox. Heinie Wagner was coaching third, but since he was due up after Stahl, Speaker had moved over to third base to relieve him. Unfortunately, Gardner saw both Wagner and Speaker first hold up Lewis and then yelling at him to score; Gardner had to hold up at second when he could well have taken third. Stahl hit back to the mound, and Marquard threw to third to cut down Gardner for the second out. Speaker wrote that he believed Gardner was nonetheless safe, believing that Herzog dropped the ball. Olaf Henriksen came in to pinch-run for Stahl at first base. Wagner hit a ball that Merkle misplayed, dropping the ball, and sending Henriksen to third—and it was first and third, two outs. Wagner stole second, putting both the tying run and winning run in scoring position. Then came the play of the game. Forrest "Hick" Cady was at the plate. It was his first time up. Carrigan had been the starting catcher but Hack Engle had unsuccessfully batted for Carrigan in the eighth.

Cady hit a long uncatchable drive to deep right-center field and hundreds of Red Sox fans went home happy, glad that the Sox had won the game. But it was a case of premature exuberation. "The Boston crowd was already celebrating a second victory … the bands were blaring, the bass drums were rumbling, and the cymbals were crashing. The grandstands were afire with waving red flags," wrote the *New York Times*. The first rush of fans harbored a false confidence and hoped to beat the masses out of the park. Right fielder Josh Devore had sprung into action with one of the greatest catches in World Series history. Tim Murnane wrote of Devore that "while under a full head of steam he leaped in the air, and, with hands extended over his head and his back to the infield, he came out of the air with the ball." There truly were fans who believed the Red Sox had won, only to learn later that the 5'6" "midget outfielder" (*Hartford Courant*) Devore had saved the day for the Giants and evened the Series at one win apiece. Chalk one up for the little guys.

The *Times* suggested that if the remaining games in the Series were anything like the first three, every one a game that went down to the wire, "New York and Boston will fill all the nerve sanitariums with their citizens."

PLAYER PROFILE: JAKE STAHL

Jake Stahl, first baseman and manager for the 1912 Sox, started his major league career the year that Boston played in its first World Series, 1903. Primarily a catcher at the time, he appeared in 40 games and hit .239. He did not appear in the World Series. Boston sold him to Washington early in 1904.

Stahl played through 1910, leading the American League in home runs with ten and hitting .27—and then decided to retire to focus on work as a bank executive in Chicago. He became a part-owner of the Red Sox in 1912 joining James McAleer's group which bought the team from John I. Taylor, with Stahl reportedly holding a 5 percent stake. He appeared in 95 games and hit .301—and led the team into the World Series and to a World Championship. In the Series, he batted .250, drove in two (both in Game Two) and scored three runs. In Game Three, Stahl reached base in three of his four plate appearances with a single, a double, and a fielder's choice, but this one went to the Giants, 2-1.

He managed the first 81 games of the 1913 season but was fired and went back to banking.

Game Four: Polo Grounds, New York / October 11, 1912

Boston 3, New York 1

Boston	010	100	001	—	3	8	1
New York	000	000	100	—	1	9	1

WP: Wood (2-0)   LP: Tesreau (0-2)

It was Wood vs. Tesreau once more, and once more Wood came out on top. Tesreau got off to a shaky start when Hooper singled through the box and Meyers pounced on Yerkes's bunt but threw wildly to second. The threat ended when Speaker hit into a double play and Lewis grounded out. The Giants got a one-out single from Doyle. He was forced at second by Snodgrass's grounder, and then Snodgrass got picked off first to end the inning.

Tesreau started off shakily again in the second frame, surrendering a first-pitch triple to Larry Gardner that went into deep right-center—and then threw a wild pitch by Meyers allowing Gardner to grab a quick run for the Red Sox. Another hit and a stolen base—but also another missed opportunity—followed for the Giants in the second.

Boston got the first two men aboard in the third (Wood with a single) but three ground balls ended that threat. A routine grounder and two strikeouts made for a quick bottom of the third for New York.

For the fourth inning in a row, the Red Sox got their leadoff man on board, this time Gardner via the base on balls. He was forced when Tesreau handled Stahl's bunt well, but Stahl stole second and then moved to third base when Wagner grounded to Merkle at first base. Cady—the man who'd hit the long ball to Devore to end Game Three, squeaked a single past Fletcher into left field to score Jake Stahl. It was the hit that proved the winning run, but there was drama yet to come in Game Four.

The Red Sox bats were pretty much silenced but for a single to Steve Yerkes (a great one-handed catch by Murray robbed Hooper of what looked like a triple), but Tesreau started a threat in the Giants' sixth, lining a single to left field. Devore followed with a single of his own—off Wood's shin—and New York had runners on first and second with nobody out. Doyle, though, swung at the first pitch and popped up to third. Snodgrass grounded to second base and the middle runner was erased, and Red Murray, too, hit into a near carbon copy 4-6 force out.

Wood was reasonably effective, though the Giants did collect nine hits, two-thirds of them after the fifth. He proved best in the pinches and may have had the Giants batters off in their timing; contemporary reports say that as the game progressed he relied much less on his smoking fastball and instead used his curve and change of pace most effectively. More than once in the Series, sportswriters commented on Heinie Wagner's defensive prowess at short-stop. Hugh Fullerton wrote that in this game alone, Wagner "made two of the greatest stops of the season." It was not until the seventh that the Giants put up a run of their own. Herzog singled, sandwiched between outs by Merkle and Meyers, but then Art Fletcher doubled down the right-field line and drove in Herzog. McGraw had McCormick bat for Jeff Tesreau and it looked like it had paid off when McCormick singled—but Yerkes knocked the ball down, gathered it in, and threw a bullet from second base to Cady at the plate, getting the speedy Fletcher (thrown out by as much as 15 feet) and keeping the Giants from knotting the score. Sending Fletcher home was probably McGraw's biggest mistake of the game, though in his column on October 15 he said he'd do it again in a two-out situation like that.

Red Ames took over pitching for New York and Speaker doubled off the top of the bleacher fence in the top of the eighth, but nothing came of it. The Giants got runners on first and third in the bottom of the inning after Wagner's error and Murray's single through the hole (vacated at short when Wagner moved to cover on the hit-and-run), but Smoky Joe struck out Fred Merkle on three curveballs. The *Globe*'s Tim Murnane observed that, though the game was played in New York, the "majority of those present seemed to favor the Boston men."

It was another 2-1 game and Wood was looking for an insurance run in the top of the ninth to give him a little breathing room. Larry Gardner singled sharply to center field, and Stahl sacrificed perfectly to push Gardner to second. Wagner walked, though, setting up a force play, and Cady obliged, grounding out 6-4 to get Wagner at second. Gardner took third, and then Wood took matters into his own hands with a single to the wall in the Polo Grounds' exceptionally short right field. Hooper flied out but it was 3-1 in favor of the visitors.

Wood settled down again on the mound. Herzog flied out to Speaker in center field, but that was the only solidly hit ball in the bottom of the ninth. Meyers lifted a foul pop-up to Cady, and Fletched popped up to Stahl at first base. The Red Sox took a 2-1 lead in the Series, and both teams hopped back on the train to head north to Massachusetts. Neither team had yet won a game at home.

As had happened after Game One, some New York fans showed their displeasure at the defeat. After Game One, the automobiles of the Royal Rooters were "stoned and deluged with dirt by the urchins lined up along the streets and avenues." After Game Four, "it was the automobiles occupied by the players that were bombarded and many of the occupants suffered from dirt being thrown." Fortunately, there were no serious injuries despite "some of the oldest of the hoodlums being particularly good marksmen." Buck O'Brien was hit in the face by a sharp stone that cut the skin. (O'Brien had a rough Series; he would be struck by one of his teammates in the aftermath of Game Six). The Red Sox complained that New York's finest stood by without intervening.

PLAYER PROFILE: HICK CADY

Forrest Leroy "Hick" Cady was backup catcher for Boston his first year in the majors, 1912. He was someone the Red Sox really wanted: in early January, they traded six players to the Jersey City Skeeters to get him. Cady played for the Red Sox through 1917, then was traded to the Athletics as part of a deal for Stuffy McInnis in early 1918.

In 1912, he hit for a .259 average and drove in nine runs in 135 at-bats. In the Series, he played in seven of the eight games and had 22 at-bats, driving in one run and hitting safely just three times, a .136 average. His RBI came in Game Four. It came in the top of the fourth inning to give the Red Sox a 2-0 lead. Jake Stahl was on third and Cady singled to left field off Giants starter Jeff Tesreau, sufficient to give the Red Sox the game as Joe Wood allowed just one seventh-inning run.

He played in the 1915 and 1916 World Series for Boston, too, with three hits in ten at-bats in the two Series combined, without any further RBIs. He scored one run.

Game Five: Fenway Park, Boston / October 12, 1912

Boston 2, New York 1

New York	000	000	100	—	1	3	1
Boston	002	000	00x	—	2	5	1

WP: Bedient (1-0)   LP: Mathewson (0-1)

It was a dark, damp, foggy, gloomy day and up until noontime, the playing of the game was still in question. Down two games to one, McGraw had his ace Mathewson up his sleeve, if not a sure bet at least even money to tie the Series. There'd only been two days off since the

11-inning tie game in which Matty had gone the distance, and there could have been questions raised as to whether the 12-year veteran's career had peaked. Whatever worries might have obtained, Mathewson pitched a great ballgame. It seemed to take him just a while to settle in; he gave up two singles in the first and one in the second, but pitched his way through to two scoreless innings.

The rookie Hugh Bedient was Stahl's selection. Winner of an even 20 games, the "modest youth" was the fourth starter for Stahl and pitched an even better game than Christy Mathewson. Bedient, too, faced a little trouble in the cold weather, walking the leadoff batter in both the first and second innings, each time on four pitches. Bedient issued free passes to three batters in all, and served up a single to Mathewson in the first three frames. Yet no Giant got past second base and Bedient didn't walk a man in the final six innings; he was fairly consistently ahead in the count, throwing a lot of first-pitch strikes. Oddly for the era, never once did either team try to lay down a bunt, nor was there an attempted steal—even though the Red Sox of the day were sometimes known as the "Speed Boys."

Harry Hooper tripled to the left-field corner to lead off the Red Sox third. The ball rolled between the stands of the temporary bleachers and Josh Devore disappeared from sight before coming up with the ball fast enough to hold Hooper to just three bases. Steve Yerkes swung at the first pitch and tripled to center field, the ball rolling to the fence to drive in Hooper. Second baseman Larry Doyle went to field Speaker's grounder but, glancing up to assess his chances of holding Yerkes at third, he lost track of the ball just long enough that it ended up in right field. It was the lone error of the game for New York. Yerkes scored the second run, of course, but Speaker was too aggressive in trying to reach second. He was thrown out, Red Murray to shortstop Art Fletcher. Both Lewis and Gardner subsequently grounded out. It was 2-0 for the Red Sox.

Mathewson retired every Red Sox batter he faced for the remainder of the game, setting down 17 in a row. He'd held Boston to but five hits, but the two runs were to prove one too many.

In the fourth, fifth, and sixth, Bedient was almost as dominant, allowing just one base runner—via a leadoff single to Meyers in the fifth, after he had fouled off six pitches. Fred Merkle doubled to start off the seventh, the ball bouncing into the bleachers for a ground-rule double. It was only the third hit off Bedient in the game, and it was to be the last. Herzog struck out. Meyers flied deep enough to Speaker in center that he had to go back to reel in the ball (Speaker traditionally played a shallow center field, and set a record for unassisted double plays by an outfielder, but fortunately this time was playing deeper than usual). Merkle was able to tag up and take third. McCormick batted for Fletcher, his fourth pinch-hit appearance of the Series. For the third time, it looked like he might have made something happen. He reached base on Gardner's error, and Merkle scored. Mathewson, though, grounded out to end the inning. It was now a one-run game.

And was to remain so. Bedient pitched a perfect eighth and ninth, only Merkle's deep fly ball in the ninth escaping the infield. Speaker had to run to haul that one in. The Red Sox starter had thrown a three-hitter, with just one unearned run allowed. Finally, the loyal hometown fans were rewarded by seeing their team win and it was a jubilant throng that left Fenway after the one hour, 43-minute game with the Red Sox up three games to one.

After the game, in a column under Doyle's byline, he took responsibility for the error that brought in Boston's second run, but blamed Snodgrass for not cutting off Yerkes's ball to center. "He could have at least stopped the ball if he had not fielded it cleanly," Doyle charged. He said he felt badly for Matty, who was pitching with a sore arm but threw a masterful game. Jeff Tesreau in his column echoed something else Doyle confessed: "We had expected to encounter a nervous youngster in Bedient, erratic and inclined to be wild on the slightest provocation, and instead we met a pitcher as cool as ice." Indeed, the Giants tried to provoke the Boston pitcher, with aggressive bench jockeying, but to no avail.

Wood put pen to paper after the game, too, praising Mathewson for not letting a Boston base runner reach base after the third, but reserving his greater praise for Hugh Bedient, who'd have pitched a shutout had not Gardner taken his eye off the ball for a split second in the seventh. Of Bedient, after the first couple of innings, Wood said, "He showed fine nerve all the way through and tightened like a steel trap on the one or two occasions that men got on bases."

It had seemed that Mathewson was the last hope the New Yorkers had and that the Series was now a lead-pipe cinch to be won by Boston.

PLAYER PROFILE: HUGH BEDIENT

Hugh Bedient was an unexpected success for the Sox in 1912. The 22-year-old right-hander turned in a 20-win season his first year in the major leagues, with a 20-9 record and a 2.92 earned run average. It was the best year he'd ever have. His 15-14 season in 1913 reflected an overall decline in Boston baseball fortunes as the team itself wound up just a few games over .500, with a fourth-place finish.

Bedient's first appearance in the World Series was to throw a scoreless 11th in the Game Two tie. He threw another scoreless frame in Game Three, the ninth inning of the 2-1 loss tagged to Buck O'Brien. In Game Five, young Hugh drew a start and was brilliant. He pitched a complete game three-hitter, allowing just one unearned run in the seventh, the only time in the game a Giant got past second base. The win gave the Red Sox a 3-1 edge in the Series.

Bedient threw the first six innings of the final game, too, again allowing just one run—this time, it was earned (and his final Series ERA became 0.50). Henriksen pinch-hit for him and doubled in the tying run.

Game Six: Polo Grounds, New York / October 14, 1912

New York 5, Boston 2

Boston	020	001	300	—	2	7	2
New York	500	000	00x	—	5	11	2

WP: Marquard (2-0)   LP: O'Brien (0-2)

The sixth game of the Series was the one that produced the most controversy. Fans wanted Stahl to go for the throat by starting Smoky Joe, but word was that owner Jimmy McAleer had ordered Stahl to start Buck O'Brien and save Wood to pitch, if necessary, in Game Seven at Fenway. [Troy Soos, *Before the Curse*, p. 139] It wasn't bad strategy, but with Sunday the 13th as a day off, Wood had had a couple of days' rest and the Sox players smelled blood. They wanted a win, and even though Buck had pitched well enough in Game Two, he'd still lost. And even though he'd won 20 games in the regular season, Wood had won 34.

Stout and Johnson contend in *Red Sox Century* that McAleer "was a shrewd businessman who knew the value of the gate he and his partners would collect if Wood were to start an additional game at Fenway Park." And victory did seem assured, which may have left the Sox owner "both confident enough and greedy enough to gamble near-certain victory and a world championship for a chance at another lucrative Fenway payday." Stahl argued, but lost the debate, and when the players heard the news their dreams of a quick wrap-up to the Series were deflated. Perhaps with a little hyperbole, Stout and Johnson suggest that "by the time they reached the Polo Grounds the Red Sox were already a beaten ballclub." It shouldn't have seemed like such a surprise, though. Murnane predicted in the *Globe* the morning of the 13th that "Joe Wood might have gone in tomorrow had the Red Sox lost out yesterday but now the chances are that they will have O'Brien for a starter … keeping a face card back in Joe Wood for the game here on Tuesday, if necessary." Hugh Fullerton's syndicated column also foresaw Wood held in reserve with O'Brien and Collins ready to go. The Associated Press wire predicted Collins to start, but agreed that Wood would be held. Several of the players writing columns expected O'Brien or perhaps Collins.

The Red Sox did little in the first and, initially, it looked like O'Brien would escape unscathed as well. Devore grounded out. Doyle singled, a slow hit to Yerkes, and then stole second, but O'Brien struck out Snodgrass. Murray singled to deep shortstop—another infield hit—but Doyle held at third base. Then O'Brien balked. Doyle was waved home and Murray was sent to second. Did the balk unnerve O'Brien? Stout and Johnson suggest he might have drunk too much the night before, not expecting to be given the ball, though the consensus in the press that he was one of the two likely starters appears to belie that notion. Nevertheless, and all of a sudden, the dike broke. Mathewson in his postgame column talked about how the two coaches were riding O'Brien from the lines. He revealed that McGraw had signaled for a double steal, but the balk rendered that academic. "The balk beat O'Brien," Matty wrote. "He could not come back. He just caved in, and right there our luck changed; we got all of the 'breaks' and, with two out, we gave O'Brien a harder whaling than any other pitcher had received in the Series."

Merkle doubled against the wall in right. Herzog doubled down the third-base line. Meyers singled, yet another infield hit. With runners on first and third, a double steal saw Herzog pilfer home with the fourth Giants run while Meyers not only stole second but took third on Yerkes's error. Fletcher bunted, squeezing in Meyers from third base. The inning was finally brought to conclusion when O'Brien picked off Fletcher—but five runs were in.

The Giants never scored again, but they didn't need to, though the Red Sox immediately struck back for two runs in the top of the second.

Marquard fumbled a ball that Gardner hit. Stahl singled on a shot to center, Gardner taking second. Wagner and Cady both made outs, a strikeout and a foul to the catcher. With O'Brien due up, Stahl took him out and put in Hack Engle, who doubled off the wall in left to drive in both Gardner and Stahl. Hooper popped up. Those were all the runs the Red Sox were to score on this day. The final was 5-2.

Ray Collins took over pitching duties for the Red Sox and pitched very well. He scattered five hits over seven innings; there were two singles in the Giants' third but both hitters erased themselves—Murray, by trying to stretch his single to a double, and Merkle, who unsuccessfully tried to steal second.

The Red Sox hit two long drives in the top of the third, but both were caught. Wagner was robbed of a homer by Snodgrass in the fourth; the Sox got a couple of singles, but Collins hit into an inning-ending double play. There were more long balls hit, and a few hard-hit grounders, but the Red Sox only got one hit in the final five innings.

Red Sox Century reports that Joe Wood's brother Paul "enraged at losing one hundred dollars on the game, sought out O'Brien and blackened one of the pitcher's eyes in a wild fistfight. Although the incident was widely reported and later denied, the team was clearly in trouble."

With an extra day of rest, though, Smoky Joe had the opportunity to close it out before the home crowd. Tim Murnane reported the Red Sox left New York "confident that they will win the game tomorrow." The Boston rooters at the game didn't seem the least discouraged; they staged an animated snake dance around the Boston bench and then paraded left to right, back and forth, making for the exits with the band blaring and shouts of "tomorrow we'll show them!"

Tesreau, in his column, said the Sox "had none of the ginger that had characterized them in the other games, and if I am not mistaken, they have shot their bolt." He thought they'd been too eager to wrap it up, and were now "beginning to stagger." That was the theme of McGraw's piece: his article about his Giants in the *New York Times* was headlined "Team Has Struck Its Stride."

PLAYER PROFILE: BUCK O'BRIEN

Local Brockton boy Thomas J. "Buck" O'Brien presented a strange Series history in 1912, the year he turned thirty; O'Brien won 20 games and lost just 13, with a 2.58 ERA. As one of the three 20-game winners on the club (well, Smoky Joe was a 30-game winner), he performed nicely in Game Three, holding New York to just two runs in eight innings of work. Rube Marquard pitched even better and allowed just one Red Sox run. O'Brien suffered a tough loss.

Then things became complicated. With the Red Sox holding a 3-1 edge in the Series after the fifth game, it looked like a sure bet they'd win it all. In fact, it may have seemed too good a bet. There are intimations that gamblers got to Buck and offered him a considerable sum to lose Game Six. If not that particular vice, one might blame him for drinking too much the night before. He'd not known he was going to get the start and reportedly imbibed rather heavily. In the bottom of the first, he did retire two of the first three batters but then the bottom fell out. A single put runners on first and third, and O'Brien balked in a run. Then followed two doubles, a single, a steal of home, and a bunt for a single. He picked off Fletcher to end the inning, but five runs were in, and Buck was taken out. Hugh Bedient finished up the game. The atmosphere in baseball at the time was such that a number of Red Sox players thought they smelled a rat, and word was that O'Brien was beaten by one or two of his teammates.

The Series ended well for Boston, of course, but O'Brien never really recovered. He spent the off-season doing vaudeville and came to camp out of shape. He only started 15 games in

1913 and wound up with a 4-9 record. The Red Sox sold him to the White Sox in early July and he was 0-2 with Chicago, and then out of baseball.

Game Seven: Fenway Park, Boston / October 15, 1912

New York 11, Boston 4

New York	610	002	101	—	11	16	4
Boston	010	000	210	—	4	9	3

WP: Tesreau (1-2)   LP: Wood (2-1)   HR: Doyle (1), Gardner (1)

If McAleer had made a bundle betting against his own team in Game Six, he may have lost it all in Game Seven when Smoky Joe failed to deliver. New York had scored five runs in the first inning the day before. Now, facing Boston's best pitcher, they scored six runs before the Red Sox even got up to bat.

Wood may have still been ticked off, or worse, from the events of the day before and Stout and Johnson claim he even beat O'Brien with a baseball bat before the game. The game was delayed by a bad mistake in ticketing. Red Sox management had sold the tickets routinely held for the team's booster club, the Royal Rooters, and the 300-strong troupe paraded into the park only to find their seats taken. This did not set well, and there was a lot of pushing and shoving on the field with five mounted policemen having to push back the team's most loyal fans. The Rooters felt aggrieved and many joined in booing Red Sox management in a demonstration after the game that even resulted in loud cheers for the New York owners who had reserved a special section for them while at the Polo Grounds. Most boycotted the ballclub the following day. It was no coincidence that about 40 percent of the park was devoid of fans on the 16th, even though it was the final game of the championship.

Wood had to pitch with a number of circumstances stacked against him, not to mention a "high cold wind" that repeatedly sent "clouds of dust over the field" and an arm he said was subpar. But he was 2-0 and Jeff Tesreau was 0-2 against the Red Sox.

The Giants came out hitting. Every one of the first seven New York batters achieved a level of success, and even the eighth and ninth batters contributed in a way. Josh Devore singled on the first pitch, fumbled a bit by Wagner but not enough for an error to be charged. Doyle hit the first pitch he saw for a single to center. Wood inexplicably took a big windup and the two base runners executed such a clean double steal that Cady didn't even throw. Snodgrass plated them both with a double to right field. Murray sacrifice bunted Snodgrass from second to third. Merkle singled, scoring Snodgrass and taking second on Lewis's errant throw to the plate. Herzog hit the ball back to Wood, who whirled and got Merkle in a rundown—but Herzog took second while Murray was being chased down. And he scored when Meyers singled. Fletcher got in the act, singling to the right side. Meyers ran to third. The pitcher, Tesreau, hit the ball off his counterpart's hand and reached safely. Meyers scored on the play and Fletcher took third. Tesreau was caught stealing second, in a rundown, but not until Fletcher had scored on the delayed double steal. The Giants had hit aggressively, all this happening on 15 or fewer pitches. New York 6, Boston coming to bat.

Boston batted but didn't succeed at it. Jake Stahl had allowed Wood to complete the first inning but wasn't about to send him out for the second. Charley Hall came in, and some adventures on the base paths ensued. Hall set the stage by walking Devore who then stole second. He walked Doyle, too, and it was getting interesting again, but Hall picked off Devore. Snodgrass singled and Doyle stopped at second. He was apparently picked off second, too—but Hall committed an error and Doyle rounded third and scored. Finally, Hall got the last two batters. 7-0 Giants.

The *New York Times* concluded after the game that Wood had needed at least one day's more rest "after his nerve-wracking games of last week. He is not tireless like Walter Johnson or 'Ed' Walsh. He needed a good rest, he didn't get it, and he cracked."

Larry Gardner bounced a home run over the center-field fence in the bottom of the second to help make the Red Sox feel just a little bit better. The next three batters were put down easily, though.

The Giants extended their lead with two more runs in the top of the sixth when Devore walked and Doyle added a "bounce" home run.

Tesreau drove in another run in the seventh, singling in Meyers.

Speaker singled after the seventh-inning stretch, and Lewis doubled. Speaker scored on Gardner's grounder to short. Larry Doyle misplayed Stahl's ball and Lewis scored. All told, the Red Sox put at least one man on in every inning. In all, 19 Red Sox reached base. Several were erased, but 12 men were left on, and the Sox failed to take advantage of the vulnerable Tesreau. Hugh Fullerton decried Boston's baserunning as "the most wretched exhibition of base running ever given a championship team. They ran bases like a bunch of farmers." Hall put more than his share of Giants on base, too, walking five—three of whom came in to score. It wasn't the prettiest of games.

In the bottom of the eighth, after Cady reached on Doyle's second error (the Giants made four in the game), the Red Sox scraped together another run on Hall's single (Cady took third on Devore's error), and a sacrifice fly to center.

The Giants made it 11-4, the final score, after Herzog walked and Wilson singled to center field. Speaker made an uncharacteristic error and Herzog was able to round the bases and score. The only lopsided game of the Series left Boston fans discouraged and presented Hugh Bedient with the responsibility of salvaging what days before had seemed a predestined World Series win for the Red Sox.

PLAYER PROFILE: CHARLEY HALL

Charley Hall started his major league career with Cincinnati in 1907 and 1908. In 1909, when he came over to the Red Sox, Charley joined Frank Arellanes as one of two Latinos in the pitching rotation. In the five seasons he pitched for the Sox, he won 46 and lost 32, with an ERA of 2.93. He contributed solidly in 1912 (15-3, 3.02). Hall was the winning pitcher in the very first game ever played at Fenway Park, on April 20, 1912.

Known as "Sea Lion" Hall, because of what Frederick Lieb called a "raucous penetrating voice like a fog horn at sea," Hall threw 2 ⅔ innings of relief of Ray Collins in Game Two, allowing one run on two hits (but walking four). His second appearance in the Series came in Game Seven, taking the ball to start the second inning after Joe Wood had been bombed for six runs in the first. Charley pitched the rest of the game—eight innings—giving up three earned runs, walking five while striking out only one. At the plate, Hall was 3-for-3 and walked once, too.

He retired with a lifetime major league 3.09 ERA and a 54-47 record.

Game Eight: Fenway Park, Boston / October 16, 1912

Boston 3, New York 2 (10 innings)

New York	001	000	000	1	—	2	9	2
Boston	000	000	100	2	—	3	8	4

WP: Wood (3-1)   LP: Mathewson (0-2)

Breaking the pattern of alternation again, because there had been no firm decision where to play an eighth game, another coin toss was held and Boston won. With the Rooters genuinely and fervently upset, and with fans discouraged by the dismal play of the Red Sox in losing the last two games, attendance dropped precipitously from an average of 32,000 to barely over 17,000.

The deciding game of the 1912 World Series was one of the great games of all time. It began with a matchup of the rookie Hugh Bedient against the veteran Christy Mathewson. The first couple of innings were a little shaky: the Red Sox committed three errors behind Bedient, who walked one and gave up a single. No New Yorkers scored. Mathewson gave up two singles and a walk, but no Sox scored.

The Giants got one run in the top of the third. Devore walked, and stood on second after Doyle's grounder to third base. Snodgrass grounded to first base, and Devore took third. Red Murray doubled, scoring Devore.

Herzog doubled in the top of the fourth and Gardner doubled in the bottom. Neither team took advantage. Two Giants singles in the top of the fifth resulted in no further scoring; the lead man was cut down stealing. But Harry Hooper made a great catch, robbing Larry Doyle of a possible home run, catching the ball in his bare hand and falling into the seats.

Bedient wasn't at his best, but all he really did was walk Meyers in the sixth, and give up a single to Mathewson in the seventh. The score remained 1-0, Giants.

In the bottom of the seventh, with time running out, Gardner flied out to center field. Then Stahl singled, a Texas Leaguer that frustratingly fell in between three New York fielders, and Heinie Wagner walked. Cady just missed getting good wood on the ball, and popped up to Fletcher at short. Hugh Bedient was due up, but Stahl knew he could get a couple of innings out of Joe Wood, so he asked their Danish-born pinch-hitting specialist Olaf Henriksen (.321 on the season) to see what he could do against Mathewson. Henriksen doubled to left field and tied the game, pushing Stahl across home plate while Wagner took third. It wasn't the most classic of doubles—the ball actually hit the third-base bag on its way and hopped on—but it did the trick. Hooper flied out. The score was tied heading into the eighth inning. And Wood toed the rubber.

Smoky Joe, looking to make up for his previous performance, kept the ball down, and induced three groundouts (around a single by Herzog). Mathewson, too, got three groundouts in succession.

It was the ninth inning of the final game of the World Series. Wood got McCormick to fly out, then struck out Mathewson. Devore worked a walk, but Doyle grounded out. Bottom of the ninth: Stahl doubled, but his hit was bracketed by three fly balls that all went for outs.

The game extended into extra innings. Some observers doubtless must have wondered if the classic battle would end in another unsatisfying tie.

Snodgrass grounded out to Wood. But Red Murray hit the ball into the left-center field stands—it only counted as a ground-rule double, since it landed in temporary seating set up for the Series. He scored when Fred Merkle singled to center field. Speaker tried a short-hop grab of the ball down near his shoestrings to fire to home plate, but instead fumbled it as the go-ahead run came in. (The Red Sox made four errors in Game Eight). Merkle took second base on the misplay—but Wood struck out Herzog and Meyers hit a hard grounder that glanced off Wood's pitching hand. Wood grabbed the ball and threw to first to record the third out. The Giants held a 2-1 lead, and only three outs stood between them and the World Championship.

Hack Engle pinch-hit for Wood. He was a mere .234 hitter but he'd doubled and driven in both Red Sox runs in Game Six. Wood hit .290 during the year, but his hand was hurting. Engle hit the ball to center field but Fred Snodgrass let the ball pop right out of his glove. Engle was safe—reaching second base on the play—and "Snodgrass's muff" went down in history, after the rest of the 10th unfolded. After flubbing a couple of sacrifice bunt attempts, Hooper flied out to center, and Snodgrass snared that one—not an easy catch—but it was deep enough that Engle tagged up and took third base. Mathewson walked Steve Yerkes. Tris Speaker hit an easy foul—but it fell in between Merkle and Meyers, and Spoke had new life. He took advantage and boosted his Series average to an even .300 with a single to right field, easily scoring Engle with the tying run. Each team had committed a 10th-inning error in center field and each time a run resulted.

Speaker took second on the late throw to the plate, and Yerkes was on third. To set up a play at any base, or perhaps a double play, McGraw had Mathewson intentionally walk Duffy Lewis (0-for-4 on the game, .188 in the Series). In the on-deck circle was Larry Gardner. He had hit .315 on the season, with a third-best 86 RBIs but only .179 in the Series. Gardner was, however, tied for the lead in World Series RBIs. He hit a fly ball to right field, to the same Josh Devore who'd made such a spectacular catch to end Game Three. Devore caught this one much more easily, but it was deep enough to serve as a sacrifice fly, and it won the game when Yerkes tagged up and scored. Red Sox 3, Giants 2.

PLAYER PROFILE: OLAF HENRIKSEN

Born in Kirkerup, Denmark, his geographically astute teammates quite naturally called Henriksen "Swede." The only Dane to make the majors, Henriksen debuted with the Red Sox in August 1911 and was a pinch-hitter par excellence who played all seven of his major league seasons with Boston. He hit .366 his first season and drew enough walks to push his on-base percentage to .449. In 1912, he hit .321 and boasted a .457 OBP. Though appearing in 321 games in his seven seasons, he only took the field in 128 games, clearly indicating his role on the team. During the Deadball Era, when runs were scarce, getting on base nearly 40 percent of the time was of prime importance; Henriksen finished his career with a lifetime on-base percentage of .392. His batting, though, declined rapidly after the first three years, hovering around or below the "Mendoza line" of .200 the final three seasons.

The Giants out-hit the Red Sox .270 to .220, outscored the Red Sox by six runs, and pitched dramatically better (an earned run average of 1.59 to Boston's 2.92). They committed 18 errors, including some key ones, to Boston's 15. But so much of it is in the timing. New York won one game by seven runs and another by three. The Red Sox won three one-run games and the other by two runs.

Olaf appeared in three World Series. In the final game of the 1912 Series, the score was 1-0 for the Giants in the seventh inning. There were runners at first and second, with two outs. Pitcher Hugh Bedient was due up, a right-handed batter who'd hit a respectable .192 during the season. Manager Jake Stahl was the base runner on second base. Henriksen doubled to left field, scoring one run and tying the score. The game ultimately went into extra innings, thanks to Henriksen's 1.000 batting average and his lone career World Series run batted in.

IN BETWEEN SERIES

For two years—1913 and 1914—the Red Sox were without a World Championship. Many of the Royal Rooters remained alienated due to the ticket problem at Game Seven of the 1912 Series, but there were still over 20,000 who flocked to Fenway for 1913's Opening Day. Attendance dropped nearly 27 percent by year's end, but significantly the number of Red Sox home wins also dropped, from 57 to 41, a decline of 39 percent. Overall, the Sox won 25 percent fewer games in 1913—from 105 to 79. Some have argued that the small turnout of 6,500 for the June 25 raising of the pennant demonstrated an ongoing boycott of sorts, but the Boston newspapers reported that the "weather was threatening and all day it looked as if it might rain." Furthermore, it was a "raw" day of "extreme cold."

Wins were down because the club just wasn't clicking. Joe Wood hurt his ankle early in spring training and then injured his thumb in mid-May, breaking it entirely later on in the season. The star pitcher with the 34-5 record in 1912 posted a mark of 11-5 in 1913. The pitcher with the best record was Collins, with a 19-8 mark. Bedient slipped from 20-9 to 15-14. Rookie Dutch Leonard won 14 games but lost 16. Team ERA increased from 2.76 to 2.94. The team batting average dipped from .277 to .268. The Athletics won 96 games and Boston was 15 ½ games behind, in fourth place.

Before the 1914 season began, the Red Sox had a new owner in Joseph Lannin. Ban Johnson was still pulling the strings and, after ensuring that Bill Carrigan had replaced Jake Stahl as manager during the season, further orchestrated Lannin replacing McAleer as principal owner.

The Red Sox finished in second place in 1914, their 91 wins still leaving them 8 ½ games behind Philadelphia. This was the year of the "Miracle Braves"—so at least one of Boston's teams captured the World Series, sweeping the Athletics. In fact, the two 1914 World Series

Mayor Boston
"Honey Fitz"
2 Forrest Cady, catcher
3 Larry Gardner 3rd base
4 Jake Stahl Mar[...]

STAHL

In the parade after the winning of the World Series, Boston Mayor Fitzgerald is shown with players Cady, Gardner, Stahl, and Wood. (Boston Public Library)

home games played in Boston were both played in the newer and larger Fenway Park, which had now hosted Series play in two of its three years of existence.

The additional 17 Sox wins were reflected in the records of their best pitchers. Leonard set a single-season earned run average mark that has never been beaten—0.96, helping him to a 19-5 record. Collins was 20-13. Rube Foster (14-8, 1.70 ERA) and Ernie Shore (10-5, 2.00 ERA) contributed. Team batting dropped to .250, but the team ERA also dropped, dramatically, to 2.36.

In 1915, the Red Sox led the league for the second half of the season. They had five 15-game winners: Joe Wood contributed again (15-5, 1.79 ERA), as did Leonard (15-7). Rube Foster and Ernie Shore each had identical 19-8 records, and the new kid—Babe Ruth—was 18-8. Team ERA was more or less the same as the prior year, 2.39. Team batting improved to .260. The rookie pitcher, Ruth, even hit four home runs, double anyone else on the team. There were four tie games, but the Red Sox won 101, while losing an even 50. They finished 2 ½ games ahead of the second-place Detroit Tigers. Boston had beaten Detroit in 14 of their 22 encounters.

In the National League, the Phillies (90-62) finished 7 ½ games ahead of the second-place Boston Braves. This year, the Braves accorded the Red Sox the use of their brand new and significantly larger Braves Field. Whereas in 1914 the Braves had played their home Series games at Fenway, now the Red Sox played at the home of the Braves.

1915 WORLD SERIES BOSTON RED SOX 4, PHILADELPHIA PHILLIES 1

The Red Sox scored only 12 runs in the five games of the 1915 World Series, but they won three games in the ninth inning and won all four games by just one run. They faced a real slugger on the Phillies—Gavvy Cravath, who slammed out a major league record 24 home runs and drove in 115 runs during the regular season. The Red Sox—as a team—only hit 14 homers; the Phillies, in large part thanks to Cravath, hit 58. He proved to be a bust in the postseason, though, with one RBI (not on a home run) and a .125 average.

Pat Moran managed the Phillies, who closed their season by sweeping a doubleheader from Brooklyn on

October 6. Three Philly batters hit home runs. The Red Sox played until October 7, their last five games in New York. On the final day in New York, Boston manager Bill Carrigan had his intended first-game starter, Ernie Shore, throw just one inning so the Philly scouts couldn't get a good read on him. Shore struck out the only three batters he faced.

The two league champs were due to open the World Series at Baker Bowl in Philadelphia the very next day. On the afternoon of the 7th, the Royal Rooters Special left Boston's South Station with nearly 350 fervid fans aboard. The Rooters—fans of both Boston teams—were looking for their second straight championship.

Hall of Fame umpire Bill Klem, holding face mask, goes over lineups with Phillies manager Pat Moran. Red Sox manager Bill Carrigan is seen behind them. Note also the megaphone man prepared to make announcements. (Library of Congress/ Bain News Service)

The Associated Press reported that Pete Alexander was well-rested and "in as good condition as he has been at any time this year." Erskine Mayer (21-15, 2.36 ERA) had also been rested. Carrigan said that he was only really worried about Alexander; he told the AP, "Outside of Alexander, I do not think any of the Philly pitchers compares with my men." Most others agreed that Boston had a real edge. Syndicated columnist Hugh Fullerton wrote on the eve of the first game, "Boston's Red Sox are the better baseball team … The figures show them superior to the Phillies in every department of the game as a team." Fullerton saw the two managers as opposites—Carrigan emphasizing offense and Moran better on defense as well as working with pitching. He felt that Carrigan's Red Sox had so many stars and were so overconfident that they took too many chances and almost blew the pennant. He figured they'd buckle down during the World Series as they had done when it counted in the final weeks of the regular season, winning 14 of 16 at one stretch in September.

Philadelphia's main catcher, Bill Killefer, had been out with a dead arm for a few weeks. As it happens, he only appeared once in the Series, in a pinch-hitting role. Backup catcher Ed Burns handled backstop duties.

Boston's Jack Barry and Larry Gardner were said to be subpar, and Duffy Lewis off a bit. Fullerton predicted the lightest-hitting World Series in a long time, and said that baserunning would be neither team's strength.

Tim Murnane was prescient when he wrote in the *Boston Globe* on the morning of the first game, "I believe that the Boston and Philadelphia teams are well matched, and luck is bound to play a very important part in the final outcome."

Game One: Baker Bowl, Philadelphia / October 8, 1915

Philadelphia 3, Boston 1

Boston	000	000	010	—	1	8	1
Philadelphia	000	100	02x	—	3	5	1

WP: Alexander (1-0)   LP: Shore (0-1)

Moran started Grover Cleveland "Pete" Alexander and Boston's Bill Carrigan countered with Ernie Shore. Alexander brought a terrific regular-season record to the game (31-10, with a 1.22 ERA) and did not disappoint in the World Series. Murnane's prediction regarding luck playing a role was reflected in the headline the following morning: "Luck-freaks and a Bit of Brain-Fog Beat Red Sox, 3-1. Shore More Than Holds His Own Against Alexander, But Breaks of Game All Go Phillies' Way." A subhead expanded on the story: "Five Fluky Hits Beat Eight Solid Ones by Boston."

The Sox got a single and a walk off Alexander in the top of the first, but couldn't cash in and Dick Hoblitzell got himself picked off first to end any threat. Shore induced three easy infield pop-ups, two of them foul. The Sox leadoff man singled for the second inning in a row, but was again left stranded. Shore walked two in the second, but a force out and a caught stealing reduced the danger and he struck out Bert Niehoff to escape it altogether. Each team got another single in the third, but nothing of real consequence happened until the Phillies were up in the bottom of the fourth.

Dode Paskert singled to right field to kick off the Phillies' fourth (it dropped in right field just over first baseman Hoblitzell's head), and moved to second base on Cravath's bunt. He took third when team captain Fred Luderus grounded out, and scored when left-fielder George "Possum" Whitted's slow roller got by Shore and was fielded by Jack Barry at second base. Whitted was safe at first and the Phillies had a 1-0 lead.

Opposing pitchers Ernie Shore (Red Sox) and Grover Cleveland Alexander (Phillies) pose at Baker Bowl prior to Game One of the 1915 World Series. (Library of Congress)

Despite one single in each of the fifth, sixth, and seventh innings, there was no more scoring until the eighth. Then the Red Sox struck back.

With one out, Speaker drew a base on balls on four pitches, and reached second base when Hobby grounded to third baseman Milt Stock. With two outs, Duffy Lewis singled into left field and drove in Speaker, taking second base on the throw to the plate. Then Larry Gardner connected with an Alexander fastball and sent it deep to center field, but Dode Paskert made a brilliant running, arms-outstretched catch that retired the side. It was the kind of catch we'd now call a "sno-cone"—he just barely held on to the ball. The Red Sox had tied the score but lost an opportunity for more. Tris Speaker was among those who felt the catch saved the game for the Phillies.

Philadelphia re-established the lead convincingly in the bottom of the eighth. Though Shore had held them to just three hits and two walks in the first seven frames, he faltered badly at this point. He got Alexander to ground out, but then walked Stock. Shortstop Dave "Beauty" Bancroft singled to second base where Barry made a bare-handed stop. Unfortunately shortstop Everett Scott failed to cover the bag and there was no chance to force Stock, let alone turn two. Some felt Scott was not at fault, Barry's catch being so spectacular it could not be anticipated. With runners on first and second, Shore walked Paskert, loading the bases with Philadelphia's slugger Gavvy Cravath coming to the plate. Cravath drove in the go-ahead run, but only by virtue of another high-bounding ball that Scott fielded after an odd bounce on a soggy patch of infield grass. With just one play left to him, Scott threw to first. The next batter, Luderus, hit a weak little roller right back to Shore, but Shore slipped and the ball got by him. It was yet another infield hit (of Philadelphia's five hits, fully four of them were infield hits, only Paskert's single in the fourth being hit well). Bancroft scored and it was 3-1, Phillies. Luderus tried to steal second but Hick Cady cut him down.

Alexander started the top of the ninth by striking out Barry. Olaf Henriksen, as in 1912 a pinch-hitting specialist, reached base when first baseman Luderus made an error on a hard-hit ball that many writers felt should have been credited as a base hit. Babe Ruth pinch-hit for Shore and grounded out to Luderus, as Shore took second base, but Harry Hooper popped up to first base to end the game. Strange as it might seem in retrospect, that groundout by Babe Ruth was the only time he appeared in the entire World Series.

Despite losing the first game, Murnane wrote, "the Boston men are tonight greater favorites than before the series started." *Globe* sportswriter J. C. O'Leary concurred: "There is now no doubt that they are the stronger club." O'Leary's story was headlined, "Red Sox Show Winning Form Though Beaten." The Sox had now faced Alexander the Great, and touched him for eight hits, two by Lewis. He had given up one single in every one of the first eight innings—far from unhittable, though he has to be credited for pitching tougher when he had men on base—which was indeed every inning throughout the game. Speaker commented after the game, "He did not look so tough to us as we expected." The Phillies were indeed fortunate that their own weak hitting off Shore resulted in three runs.

PLAYER PROFILE: DUFFY LEWIS

The Red Sox boasted one of the greatest outfields of all time in right-fielder Harry Hooper, Tris Speaker (center), and Duffy Lewis in left. Lewis saw World Series action in 1912, 1915, and 1916. His .444 average in the 1915 Series led all regular position players on both teams. He drove in five of Boston's 11 runs, the only player other than Hooper (3) to knock in more than one. Lewis hit one of Boston's three home runs. During the 1912 regular season, his 109 RBIs led the team, well above Speaker's second-place 90 and Larry Gardner's 86.

Lewis was in the Navy during 1918, and at the end of the year was traded with Ernie Shore and Dutch Leonard to the New York team that became the Yankees in a lopsided deal that looked like an early Harry Frazee housecleaning. After his playing days were done, Duffy served as traveling secretary for the Boston Braves for 26 years.

Pete Alexander held the Red Sox to just one run on eight hits in his 3-1 Game One win. Lewis drove in the one run. Lewis's ninth-inning single was a walkoff in Game Three and his sixth-inning double won Game Four of the Series for the Sox.

Game Two: Baker Bowl, Philadelphia / October 9, 1915

Boston 2, Philadelphia 1

Boston	100	000	001	—	2	10	0
Philadelphia	000	010	000	—	1	3	1

WP: Foster (1-0)   LP: Mayer (0-1)

It seemed like the Red Sox didn't want to waste time coming out of the gate against Philadelphia's Erskine Mayer. The first pitch was a ball, though, and after Burns caught it, the souvenir was presented to President Woodrow Wilson, who was the first President ever to attend a World Series game. He had rejected the offer of complimentary tickets, preferring to purchase his own.

The sharp-eyed Hooper worked himself a walk. Scott predictably tried to bunt him to second, but failed to execute properly and popped up to the first baseman. Mayer had his eye on Hooper and threw a couple of near pitchouts, but the man they called "Hoop" stayed put and Mayer had to throw the ball over or risk walking Speaker, too.

Speaker took advantage and "dropped it to right field"—and that's when Hooper took off, advancing from first to third on the relatively routine single. Attempting to get two men into scoring position for Hoblitzell, the two runners tried to pull off a delayed double steal but it almost turned into a double killing. Speaker was cut down, the catcher Burns throwing to Niehoff at second, and the return throw to the plate was in time to get Hooper for a double play—but Burns dropped the ball and let it squirt away from him. Hooper scored, though only after missing the bag initially and having to crawl back quickly before Burns recovered the ball. And then Hobby hit a single to center. Continuing to run the base paths aggressively, Hoblitzell was thrown out at second—just barely.

Rube Foster, pitching for the Red Sox, was the star of the day. The sophomore pitcher was nevertheless a veteran of a decade of minor league ball. He struck out five of the first nine Phillies batters he faced and retired the other four on infield grounders, though the one that closed out the first saw Sox second baseman Barry rescue Hoblitzell on a 3-4-1 play at first base. Only in the fourth inning did a couple of fly balls give Red Sox outfielders some routine action. Foster was perfect through four.

Strikeouts suddenly seemed the order of the day; Mayer struck out five of the six Boston batters in the second and third. The Sox only singled once, Lewis in the fourth.

In the fifth, Foster aided his own cause with a double—the first extra-base hit in the Series. Hooper walked, but Scott flied out to end the inning. Then Foster got flustered and gave up back-to-back doubles—to Cravath down the left-field line and Luderus to right-center—to lead off the bottom of the fifth. Although the Rube soon settled down, the Phillies had tied the score, 1-1.

Boston bats turned anemic in the sixth, producing a couple of weak pop-ups and a strikeout. In the seventh, they recovered to tap out three singles. None of the hits plated a run, however, and neither team was able to produce until the Red Sox came up in the top of the ninth, the score still tied.

Larry Gardner singled to left field, his second hit of the ballgame. Jack Barry flied out to Paskert in center field. Hal Janvrin, who'd entered the game to play shortstop after Henriksen pinch-hit for Scott, grounded one weakly back to Mayer, who had but one play. Gardner took second base on the very close bang-bang throw to first. Then Rube Foster singled solidly to center field, the Boston pitcher's third hit of the game. Paskert grabbed the ball as quickly as he could and threw a strike to the plate, but it was wide of the mark and Gardner scored the go-ahead run. Foster took second on the throw, but Hooper struck out and it was up to Foster to see if he could hold the 2-1 lead he'd just given himself.

He got the first two outs with ease. Stock lifted a fly to left field. Bancroft struck out for the second time, and Paskert hit a long fly ball to deep center field. Speaker made a sensational catch to save the game, his back against the low fence. With just a moment to set himself, he leaped to rob Paskert of a game-tying homer.

The Royal Rooters spilled onto the field and paraded around as their band played "Tessie" and the two teams prepared to head to Boston for the next two games with the Series tied one game apiece.

Foster had struck out eight, and Mayer seven, but Mayer had allowed ten hits and Foster but three—matching the number of hits he'd had himself. Grantland Rice wrote that "Only Mayer's coolness and his support kept the game a contest." Hugh Fullerton felt that the Boston bats had shown a "lamentable lack of punch [and] should have won by at least five runs."

It was a very well-played game, though, and thanks to the solid defensive efforts of Stock and Bancroft in particular, Philadelphia was fortunate to keep the score as close as it did. A loss is a loss, however, and the Phillies were forced to rely on Alexander the Great to win Game Three.

Noting how much more productive Boston had been at the plate, albeit without demonstrating much in the way of runs, Grantland Rice concluded that the Sox had reasserted themselves as favorites and that Boston boosters "can't see where the Phillies are going to make enough runs to win, and they can't see how anyone except Alexander can stop Boston batting."

After the game, some suggested that Moran pitched Mayer rather than George Chalmers because he knew the plate umpire was going to be NL umpire Cy Rigler and Moran didn't believe he was very good on calling low pitches, Chalmers's strength.

PLAYER PROFILE: RUBE FOSTER

The Red Sox evened the Series with a 2-1 win at Baker Bowl in Game Two, thanks in large part to the pitching of twenty-four-year-old right-hander George "Rube" Foster. He helped Boston reach the Series again in 1915 with a 19-8 (2.11) record.

He pitched and won Game Five for the Red Sox, 5-4, the only Boston pitcher to win two games in the five-game Series. Game Two was the gem, though. Foster retired the first 12 men in order, then gave up back-to-back leadoff doubles to Gavvy Cravath and Fred Luderus, for the only Phillies run. The only other hit he allowed in the tight 2-1 Boston win was a harmless single to Dave Bancroft in the sixth. He finished the Series with a

2.00 ERA—and a .500 batting average (4-for-8), going 3-for-4 in Game Two—supplying the winning run by singling in Gardner in the top of the ninth.

Foster threw a no-hitter on June 21, 1916, and put up decent stats (14-7, 3.06), but only had one three-inning scoreless relief stint in Game Three of the 1916 Series. In 1917, he showed up out of condition, and his first start didn't come until June 18. When he was traded to the Reds in 1918, he refused to report and never played another major league game.

Game Three: Braves Field, Boston / October 11, 1915

Boston 2, Philadelphia 1

Philadelphia	001	000	000	—	1	3	0
Boston	000	100	001	—	2	6	1

WP: Leonard (1-0)   LP: Alexander (1-1)

Hick Cady wins a spontaneous footrace in practice before one of the 1915 World Series games. (Library of Congress)

Once again, the game would go into the ninth inning tied 1-1. Pat Moran started Alexander, and Bill Carrigan responded with the left-handed Dutch Leonard (15-7, 2.36 ERA). A loss for the Red Sox wouldn't cut deeply, since they'd still have other pitchers to choose from, but a loss for Philadelphia could potentially be devastating since they relied so heavily on Alexander.

Once again, the Red Sox starter went the distance and, once again, held the Phillies to just three hits—a total of 11 hits in three games.

Once again, the Red Sox scored the winning run in the ninth inning, and once again the final was 2-1.

This time the action took place at Braves Field, and the decision to move from Fenway to the larger facility paid off in attendance of more than 42,300. Just as Philadelphia fans had applauded the better plays of the Red Sox in Philadelphia, Boston fans frequently showed their appreciation for the fine work turned in by the Phillies.

Milt Stock flied to straightaway center field off Leonard to begin the game, but playing in an unfamiliar "home field" caused Speaker to lose the ball in the sun; it fell right in front of him for a two-base hit. Bancroft bunted to send Stock to third, but Paskert fouled out to third baseman Gardner and Cravath struck out.

Neither team did much until the third, when Ed Burns singled over second baseman Barry to lead off. Alexander sacrificed him to second, but Hoblitzell's failure to hold Gardner's throw resulted in men on first and second with nobody out. Bunting duties fell to Stock, who executed a perfect one. When Bancroft singled to center, it was 1-0 for the Phillies. Nobody knew it at the time, but that was the last hit the Phillies would get. Leonard retired every one of the final 20 batters he faced from that point on.

The first two were not easy to get, though. Paskert hit a ball that looked sure to drop into right-center field, but Jack Barry—running full-tilt with his back to the ball—caught it "as it popped over his shoulder … the most sensational catch of the series." (*New York Times*) Two runs would have scored, but for the catch. In a separate story by Hugh Fullerton, the *Times* headline read "Barry Saves Sox From Defeat."

Cravath made the last out of the third, but only because Duffy Lewis played him unusually deep and was able to run down and snare the ball a few scant feet from the cement wall—at a distance that would have been a home run in Philadelphia and off the left-field wall at Fenway Park. With runners on second and third, and two outs, Lewis, too, had saved at least two runs.

The Red Sox scored for the first time in the bottom of the fourth. With one out, Tris Speaker tripled over the first-base bag and just inside the right-field foul line. Hoblitzell, up next, hit the ball deep enough to center that Paskert didn't even try to get Speaker at home plate.

Nothing of much note happened until the seventh when Speaker singled, but Hobby hit into a 2-6-3 double play. Duffy Lewis then singled, but Gardner flied out to end the frame.

Leonard continued to retire batter after batter, and the Red Sox didn't score again through eight full. After the three Phillies were retired efficiently in the top of the ninth, Alexander returned to the mound after scattering just four hits. Harry Hooper greeted him with a single to right field on a 0-2 count. Scott sacrificed him to second base to bring up Tris Speaker with just one out. After conferring on the mound, Alexander walked Speaker intentionally. Hoblitzell grounded out but both runners moved up a base. With two outs and two on, Duffy Lewis swung at the first pitch and hit a "screaming line drive" up the middle, over Bancroft's head, to drive in the winning run.

Speaker said that Alexander had pitched a better game than in Game One, but he was still tagged with a loss. Lewis was 5-for-8 against Alexander.

It was reportedly the largest crowd in baseball history to date, but it was estimated that perhaps an additional 10,000 were turned away. Three brass bands, a drum corps, and a band of Scottish bagpipers added to the din inside the park.

Tim Murnane said he expected that Carrigan would start Babe Ruth in Game Four.

PLAYER PROFILE: DUTCH LEONARD

One of the many major leaguers to come out of St. Mary's College in Oakland, Hubert "Dutch" Leonard first made his mark in 1914, however, 19-5 with a microscopic 0.96 earned run average that remains the major league record 100 years later.

In 1915, Leonard was 15-7 (2.36) and got the Game Three start in the Series. Facing Pete Alexander, making his second start after just two days off, he matched the Phillies ace through eight full innings with a 1-1 tie. When Boston came to bat in the bottom of the ninth, Alexander had allowed just four hits and Leonard had permitted just three. A single by Hooper, a walk, and a two-out single by Duffy Lewis turned the game in Boston's favor and Leonard had himself a World Series win.

He won his only start in the 1916 World Series, a five-hitter in Game Four over Brooklyn, 6-2 (one of Brooklyn's runs was unearned).

Leonard and Cy Young are the only Red Sox pitchers to have thrown two no-hitters; Leonard's came on August 30, 1916, and June 3, 1918. His 25 shutouts still leads all Red Sox left-handers. Not long after the 1918 no-hit game, Leonard quit the Sox and signed up with the Fore River Shipyard in Quincy, playing with the shipyard ball team.

Game Four: Braves Field, Boston / October 12, 1915

Boston 2, Philadelphia 1

Philadelphia	000	000	010	—	1	7	0
Boston	001	001	00x	—	2	8	1

WP: Shore (1-1)   LP: Chalmers (0-1)

For the third game in a row, the Red Sox posted a 2-1 victory. Those six Sox runs were sufficient to give Boston three World Series wins, because Foster, Leonard, and Shore threw three complete games, allowing just one run per game. Surely this was one of the most efficient uses of runs in World Series history.

Shore evened his record at 1-1, avenging his defeat in Game One. "Moist ball" pitcher Chalmers pitched for Philadelphia, and he was very good—though without run support, he was not good enough.

The first inning saw frustration build for the Phillies. Stock singled to left field off Shore, but was thrown out by Duffy Lewis when he tried to take two bases on the hit. Then Bancroft walked, but he was—seemingly—thrown out stealing. However, Barry dropped the ball during a collision at second base and was charged with an error. After finally succeeding in getting a man on second, Philly's two best batters—Paskert and Cravath—both struck out.

Chalmers struck out the first two Red Sox, but walked Speaker—who was thrown out trying to steal second.

The Phillies got two men on in the top of the second, too. Luderus singled, and moved to second base on a bunt. After Niehoff's foul pop-up to the catcher, Burns walked on four pitches, but that brought up Chalmers with two outs and Shore struck him out, stranding two men on base. With one on in the Philadelphia third, Lewis ran down Cravath's drive and grabbed it just before he would have hit the wall in left. Grantland Rice said it would likely have been a homer almost anywhere else—the same comment he made about another drive the Phillies slugger hit to Speaker in the sixth.

The first score came in the bottom of the third. Barry walked to lead off. Cady bunted for a single when Chalmers fell down while trying to field it. While Shore was batting, one umpire called a balk, but the call was soon reversed. Shore sacrificed and executed perfectly, moving both runners up. Hooper singled in Barry with an "ugly bounder" that second baseman Niehoff charged but could only swat down as Barry scored. With Cady on third, Scott fouled out and Speaker grounded out to Luderus at first. It was 1-0, Boston.

Philadelphia left two more men on in the top of the fourth—Niehoff, who walked, and Burns, who singled. Two attempts to bunt came to naught, both going foul. Shore obviously had something on the ball that prevented the Phillies from successful sacrifices. With two outs and two on, Chalmers again made the third out.

The Sox increased their lead by a run in the bottom of the sixth when Hoblitzell hit a one-out single to center field and Lewis doubled him in with a ball that rolled all the way to the wall in left field. It was the seventh hit for Lewis in the Series and gave Boston a 2-0 lead. Left-fielder Whitted had just been waved over to play closer to the line, and the ball shot into the gap in left-center. The strategic placement, and his quick fielding, held Lewis to two bases.

In truth, the Sox had a bit of luck, too. In the seventh, they retired two Phillies on one play, Scott throwing to Barry for a forceout at second. Barry's throw to first went through Hoblitzell's legs but rebounded off the wall hard enough that Hobby recovered and threw to second in time to get Stock, who tried to take the bag on the evident error.

In the top of the eighth, Cravath hit a two-out triple to center field. The ball had bounded over Speaker's head in center; fortunately Hooper had been backing up the play, or Cravath would surely have scored. Cravath trotted in on Fred Luderus's single to center, which had itself taken an odd bounce, coming up to hit Speaker in the face. Moran had Oscar Dugey pinch-run for Luderus, and Dugey stole second base, but was stranded when Whitted hit the ball back to Shore, who threw him out at first base. The Phillies had pulled to within a run.

The Red Sox wanted an insurance run in the bottom of the eighth, and Speaker came through with an infield single to third base. Hobby hit to right—his third hit of the game—and Speaker took third on the play. Lewis walked, loading the bases with one out. But Larry Gardner chopped the ball back to Chalmers, who initiated a 1-2-3 double play.

Carrigan had Joe Wood warming up as the Red Sox were batting in the eighth, but never needed him. Shore kept his cool and more or less breezed through the ninth, getting Niehoff on a grounder, Burns on a pop-up to Scott at short, and getting pinch-hitter Bobby Byrne (batting for Chalmers) to fly out to Lewis in left.

Lewis made more than one "phenomenal" catch in the game. Afterwards, Tim Murnane declared that Lewis "carried off the honors. In fact, his all-around performance was absolutely the finest ever recorded in a World's Series game."

The Phillies were facing sudden death; they hadn't scored more than one run a game for three games in a row. They were going to have to get something going on offense. At least they were headed back to their home ballpark. But, Hugh Fullerton, an astute observer, wrote, "the Phils seem beaten."

PLAYER PROFILE: DICK HOBLITZELL

In a bizarre twist, he began his baseball career as a "Bloomer Girl" ballplayer (the touring female teams were allowed a certain number of men who dressed as women), by September 1908 Dick Hoblitzell became first baseman for the Cincinnati Reds. He played for the Reds for parts of seven seasons, but seemed to have lost it in early 1914; he was hitting just .210 and placed on waivers. The Red Sox grabbed him and he hit .319 in the remaining 69 games of the season. As Boston's starting first baseman, he hit .283 in 1915 and found himself in the World Series.

In Series play, Hobby hit .313, though his only RBI came in Game Three—a key sacrifice fly that kept Boston in the 1-1 game until the bottom of the ninth. In Game Four, he had himself a 3-for-4 day in another 2-1 Red Sox win.

Over 11 seasons in major-league ball, he had compiled a strong .278 average with 1,310 hits in 4,706 at-bats.

Game Five: Baker Bowl, Philadelphia / October 13, 1915

Boston 5, Philadelphia 4

Boston	011	000	021	— 5	10	1
Philadelphia	200	200	000	— 4	9	1

WP: Foster (2-0)   LP: Rixey (0-1)   HR: Hooper 2 (2), Lewis (1), Luderus (1)

With their backs to the wall, Moran started Erskine Mayer again. Carrigan countered with Rube Foster, who'd beaten Mayer in Game Two but only by 2-1. After three consecutive games, each won by Boston by the same 2-1 score, all of a sudden there were four home runs banged out of Baker Bowl.

Though Hooper singled on the first pitch of the game, nothing came of it. After a forceout, Speaker was caught stealing for the third time in the Series for the third out of the inning.

Then the Phillies jumped out to a quick lead by scoring twice in the bottom of the first. Foster hit Stock with a pitch. On the hit-and-run, Bancroft singled and the Phils had men on first and second with nobody out. Paskert laid down a perfect bunt and was ruled safe on a close play at first, loading the bases. Both Babe Ruth and Carl Mays started warming up on the sidelines.

Gavvy Cravath strode to the plate. His 24 home runs led the majors and were ten more than the entire Red Sox team managed in 1915. Cravath had only batted in one run in the prior four games, though his 115 regular-season RBIs had led both leagues. If there was a time for him to come through, this was it. Instead he hit a "puny grounder" right back to Foster, who threw home to catcher Pinch Thomas, who forced Stock and then threw to first to get Cravath. Two outs. Fortunately for Philadelphia, Fred Luderus came through with a double to left-center field and the Phillies were up 2-0.

Larry Gardner hit a two-out triple to the center-field fence and Jack Barry singled him in with a Texas Leaguer to left, as the Red Sox cut the lead in half in the second. Two Phillies struck out and another hit a high pop-up to third base.

Boston tied up the game thanks to a Harry Hooper homer. It was one of the bounce variety—hopping into the center-field bleachers for a home run. As in the 1912 World Series, a hit of this sort was not a ground-rule double as it would be today but counted as a home run. After Speaker hit a one-out single, Moran pulled Mayer and brought in the left-handed Eppa Rixey (11-12 on the season, but with a 2.39 ERA) to pitch to Hoblitzell. It was the first and only time in the 1915 World Series that a relief pitcher was used. Carrigan had Del Gainer pinch-hit for Hobby, but he grounded into a double play. Suddenly it was a 2-2 game.

Each team got one man on base their next time up, but the next two runs scored were for the Phillies in the bottom of the fifth. Cravath whiffed but Fred Luderus homered over the 35-foot-high right-field wall into Broad Street beyond. Then Niehoff singled to center and Burns singled to right. Niehoff took third on the single, but scored the fourth Phillies run when Hooper's throw to third sailed past Gardner. At first he held up, but when Gardner frantically scrambled to throw the ball home, Thomas had to lunge for it and chase it down, leaving the plate uncovered—an alert Niehoff bolted home and made it. Phillies 4, Red Sox 2.

For the next three innings, neither team scored. Foster tried to kick things off with a leadoff single in the fifth and when Hooper was hit, the Sox had two men on and no one out. But Rixey squelched the threat. The Sox got two on in the sixth, too, but to no avail. The Phillies got men on, but Bancroft was caught stealing in the fifth and Luderus was caught stealing in the sixth.

The only man from either team to reach in the seventh was Rixey, who singled but was stranded.

In the top of the eighth, after Gainer reached on an infield single, Duffy Lewis hit a home run into the bleachers set up in center field, tying the game at 4-4.

After there were two outs in the bottom of the inning, the Phillies gave the Red Sox a scare when Foster pitched around Cravath and walked him, then hit Luderus with a pitch, but Carrigan stuck with his pitcher and Foster induced Whitted to ground out to him.

Foster was up first in the top of the ninth. Carrigan had still not given Babe Ruth more than the one at-bat back in Game One. He let Foster hit (he was 4-for-7, with one RBI in the Series), but Foster struck out. Harry Hooper swung on an 0-2 count and bounced a ball into the bleachers in right-center field for his second home run of the game. Foster didn't let a ball out of the infield and won the game, while the Red Sox won the World Series with the 5-4 finish.

Though the Series may have felt like a bit of a rout, Game Five was the fourth game in a row won by just one run. And the Phillies' one win back in Game One was just a 3-1 victory. Any one of the games could have gone the other way very easily. Philadelphia pitchers held the Red Sox to 2.27 earned runs per nine innings, but Boston's 1.84 ERA made a big difference. The Red Sox hit better, too, .264 to a weak .182 for the Phillies. All the home runs came in the final game, three of them hit by Boston's batters. Luderus was the star for the Philly offense, driving in six of their nine runs. Duffy Lewis drove in five of Boston's 11 runs and Hooper drove in three. Both managers spoke highly of the other, but Moran admitted, "When you are beaten four in a row, there isn't any excuse to offer. … They naturally should be regarded as the best ball club in the country."

It was an odd World Series in that Boston manager Bill Carrigan never used Smoky Joe Wood and he never used Babe Ruth. Wood was the American League leader with his 1.49 ERA and a 15-5 record. And Ruth was 18-8 (2.44) as well as Carrigan's leading home run hitter.

PLAYER PROFILE: HARRY HOOPER

Signed by the Red Sox in November 1908, right-fielder Harry Hooper played in all four World Series from 1912-1918, with an aggregate .293 average, two home runs, and six runs batted in. The two home runs both came in 1915's Game Five. No other Red Sox player has yet appeared in more than three World Series.

The Phillies had taken an early 2-0 lead, but a run in the second and Hooper's leadoff home run in the third off starter Erskine Mayer tied the game. He'd singled in the first, and was hit by a pitch in the fifth. In the top of the ninth inning, with one out and the score tied 4-4, Hooper was up facing reliever Eppa Rixey. Hooper hit another home run. This one, like the first, was a "bounce home run"—today we would call it a rule-book double, but in those days it was a home run—and it counted, and made all the difference in Boston's 5-4 win, which won them the World Series. Sometimes the bounces just go right for you. Just three years earlier, his spectacular catch had saved the win for the Red Sox in the final game of the 1912 Series. In 1915, he scored four runs, twice as many as anyone else in this low-scoring Series.

1916 WORLD SERIES
BOSTON RED SOX 4, BROOKLYN ROBINS 1

The 1916 season began with the reigning World Champions featuring much the same roster as the year before. The two major changes were the loss of Tris Speaker and Smoky Joe Wood. Considering their iconic status, one might have expected the losses to have hurt more than they did.

Tillie Walker took over for Speaker in center field, but that was really the only significant change in the lineup. Before the 1914 season, the Red Sox had offered Speaker a rather large salary in order to prevent him from jumping to the Federal League (1914-15). When the rival league collapsed, there were fewer bidders for

Managers Wilbert Robinson (Brooklyn Robins) and Bill Carrigan (Boston Red Sox) before the playing of the 1916 Series. (Bain Collection/The Library of Congress)

players' services and Sox owner Lannin cut his offer to Speaker for 1916 in half. Speaker's batting average had fallen for three years in a row, and that provided a bit of a rationale for the revised offer. When he didn't sign, Lannin sold him to Cleveland for the princely sum of $50,000 and a couple of ballplayers to boot.

In truth, Wood didn't have much to offer at this point. His arm was bad and, when he finally did sign with the Indians, he only threw 15 ⅔ innings. After 1915, he never won another game, though he resurfaced as a decent hitter with Cleveland beginning in 1918. Speaker improved on his 1915 average, but with fewer RBIs. Walker made up enough of the difference that the loss was not a grievous one.

Stout and Johnson write that despite a slow start, "Once the club adjusted to Speaker's absence, they began to respond to Carrigan, a master motivator."

The team as a whole performed as well relative to the other contenders as it had in 1915, finishing two games ahead of second-place Chicago. The team batting average and the team ERA were .248 and 2.48 respectively, compared to .260 and 2.39 the year before. The run differential between the Red Sox and their opponents was 170 (669 runs scored—499 runs allowed) in 1915 and a tighter 70 runs (550 RS—480 RA) in 1916. It was only on September 18 that the Red Sox climbed into first place for good.

They won 91 games, as opposed to 101 in 1915, but it was enough to allow them to hoist another pennant at Fenway.

Two different pitchers threw no-hitters, both at home. Rube Foster beat the Yankees on June 21 and Dutch Leonard beat the Browns on August 30. Babe Ruth truly came of age as a pitcher, posting a record of 23-12 on the strength of a league-leading 1.75 ERA. Carl Mays had also come into his own, with an 18-13 record (2.39 ERA), matched in wins by Leonard's marginally better 18-12 (2.36). Shore and Foster both tailed off some, but still won 16 and 14 games respectively.

In the World Series, the repeating Red Sox faced the Brooklyn ballclub, the Robins, who beat out the Phillies by 2 ½ games. Once again, the Sox borrowed Braves Field for their home games. Brooklyn, of course, played at Ebbets Field.

The Brooklyn lineup featured some good hitters as well, with Zack Wheat's .312, nine homers, and 73 RBIs leading his team in the two latter categories and only four points behind Jake Daubert in batting average; Wheat led the National League in slugging percentage.

Jake Pfeffer was a 25-game winner (25-11, 1.92 ERA); Larry Cheney had an identical ERA and an 18-12 record. Sherry Smith, Rube Marquard, and Jack Coombs had 14, 13, and 13 wins. The team ERA was much better than Boston's, at 2.12, and the .261 team batting average was higher as well. They looked to be a formidable opponent.

The *Boston Globe*'s Tim Murnane expected Brooklyn to break through first, to "start with a rush." He added, "The Red Sox seldom start like winners, but manage to tighten up and show as the game and contests lengthen out."

Neither manager announced his pitcher beforehand. Marquard was expected to face the unorthodox submariner Carl Mays, according to the newspapers the morning of the first game. Boston's Jack Barry had a hand injury and was not thought likely to play. Columnist Hugh Fullerton picked the Red Sox to win in five games with Coombs pitching and winning for Brooklyn in the third game of the five. He didn't expect Foster to be used at all, given that he'd had an off year. He anticipated a Ruth/Marquard matchup in Game Two that would prove to be the tightest one of the Series.

Game One: Braves Field, Boston / October 7, 1916

Boston 6, Brooklyn 5

Brooklyn	000	100	004	—	5	10	4
Boston	001	010	31x	—	6	8	1

WP: Shore (1-0)   LP: Marquard (0-1)   SV: Mays (1)

Though Boston's Bill Carrigan had Ernie Shore warming up, the Robins expected Carrigan to call on Babe Ruth at the last minute, so they took batting practice as though they'd be facing the left-hander. Carrigan chose Shore and Brooklyn manager Wilbert Robinson led with Rube Marquard. The Robins made a weak showing of it in the top of the first. In Boston's bottom of the first, after two men were out, Tillie Walker tripled to the wall in left, but Dick Hoblitzell grounded out to end the inning.

The Robins got two men on base in the second, and didn't score. The Red Sox put three men on—two on Marquard walks—but didn't score, though only after Hooper's two-out smash to Myers in deep center field saw the Brooklyn man "fairly robbing" Hooper of a bases-clearing hit.

Hi Myers singled in Brooklyn's third, but was left stranded. With two outs, the Red Sox put a run on the board with back-to-back extra-base hits—a triple by Hoblitzell and a "fierce liner" of a double by Lewis. Lewis was then picked off second base when Brooklyn's catcher Chief Meyers fired to shortstop Ivy Olson.

Right-fielder Casey Stengel singled to center field to lead off the fourth, and Zack Wheat banged one of Shore's pitches for a triple that hit the right-field wall. George Cutshaw hit into an unusual double play, when Harry Hooper raced in and—as he slipped and fell—caught Cutshaw's shallow fly ball, and then hopped up in time to throw on the fly directly to Cady, who erased Wheat at the plate. The *Washington Post* correspondent termed it "one of the most brilliant plays ever witnessed on a ball field." With just one out, Meyers tripled in Brooklyn's fifth but couldn't get home. The Red Sox re-established the lead in the bottom of the fifth when Hooper led off with a double to center that Myers lost in the sun, took third on Hal Janvrin's bunt, and scored when Walker singled to left field.

The Red Sox broke the game open in the bottom of the seventh. Janvrin doubled down the left-field line to kick things off. Walker reached safely as Ivy Olson's error allowed Janvrin to get to third; he may have been a bit hasty in anticipating the double play and flubbed the catch. Then it was Cutshaw's turn for an infield error as he tried to scoop up a grounder and throw to home plate, but merely knocked the ball down instead; Hoblitzell reached first and Janvrin scored. After Lewis pushed both runners up a base with a successful sacrifice, Larry Gardner reached on a fielder's choice and Walker scored. Everett Scott's sacrifice fly brought in Hobby. It was 5-1, Red Sox.

One of the four double plays the Sox turned wiped out another Robins runner in the eighth. It was quite a play, a rocket of a ball that caromed off Shore's glove and off Shore's ankle directly to Janvrin, who stepped on second and threw to first. With Jeff Pfeffer now pitching for Marquard, the Red Sox ran the score to 6-1 in the bottom of the eighth as Hooper walked and Janvrin singled. Stengel committed the fourth error of the game by throwing the ball in so far from any possible fielder that it allowed Hooper to come all the way home.

It was a good thing for the Red Sox that they'd built up a five-run lead, because the Robins pecked away at Shore in the top of the ninth. After walking Brooklyn team captain Daubert on four pitches and giving up a single to Stengel, Shore hit Cutshaw in the ribs, loading the bases with one out. Janvrin's error on Mike Mowrey's drive allowed two runs to score. Olson hit one on a hop to Gardner, who gloved the ball but couldn't make a play. The bases were loaded. Meyers popped out to Hobby at first for the second out, but Shore walked pinch-hitter Fred Merkle. Carrigan had seen enough, and changed the whole battery, bringing in Carl Mays to pitch and Pinch Thomas to catch. The next batter, Hi Myers, bounced a single over Mays's head to bring the score to 6-5 with the bases still loaded. Daubert hit a hot grounder that got by Gardner, but Scott ranged far to his right, snared the ball, and threw a perfect strike to Hoblitzell to just nip Daubert and save the game.

Scoring four runs in the top of the ninth, and leaving the bases full of Robins, had put a scare into the Red Sox and Sox fans, too. Red Sox fans left Braves Field somewhat subdued, but very relieved.

PLAYER PROFILE: TILLIE WALKER

When Tillie Walker hit 11 homers for the Athletics in 1918, it was the third year in a row he'd matched The Babe in homers. They both hit three for Boston in 1916 and two in 1917. Oddly, Walker's home run of June 20, 1916, was the only homer hit at Fenway Park during the entire 1916 season.

Walker played center field in Games One, Two, and Four. Walker hit .273 in his 11 Series at-bats, but was 2-for-4 with an RBI (his only one) in the first game. Batting third, he tripled in the bottom of the first, but was left stranded. He whiffed in the third, but singled in Hooper with the go-ahead run in the fifth, giving Boston an early 2-1 lead. In the seventh, he reached on Olson's error and scored three batters later on a fielder's choice. He walked in the eighth, reaching base for the third time in four plate appearances. He was flawless in the field throughout the Series, his one assist cutting down Sherry Smith who tried to stretch a double into a triple in Game Three on a nifty 9-8-5 play.

Game Two: Braves Field, Boston / October 9, 1916

Boston 2, Brooklyn 1 (14 innings)

Brooklyn	100	000	000	000	00	—	1	6	2
Boston	001	000	000	000	01	—	2	7	1

WP: Ruth (1-0)   LP: Smith (0-1)   HR: Myers (1)

As was so often the case in the era, both managers tried to keep secret who their starting pitchers would be. It seemed obvious it would be Ruth for the Red Sox but Christy Mathewson predicted he'd be faced by spitballer Larry Cheney and Hugh Fullerton predicted Jack Coombs, who could boast a 4-0 record in World Series play.

Babe Ruth, who only appeared for one pinch-hitting cameo in the 1915 Series, was the Red Sox mound ace in 1916, leading the league with his 1.75 ERA and with 23 wins to his credit. He'd lost but 12. Ruth squared off against Brooklyn's Sherrod Smith (12-12, 3.32 ERA) in a battle of southpaws.

Ruth retired the first two batters in the top of the first, but Hi Myers hit a "savage wallop" (Grantland Rice) of a low liner that Hooper dived for in vain. It skittered between him and the stumbling Walker to the fence in right-center field for an inside-the-park home run and an early 1-0 lead for Brooklyn. Ruth allowed a double and a single in the third but escaped the inning without allowing a second run, in good part due to a Hooper to Walker to Scott (covering third) relay that gunned down Sherry Smith who had a bit recklessly tried to stretch his double into a triple.

Smith retired the side in order in the first, allowed just a single in the second, but let the Red Sox tie it in the third. Leading off, Scott tripled to left-center and scored on Ruth's ground ball to second base which Cutshaw juggled just long enough to let Scott score before he threw to first to get Ruth.

That's where the score stood, 1-1, for a very long time. Daubert walked in the Brooklyn fourth, and Carrigan asked Rube Foster to start warming up, but Daubert was erased by a double play. Hoblitzell walked in the Boston fourth but was erased by a double play.

The Robins got a nest egg single in the fifth but it failed to hatch a run. Thomas tripled for the Red Sox with two out in the fifth (he was awarded third base on the play by umpire Quigley, who saw Olson interfere by tripping the Red Sox batter), but failed to score as Ruth struck out on three pitches. In the top of the eighth, the Robins almost scored when Mowrey singled and moved to second on Olson's sacrifice. Miller singled to center, but Walker's heave to home plate caused Mowrey to hold at third. Miller took second. Pitcher Smith almost earned himself an RBI of his own, to match Ruth, but Scott fielded his ball to short and threw to the plate in time to entrap Mowrey in a rundown, Ruth making the putout. Ruth knocked down Jimmy Johnston's high bouncer back to the mound, recovered it, and threw to first for the third out.

The Sox almost put it away in the bottom of the ninth. Leading off, Hal Janvrin hit the ball to left field and Wheat almost made a great play on the ball. It was deemed a double, not an error. Jimmy Walsh pinch-hit for Tillie Walker; there was an error on the attempted sacrifice when Smith threw to Mowrey but Janvrin jarred the ball loose from the third baseman's grip, and the Sox found themselves with two runners on and nobody out. Hoblitzell lashed the ball hard to center, but Myers caught it and pulled off a game-saving double play by firing the ball to home on one bounce to nail Janvrin. Always appreciative of great baseball, the "Boston crowd cheered him vociferously." (*New York Times*) Walsh took second on the throw, so Smith walked Lewis intentionally. Gardner fouled out to the catcher, and the game proceeded into extra innings.

Ruth walked Olson in the top of the 10th, but nothing came of it. The Red Sox almost won it again in the bottom of the 10th. Scott singled to lead off, and took second on Thomas's sacrifice. After Ruth whiffed for the second out, Hooper hit the ball deep to third base but Scott was thrown out on a wonderful play as he turned for home. He was caught off guard when third baseman Mowrey bluffed a throw to first, deking Scott, who quickly realized Mowrey might throw him out at the plate. He scurried back toward third, but Mowrey threw the ball to the shrewd shortstop Olson, who had rushed in behind Scott to cover the bag. The play wiped Scott off the base paths. For two innings in a row, foolhardy and substandard baserunning had cost the Red Sox an opportunity.

The next three innings were fairly uneventful, and nothing but zeroes populated the scoreboard—though only a spectacular catch by left-fielder Lewis prevented Smith from winning the game for himself in the 13th. At one point in the bottom of the 11th, the band was playing "Tessie" so incessantly that the Robins took the unusual step of complaining, even threatening to deny the Royal Rooters entry into Ebbets Field if they didn't stop. Plate umpire Bill Dinneen actually ordered the band to stop playing, a bit ironic in that Dinneen had been on the 1903 Boston team that won the first World Series in part thanks to the "Tessie" rally song.

Ruth, throwing his 13th consecutive scoreless inning and seeming to get stronger after the ninth, faced the top of the Brooklyn lineup and retired the Robins in order in the top of the 14th.

It was getting dark. This was perhaps the last inning that could be completed. As first man up for Boston in the 14th, Hobby walked for the fourth time in the game. Lewis sacrificed him into scoring position. The swifter Mike McNally came in to pinch-run for Hoblitzell and the right-handed-hitting Del Gainer batted for Larry Gardner. Gainer hit a line drive between short and third that took two hops into left field but hooked just enough away from left-fielder Wheat that McNally was able to score the winning run ahead of Wheat's desperate throw to the plate.

Grantland Rice was particularly impressed with Boston's "impregnable defense" on the left side of the infield, which he termed "a wall of human flesh that shifted and swerved to meet every point of Brooklyn's blind, but game, aggressive attack." Many writers thought that Smith threw a better game than Ruth, but the Boston defense saved the day.

Both Ruth and Smith had pitched excellent games, and neither team had any reason to be ashamed of their effort. The special to the *New York Times* called the contest "a hard game to win, but a yet harder one to lose." The Red Sox held a 2-0 edge in the Series.

PLAYER PROFILE: BABE RUTH

Many Red Sox fans have heard of George Ruth, though even after completing the 1916 season—his third—he only had seven home runs to his name and a .272 batting average. But he was a pitcher who never in his career had a losing record. By the time he entered the 1916 Series (manager Bill Carrigan had elected not to pitch him at all in the 1915 World Series), he had a 43-21 won-loss record and had just completed his first 20-win season (23-12, with a spectacular league-leading 1.75 earned run average).

It was time to give the left-hander a start. It was the only one he had, but it was magnificent. Ruth went the distance against Brooklyn's Sherry Smith, throwing 14 innings without relief, winning 3-2 on Del Gainer's pinch-hit single. Ruth had allowed just six hits, while recording 42 outs. And just one run, way back in the first inning on Hi Myers's inside-the-park home run. Settling down, he allowed just three hits in the final 11 frames. It remains the longest complete game win in World Series history, and likely will never be challenged. Ruth had initiated a streak of scoreless Series innings that extended into 1918 and totaled 29 ⅔ innings before it was over. The Red Sox had taken a 2-0 lead in the World Series.

As for Ruth, he finished his career with 94 wins against 46 losses and a career 2.28 ERA. Three years later, in 1919, he transitioned to play outfield and occasional first base and showed prowess and power offensively as well.

Game Three: Ebbets Field, Brooklyn / October 10, 1916

Brooklyn 4, Boston 3

Boston	000	002	100	— 3	7	1
Brooklyn	001	120	00x	— 4	10	0

WP: Coombs (1-0)   LP: Mays (0-1)   SV: Pfeffer (1)   HR: Gardner (1)

Brooklyn started right-hander Jack Coombs, a major league veteran since 1906 who'd won three games for the Athletics in the 1910 World Series and another game in the 1911 Series. In 1910, he'd been 31-9 with a 1.30 ERA. Coombs was 13-8 with a 2.66 ERA in 1916, but was really the fifth starter on the staff.

Boston put their trust in Carl Mays, who had finished his second season 18-13 with a 2.39 earned run average. Mays had not appeared in the 1915 Series and was far from his best in his first Series start.

Chick Shorten played center field, batting left against the righty Coombs. Both he and Hoblitzell singled in the top of the first, but Shorten was thrown out at third on Hobby's hit for the final out of the inning. Mays hit the first batter he faced, Myers, then failed to field Daubert's bunt smoothly and there were two on. Stengel sacrificed both runners up, prompting Mays to intentionally walk Wheat. It paid off. Hobby came in to field Cutshaw's grounder and threw home to get Myers. Mowrey then struck out.

Mays got through the second easily, but gave up the first run of the game in the bottom of the third. With one out, Daubert and Stengel both singled, and—after Wheat lined out to left—so did Cutshaw, whose base hit along the right-field foul line brought Daubert home. 1-0, Brooklyn.

A caught stealing in the third and another in the fourth (a missed hit-and-run) robbed the Red Sox of base runners. They fell behind 2-0 when the Robins scored in the bottom of the fourth. Olson led off with a swinging bunt for a base hit (taking second base on Gardner's throwing error). Miller advanced Olson with a bunt, which Mays fielded but—despite a clean play awaiting him at third base—threw instead to first base. The Brooklyn pitcher, Coombs, singled Olson in with a hit to Hooper.

Brooklyn seemed to put the game away, taking a 4-0 lead in the bottom of the fifth, scoring in their third consecutive inning. Mays walked both Wheat and Mowrey. He had two outs, but then Olson tripled into the temporary bleachers in left field and both runners scored on what might have gone for a homer but for the ground rule.

The Red Sox weren't going to give up as easily, though manager Carrigan was glad enough to take Mays out of the game. With one out in the top of the sixth, Olaf Henriksen pinch-hit for Mays and never swung at a pitch as he drew a walk. Harry Hooper tripled to the fence in center field. Janvrin tried to hit away, rather than squeeze, and popped out to second base. Shorten scored Hooper, though, with his third single of the game.

Rube Foster took over for Mays on the mound. Daubert tripled in the bottom of the sixth and the ball got past Lewis. The throw to the plate, relayed by Scott, reached home just a bit too late, but Daubert was nevertheless ruled out. His leg had been blocked from the plate by Thomas, who pointed out the situation to the home plate umpire and tagged him out. Had Daubert even bounced up and run to dugout, he'd have likely been called safe. But by staying at the scene of the crime, his failure to reach home was all too evident.

The Red Sox cut the lead to one run in the top of the seventh when Larry Gardner crashed a long home run off Coombs that passed over the right-field wall into Bedford Avenue beyond. Coombs called his fielders in for a mound conference and took himself out of the game in favor of reliever Jeff Pfeffer. Pfeffer retired the last eight men he faced and closed out the win, but not before Wheat made a great play by hauling in Shorten's long foul fly ball to left.

It was the seventh game in a row the Red Sox had played that had been won or lost by just one run. Coombs didn't know it yet, but he'd pitched his final Fall Classic game, a perfect 5-0 in World Series competition. He'd given Brooklyn hope.

PLAYER PROFILE: CHICK SHORTEN

Shorten only hit .205 in 1916, and only two doubles and one triple were of the extra-base variety. In his only World Series, he was the starting center fielder in Game Three facing Jack Coombs in Ebbets Field, batting third in the order. Brooklyn had built a 4-0 lead before the Red Sox started scoring but Shorten had done what he could at the plate. On the base paths, it was another matter. He singled to center in the first inning and singled to left in the fourth, though he was cut down at third trying to take two bases on Hoblitzell's single and was thrown out stealing in the fourth. In the sixth, he singled for the third straight time, this time driving in Hooper and getting Boston its second run. In the top of the ninth, he led off. The Sox were short just one run. Jeff Pfeffer had taken over for Coombs in the seventh and retired every batter he faced. Shorten flied out foul down the left-field line. It took Zack Wheat to turn in "one of the greatest catches of the day" to get Chick out.

His only other Series appearance was back in center for Game Five, and he was 1-for-3 with a two-out RBI single in the third. Beaten again on the base paths, he was thrown out trying to get into scoring position for the cleanup hitter Hoblitzell.

Game Four: Ebbets Field, Brooklyn / October 11, 1916

Boston 6, Brooklyn 2

| Boston | 030 | 110 | 100 | — | 6 | 10 | 1 |
| Brooklyn | 200 | 000 | 000 | — | 2 | 5 | 4 |

WP: Leonard (1-0)   LP: Marquard (0-2)   HR: Gardner (2)

The Red Sox hoped to take Game Four by starting Dutch Leonard (18-12, 2.36) against Brooklyn's Rube Marquard. For his part, Marquard was looking to avenge the defeat he'd suffered in Game One. Carrigan had tried to trick Brooklyn by warming up Shore as well as Leonard, and seeing to it that a rumor was spread that Leonard wasn't in good shape. Brooklyn's Robinson warmed up Cheney, Marquard, and Pfeffer—and, as it happened, before the game was over he'd used each of them one way or another.

Marquard took the mound, though, and retired the Red Sox with ease in the first, inducing Hooper to bounce one back to the mound and then striking out Janvrin and Walker.

And Brooklyn started out strong, with Jimmy Johnston tripling on the very first pitch of the game to the center-field fence. He was driven in by Myers with a single past Janvrin and into right. Merkle walked on five pitches. Finally, Leonard got an out as Gardner nipped the middle runner on a force play that could have been a double play had Janvrin reached the bag more quickly. Wheat reached first on the play. Leonard threw a wild pitch, and there were men on second and third. Cutshaw reached on Janvrin's error while Myers scored. The scoring might have continued, but the Red Sox sussed out a double-steal attempt and Janvrin took a short throw from Carrigan, firing over to third base to nab the retreating Wheat.

The *New York Times* noted the enthusiasm of the Brooklyn fans: "They rent the air with shrieks and stentorian cachinnations such as no theatrical noise creator ever dreamed of … warwhoops and vocal outbreaks … accompanied by frenzied dances and gesticulations which threatened the dislocation of perfectly good arms and legs from presumably useful bodies. Hats went into the air in clouds, and one was almost led to fear a shower of arms and legs dismembered from the wild demonstrations."

A 2-0 lead was a meaningful lead in the Deadball Era, though Tim Murnane called it a "proper handicap" to spot the Robins.

Of course, a lead's only good if you hold it, and the Red Sox promptly wrested it from their grasp and took it for themselves in the top of the second. Hoblitzell walked on the first four pitches. Lewis doubled off the right-field wall, and Larry Gardner hit a 3-2 fastball over Myers's head for an inside-the-park home run; Myers had been playing the lefty to hit to the opposite field, but Gardner hit it to right-center instead. It was universally described as the hardest-hit ball of the Series. Murnane wrote that "the sound that went echoing across the field was like the breaking of a bed-slat after midnight." All this with nobody out. The next batter, Scott, took two bases when Wheat dropped his liner, and some of the Brooklyn fans started shouting that Marquard should be removed. He got through the inning without further scoring, but it had become Boston 3, Brooklyn 2. They'd taken a lead they never gave back.

Murnane declared that Gardner's three-run homer gave Leonard "back his nerve, which was shaken in the first inning, and also took the confidence away from the home team." As for the Ebbets Field faithful, so boisterous in the bottom of the first, after the explosion of Gardner's bat driving the ball for the three-run homer, the *Times* noted that "a great silence fell on the throng."

Two innings later, Boston added another run on Lewis's single, Gardner's sacrifice, and a Texas League single by Carrigan—who was catching in his only game of the 1916 Series.

Marquard was sufficiently shaken that he even walked Leonard on four pitches, but got himself through the inning with just the one run. The inning was his last. In the fifth, the Bostonians made it 5-2 when, facing pitcher Larry Cheney, Hooper walked, then stole second as Janvrin whiffed, and scored easily on Hoblitzell's double to left.

In the seventh, the relentless Red Sox added one more. Hooper led off again, this time singling. He was forced out at second on Janvrin's bunt, but Janny took second on Walker's grounder, then scored on Hobby's weak infield squibber, thanks to a Cheney throwing error that hit Hoblitzell in the back.

Leonard didn't pitch his best. He walked four Robins, but he only allowed five hits and quite evidently settled down after the first inning to earn himself a complete game win. The Robins tried three pinch hitters, all in vain, and a pinch runner in Casey Stengel, but didn't score another run after the pair in the first.

The *Times* was not impressed by Brooklyn's showing. In its account of the game, the paper praised the spirit they'd shown in prior games but concluded that "all the punch they had after the first inning could have been applied to a baby's cheek without inflicting serious damage, and their spirit was the reverse of formidable." Instead, they gave the impression of "utter helplessness."

PLAYER PROFILE: LARRY GARDNER

In Game Four, it took Dutch Leonard an inning to settle down, but Boston faced a 2-0 deficit by the time he did. Rube Marquard had dominated in the first—a grounder back to the mound and two strikeouts—but he faced troubles in the top of the second. Hoblitzell walked, then took third on Lewis's double. Vermont's Larry Gardner hit an inside-the-park home run to center field and the Sox took a 3-2 lead. That was all they needed for the win.

For Gardner, it was the second game in a row in which he'd homered. After that game, he told reporters that he had been angry at himself for not hitting better and had actually swung with his eyes closed. It was his 17th World Series game; he'd played in every game for Boston in 1912 and 1915, too. His Series average, after completing the 1916 Series and playing in seven games for Cleveland against Brooklyn in the 1920 Fall Classic, was just .198 but he'd been steady in the field and contributed big time in moments like this.

He was a World Champion again in 1920 for the Indians.

Game Five: Braves Field, Boston / October 12, 1916

Boston 4, Brooklyn 1

Brooklyn	010	000	000	—	1	3	3
Boston	012	010	00x	—	4	7	2

WP: Shore (2-0)   LP: Pfeffer (0-1)

First baseman Dick Hoblitzell played in both the 1915 and 1916 World Series. (Library of Congress)

It was Columbus Day and the biggest crowd of the Series, some 43,620 turned out to see if the Red Sox could win their second World Championship in a row. The Brooklyn crowds were only half the size of Boston's, despite it being their first appearance in a World Series. Owner Charles Ebbets charged much higher prices than were customary at the time—all the way up to $5.00. And the weather was very cold. It may be, too, that few thought the Brooklyns had much of a chance to win.

The fifth game in Boston saw Jeff Pfeffer start, facing Game One winner Ernie Shore. For Pfeffer, it was his fourth appearance of the Series. He'd thrown the last inning in relief of Marquard in Game One, the last 2 ⅔ innings saving the game for Coombs in Game Three, and had pinch-hit for Marquard in Game Four (striking out) before Cheney came in to pitch. Pfeffer was a formidable 25-11 in 1916, with a 1.92 ERA.

For the fourth game in a row, Brooklyn scored first—a single run, without benefit of a hit, in the top of the second. George Cutshaw walked on four pitches and then advanced one base at a time on Mowrey's sacrifice, Olson's high-bouncing grounder to third that Gardner hauled down, and a passed ball charged to Cady.

In no time, the Red Sox tied the score when Lewis hit a one-out triple down the left-field line and Gardner flied one just barely deep enough to left that Lewis was able to tag and score when Wheat's throw went wide.

After the Robins (some accounts were already calling them the Dodgers, though they were more frequently termed the Robins in reference to manager Robinson) failed to get the ball out of the infield, the Red Sox took advantage of their next opportunity to score as well.

Cady singled to lead off the third. Ernie Shore fouled off a bunt attempt to the catcher Meyers. Pfeffer missed with four in a row and walked Hooper. Janvrin hit a ball to shortstop Olson that looked like a sure double play, but Olson tried to rush the throw and couldn't maintain his grip on it. After finally corralling it, his only play was to first but the ball flew out to right field, enabling Cady to score and Hooper to reach third, Janvrin stopping safe on first. Janny was caught stealing, but Chick Shorten then singled up the middle and into center field, and Hooper trotted home. Shorten was then caught stealing, too, the second Red Sox base runner erased in the inning.

Brooklyn finally got its first hit of the game in the fifth, a meaningless single by Chief Meyers. And, as if to punish them, the Red Sox added an insurance run when Hooper singled and Janvrin doubled, both of them first pitch swinging—a strategy employed by several Sox throughout the game. It was 4-1, Red Sox, after five.

Neither team scored again. Brooklyn added one single in the seventh and one in the ninth. A subsequent error in the seventh saw Robins runners on second and third, but there were two outs and Meyers hit one back to Shore, who threw him out at first. Shore threw a three-hitter, the only run an unearned one, and won his second game of the Series while the Red Sox won their second Series in succession.

Never once playing on their true home field, the Red Sox had nonetheless taken the Series with ease. The *New York Times* column on the game said acidly of the 4-1 final that if the score "had been 40 to 1 it would have represented more accurately the respective merits of the two contending teams." The game was said to be so lacking in drama that even the hometown fans didn't get worked up during the competition. The *Times* said it "resembled a tug of war between an elephant and a gold fish."

The Boston fans were so jaded that Wallace Goldsmith's sports page cartoon of the game in the *Globe* depicted a tradition apparently more long-standing than heretofore appreciated—fans on the first-base side "so sure of the outcome that it amused itself batting toy balloons about."

At the very end, though, there arose such a loud shout from all those present that its effect was all the more startling, given their quiescence throughout. Winning the World Series was apparently still a big thing in Boston, though the Red Sox had now won three of the last five played.

Widely syndicated columnist Hugh Fullerton proposed abolishing the World Series. The American League was superior, he wrote, and the Brooklyn "team was licked, beaten, and dogging before it went to the park." He claimed they'd held a team meeting before the game to decide how to divide the loser's share, a telling and self-fulfilling attitude. Overriding the play of the losers was Fullerton's feeling that "baseball has ceased to be a sport and has become a commercial enterprise." The players were, he felt, more interested in the money than the result on the field. Fullerton closed his column recounting what Christy Mathewson had told him: "I don't know whether the best team won or not, but I am satisfied that the worst team lost. You've got to give it to Brooklyn—they finished the game—and it looked to me as if that was about all they were trying to do."

PLAYER PROFILE: ERNIE SHORE

Ernie Shore pitched as perfect a game as one could ask for on June 23, 1917. He retired 27 men in order, but he'd come on with a runner on first after starter Babe Ruth had been ejected for arguing. While Shore was pitching, the runner Ruth had walked was cut down. Shore went on to get out the 26 batters he faced. Today it's considered an "unofficial" perfect game.

His contract had been bought by Boston on July 9, 1914, the same the Sox bought Babe Ruth. Shore was 10-5 with a 2.00 ERA in what remained of the season, and a stellar 19-8 (1.64) in 1915. He was 1-1, with a 2.12 ERA in the 1915 World Series, with a 3-1 loss in Game One and a 2-1 win in Game Four.

In 1916, he had a rough outing in Game One but came away with a win. He had come off a 16-8 season (2.63 ERA). In Game Five, he excelled, giving up just one unearned run in the second on Cady's passed ball. He allowed but three singles, in the fifth, the seventh, and Stengel's leadoff single in the ninth. With Casey on first, Shore buckled down and didn't let the ball out of the infield, walking off the mound triumphant as the Red Sox won the game, 2-1, and captured their fourth World Championship.

After a good year in 1917, he spent 1918 in the Navy before being traded to the New York Yankees in December, but his better years were behind him.

1917—THE YEAR BETWEEN CHAMPIONSHIPS

You could call 1917 an "off-year"—the Red Sox didn't win the World Series. After winning it in 1915 and 1916, and making the Series again in 1918, it really was a bit of anomaly not to be playing the National League in the postseason.

Bill Carrigan, manager the two championship years, had definitively retired. The Red Sox had a new owner in Harry Frazee, who'd purchased the ballclub from Joseph Lannin just a very few weeks after the second World Series win. Grantland Rice predicted another Series between the Giants and the Red Sox, writing that the Sox would be "as hard to beat in 1917 as they were in 1915 and 1916."

The Red Sox finished a full nine games behind the White Sox, in second place. Boston had the best pitching in the league, but the White Sox bats carried the day.

The World War was in progress and soon after the season was over, Jack Barry, Del Gainer, Duffy Lewis, Mike McNally, Herb Pennock, Ernie Shore, and Chick Shorten all reported for duty with the US Navy. Hal Janvrin joined the Signal Corps on December 1. Many others were preparing to serve. There was a lot of roster movement as many players from other teams made their plans, too. Harry Frazee was able to acquire Bullet Joe Bush, Wally Schang, and Amos Strunk in a December trade with the Athletics. He picked up Stuffy McInnis in January. The Red Sox swapped out, among others, Hick Cady, Larry Gardner, Pinch Thomas, and Tillie Walker. It was going to be a very different team in 1918 than the team that had won in prior years.

Author Allan Wood points out in his introduction to *When Boston Still Had the Babe: The World Champion 1918 Red Sox*, Frazee was making numerous moves to improve the ballclub, and so aggressively that he was effectively accused in a *New York Times* editorial of trying to buy a pennant for the Red Sox.

This was a team with a tradition, of course. There had only been 14 World Series played to date and the Red Sox had won four of them.

1918 WORLD SERIES BOSTON RED SOX 4, CHICAGO CUBS 2

1918—AN IRREGULAR SEASON

The regular season in 1918 was, due to the world war, far from a typical one. The season only lasted 126 games for the Red Sox, who won the pennant with a 75-51 record. They finished 2 ½ games ahead of the Cleveland Indians and four games ahead of the Washington Senators. The White Sox, who'd won the 1917 World Series in six games, finished in sixth place, 17 games behind Boston.

One of the oddities of the season was that, for the first several months, no one knew when the season

OFFICIAL SCORE CARD

WORLD'S
SERIES
1918
—
FENWAY
PARK

BOSTON
(RED SOX)
American
League vs.
CHICAGO
(CUBS)
National
League

HARRY H. FRAZEE, President
Boston American League B. B. Club

BETWEEN the ACTS
(ALL TOBACCO)
LITTLE CIGARS

IT'S WASTE TO LIGHT A BIG CIGAR
WHEN YOU'VE ONLY TIME FOR A LITTLE ONE
ASK THE BOY

PRICE TEN CENTS

1918 World Series scorecard for game at Fenway Park. (National Baseball Hall of Fame Library)

would really end. As late as the first week in August, the two leagues were still working out plans as to when to cut off the season and comply with a "work or fight" order that came down from the War Department. It was finally determined to end the regular season on September 2, playing out the schedules until that date.

The Chicago Cubs won the pennant in the National League and won it with ease, looking back 10 ½ games to find the distant second-place New York Giants.

The core of the Boston pitching staff that had seen success over the prior years remained: Carl Mays was the only 20-game winner, but this was a season of just those 126 games. Mays was 21-13, 2.21 ERA with a league-leading eight shutouts and 30 complete games. Joe Bush was best among the regular starters with a 2.11 mark but a mediocre 15-15 won-loss record. Second-most in wins was Sad Sam Jones (16-5, 2.25 ERA). Babe Ruth was 13-7 with a 2.22 ERA. The only other man with more than four decisions was Dutch Leonard at 8-6; Leonard left midseason to take a shipbuilding job as part of the war effort.

The staff ERA as a whole was a miserly 2.31. A full 26 of the Red Sox's games (more than 20 percent of the schedule and more than one-third of the team's wins) were shutouts. Eight of Boston's shutouts were by a 1-0 score.

It was with pitching that the Red Sox won the season. The team ranked tops in fielding as well, concomitant to a good year for pitching, but they had one of the lowest team batting averages (.249) and only ranked more or less in the middle of the pack in on-base percentage, slugging average, and in runs batted in.

Because of the truncated schedule, they played many more games at home (70) than on the road (56), and they had a losing record on the road (26-30), but excelled at Fenway, winning 70 percent of their home games (49-21). After bolting out of the gate with an 11-2 mark in April, they truly never looked back, though there were some 12 days that they weren't atop the standings. Nonetheless, there were only two days in the entire season that they were even as much as one game behind the league leader. From July 5 on, first place was theirs—though it remained a competitive race to the finish.

With all the coming and going on bit-part players (ten of the Red Sox appeared in six or fewer games and for four of them, they were the only major league games in which they ever appeared), credit must be given to Barrow and Frazee for keeping the team on a fairly even keel.

In this year's World Series, unlike the last two times, the Red Sox played their home games at home—in Fenway Park—but the Cubs played theirs at the larger park on the South Side, Comiskey Park.

The Cubs were the favorites on the eve of the Series. They were a better hitting team (.265 eclipsing Boston's .249 team average) and had a much lower earned run average, too (2.18 to 2.31). The games, though, still had to be played.

Game One: Comiskey Park, Chicago / September 5, 1918

Boston 1, Chicago 0

Boston	000	100	000 —	1	5	0
Chicago	000	000	000 —	0	6	0

WP: Ruth (1-0)   LP: Vaughn (0-1)

Jim "Hippo" Vaughn started Game One for the hosting Cubs. The 6'4", 215-pound left-hander led the National League in all sorts of stats: wins (he was 22-10), ERA (1.74), strikeouts, starts, innings pitched, and shutouts, with eight. The Red Sox bats were going to be challenged.

Red Sox second baseman Dave Shean singled in the first. Left-fielder George Whiteman singled in the second. Harry Hooper singled in the third. No one scored.

It was a battle of southpaws. Babe Ruth started for Boston. His last Series appearance was in Game Two of the 1916 World Series, the 14-inning game in which he'd allowed one run in the first but not one run for the final 13. Ruth gave up two singles and a walk in the bottom of the first, but got out of the inning with all three men still on the bases.

No one reached in the second. With a lone leadoff single, Max Flack was the only runner to reach base in the third.

Shean got on base again in the top of the fourth, walking on a 3-2 count to get to first. Amos Strunk prepared to bunt him into scoring position but instead popped up to Vaughn on the very first pitch. George Whiteman—his name crops up often in the 1918 World Series— singled just over shortstop Charlie Hollocher's glove and Shean ran to second. Stuffy McInnis singled to left on a hit-and-run play, Les Mann fielded it on one bounce, but Shean's running start paid off and he scored sliding across home plate just barely ahead of Mann's throw. Third baseman Charlie Deal made a shoestring catch of Everett Scott's soft looping bunt attempt and Fred Thomas struck out. It was 1-0, Boston.

The weather had helped the Red Sox. Shean, who got on base three times in the game and scored the lone run, had suffered an injury to the middle finger of his throwing hand the day before and would have been unable to play, but the initially scheduled September 4 game was postponed due to rain, giving him enough time to heal. The grounds were covered by a tarpaulin and were reported by the *Chicago Tribune* as dry and accurate. McInnis's hit, though, may have taken just a bit slower of a bounce on the outfield grass than usual. It was the last hit of the game that Vaughn allowed the Red Sox.

Ruth retired the Cubs in order in the fourth.

The Red Sox never even got another base runner until the top of the ninth, when Shean reached base for the third time on a base on balls. (Vaughn walked six patient Sox in the game). This time, Strunk laid down a good bunt and Shean was poised at second with just one out. But Whiteman whiffed and—after walking McInnis to set up a force at any of the bases, Scott just hit a grounder back to Vaughn, who made the routine throw to first base.

The game entered the bottom of the ninth, 1-0 in favor of the Red Sox. The slightest slip would tie the game or give it to the Cubs.

The Cubs had been unable to score on Ruth, though he was far from perfect. He hit Flack in the head with a pitch in the fifth, but Flack didn't seem the least bit fazed. In the sixth, Ruth surrendered one-out singles to both Dode Paskert and Fred Merkle (Series opponents from prior years, the Phillies and Giants respectively). Barrow had a couple of men start to warm up. Charlie Pick unintentionally moved both runners up when he grounded out slowly to McInnis at first base, but Deal swung at what would have been ball four and hit a high fly ball to Whiteman in left.

The seventh and the eighth were easy enough for the Babe, though it took a great bare-handed catch by Scott to retire Vaughn in the seventh. And Ruth got the first two batters in the ninth easily enough, too. Then Deal hit a little roller to Thomas at third and just made it to first base on time. Cubs manager Fred Mitchell, whose major league career began with the Boston Americans in the very first year of the franchise, 1901, put in Bill McCabe—no relation to pitcher Dick McCabe who'd appeared in three games for the 1918 Red Sox—as a pinch runner. Cubs catcher Bill Killefer lofted a high fly ball to Harry Hooper in right-center field. Hooper called off center-fielder Strunk at the last moment to avoid a collision but secured the ball. McCabe ran around second and straight into the Cubs dugout. The game was over. Babe Ruth had thrown a 1-0 shutout in Chicago and, in so doing, ran his World Series scoreless streak to 22 ⅓ innings of work.

He hadn't done much at the plate, striking out two times in an 0-for-3, but no one was going to hold that against him. Whiteman got two of Boston's five hits; McInnis had the lone

RBI. The Cubs feared Ruth nonetheless; they were well aware he'd led the American League in home runs with 11 despite being a pitcher. Barrow had used Ruth at first base and the outfield, and he'd accumulated 251 at-bats as a position player. Ruth was a good-fielding pitcher, who led his league with 19 putouts. He was the only batter the Cubs truly feared, yet Barrow never used him for pinch-hit duty and he only played one inning in the field, after he'd left off pitching in Game Four.

PLAYER PROFILE: STUFFY McINNIS

There was only one run in the first game of the 1918 Series. Babe Ruth extended his scoreless innings streak with a 1-0 shutout of the Cubs. The run came in the fourth inning. Dave Shean walked, but had to hold at first on Strunk's failed sacrifice to the pitcher. George Whiteman singled, pushing Shean to second, and first baseman Stuffy McInnis singled to left, scoring Shean. McInnis helped win another game in the 1918 Series, also in the fourth inning. In Game Three, Stuffy singled and soon scored the second and deciding run of Carl Mays's 2-1 win.

Gloucester native McInnis was an exceptional fielder at first base, with a .993 lifetime fielding average helped considerably by his 1921 season when he made just one error in 1,651 chances. It took Kevin Youkilis to top him in 2007, not making a single error at first base. He was a great hitter as well, leaving the game with a .307 career average after appearing in 2,128 major league games.

McInnis had played in three World Series with Philadelphia, for Boston in 1918, and then played in 1925 for the Pirates. He never made an error in 202 chances during his 19 World Series games. He hit .200 in Series play, each year hitting higher than his previous Series.

Game Two: Comiskey Park, Chicago / September 6, 1918

Chicago 3, Boston 1

Boston	000	000	001	—	1	6	1
Chicago	030	000	00x	—	3	7	1

WP: Tyler (1-0)   LP: Bush (0-1)

The pitchers for Game Two were no surprise. Mitchell had let the Red Sox think Lefty Tyler was going to pitch Game One, and Barrow had made a show of warming up Joe Bush before the first game. Now both managers used the men they'd decoyed with before the Series began.

Oddly, both men had faced each other before in the 1914 World Series—Bush pitching for the Athletics and Tyler pitching for the Braves. Allan Wood further notes: "In that game, Bush's 12th-inning error allowed the Braves' winning run. Seven players from that Series were in uniform today, including Mann, Charlie Deal, Stuffy McInnis, Wally Schang, and Amos Strunk. Cubs manager Fred Mitchell had been the Braves' manager in 1914."

Tyler walked the leadoff hitter Hooper, but he was called out on interference when batter Dave Shean stepped out in front of catcher Killefer while striking out as Hooper was trying to seal a steal of second base.

Flack singled to lead off for the Cubs but he, too, was cut down when rookie shortstop Charlie Hollocher bounced back to Bush, who threw to get the lead man. Then Hollocher, whose 26 stolen bases reflected some real speed, was forced at second base on Mann's fly to center field which Strunk lost in the sun and let fall—but which he recovered quickly enough to peg to second. Paskert flied out.

The Red Sox mounted a real threat in the top of the second. Again, Tyler walked the first batter, this time Whiteman. McInnis bunted safely. Then Scott bunted, and both runners moved up. Whiteman was cut down at home, trying to score on Thomas's grounder to second base. Agnew flied out foul to right field.

The Cubs scored three times in the bottom of the second. Merkle walked. Pick singled on a swinging bunt, when his ball took an odd skitter and got past Thomas at third. After Deal popped up, Killefer hit a double to right field, driving in Merkle. Tyler singled to center to drive in two more runs—Pick and Killefer—but was thrown out trying to take second when Agnew fired the ball back from the plate to Scott covering second. Flack singled but was caught stealing.

Tyler had driven in all the runs the Cubs needed.

In the top of the third, Tyler walked the lead man for the third consecutive inning. This time it was Joe Bush. But Hooper forced Bush at second, and Shean forced Hooper at second, and Strunk fouled out to the catcher.

Neither the Cubs nor the Red Sox got the ball out of the infield in their next time up. The bottom of the fourth was a little messy, but Boston escaped unharmed. There was a two-base error that let Merkle reach, but he was thrown out at third when Pick hit back to Bush for a fielder's choice. After Deal flied out to Hooper in right, Pick was gunned down while trying to steal second.

Both teams got a hit in the sixth, but Shean's single went for naught when he was retired on a fielder's choice and the next batter hit into a double play. Hollocher tripled into the right-field corner in the bottom of the sixth, but had to hold when Mann grounded out hard to

Scott at short. He was out at the plate, when Scott fielded the next ball, too, and threw home to Agnew. Merkle singled, putting runners on first and third, but then was cut down on the base paths, retired in a rundown before the runner on third had any chance to try and score.

The Sox got two hits in the top of the eighth, Schang pinch-hitting for Agnew and singling and then—after Bush flied out—Hooper singling to third. But Schang was thrown out for trying to challenge Flack's arm and take third on Hooper's hit to right, and Shean grounded out to first, Tyler covering.

For the sixth time, the Sox got their lead man on base. Strunk kicked off the ninth with a triple off the fence in the right-field corner. Whiteman tripled right after him, all the way to the center-field fence. Had Whiteman been faster, he might well have had a homer. The Red Sox were on the board and the score was 3-1. McInnis grounded out to Tyler, though, for the first out. Scott walked and the tying runs were on base. Fred Thomas was due up. He was 0-for-3 on the day. Barrow followed his gut and tried Jean Dubuc (who'd had just one hit all year long, batting .167 in six at-bats), though Thomas had hit above average for the team at .257. Dubuc was a pitcher and not a bad-hitting one throughout his career, but if Barrow wanted a pinch-hitter with some pop, he might have tried Babe Ruth.

Ruth hadn't looked good against the Cubs' other left-hander in Game One, though. Dubuc almost walked, which would have loaded the bases. It took Tyler eight pitches but he finally struck out the batter when Dubuc swung at a ball that the *Globe* felt was "so wide that it was nearly out of the game." It was the only appearance Dubuc made in the Series.

Schang was last up, but he swung at the first pitch and popped up to the shortstop.

The game had been enlivened early on as some bench-jockeying got a little out of hand and in between the second and third innings, coaches Heinie Wagner of the Sox and Otto Knabe of the Cubs wound up grappling with each other on the floor of the Cubs' dugout. When Wagner emerged, just before a rescue party of Red Sox players arrived, the back of his uniform "looked as if he had been repairing a flivver." (*New York Times*)

PLAYER PROFILE: JOE BUSH

He'd been an even 15-15 in 1918, with a 2.11 ERA—his best ERA ever. In the Series, except for a brief meltdown in the bottom of the second, Joe Bush pitched a good Game Two. Unfortunately, the three runs on four hits sank the Red Sox, who only scored twice. A walk, single, double, single, and a single was not a good inning. Bush lost the game; he appeared again in Game Four and earned a save in relief of Babe Ruth. After the first two runners reached base, Ruth changed positions and went out to left field. Bush came in, inserted in Whiteman's place in the order. He faced two batters and got three outs; the first man up bunted to first, and McInnis fielded it and threw to Fred Thomas at third to get the lead runner. Then he induced pinch-hitter Turner Barber to ground into a 6-4-3 game-ending double play.

Bullet Joe Bush had several opportunities to pitch in the World Series. He pitched for the Athletics in 1913 (starring as a 20-year-old) and 1914, and later threw for the Yankees in 1922 and 1923. All told, he started six games and relieved in three others. His Series ERA was 2.67, which belied a disappointing 2-5 record.

Game Three: Comiskey Park, Chicago / September 7, 1918

Boston 2, Chicago 1

Boston	000	200	000	—	2	7	0
Chicago	000	010	000	—	1	7	1

WP: Mays (1-0)   LP: Vaughn (0-2)

The third game of the Series drew more fans, but there were still thousands of seats empty as the wartime Series progressed. Right after Game Two, Mitchell had announced he would be starting Claude Hendrix so everyone was surprised when Vaughn was back again after just the one day off. The conventional wisdom was that the Red Sox couldn't hit lefties, and both Vaughn and Tyler had held them to just one run in each of the first two games. After seeing Ruth hit ball after ball to the right-field bleachers during batting practice, Mitchell may have figured he'd throw the third left-handed starter in a row at them by starting Vaughn once more. As the Series wore on, Mitchell never did start a right-hander. Vaughn and Tyler alternated starts—just the two of them.

Hooper dropped a single into short left field to start the game, and Flack walked to lead off for the Cubs but neither team did anything else in the first round. Whiteman singled to lead off the second and then both teams offered a minor display of ineptitude. McInnis struck out bunting. Then Schang struck out, too, but the far-from-fleet Whiteman stole second. Whiteman got to third and Scott was safe when Hollocher bollixed a play. Thomas flied out, though.

The Red Sox put two runs on the board in the top of the fourth, though the inning started with Strunk striking out. Whiteman got hit in the small of the back by Vaughn's pitch. McInnis slapped a single into left field, a bit of a swinging bunt between short and third. First and second, one out, and Schang singled over the second-base bag, which drove in Whiteman and found McInnis on third. Scott executed a suicide squeeze on the first pitch, and it worked as intended when Vaughn seemingly froze after fielding the ball. McInnis had been off before the delivery, and scored the second run—it turned out to be the winning run. Then Thomas singled to right field—the fourth single in a row—but Flack's throw got Schang at the plate. He'd run through Wagner's stop sign and paid the price. It was the second time in two games that Flack had thrown out Schang. Mays hit the ball hard but he was out on a liner to center field.

The Cubs collected their first hit when Mann doubled to left, but he stayed on second—thanks in large part to a leaping catch that Whiteman made against the wall in left field. Paskert's blow might well have bounced into the bleachers for a home run. The *Globe*'s Martin, at least, was taking note of Whiteman: "There is not a ballplayer on the Sox fighting harder or showing any more gameness or confidence." He'd made a number of key plays and gotten on base more than half the times he'd been up.

Mays baffled the Cubs early on with his sidearm "uplift" pitch, and the submariner had hardly let a man on for the first three innings. Vaughn settled down for the rest of the game with the only hit a Schang single in the top of the ninth.

The Cubs began to pick away at Mays. Leading off the fifth, Charlie Pick took two bases when his grounder skidded by Scott and died in center. After Deal flied out to Whiteman, Killefer singled and Pick scored on the play. Vaughn struck out and Killefer was caught trying to steal second. It was 2-1, still in Boston's favor.

In the sixth, two Cubs hit back-to-back two-out singles—Mann and Paskert, but Merkle struck out leaving both on the bags.

After Deal singled in the seventh, Mays set down seven in a row, which put him in the bottom of the ninth with a one-run lead and two outs with nobody on base. Then Pick singled, an infield hit that Shean was lucky to stop but that left him without a play. Mitchell had Turner Barber pinch-hit for Deal. Pick was thrown out trying to steal second—but Shean couldn't handle the ball and Pick was safe. Barber hit a liner down the third-base line that would have tied the game, but it was foul by half a foot. A passed ball off Schang's glove let Pick sprint to third. Schang recovered the ball and fired to Thomas, who looked to have Pick out, despite Pick sliding in with spikes flashing—but the third baseman couldn't keep a hold of the ball and it squirted away. The runner picked himself up and bolted for home. Thomas, arguing that Pick had kicked the ball from his grip and should be ruled out, realized he'd better recover the ball and did so, and regained his composure well enough to throw home "straight and true and swift as a bullet." (*New York Times*) And in the nick of time Schang gloved the ball and slapped the tag on the sliding runner. Pick was out at the plate, the game was over, and the Red Sox had won, 2-1, giving them a 2-1 edge in the Series. It was later learned that Pick had spiked home plate umpire Bill Klem on the play, fairly seriously.

The Cubs had scored a total of one run for Vaughn in the two games he'd pitched. As in Game One, he'd been scored on in the fourth, but was pretty untouchable for the final five.

Under an agreement designed to minimize travel during wartime, the first three games were played in Chicago. The rest of them—however many it took—would be in Boston.

PLAYER PROFILE: WALLY SCHANG

The first game in Chicago, played at Comiskey Park, was a 2-1 win for the Red Sox. Both Sox runs scored in the fourth. After Strunk struck out, Whiteman was hit by a pitch and McInnis singled. Boston catcher Wally Schang was up next and he singled into center field, scoring Whiteman from second and sending McInnis to third. When Everett Scott singled, McInnis crossed the plate. Those were the only two runs submarining Carl Mays needed.

Schang led all Boston batters in the Series, by a big margin, in the five games he played. He hit .444 (4-for-9, with two walks), Agnew started four of the games behind the plate, and Schang just two, but Schang's was the bigger contribution on offense.

The switch-hitting catcher had a long major league career stretching from 1913 (with the Athletics) to 1931 (with the Tigers), He was a real star in the 1913 World Series for Philadelphia, with seven RBIs, and played for six World Series teams, hitting .287 in 94 Fall Classic at-bats.

Game Four: Fenway Park, Boston / September 9, 1918

Boston 3, Chicago 2

Chicago	000	000	020	—	2	7	1
Boston	000	200	01x	—	3	4	0

WP: Ruth (2-0)   LP: Douglas (0-1)   SV: Bush (1)

As both teams traveled east on Sunday on the same train, they discussed the lower attendance and the diminished revenues due to lowered prices. Despite a written agreement as to what they'd be paid, the revenues weren't coming in and they were being asked to take a dramatic cut. They demanded a hearing in front of the National Commission that ruled baseball. There was even talk of calling off the Series.

The Commission, which represented the owners, wanted nothing to do with player demands and asked to defer any discussion until they saw how well Game Four drew at Fenway. It was clear enough that there'd be no need to request the use of the larger Braves Field.

Babe Ruth started again for the Red Sox, and Tyler for the Cubs. Ruth was fortunate to have a start. He'd been roughhousing with Walt Kinney on the train from Chicago and hurt a finger on his pitching hand. The injury couldn't have been more evident; the *Boston Globe* mentioned the "iodine-painted finger" in the second paragraph of its front-page game story, and observed that it "bothered him constantly, causing the ball to shine and sail."

Kinney's role in the Series was to throw batting practice to Boston's batters so they'd be accustomed to facing the relentless onslaught of left-handed pitching the Cubs presented. Only two of the ultimately 52 innings saw a Chicago right-hander on the mound.

Yet again, a leadoff man got on base—Max Flack, singling for Chicago. Shortly after Hollocher lined out to Scott at short, Sam Agnew fired the ball to McInnis at first and picked off Flack. The Cubs got to Ruth for two singles in the second, but there were two outs and the pitcher got Killefer to ground into a 6-5 force play at third base. Tyler walked to lead off the third, but Flack forced him at second. Hollocher moved Flack to second on a grounder that McInnis handled by himself at first, and then Ruth picked off Flack—for the second time in three innings by wheeling and throwing to Scott.

Dave Shean doubled for the Red Sox in the bottom of the first, but he was the only Red Sox to reach base.

Shean led off in the Boston fourth, and Tyler walked him. Strunk couldn't execute the sacrifice and then flied out. Shean saw an opportunity and stole second base without drawing a throw, as the ball got a bit away from Killefer. Whiteman walked. McInnis hit back to Tyler, who had time to throw out the lead runner at third. With two outs, Babe Ruth was up. Ruth was batting sixth in the order, and it seemed that the Cubs had gone to unusual lengths not to have to pitch to him. "The Tarzan of the Boston tribe" strode to the plate "swinging his savage looking black bludgeon." (*New York Times*) But despite the buildup, Ruth had accumulated ten at-bats in three World Series (1915, 1916, and this one) and had yet to hit safely. Rather than walk the bases loaded, Mitchell decided to pitch to him.

Tyler tried to get Ruth to swing at outside pitches and didn't give him much to hit, missing with the first three pitches, and seeming to walk him on an outside pitch at 3-1. The umpire called it a strike. Tyler knew what he planned to throw and twice tried to reposition Flack more deeply, but the right fielder held his position. This is the same Flack who'd already been picked off base twice in the game. It was not his best day in baseball.

On a 3-2 count, Ruth drove a fastball into deep right field. He tripled over Flack's head and almost to the center-field bleachers to drive in both Whiteman and McInnis, and might have scored but for the backup by Tyler when the throw to third was wide of the bag. Scott flied out to center to close the inning. It was the third time in the Series that the Red Sox had come through big in the fourth inning; the score was 2-0.

The Cubs got the lead man on in the fifth (Pick, with a single) and the sixth (Tyler, with a walk), but Ruth got Killefer to hit into a double play in the fifth and three grounders one after the other in the sixth. The Red Sox saw Tyler retire all six batters.

Credit Shean with a heads-up play in the sixth. With Tyler on base, Flack bounced one to Ruth, who threw badly to second. The ball got away from Scott. Allan Wood tells it well: "Shean, however, was positioned only a few feet behind the base. He was on his knees when he gloved Ruth's errant toss, then crawled on his stomach in the dirt, tagging the bag with his mitt just ahead of Tyler's foot." Had the ball gone astray, it might have put the Cubs back in the game.

In the seventh, with one out, Ruth walked Fred Merkle and then walked pinch-hitter Rollie Zeider (batting for Pick), but a second pinch hitter, Bob O'Farrell, grounded into a 6-4-3 double play.

Stuffy McInnis singled in the Sox seventh, and Ruth bunted him to second. Scott reached on a fielder's choice—but McInnis was out at third—and Thomas popped up to second base.

Ruth seemed to tire in the eighth. He walked Killefer, then allowed pinch-hitter Claude Hendrix to single to left field. Hendrix was a pitcher, but not a bad choice; he'd hit nine extra-base hits (three home runs, three triples, and three doubles) and batted .264 during the regular season. With runners on first and second, Ruth threw a wild pitch and there were two men in scoring position with nobody out. Throughout the game, the *Globe* noted, Ruth was "ever on the brink of danger."

Max Flack was having a tough game and it only got worse when he grounded out to first baseman McInnis, who looked Killefer back to the bag at third while tagging out the oncoming Flack. Mitchell made his fifth substitution of the game after he saw that Hendrix seemed a little sketchy on the base paths (he almost got caught off second base); he had the rookie Bill McCabe run for Hendrix, who was already primed to pitch. Mitchell had Phil Douglas start warming up; he'd been 10-9 with a 2.13 ERA during the regular season. Hollocher grounded out to the second baseman, whose only play was to first base; Killefer scored. Les Mann singled to left, scoring McCabe from third base. The game was tied, 2-2.

And Ruth's World Series scoreless innings streak was snapped at 29 ⅔ innings. He'd surpassed the previous record (Christy Mathewson, with 28) and established a new record that stood for decades until Whitey Ford upped the ante by pitching 33 consecutive scoreless innings in the 1960, '61, and '62 World Series. Paskert grounded out to end the eighth.

Faced with a tied ballgame, and with a right-handed pitcher on the mound for the first time in the entire Series (Mitchell brought in the big righty Douglas), the Red Sox countered by having switch-hitter Wally Schang bat left-handed in place of Agnew. Agnew was 0-for-7 and hadn't gotten on base yet in the three games he'd played. Schang came through with a single to center field—and then took second base when Killefer allowed a ball to get away from him. After the passed ball, and with nobody out, Hooper tried to bunt Schang to third base—and more than succeeded. Douglas pounced on the ball but threw it away. Schang scored on the misplay and Hooper wound up on second base. Douglas then retired the next three batters and Hooper stayed on second throughout. But the damage was done: it was Boston 3, Chicago 2.

All the newspapers understandably saw Douglas's throw as the tipping point in the game; the *Times* in particular suggested that his spitball was still wet when he fired an "impetuous, violent" throw toward first base. The "wet, slippery sphere skidded in his hand as he threw and went hopping to the right-field stand."

Game Four, bottom of the ninth inning: the score was 3-2, Red Sox, and the Cubs had men on first and second and nobody out. Chuck Wortman bunted but Sox 1B Stuffy McInnis fired the ball to third base and caught Fred Merkle after he'd rounded third base. (Boston Public Library)

Schang took over behind the plate for Boston. Barrow waited it out as Ruth got in trouble again, seeing Merkle single into center field and Zeider walk. Finally, he'd seen enough and brought in Bullet Joe Bush to relieve Ruth. Rather than head to the showers, though, Ruth took over for Whiteman in left field. Chuck Wortman, who'd come into the game to play second in the seventh inning, bunted to first base—but McInnis had anticipated well and played in daringly close. His boldness worked and McInnis fired across the diamond to Thomas who got Merkle at third base. It wasn't even close. Turner Barber pinch-hit for Killefer, and grounded into a 6-4-3 double play to end the game and secure the win for Ruth and the Red Sox. Boston held a 3-1 margin in the World Series and hoped to wrap things up the next day.

Ruth hadn't pitched all that well, with six bases on balls mixed in with seven hits—and the wild pitch—while the Red Sox only had four hits. But the Red Sox infield defense had been error-free and turned three double plays, including a couple of crucial ones in the seventh and ninth. McInnis was credited for digging at least a couple of tough throws out of the dirt, and Scott handled 11 chances at short without an error.

PLAYER PROFILE: GEORGE WHITEMAN

The case has been made in other books that veteran left-fielder George Whiteman was the key Red Sox player in most of the action, both defensively and offensively. Whiteman broke in with Boston in 1907, then spent five years in the minors before surfacing with the Yankees in 1913, spent four more years in the minors, and then re-emerged with the Sox in 1918.

In a Series without much offense, Whiteman's .250 average doesn't sound like anything special, but it was (tied with McInnis) the highest of any of the regulars. The team average was .186. In all, Whiteman reached base nine times out of 24 plate appearances for a Series OBP of .375 and was involved—one way or another—in scoring five of Boston's nine runs.

Game Four was a 3-2 win for Babe Ruth, with a save by Bush, but Whiteman was in the thick of it. Whiteman's was the second of two bases on balls, but Shean was forced at third base when McInnis grounded back to the pitcher. Babe Ruth tripled and both Whiteman and McInnis scored. The Sox were on the board, and any run scored in this World Series was a big one.

Two dramatic running catches were cited by the Boston papers in their Game One accounts, and his catch in Game Six was said to have saved the game for the Red Sox.

Whiteman went on to play for another ten years in the minor leagues but never got a fourth call to the majors.

Game Five: Fenway Park, Boston / September 10, 1918

Chicago 3, Boston 0

Chicago	001 000 020	—	3 7 0
Boston	000 000 000	—	0 5 0

WP: Vaughn (1-2)   LP: Jones (0-1)

After Game Four, the player representatives from the two teams traveled to the hotel to meet the members of the National Commission, only to learn that the men had gone out for an evening of theater. They met the following morning, and were now told that a final decision would be made after Game Five. Of course, should the Red Sox win, the World Series would be over and any leverage the players had would be moot. As game time approached, the players decided not to play until the matter was resolved—but a couple of the Commissioners had imbibed far too much at lunch and were in no condition to meet. The frustrated players, hearing how restive the fans were becoming at the delay of the game, threw in the towel and agreed to play the game after it was delayed a little more than an hour. The Commission had nearly prompted a player strike by continually dodging the issue before them, but had successfully deferred the decision.

The players were looking to ensure, among other things, that the loser in the Series would at least take home more than the second-place teams in each league. It was looking as though receipts were going to leave each player with less than half of what they'd expected. With the season ending early, and an end to the war not clearly in sight, it was possible that the 1919 baseball season would be canceled. The *Chicago Tribune* likened the squabble to a "wrangle over the pennies on the corpse's eyes." The corpse, of course, being organized baseball.

Harry Frazee was no fan of baseball's leading body; the *New York Times* said he called it the National Omission.

The band struck up the "Star Spangled Banner" and then the game began. Regular playing of the tune before ballgames reportedly began at Fenway Park during the wartime World Series of 1918.

Sam Jones was the starter for the Sox. The right-hander was in his fifth year of major league ball and had recorded a 16-5 (2.25 ERA) season in his first full year of work since 1915 with Cleveland. The game started poorly for Sad Sam, when he walked Flack on the minimum four pitches and then saw Hollocher single. Mann's bunt put runners on second and third with one out. George Whiteman then made one of the plays of the Series that led many to feature him as one of the more valuable players—he raced in on Paskert's drive into left field, caught the ball off his shoestrings, and immediately threw to second base to double off Hollocher for an inning-ending double play—all before Flack could cross home plate.

In their alternating sequence, it was Vaughn back on the mound for the Cubs. He'd already lost two games, 1-0 and 2-1, but clearly pitched well enough to have won both. Back for a third crack at a win, he bore down from the beginning, in the first third of the game giving up only a leadoff single to Hooper in the first and a base on balls to Sam Jones in the third.

Vaughn found himself with a lead, albeit a thin one, for the first time in the Series, after the Cubs batted in the top of the third. He grounded out to start the inning, and Flack did the same. But then Jones walked Hollocher, and the base runner took such a long lead that he drew a throw behind him from Agnew to first baseman McInnis, who whipped his glove down and tagged … nothing at all. Hollocher hadn't returned to the bag; he'd stolen second. Mann doubled over third base into left field, driving in Hollocher. Paskert hit the third short-to-first grounder of the inning to end it. Cubs 1, Red Sox 0.

Amos Strunk doubled to right field to lead off the Boston fourth, but Whiteman popped up in the infield and McInnis hit into a double play that caught Strunk off second. After Thomas singled in the fifth, it was Agnew's turn to hit into a double play which ended that inning.

The Cubs collected another couple of hits in the sixth, bookending a fly out and a walk. Hollocher singled to center, Mann flied out, and Paskert walked. Then Merkle singled to center, but Whiteman earned his second assist of the game throwing out Hollocher at home plate. The runners took advantage—Paskert going to third and Merkle to second—but there they languished as Pick flied out to center.

Whiteman singled in the seventh, but McInnis hit into his second double play of the game, the third one the Cubs had completed in four innings.

Flack walked again to lead off the eighth. Hollocher reached, bunting for a base hit—his third hit of the game, a slow roller that seemed headed foul but came to a stop in fair territory. Barrow had fully three pitchers start warming up—Dubuc, Mays, and Bill Pertica. Though Mann popped up to second, Paskert doubled with a ball that came to rest against the wall in left-center field and drove in both base runners, giving the Cubs a 3-0 lead. Barrow left Jones in and he struck out Merkle. Pick singled, but Paskert got caught in an odd rundown that saw first baseman McInnis tag him out at home plate, and the Cubs were retired. The Red Sox went down in order.

In the top of the ninth, Jones got all three Cubs on a couple of grounders and a strikeout of Vaughn. The Cubs pitcher faced a pinch hitter in Hack Miller. Four years later, Miller starred with the Cubs, but now he flied out to left—a little dramatically. It was a solid smash that might well have fallen for two bases, but Les Mann raced up the sloped bank in left-center (still known by fans as "Duffy's Cliff"), hit the boards of the wall and then fell, saw the ball drop providentially into his glove, juggled it, and held on. Hooper popped up to Hollocher at short, who ranged back to steal a single away. Though Shean singled—an infield hit to short—Strunk struck out on three pitches, striking out for the fourth time in the game.

Jim Vaughn had himself a five-hit shutout. Vaughn had thrown 27 innings in three starts and now boasted a 1.00 earned run average, but had only improved his record to 1-2. Nonetheless, the Cubs had recovered. If they could win the next day's game, the Series would be tied.

Mitchell was pleased. "The men were more like themselves than in any one game of the series and I am confident they will maintain the same pace tomorrow." A supremely confident Ed Barrow said the Cubs victory just postponed the inevitable: "[M]erely prolongs the series. We expected to end it today, but things broke too well for Chicago. We will win tomorrow."

PLAYER PROFILE: SAD SAM JONES

Game Five was Jones's only Series start in 1918 and he pitched a complete game, allowing three runs on seven hits. Not bad, but not good enough. It was the largest margin of defeat in any of the 1918 games. Hippo Vaughn dominated, pitching for the Cubs, earning his first win after two losses in the prior four games, holding the Red Sox to just four hits. Though he only gave up five hits, Jones played with fire, walking five. It was a walk, a stolen base, and a double that gave the Cubs a 1-0 lead in the top of the third. He walked the lead batter in the eighth, and he scored, too.

After the 1921 season, Jones was traded to the Yankees and appeared in three World Series for them. He lost his only other start, though, another sad one, pitching eight innings and giving up just one run to the Giants, and losing 1-0. After 22 innings of World Series pitching, and an excellent 2.05 ERA, his career mark was 0-2.

Game Six: Fenway Park, Boston / September 11, 1918

Boston 2, Chicago 1

| Chicago | 000 | 100 | 000 | — | 1 | 3 | 2 |
| Boston | 002 | 000 | 00x | — | 2 | 5 | 0 |

WP: Mays (2-0)   LP: Tyler (1-1)

Attendance was down dramatically for Game Six. It was cold, but more likely there was confusion over whether the game would be played at all, given the ongoing dispute. The official attendance for the possible final game was 15,238—less than half of capacity.

Game Three winner Carl Mays was given the game ball. With Tyler starting a third time for the Cubs, Barrow again had Whiteman in the game and had Ruth grab some bench.

Only one batter reached first base off Mays in the first three innings—Pick, who singled to left field but then was picked off first base. Mays faced the minimum nine.

Strunk singled in the first and Thomas walked in the second, but the Red Sox really didn't have anything going, either. Mays was quite a good hitter, with a .288 average in 1918, but walking the opposing pitcher never really does a lot for one's confidence, and Tyler walked Mays on four pitches to lead off Boston's bottom of the third. Hooper did his job, bunting Mays to second. Shean walked. Strunk grounded out to second, but moved up both runners. Whiteman was up. He hit the ball to Flack, who was becoming a bit of a hapless character in this Series when not at the plate. The right fielder let Whiteman's liner play him, a routine catch glancing off his glove, and both Mays and Shean scored on the error.

Perhaps it was, as the *Washington Post*'s J. V. Fitz Gerald suggested, that Flack had run in too fast. Whatever the reason, he dropped the ball. Flack's .263 average was third-best among Cubs batters and better than any Red Sox regular save Schang; his .417 on-base percentage was second-best on the Cubs. But he'd dropped a two-out fly ball that should have ended the inning. It was the only time the Red Sox would score, unearned runs but enough.

The Cubs wasted no time before scoring themselves, and it was Flack who did so. He led off with a single, taking second on Hollocher's grounder to the second baseman. Mays then hit Mann, and the Cubs had runners on first and second. Mann got careless and got picked off first on a throw from Schang; it was the fourth time in the Series a Cubs runner had been picked off base. The Cubs otherwise would have had the bases loaded when Paskert walked. Flack then stole third base, but Paskert stayed rooted on first. Merkle's single to left easily scored Flack, but Pick lined out to Hooper. It was Red Sox 2, Cubs 1.

The Red Sox also got men on first and second with one out, on Scott's single and Schang's walk. Mays bunted safely and loaded the bases, but Hooper's grounder to first base forced Scott at home plate and Deal gathered in Shean's grounder and stepped on the bag at third to force Mays. The scored stayed as it was.

After three ground ball outs in the fifth, Mays walked Flack to lead off the sixth. But Hollocher forced Flack and then Mann forced Hollocher. And when Mann tried to steal, he was thrown out at second base. To go with their four pickoffs, the Cubs now had been caught stealing five times in the six games. The Cubs were hitting the ball with a bit of authority, but the Red Sox fielders—including Mays himself, who had six assists in the game—plugged any holes. After the fourth inning, Chicago never hit safely again.

For that matter, the Red Sox were hitless as well after the fourth, save for a seventh-inning single by Strunk.

Whiteman had one more big play in him. Mitchell turned again to Turner Barber to pinch-hit to lead off the eighth. He almost came through, hitting a ball that just got over Scott at shortstop. Seemingly a sure single, representing the tying run, the Cubs were stunned when Whiteman came out of nowhere and grabbed the ball just above the grass, tumbling forward but holding onto the ball. It was such a spectacular catch that the thin crowd at Fenway cheered for as long as three minutes.

Another pinch hitter, O'Farrell again, batted for Killefer. He hit another ball that also looked sure to fall in, also into short left. Whiteman was still woozy and, in any event, not positioned to be able to get this one, but this time it was Scott who appeared to make a dramatic catch. Barrow prompted the crowd to offer up back-to-back ovations, once as Whiteman ran in to take a seat and again as Babe Ruth ran out to take his place in left. The third pinch hitter of the inning, McCabe, fouled out; it was shortstop Everett Scott who had run all the way into foul territory to make the catch.

Hendrix was back, this time as the pitcher he was, and he got all three Boston batters to fly out.

Mays was prepared to close it out, facing Flack again in the leadoff slot. He had reached base twice in three plate appearances, but popped up foul to Thomas at third. Hollocher flied out to Ruth in left, and Mann grounded out to Shean, who tossed to McInnis—and the Red Sox had won their third World Series in four years, fourth in the last seven seasons.

The final ball from the 1918 World Series, caught by Fred Thomas and retained by his son Warren. (Sportsworld USA and Phil Castinetti)

Only one Cub reached second base after the fourth; Mays had thrown a masterful three-hitter. Tyler had only allowed five hits, but as the *Globe* noted, it was "a pair of walks, a sacrifice and Flack's muff that developed the runs."

It was a surprising World Series. Lasting six games, the Red Sox had only scored nine runs—but won the requisite four games. They won with a team batting average of .186. Perhaps more importantly, they'd only committed one error in the entire six-game stretch and made the plays that counted. They had received excellent pitching from Mays (2-0) and Ruth (2-0) in particular. The team ERA was a collective 1.70.

The Cubs stats were similar enough; a remarkable ERA of 1.04 but a team batting average of only .210. Fred Mitchell was just being frank when he allowed, "I'd like to play the series over again if such a thing were possible. … I shall always contend that with an even break, we would have won." He didn't mean to detract from Boston's win. "It was a tough series to lose," he admitted. "All the glory that goes with winning the world championship belongs to Boston. The pitching on both sides was the best in years. … They are a great team and proved it."

Numerous columnists agreed that luck played a big role in such a close Series, and that the Red Sox had the better luck.

Boston kept tradition alive—no Boston team had ever lost a World Series. Of the 17 Series played to date, the Braves had won their one in 1914 and the Red Sox had won all five of theirs.

It wasn't yet mid-September, but there was a war to win. Everyone hoped baseball might resume in the springtime.

PLAYER PROFILE: CARL MAYS

Carl Mays started two games in the 1918 Series and won them both, each time holding the Cubs to just one run. Boston took both games by the score of 2-1. Where Mays allowed the Cubs seven hits in Game Two, he only doled out three in Game Six. And Mays primed the pump by drawing a leadoff walk in the bottom of the third, making his way around the bases and coming in as one of two runs that scored when Whiteman's ball was misplayed. Two of the three Chicago hits came in the top of the fourth and Mays flirted with disaster, hitting one man (but then picking him off) and walking another. One run scored, but only the one. For the next five innings, he faced the minimum 15 batters; only one batter reached base—on a walk—and he didn't last long. For Mays, who'd lost Game Three in 1916, the two wins had to feel good. His ERA in the 1918 Series was 1.00.

The submarining right-hander started with the Red Sox in 1915 and compiled a 72-51 record, helping the Sox reach the Series three times in a four-year stretch.

Mays had a combative personality that alienated many a player. He tired of the Red Sox and they tired of him, and he was dealt to New York in midseason 1919. Mays appeared in two more Series, for the Yankees, pitching well (1.73 ERA) in 1921, but with only a 1-2 record to show for it, and losing another game in 1922. He had five 20-win seasons, two with Boston and three with New York. He has gone down in history as the man who threw the August 1920 pitch that killed Cleveland's Ray Chapman.

IN BETWEEN SERIES

The years between 1918 and 1946 were not kind to the Boston Red Sox. Owner Harry Frazee famously sold Babe Ruth to the Yankees after the 1919 season (in which the Babe hit an unheard of 29 homers for Boston) and the franchise quickly stumbled, staggered, and fell so low that at times it seemed they would have to ascend a flight of stairs to reach the basement. Indeed their change in fortunes was so abrupt that it is still shocking, even when observed in cold statistical form. During one ten-year span, from 1922 to 1932, they finished dead last eight times and seventh (1924) and sixth (1931) the other two times. This was in an eight-team American League, it should be noted.

1918—The Red Sox had won the only September World Series ever played, by scoring a total of just nine runs. The Cubs had scored 10, but it's when you score them that counts. The total of nine was lower than the 12 the Sox had scored to win the 1915 Series, and still stands as the fewest runs scored by the winning team in the Fall Classic. (Strictly speaking, of course, this was not a Fall Classic, since the first day of autumn hadn't yet arrived when the Series was over).

Frazee had also mortgaged Fenway Park—to the Yankees owners, no less—as part of the Ruth deal. And then he sold player after player, to the extent that most of the Yankees who won their first World Championship were former Red Sox. Then Frazee sold the ballclub, too! J. A. Robert Quinn bought the team in August 1923.

Before emerging from this primordial ooze in the late 1930s, the Red Sox were, in a word, pitiful to behold. A financial angel appeared on the scene in the person of Tom Yawkey, who inherited enough money to be able to buy the club in February 1933. Finally, there were signs of life as owner Yawkey went ashoppin' and brought in Joe Cronin from the Washington Senators, and a number of other players. His GM, Eddie Collins, set up a farm system and signed players such as Bobby Doerr and Ted Williams, and in 1938, Yawkey financed the purchase from the Philadelphia Athletics of both Jimmie Foxx and Lefty Grove. Foxx led the AL in RBIs (175) and batting average (.349), and second in homers with a then–Red Sox record 50. Grove led the league in ERA with a 3.08 mark. The result was a second-place finish and the beginning of the evolution (or intelligent design) of the new Boston Red Sox

With Williams joining the team in 1939, and Johnny Pesky in 1942, they seemed to have a core that would see many good seasons ahead—but the country became embroiled in a world war and many of the Sox saw a number of years in military service.

1946 WORLD SERIES ST. LOUIS CARDINALS 4, BOSTON RED SOX 3

T he long war was finally over and it was as if America was emerging from a dark nightmare into a morning of vibrant color and fresh hope for the future. The world of Major League baseball was also emerging from the shadows of American life.

Baseball had continued during the war years but no one would confuse it with the pre-war variety. Gone were the stars: Joe DiMaggio, Ted Williams, Stan Musial, Hank Greenberg, and Bob Feller. In their place was a motley array of older, less talented, sometimes even physically disabled (valiant, one-armed Pete Gray of the St. Louis Browns, for instance) fill-ins. In

Photographer Leslie Jones captured six of the Red Sox in the dugout during the workout game prior to the 1946 World Series. L to R: Rudy York, Bobby Doerr, Johnny Pesky, Pinky Higgins, Rip Russell, and Don Gutteridge. (Boston Public Library)

1945, the toothless Detroit Tigers and the clawless Chicago Cubs met in the World Series, prompting Chicago writer Warren Brown to quip "I can't conceive of either team winning a single game." Fortunately for the Tigers, Hank Greenberg's July return from service enabled the Tigers to eke out a 4-3 Series win.

But now the baseball diamonds shone again and fans flocked to the ballparks (18.5 million in '46) to renew their love affair with the national pastime. Fenway was no exception as a record 1,416,944 fans came out to see their returning heroes.

The 1946 World Series pitted the Boston Red Sox against the St. Louis Cardinals. No roster had been hit harder by World War II than the Red Sox. In total, the Sox had at least 24 players enter the service, including Williams, Johnny Pesky, Bobby Doerr, Dom DiMaggio, Joe Dobson, Hal Wagner, Tex Hughson, and Mickey Harris. The Cardinals welcomed back 15 veterans, including Musial who had led the league with a .365 average and captured the MVP Award. Named AL MVP after the Series, Williams had batted .342 with 38 homers despite the introduction by Cleveland manager Lou Boudreau of an exaggerated "Ted Williams shift" in game two of a July 14 doubleheader. Soon every team in the AL would feature a version of the shift in their defensive repertoire.

Both teams possessed great star power, most notably in the persons of Bosox star Williams and Cardinals standout Musial. The Red Sox had cruised to the postseason on the strength of a 104-50 record (the Red Sox managed only 71 wins in '45), finishing an even dozen games ahead of the runners-up Detroit Tigers. (One industrious writer has estimated that the returning Red Sox servicemen were responsible for at least 65 percent of the 104 wins and almost 60 percent of their hits). Ironically the Red Sox clinched the pennant on an inside-the-park home run dash by Ted Williams who was much more accustomed to trotting around the bases at a leisurely pace. Meanwhile the Cards had stumbled across the National League finish line in a dead heat with the Brooklyn Dodgers, forcing a best-of-three tiebreaker. St. Louis won two straight to capture the pennant but smart money was on the fresh Red Sox to win the Series. The AL was seen as vastly superior to the senior circuit and that year's All-Star Game, a 12-0 shellacking of the NL, only underlined the disparity that existed between the two major leagues. Experts predicted the Sox would win in four or five games.

But there was one piece of information that the public was not privy to. In an effort to keep his team sharp during the wait for the NL title to be decided, Red Sox manager Joe Cronin set up a three-game series against a team made up of AL players. Ironically the ploy may have backfired. Ted Williams was struck in the elbow by a pitch thrown by pitcher Mickey Haefner. Williams experienced intense pain and even though x-rays were negative the elbow ballooned to twice its natural size. Just how much this injury impacted Williams and the fortunes of the Red Sox is open to conjecture.

Game One: Sportsman's Park, St. Louis / October 6, 1946

Boston 3, St. Louis 2

Boston	010	000	001	1	—	3	9	2
St. Louis	000	001	010	0	—	2	7	0

WP: Johnson (1-0)   LP: Pollet (0-1)   HR: York (1)

Despite being a squeaker, the first game seemed to confirm the popular line that the series would be a walk-through for the Red Sox. After all, the Red Sox had never lost a World Series and they were the team with the big bats.

Playing in St. Louis' Sportsman's Park in front of a crowd of 36,218, Sox top starter and 20-game winner Tex Hughson squared off against St. Louis ace Howie Pollet, a 21-game winner with a league-best 2.10 ERA during the regular season.

The Sox struck first scoring a lone run in the second inning when Pinky Higgins drove in Rudy York from second base. The Cardinals answered back in the bottom of the sixth when a Musial double drove in the tying run in the person of Red Schoendienst. Musial reached third on an error and Hughson intentionally walked Enos Slaughter to pitch to Whitey Kurowski, whom he promptly hit with a pitch to load the bases. He escaped a tight situation by striking out Joe Garagiola.

The Red Sox threatened to re-take the lead in the eighth but DiMaggio was thrown out trying to stretch a single into a double. In the bottom of the same inning, the man they called the Little Professor lost a Joe Garagiola flyball in the Missouri sun giving Garagiola a sun-assisted double and allowing Kurowski to score the go-ahead run.

Pollet appeared to be in complete control, having surrendered only four hits going into the ninth. He opened the ninth by whiffing Bobby Doerr. Only a sharp single by Mike "Pinky" Higgins kept the faint Red Sox hopes alive. Manager Joe Cronin inserted Don Gutteridge to run for Higgins. He then pinch-hit for catcher Hal Wagner, sending Rip Russell to the plate. Russell singled to center moving the runner to third. Pinch-hitter Roy Partee struck out and the Red Sox were down to their last out. Tom McBride hit a grounder at shortstop Marty Marion that looked like out number three, but the ball took an erratic bounce and went between Marion's legs to allow Gutteridge to score, knotting the score 2-2. Red Sox reliever Earl Johnson kept the Cardinals off the board in the bottom of the ninth and the game went into extra innings.

After Pollet retired DiMaggio and Williams in the top of the tenth, the Red Sox bench erupted as Rudy York hit a solo home run. The ball landed in the upper reaches of the left-field bleachers scattering fans gathered at a refreshment stand. The Cardinals rallied in the bottom of the tenth when Johnny Pesky's error allowed leadoff man Schoendienst to reach first. The potential tying run was sacrificed to second and Schoendienst moved to third on a groundout by Musial. The rally fizzled as Slaughter flied out to Wally Moses in right field. The final score was 3-2 for the Red Sox.

Ted Williams went 1-for-3 with a single and added a pair of walks despite the fact that Cardinals rookie skipper Eddie Dyer premiered his own version of the Williams shift. The third baseman, Whitey Kurowski, was moved to the right of second base and shortstop Marty Marion remained just to the left of the bag.

Hughson allowed just seven hits before being replaced by reliever and eventual winner Earl Johnson, who turned in a perfect two innings in a pressure situation. Of course pressure is a relative thing. Johnson had fought in major engagements in WW II and been awarded a battle-field commission as a rifle platoon sergeant. He won the Bronze Star before being commissioned second-lieutenant. Hard-luck loser Howie Pollet went the distance for the Cardinals side, also giving up nine hits.

PLAYER PROFILE: RUDY YORK

Rudy York is the answer to a pretty obscure trivia question: Who was Ted Williams' only strikeout victim? In 1940, in the midst of a 12-1 drubbing by York's Detroit Tigers, Ted took the mound for Boston and struck out York on three pitches. Of course, despite Ted's feat, York still drove in five of Detroit's runs in the game.

There is nothing trivial about York's major league accomplishments. The 6'1", 209-pound part-Cherokee from Ragland, Alabama, enjoyed a 13-year career in which he hit 277 home runs and maintained a .275 batting average. He was a seven-time

All-Star. In August of 1937 he slugged 18 homers to break the record of 17 home runs in one month held by Babe Ruth. In 1943, York led the American League in homers with 34, in RBIs with 118, and in slugging percentage with a robust .527 mark. He finished third in that year's MVP voting.

A notoriously bad fielder, York would be an ideal candidate for designated hitter in today's game. The Tigers tried him in the outfield, at third, catcher, and first base with various degrees of success. One wit declared that he was "part Indian and part first baseman." York played for the Tigers from 1934 to 1945. In 1946, he came to Boston in a trade for Eddie Lake. He was one of the few who dared to challenge Ted Williams to play harder. "I told him that anyone on the team who loafed would have to answer to me," said York (*The Picture History of the Boston Red Sox*, George Sullivan, Bobbs-Merrill, 1980). So respected was York that Williams took it in stride, apologized, and their friendship remained intact.

He had such an encyclopedic knowledge of pitchers that even Ted was impressed. Installed at first base, he made an immediate impact with the Red Sox and was a key contributor in their drive to the AL pennant. On July 27, he hit two grand slams against the St. Louis Browns (he had 12 career grand slams). He hit 17 homers in that '46 season and drove in 119. Once in the Series, he excelled in a losing cause, hitting two dramatic homers, including the Game One winner.

Game Two: Sportsman's Park, St. Louis / October 7, 1946

St. Louis 3, Boston 0

Boston	000	000	000	—	0	4	1
St. Louis	001	020	00x	—	3	6	0

WP: Brecheen (1-0)   LP: Harris (0-1)

Pitching was the name of the game at Sportsman's Park in Game Two as St. Louis' Harry "The Cat" Brecheen crafted a 3-0 victory against the suddenly silent Red Sox bats. Brecheen's deadly concoction of screwballs, fastballs, and curves kept Red Sox batters off balance, and off the bases, throughout the contest. The left-hander had only a mediocre 15-15 regular-season mark but with an impressive 2.49 ERA. He also had World Series experience having played in two previous postseasons. The Sox managed a paltry four base hits all day.

Southpaw Mickey Harris, a 17-game winner during the regular season, was the hard-luck loser for Boston, going seven innings. Ted Williams was unable to get a ball out of the infield.

The first hit of the game came from the first batter, Red Sox leadoff man Tom McBride. Swinging at the very first pitch of the game, the right fielder singled to right field. Brecheen struck out Pesky on three pitches and got Dom DiMaggio to ground into a double play, leaving Ted Williams in the on-deck circle.

Ted grounded out to first base leading off the second. Brecheen walked two, but nothing came of it. A native of Broken Bow, Oklahoma, Brecheen had led the National League with five shutouts during the regular season and showed his stuff against the Sox. The Red Sox had been shut out only four times all season long.

Brecheen also starred at the plate, driving in what proved to be the winning run in the third inning. Catcher Del Rice led off the inning with a double that bounced off the fence in left field, just inside the line. Brecheen singled between York and Doerr, and Rice scored standing without even drawing a throw. The Cardinals padded their lead in the fifth inning when Rice—starting in place of Garagiola—singled over Pesky at shortstop, bringing Brecheen to the plate again. This time, Brecheen bunted a hard grounder to Higgins at third. Pinky bobbled the ball, then threw hurriedly to second base, so high that it glanced off the leaping Pesky's glove and rolled out into right field. Rice was safe at third and Brecheen at second. Red Schoendienst grounded out to Doerr at second, who held Rice at third with a look and threw out Red at first base. But Terry Moore's infield single to Doerr was too weakly hit and scored Rice, and Musial's grounder—also to Doerr—forced Moore but plated Brecheen.

With a 3-0 lead, Brecheen tightened the screws even more. DiMaggio, with a single in the top of the ninth was the only Boston batter to reach base after the fifth, and Ted Williams—a strikeout victim in the fourth and unable to get a ball out of the infield at any point in the game—tried to hit to left, but swung and missed. He followed that by fouling out to shortstop Marty Marion.

Cards manager Eddie Dyer told reporters after the game that he'd been advised simply to walk Ted Williams every time up, since conceding one base was better than allowing a double or a homer. He said their plan was to pitch him, unless he really started hitting, but to use the shift against him. He'd rather concede a possible double to left than a home run to right. He added, "You know, it's funny how eager my boys were to get at Ted. I mean, they wanted a chance to show him up. I suppose they'd feel that way about any standout hitter." [*Christian Science Monitor*, 10/8/1946] Brecheen didn't take too many chances with Rudy York, though, twice giving him a free pass to first base.

Pesky spoke up in admiration of Brecheen's effort: "The way he pitched to spots made you wonder how he ever lost 15 games during the regular season." In the *Los Angeles Times*, Brecheen gave credit to his fastball having "the extra hop." The *New York Times* quoted him as saying that the screwball was his most effective weapon causing Williams to swing so wildly at a sixth-inning offering that his bat sailed into the Red Sox dugout (barely missing Sox owner

Tom Yawkey, who was sitting in temporary field seating). The Red Sox batters all praised a glum Mickey Harris, assuring him that he'd pitched a game he could well have won.

PLAYER PROFILE: MICKEY HARRIS

Mickey Harris was a 6'0", 195-pound southpaw pitcher who played in the major leagues for nine seasons. His record was an unimpressive 59-71 with a 4.18 ERA and 534 strikeouts.

Returning from four years in the army in 1946, he compiled a 17-9 record with 3.64 ERA and 131 strikeouts. As part of a starting rotation that also included Tex Hughson, Boo Ferriss and Joe Dobson, he played an important role in the Red Sox pennant drive. He was selected to the American League all-star team, although he did not play in the game.

Although he suffered throughout his career from chronic arm problems, he had his moments of glory. In 1950 as a member of the Washington Senators, he was 15-1 in save situations, best in the league.

In the second game of the Series, he held the Cardinals to just one earned run and was 1-for-2 at the plate, in a game where the Sox only hit four safeties.

Game Three: Fenway Park, Boston / October 9, 1946

Boston 4, St. Louis 0

St. Louis	000	000	000	—	0	6	1
Boston	300	000	01x	—	4	8	0

WP: Ferriss (1-0)   LP: Dickson (0-1)   HR: York (2)

Returning to the friendly confines of Fenway Park (their regular-season record had been 61-16 at Fenway) for Game Three, the moribund Red Sox bats flickered back to life. Boston's 25-game winner Dave "Boo" Ferriss kept the Cardinals off the base paths and off the scoreboard, putting up a perfect row of nine zeroes on the Green Monster's tote. He pitched the complete game and allowed only six hits.

Pitching for the Cardinals was Murry Dickson. The right-hander was 15-6 on the regular season, the best winning percentage on his team. His 2.88 ERA was third-lowest on the

In Game Three at Fenway, Ted Williams faced the shift and laid down a bunt toward third base, reaching on a single. He was 5-for-25, all singles, in his only World Series. (Associated Press)

St. Louis ballclub. This time, though, it was the Red Sox who registered the shutout—their first in World Series competition since Babe Ruth shut out the Cubs in Game One of the 1918 World Series.

The game was decided in the first inning. After Wally Moses flew out to left, Johnny Pesky singled over third base—his first hit of the Series—and Dom DiMaggio moved him to second with a groundout down the first-base line. Ted Williams drew an intentional walk, bringing Rudy York to the plate. Brecheen had pitched around him in Game Two, but Dyer had Dickson take his chances against York instead of Williams. He didn't give York anything good to hit, but when the count got to 3-2, he put one over and the "clouting Cherokee"—the hero of Game One—blasted a three-run homer that nicked off the top of the fence and flew into the netting in left-center field to put the Red Sox back on victory road. Dickson struck out Doerr on four pitches, and pretty much matched Ferriss the rest of the game.

The Red Sox added an insurance run in the eighth against Ted Wilks who had come on after the Cards pinch-hit Sisler for Dickson. With one out, York singled and Bobby Doerr doubled high off the wall in left, sending York to third. Higgins hit a ball back to the box and Wilks froze the runners before making the out at first. Schoendienst then fumbled an easy ground ball off the bat of catcher Hal Wagner (Roy Partee's finger had been injured in Game Two, and Wagner had taken his place) and the Red Sox had their fourth run. The final score was 4-0 and the Red Sox had shown that they had some pretty fair country pitching too.

Ferriss (a 25-game winner for the Red Sox during the regular season—only Cy Young and Joe Wood had ever won more) gave up just two extra-base hits, a leadoff double by Cardinals pitcher Dickson in the sixth and a triple by Stan Musial in the top of the ninth. He walked just one. The Cardinals never once got two men on base in the same inning. Eight men reached base, but thanks to solid Sox defense including two double plays, a force out, and a pickoff, St. Louis only left four men on base. Musial's triple off the front of the Red Sox bullpen in right was his first hit of the Series, but he was stranded on third as Ferriss struck out Enos Slaughter to end the game. Ferriss had been 13-0 at Fenway during the regular season; now he'd added one in the postseason.

Despite the convincing win, fans were nervously noting the lack of production from the biggest bat in baseball—the Louisville Slugger belonging to one Theodore Samuel Williams. Aside from the walk, Ted's lone offensive contribution was a bunt single against the shift in the third inning. The fans appreciated it; the *New York Times* said the hometown crowd cheered it "as lustily as though it had sailed out of the park." Williams was on first, "chuckling like a youngster who had just pulled the chair out from under the teacher." As backdrop to the Series, rumors were rampant in the sporting press about a proposed trade of Williams—either to New York for DiMaggio, to Cleveland for Feller, or to Detroit for Hal Newhouser and Dick Wakefield. Whether it was the elbow injury, the Williams shift, or the distraction of trade talk, something was definitely bothering the Kid. Typically Ted refused to use any of these excuses. Instead, he talked up Ferriss.

Though he was really only guilty of one bad pitch (a half-speed curveball to York), Dickson offered a bit of an excuse after the game. "I was far from ready when I took the mound," he told the Associated Press. "There wasn't enough room for me to warm up with the photographers running back and forth before the game. I couldn't throw because I was afraid of hitting them." The Red Sox were reported to now be 5-1 favorites to take the Series.

PLAYER PROFILE: BOO FERRISS

Boo Ferriss was born in Shaw, Mississippi. He pitched for Mississippi State University for two years before being drafted by the Red Sox in 1942. Almost immediately he was called to military duty but due to his asthma his military stint was cut short. He was brought up to the Red Sox from Louisville to start the 1945 season and his debut was nothing short of spectacular.

On April 25th, the 6'2" right-hander took the mound for the first time in the majors and spun a two-hit shutout. In fact, relying on a wicked sinking fastball, he went on to set a rookie record for most scoreless consecutive innings to begin a career—22. But it didn't end there. In his first eight games with Boston, Ferriss pitched against and defeated every other American League team. Boo was a workhorse for Boston, throwing 264 ⅓ innings (second only to Hal Newhouser's 313 ⅓ for Detroit) and 26 complete games. He went on to notch a 21-10 record on the strength of a stellar 2.96 ERA and in the process was selected to the American League All-Star squad. It was an amazing feat, especially in light of the fact that the 1945 Red Sox were a war-decimated team that had won the grand total of 71 games, while losing 83.

There would be no sophomore jinx for this easygoing Southerner. In 1946, with the Red Sox stars back from war, Ferriss improved his record to 25-6 with a 3.25 ERA. Once again he was named to the AL All-Star team. He topped off the season with his complete game shutout in Game Three of the World Series.

Unfortunately, recurring attacks of asthma and assorted arm problems cut short what promised to be a brilliant major league career. In 1947, suffering from torn cartilage in his shoulder, his record dipped to a mediocre 12-11 as he started just nine games. By 1950 he pitched in just one game and was finished. But what he had accomplished in his brief tenure in Boston has won him a permanent spot in Red Sox history and folklore. It was a short but incandescent career that flared briefly and was extinguished just as quickly. He is a member of the Red Sox Hall of Fame (inducted on November 14, 2002) and will always be remembered for his red hot freshman campaign.

Game Four: Fenway Park, Boston / October 10, 1946

St. Louis 12, Boston 3

| St. Louis | 033 | 010 | 104 | — | 12 | 20 | 1 |
| Boston | 000 | 100 | 020 | — | 3 | 9 | 4 |

WP: Munger (1-0)   LP: Hughson (0-1)   HR: Slaughter (1), Doerr (1)

Just when it seemed that the Red Sox pitching and hitting were in sync, the Boston pitching went south. The Cardinals treated the Red Sox starter Tex Hughson—so commanding in Game One—and a parade of relievers, as if they were tossing batting practice. When the barrage was over, the Cards had hammered out a Series record 20 hits and humiliated the home team, 12-3. Six Sox pitchers made the trek to the mound and six were quickly dispatched to the shower. Hughson absorbed the loss.

Notable among the offensive stars for St. Louis were Enos "Country" Slaughter, whose name would soon become synonymous with this Series and would someday be posted on the New England wall of infamy alongside Bucky Dent, Aaron Boone, and other nemeses. Slaughter homered in the second to give the Cards the lead. Kurowski followed with a double. Harry Walker hit a one-out single to score Kurowski. Walker appeared to be hung up between second and third on a steal attempt but Pesky bobbled the throw from catcher Hal Wagner and Walker was safe at third. Marty Marion and Walker combined on a well-executed squeeze play to make the score 3-0 and the rout was on. The Cardinals scored another trio in the third as Schoendienst singled, and Hughson misplayed the sacrifice bunt, leaving runners on second and third. Musial doubled them in. Jim Bagby came on in relief, and got the first two batters he faced before Garagiola's single scored Musial.

With the Cardinals leading in Game Four, and the score 12-3 in the top of the ninth, Ted Williams leans on the scoreboard as the Sox bring in their sixth pitcher of the game. (Associated Press)

The Cardinals added single runs in the fifth and seventh while the Red Sox relief pitching was trying to tread water in a lost cause. Bobby Doerr showed a flash of Boston's vaunted offense, hitting a two-run homer in the eighth but it was much too little much too late. To add insult to injury, the Cardinals scored four ninth inning runs against three different Sox relievers. The appropriately named Slaughter scored four runs for the red birds.

Meanwhile Teddy Ballgame was barely visible in the next day's box score.

The Cardinal starter wasn't exactly a household name but George "Red" Munger was in control throughout, scattering nine hits and pitching a complete game.

Light-hitting Joe Garagiola collected four hits, and George Kurowoski and Slaughter added another four each. Garagiola later called this game the high point of his career as a hitter. The twenty-year old rookie catcher not only collected four hits in five trips to the plate, including a double, but he drove in three and scored one. The four hits tied the World Series record. A born entertainer, the articulate Garagiola later made a career out of denigrating his abilities (and building the comic legend of his friend Yogi Berra) and this game was to become one of his comedy circuit staples. According to Joe, he was very excited after the game and couldn't wait until the newspapers came out the next day to see how his hitting feats were described. When he finally found a paper he was deflated to find the headline writer still obsessed with Ted's shocker in Game Three: WILLIAMS BUNTS!

PLAYER PROFILE: BOBBY DOERR

Robert Pershing "Bobby" Doerr played for the Red Sox from 1937 to 1951 with the exception of his military absence in 1945. He finished his 14-year career with a .288 batting average, 223 homers, and nine All-Star team selections. In 1944 he slugged a league best .528 and in 1950 he led the junior circuit in triples with 11 (tied with teammate Dom DiMaggio). Six times his batting average surpassed the .300 benchmark and in total he hustled for 381 doubles and 89 triples. He was a superb situational hitter and could lay down a perfect bunt to set the table for sluggers such as Ted Williams.

In addition to his offensive contributions, Doerr was generally considered to be the best defensive second baseman of his time. During one stretch of perfection, he fielded 414 chances without committing an error, establishing an American League record in the process.

Doerr, dubbed "the silent captain of the Red Sox" by Williams, was named AL MVP and AL Player of the Year in 1944 by *The Sporting News*.

The 5'11", 175-pound second baseman from Los Angeles was a part of Boston's West Coast connection that included fellow Californians Ted Williams and Dom DiMaggio, and Oregon's own Johnny Pesky.

Doerr excelled in the pressure cooker of the 1946 World Series, batting .409 to lead all Red Sox batters (9-for-22). He also chipped in with a homer and three RBIs. Bobby drove in two of the three runs in the Game Four loss.

Ted Williams lobbied for Doerr's election to the Baseball Hall of Fame and that honor was finally bestowed in 1986. His uniform's familiar Number 1 has been retired by the Red Sox (May 21, 1988) and is prominently displayed alongside those of Williams (9), Cronin (4), Yastrzemski (8), Fisk (27), and Jackie Robinson (42) at Fenway. They are in good company.

Game Five: Fenway Park, Boston / October 11, 1946

Boston 6, St. Louis 3

St. Louis	010	000	002	—	3	4	1
Boston	110	001	30x	—	6	11	3

WP: Dobson (1-0)　　LP: Brazle (0-1)　　HR: Culberson (1)

Game Five, bottom of the second: catcher Roy Partee of the Red Sox slides across home plate while an animated Johnny Pesky seems to signal him safe. (Associated Press)

The Cardinals could have used some of the score of hits they had tapped out on the previous day. Unheralded Joe Dobson, 13-6 during the regular season, spun a gem, keeping the Cardinals hitters at bay and allowing only two hits to pick up the win. Only two errors by shortstop Johnny Pesky allowed St. Louis to score.

With 11 hits, the Red Sox bats were suddenly pounding the ball again. Game One starter and Cardinals stopper Howie Pollet was driven from the mound in the first inning when Gutteridge and Pesky hit consecutive singles. Gutteridge was forced at third on a groundout by DiMaggio. Williams singled to score Pesky and made it to second on the throw to the plate. Pollet was replaced by Alpha Brazle who pitched through the eighth. Brazle intentionally walked the always dangerous Rudy York. Pinky Higgins hit a grounder to third and the throw home forced DiMaggio for out number two. The bases were still loaded. Culberson grounded out to end the threat.

With two out in the top of the second, Pesky bobbled a ball hit by Garagiola and the catcher scored the tying run on a double by Harry Walker. The Red Sox quickly regained the lead in the bottom of the second. Partee singled and Dobson was safe on a sacrifice bunt when the Cardinals unsuccessfully tried to get the lead man. Both runners were safe. Gutteridge singled to make the score 2-1.

Culberson hit a leadoff homer in the sixth to make it 3-1 and the floodgates opened in the seventh. DiMaggio doubled. With one out, York was issued a free pass. Higgins doubled to score DiMaggio. Culberson drew an intentional walk to load the bases. Partee hit a sharp ground ball toward short that handcuffed Marty Marion who was unable to make the play. Two more runs crossed the plate to make it 6-1 and despite a costly Johnny Pesky fielding miscue in the top of the ninth (his fourth of the Series) which resulted in two unearned runs—the Red Sox went on to win 6-3.

Now up three games to two, the Red Sox were on the brink of winning their first World Series since 1918 and the fact that Ted Williams was in a serious slump hardly seemed to matter anymore.

PLAYER PROFILE: JOE DOBSON

Joe Dobson was a 6'2", 197-pound native of Durant, Oklahoma, with the distinctive nickname "Burrhead." He had 13 brothers and sisters. The big right-hander came to the Red Sox in 1941 after two seasons in Cleveland and was to be a mainstay of the Boston pitching staff for eight seasons before joining the Chicago White Sox in 1951 (he returned to Boston in 1954 but quickly retired after appearing in only two games). He spent 1944 and 1945 in the military.

At the age of nine, Dobson was playing with a dynamite cap that exploded and blew off his thumb and left forefinger. Despite this temporary setback, he excelled as a pitcher and eventually won 106 games as a member of the Sox.

Dobson's overall career record is 137-103 with a 3.62 ERA and 992 strikeouts over 14 regular seasons. In 1946 he was 13-7 as the Red Sox swept to the pennant. He won Game Five without allowing even one earned run, and parceling out just four hits. The following year, he improved to 18-8 with a 2.95 ERA. He earned a trip to the All-Star Game in 1948 with a 16-10 record and a 2.65 ERA.

Game Six: Sportsman's Park, St. Louis / October 13, 1946

St. Louis 4, Boston 1

Boston	000	000	100	—	1	7	0
St. Louis	003	000	01x	—	4	8	0

WP: Brecheen (2-0)   LP: Harris (0-2)

The Boston Red Sox returned to the Show Me State ready to show the world the real Boston Red Sox. They were brimming with confidence, but that confidence was shaken in the third inning.

This game was all about Harry Brecheen. Brecheen turned in another brilliant performance for the Missouri franchise, distributing seven harmless hits in the 4-1 victory.

Although the first two innings were scoreless, Brecheen escaped from more tight spots than Houdini. He gave up two hits and a walk in the first and two more hits in the second but emerged unscathed. In the bottom of the third, the Cardinals once again executed the small ball that had become their trademark. Rice singled. Brecheen bunted but Rice was forced at second. Schoendienst doubled. Terry Moore sent a sac fly to right and Brecheen scored with the manufactured run to give St. Louis a 1-0 lead. Consecutive singles by Musial, Kurowski, and Slaughter made it 3-0 and the Red Sox summoned Tex Hughson from the bullpen.

The experienced Brecheen had the lead he needed and he wasn't about to give it up. Entering the seventh inning, he had not allowed a run in 15 innings of work. A Rudy York triple and a sac fly from Doerr ended the streak, making it 3-1, but that was as close as the Red Sox were to come. In the home half of the eighth Slaughter walked but Walker's grounder forced him at second. Walker then crossed the plate courtesy of a double to right field by Marion.

The Red Sox went quietly in the ninth as Williams singled with one out but was slickly doubled up on a ball hit back to game hero Harry Brecheen. He had done it all, on the mound, at the plate, and in the field. The Series was now tied at three games each.

PLAYER PROFILE: TED WILLIAMS

By almost anyone's standard, Ted Williams has to be considered the greatest hitter who ever lived. The statistical evidence is plentiful and convincing. Ted maintained a lifetime .344 batting average while hitting 521 home runs. His career slugging percentage was .634 and his on-base percentage was .482. He was a 17-time All-Star who led the American League in home runs four times, RBIs four times, and batting average six times. He was tops in slugging average nine times and in walks on eight occasions. He is the last man to hit .400 in the major leagues, hitting .406 in 1941, and when he swung a bat for the last time in the majors, the result was a home run.

The 6'3" native of San Diego, California, won two Triple Crowns (in 1942 with 36 HRs, 137 RBIs, .356 average; and in 1947 with 32 HR, 114 RBIs, and .343 average).

He won two MVP awards (1946—after missing the three prior seasons to military service—and 1949) and arguably would have had a few more if not for his enemies in the press. He was named Player of the Decade (Fifties) by *The Sporting News*.

The fact that he batted only .200 (5-for-25) in the 1946 World Series was his biggest disappointment in a magnificent 19-year baseball career. Williams is chosen here as player of the game for Game Six because it is symbolic of his lack of production in the Series. He contributed a walk in the first, popped up in the fourth, struck out in the sixth, and when he finally singled in the ninth, nothing came of it. In the dressing room after the final game, he was inconsolable.

Game Seven: Sportsman's Park, St. Louis / October 15, 1946

St. Louis 4, Boston 3

Boston	100	000	020	—	3	8	0
St. Louis	010	020	01x	—	4	9	1

WP: Brecheen (3-0)   LP: Klinger (0-1)

The final game of the 1946 World Series was played on October 15 at Sportsman's Park. It has gone down in Red Sox and baseball history as one of the most controversial games in the history of the Fall Classic.

The game mirrored the series. First one team took the lead and then the other. The Red Sox had been wandering in the baseball wilderness for 28 years and it seemed only right that Moses would lead the way out; Wally Moses that is. The 36-year-old veteran singled crisply past second. Pesky followed Moses with a carbon copy single up the middle. Dom DiMaggio hit a sacrifice to right, scoring Moses from third. Ted took six games worth of frustration out on a towering drive to center field that center-fielder Charlie Moore tracked down and caught. Williams nipped a Cardinals threat in the bottom of the inning, gunning down Red Schoendienst who foolishly tried to turn a single into a double.

But St. Louis answered back in the bottom of the second as Whitey Kurowski doubled. Hitting behind the runner, Garagiola moved him to third on a groundout. Walker then powered a sacrifice liner to Williams in left and the score was tied.

With Williams and Pinky Higgins both being robbed of base hits by the fired up Cardinal outfield, the teams remained deadlocked until the bottom of the fifth. The Cardinals finally got to Boston starter Boo Ferriss for two runs and chased him from the mound. Joe Dobson came on in a relief role to quell the uprising.

Down 3-1, the never-say-die Sox rallied in the eighth inning as manager Joe Cronin tried to manufacture some runs. He batted utility infielder Rip Russell in place of catcher Hal Wagner. The move paid immediate dividends as Russell ripped a single up the middle. He then called back Dobson to the dugout and sent Catfish Metkovich to the plate. Catfish came through with a two-bagger to left field. And Russell scurried to third. Rookie Cardinal manager Eddie Dyer promptly lifted his starter and inserted workhorse Brecheen into the breach. The man they call "the Cat" quickly retired Moses and Pesky on a strikeout and line out.

With the two pinch hitters on the bases, little, bespectacled, professorial Dom DiMaggio doubled off Brecheen and tied the score for Boston. Williams came to the plate and hope sprang eternal among the Boston contingent. The hope quickly died as Ted could only manage a weak pop up to second base for out number three.

Cronin brought on Bob Klinger to replace Dobson in the bottom of the inning. With the clarity of hindsight, many observers have questioned why Cronin would bring on a right-handed pitcher to face left-handed hitting Enos Slaughter, when southpaw Earl Johnson was available. Klinger had not seen action in the postseason and now he was being asked to perform in the most crucial situation imaginable.

And then disaster struck in the person of "Country" Slaughter. Slaughter reached base on a single but was stalled there when the next two batters failed to advance him. Harry Walker, who would finish with a .412 World Series average—and would inexplicably be traded to the Phillies the next spring (where he proceeded to win the NL batting crown)—came to the plate and drove the ball on a line toward left-center field where Leon Culberson was patrolling (the hit was officially ruled a double). Yes, Leon Culberson. Speedy, quick-thinking, smooth fielding Dom DiMaggio should have been in center field but had sprained his left ankle legging out the very double that had given Boston new life back in the eighth. Journeyman Culberson was also very fast, but as a center fielder, he was no Dom DiMaggio. This is where the controversy comes in.

Leon Culberson had been playing the left-handed Walker to pull and the outfielder had to run a fair distance to field the ball. When he did, he threw to cutoff man Johnny Pesky, who had moved toward center to receive the throw. Of course some argue that had DiMaggio, and not Culberson, been in center field, he might actually have thrown directly to the plate, or at least gotten the ball to Pesky sooner. Some newspapers even conjectured that Slaughter would never have tried to score on DiMaggio.

At the end of his "Mad Dash" Enos Slaughter crosses the plate with what proved the World Series–winning run in the bottom of the eighth of Game Seven. (Associated Press)

Reports differ widely as to what actually took place, but it has entered the lore of Boston baseball that Pesky hesitated for a split second before relaying the ball to home plate. A split second was all it took because as soon as ball left the pitcher's hand, Slaughter took off from first base and never once broke stride, sliding home with the winning run ahead of the desperate relay throw from Pesky. The *New York Times* of October 16, 1946, reported that "(Pesky) had delayed on the relay … long enough to let Slaughter slide home with the winning run." Nor did Pesky himself try to avoid the blame. "I'm the goat," he said. "I never expected he'd try to score. I couldn't hear anybody hollering at me above the noise of the crowd. I gave Slaughter at least six strides with the delay. I know I could have nailed him if I had suspected he would try for the plate. I'm the 'goat.' No mistake about that."

Mel Allen's broadcast of the play is revealing. Never once does he mention that Pesky hesitated. *"There goes Slaughter. The ball is swung on. There's a line drive going into left-center field. It's in there for a base hit. Culberson fumbles the ball momentarily and Slaughter charges around second. Heads for third. Pesky goes into short left field to take the relay from Culberson. And here comes Enos Slaughter rounding third! He's going to try for home! Here comes the throw … and it's not in time! Slaughter scores!"*

The Cardinals had a 4-3 lead and the Red Sox had their backs against the wall. The Red Sox tried to claw back on top in the ninth. Singles by Rudy York and Bobby Doerr set the table. York was removed for a pinch runner named Paul Campbell. Higgins successfully bunted Campbell to third as Doerr was forced at second. With runners at first and third and only one out you had to like Boston's chances but Roy Partee (who'd taken over for Wagner behind the plate) hit a foul ball to Musial for the second out. Batting for reliever Johnson, Tom McBride grounded the ball to second baseman Red Schoendienst. The infielder bobbled the ball for a tantalizing second that seemed to embody the frustration of the entire series, and then calmly threw to second base to force Higgins.

Harry Brecheen was the winning pitcher for the new champions of baseball while Bob Klinger was the loser for Boston. Brecheen won three decisions in the series and posted a microscopic ERA of 0.45.

Ted Williams, in the biggest disappointment of his major league career, batted .200 with five singles, one a bunt. There may be no crying in baseball but reliable sources reported that Ted Williams cried that day. He would never get to play in another World Series. For the record, Stan Musial also underperformed, managing only a .222 batting average, but the fact that he was on the winning side defused any criticism.

The 1946 Boston Red Sox carry the stigma of the first Boston team to lose a World Series.

After losing Game Seven, and the Series, Ted Williams and pitcher Mickey Harris both slump downhearted in Boston's dressing room. (Associated Press)

PLAYER PROFILE: JOHNNY PESKY

Of all the baseball immortals who have played for the Boston Red Sox American League franchise, a 5'9" shortstop named Johnny Pesky is the man recognized throughout Red Sox Nation as "Mr. Red Sox." Although he is not yet in the Hall of Fame in Cooperstown, one suspects that this unofficial title is just about as sweet. Naturally Pesky is a member of the Red Sox Hall of Fame, having been inducted in the inaugural 1995 class.

Pesky played for the Sox from 1942 to 1952, spending 1943-45 in the military. He led the American League in hits in '42 (205), '46 (208), and '47 (207). His 1942 total remained the rookie record until Nomar Garciaparra broke it in 1995 with 209.

The native of Portland, Oregon, was named an American League All-Star in 1946 as he helped lead the Sox to the pennant. On May 6 of that year he equaled an American League record by scoring six runs in a nine-inning game. Typical of his unselfishness was his agreeing to move from shortstop to third base to make room for Vern Stephens in 1948. Not surprisingly this ultimate team player led the AL in sacrifice hits in 1942.

He is forever linked with Game Seven of the 1946 World Series, and unfairly so. The charge that "Pesky held the ball" seeks to blame a Boston fielder for the go-ahead run that won the Series for St. Louis, rather than to credit Slaughter for his bold baserunning. Film of Pesky's play is by no means conclusive as to any meaningful delay, and no one ever charged him with an error.

Pesky finished his career with a .307 batting average and batted better than .300 on six occasions. Despite the fact that he hit 504 fewer homers than Ted Williams' 521, it is Pesky, not Teddy, who lends his name to the Fenway Park foul pole in right field. Pesky's Pole is as much a part of Red Sox lore as the Green Monster. And so is Johnny Pesky.

Pesky knew his role was to get on base for the bigger bats to drive home. He led the AL in hits three times and was almost invariably among the top ten in on-base percentage.

In 1963, Pesky became the Red Sox manager and held the position for two seasons. Unfortunately the Red Sox teams who played for him were not pennant caliber outfits and Pesky was released with two games to go in 1964. He later served as a color man for Red Sox radio and TV before once again donning the Red Sox uniform as a coach under Darrell Johnson in 1975. With only a few pauses, he remained a presence at Fenway, in one capacity or other, practically until the time of his death.

IN BETWEEN SERIES

With the exception of a spectacular 1947 plummet to third place, 14 games behind the pennant-winning Yankees, the Red Sox continued to flirt with the postseason for the remainder of the decade. In 1948, it took a one-game playoff with Cleveland to decide who would represent the American League.

The Indians decided to start a young rookie named Gene Bearden. In a move that is still being second-guessed, Boston's manager Joe McCarthy settled on Denny Galehouse (8-8 during the regular season). Cleveland player-manager Lou Boudreau looked like a genius as Bearden allowed one earned run and struck out six, though the five walks he dealt out offered Boston opportunities they often failed to redeem. Boudreau's high IQ was confirmed when he hit two home runs and added two singles to lead the Tribe to an 8-3 win. Galehouse was gone by the end of the fourth, leaving Red Sox fans to forever wonder why Mel Parnell (15-8, 3.14 ERA) had not been given the crucial start. A win for the Red Sox would have meant an all Boston World Series. Instead, Cleveland went on to defeat the Boston Braves four games to two.

In 1949, the Sox lost out by a single game to the Yankees. With just two games remaining in the regular season the Red Sox clung to a one game lead over the New Yorkers. With the Sox leading 4-0, it looked like they would clinch the pennant on Saturday and rest their top players on Sunday. Instead the Red Sox got much more rest than they wanted. The Yankees rallied to win the game and went into the final game deadlocked with their rivals. The Yankees, behind the clutch hitting of rookie second baseman Jerry Coleman, then won the season-ending game, 5-3.

In 1950, the long spell of Yankee domination began in earnest, although the Red Sox finished a respectable four games out of first behind New York and Detroit.

From 1951 to 1966, the closest the Red Sox would get to an American League pennant winner was 11 games. The numbers are staggering. In 1951 they finished 11 games out of first, in 1952 it was 19, then 16, then 42 (!), 12, 13, 16, 13, and 19. They ushered in the 1960s by finishing 32 games out of first place, were 33 games out in 61, then 19, 28, 27, 40 (!), and finally 26 games in 1966. If the Red Sox were a poor organization with a laissez-faire owner this record of mediocrity might be understandable, but Tom Yawkey had tons of money and he wanted a winner so bad he could taste it.

Individual stars came and went in this period: Jackie Jensen, Billy Goodman, Frank Malzone, Pete Runnels, Dick Radatz, and Harry Agganis just to name a few. In 1960, Ted Williams retired and then the Red Sox didn't even have a star player to make all the losing tolerable. In 1961 an undersized rookie with an unpronounceable name arrived in Boston and was touted as the next Ted Williams. He was given number 8 and asked to patrol Boston's hallowed left field. Carl Yastrzemski was a great young player with loads of potential, but he wasn't going to make anyone forget Number 9, and he certainly wasn't going to lead them to a World Series. Not on his own at least.

And then the youth movement began. Local hero Tony Conigliaro joined the team in right field. Meteoric Reggie Smith was added in center. First baseman George Scott was making fans pay attention with his booming homers and his golden glove. Rico Petrocelli played well at shortstop and proved to have a perfect Fenway swing. Jim Lonborg, a 6'5" right-handed right-handed pitcher was coming into his own. Other Red Sox farmhands ready to contribute included Mike Andrews and Ken Brett. By 1966, the Red Sox were a fun team to watch … much too early to think about a challenge for the top, of course, but still, an interesting team to watch. The Red Sox record in 1966 was 72-90 as they finished in ninth place in a ten-team league. The only consolation was that the mighty Yankees had also fallen from glory in the last two seasons and finished dead last in the American League in 1966 with a record of 70-89. So far had the once proud Red Sox plummeted that this was considered a victory of some sort.

Not that any bettor was crazy enough to take advantage of the fact but the odds on the 1967 Red Sox winning the pennant were 100-1. The Red Sox had long had the reputation of being a country club team with little or no discipline and ownership all too willing to indulge the players' every whim. Rookie manager Dick Williams was about to change all that. Williams was to country clubs what Leona Helmsley was to hotel hospitality.

1967 WORLD SERIES ST. LOUIS CARDINALS 4, BOSTON RED SOX 3

The season would later become known as the Impossible Dream and the Red Sox were variously referred to as the Cinderella Sox and the Cardiac Kids, among other things. Overall the Red Sox pitching staff was mediocre at best, finishing the season eighth in ERA with a 3.36 mark. Their ace in the hole was right-hander Jim Lonborg who won 22 games and led the league with 246 strikeouts to earn the Cy Young Award. Lonborg also topped the circuit in games started with 39.

Carl Yastrzemski captured the Triple Crown on the strength of a league-best 44 homers (tied with Harmon

Killebrew), 121 RBIs, and a .326 batting average. He would later be named AL MVP. Every game was played out like a morality play. Hometown hero Tony Conigliaro, who was leading the league with 20 long balls, was the tragic hero. The right-hand power hitter with the Hollywood good looks and the matinee idol voice was the toast of the town until August 18 when he was felled by a Jack Hamilton beanball and missed the rest of the season. Within ten days the Red Sox brain trust had signed colorful Ken Harrelson, late of the Kansas City Athletics, to replace Tony C.

Every successive day produced a new Red Sox hero for the infatuated New England fans. On April 14, a rookie left-hander named Bill Rohr pitched eight and two-thirds innings of no-hit ball until Elston Howard's two-strike hit marred the pitching gem. (By August, Howard would be playing in a Red Sox uniform). But ultimately it was the Carl Yastrzemski show. His heroics in the field, on the bases, and at bat seemed almost mythical. He played like a man possessed and carried the team on his back game after game. Throughout the season—which some have called the greatest pennant race in baseball history—four teams were serious pennant challengers: Chicago, Minnesota, Detroit, and Boston.

Going into the final weekend of the season, the White Sox had faded and the Minnesota Twins held a two-game lead over the Red Sox and Tigers. But the American League pennant winner was not to be decided until the very last day of the campaign. Going into play on October 1, the Red Sox faced the possibility of a three-way tie with Minnesota and Detroit. Fittingly, ace Jim Lonborg was on the mound for Boston against the Minnesota Twins. Lonborg pitched brilliantly in the biggest game of his career, winning 5-3. Carl Yastrzemski had gone an incredible 7-for-8 in the final two pressure cooker games.

The 35,770 Fenway throng were delirious with joy but the Red Sox couldn't celebrate just yet. They had to sit in their clubhouse and listen to the out of town results come in from Detroit where the Tigers were trying to claw their way past the California Angels to a single game playoff for the pennant. Not until Dick McAuliffe bounced into a game ending double-play were the Red Sox able to pop the champagne corks and symbolically release the pressure that had been building steadily since the season opener.

After 21 years of futility, frustration, and failure, the Red Sox were going back to the World Series.

Not only were the Red Sox in their first World Series since 1946, but they would be facing the same St. Louis Cardinal franchise that had taken them to seven games before capturing the world championship. Of course, both teams were quite different from the forties version. This time it was the Cardinals who had coasted to the pennant, winning 100 games and finishing ten and a half games in front of the San Francisco Giants. St. Louis featured fearsome right-handed fastballer Bob Gibson whose glare alone was good for two strikes. Gibson was fully recovered from a broken leg he suffered in the early part of the season. Their rotation was bolstered by Nelson Briles and a promising youngster named Steve Carlton.

The Cardinals offense included first baseman Orlando Cepeda who batted .325 and drove in a league-leading 111 runs en route to a unanimous selection as National League MVP. Professional distraction Lou Brock added 21 home runs to his league-leading 52 steals, the first time a player had reached the 50/20 plateau. He batted .299 and drove in 76 runs *from the leadoff slot*. Proven hitters like Roger Maris and Curt Flood added punch to a strong defensive lineup and along with Brock, infielders Mike Shannon and Julian Javier and backstop Tim McCarver were postseason veterans from 1964. The Cardinal lineup included four future Hall of Famers.

Game One: Fenway Park, Boston / October 4, 1967

St. Louis 2, Boston 1

St. Louis	001	000	100	—	2	10	0
Boston	001	000	000	—	1	6	0

WP: Gibson (1-0)   LP: Santiago (0-1)   HR: Santiago (1)

The 1967 World Series opened at Fenway Park in Boston. It was one of those pristine October days that bring tourists flocking to New England to view the splendor of the fall foliage. Fenway was also decked out in her finery, with the red, white, and blue World Series bunting adorning the railings and complementing the emerald green of the diamond.

Because the Cardinals had clinched the NL pennant early they had been able to rest their key players and pitching staff in preparation for the postseason. Meanwhile Dick Williams and the Red Sox had been required to use everyone and anyone in their desperate quest for AL honors. This would prove to be a huge factor as the series wore on.

In game one, St. Louis manager Red Schoendienst, a significant cog in the victorious 1946 Cardinal team, handed the ball to Bob Gibson and sent him to the mound. Any other decision on Red's part would have resulted in his institutionalization. A rested Gibson was virtually unhittable.

Dick Williams' ace Jim Lonborg had been called into action for the last game of the season just three days earlier and was unavailable to start against Gibson. In his place, Williams went with 12-game winner Jose Santiago.

Lou Brock, well rested from his 52 successful baseline larcenies, proved to be a one-man wrecking crew. Brock wasted no time, singling to left field to open the game and then stealing second. The threat died but a loud message had been sent to Red Sox pitchers: keep Lou Brock off the bases.

In the third inning, Brock once again singled to open the inning. Curt Flood doubled, moving him to third, and Roger Maris grounded out sending him home with the first run of the World Series.

In the home half of the third, the Red Sox got some offense from an unexpected source as pitcher Jose Santiago hit a Gibson offering over the fence to tie the game. In the fourth, with two out and Javier on second base, Brock collected another base hit and only a great peg to the plate by Yaz prevented another run from scoring. In the top of the next inning, Captain Carl robbed Flood of a hit with an improbable catch of a sinking liner. The teams battled through three scoreless innings until Lou Brock struck again in the top of the seventh.

Santiago had kept the Red Sox in the game and given them a chance to win, but Brock once again was his nemesis. He singled for his fourth hit but didn't loiter long at first. He chose his pitch and slid into second under catcher Russ Gibson's accurate throw. The Red Sox protested the call but to no avail. Flood expertly moved him to third with a groundout to the right side of the infield. Once again Brock scored on a grounder by Maris to second baseman Jerry Adair. St. Louis took a 2-1 lead. It was classic Cardinals baseball executed to perfection by a well-tooled machine.

The Red Sox were unable to answer in the bottom of the inning and Gibson was his dominant self the rest of the way. He struck out ten and allowed just the one run as no Red Sox runner got beyond first base after Santiago's fourth inning dinger. However, if a postmortem had been conducted on the demise of the Red Sox in Game One, it would come back marked Death by Brock. He went a perfect 4-for-4, stole two bases and generally created havoc on the base paths. He also scored both St. Louis runs.

Roger Maris, the man who broke Babe Ruth's single season home run record by clouting 61 in '61 was still flexing his offensive muscle.

PLAYER PROFILE: JOSE SANTIAGO

Jose Santiago's major league record was 34-29 with a 3.74 ERA. Game One of the 1967 World Series may have represented the high point of his career. In that contest he was pitted against the formidable Bob Gibson and performed above and beyond the call of duty, holding the Cardinals to just one run while notching the only Red Sox tally with a home run off Gibson in the third inning. Although he lost the game 2-1, he sent a clear message to the cocky Cardinals that this Series would be no cakewalk.

Blessed with a superior curveball, Santiago's career ended prematurely when he suffered an elbow injury during the 1968 season. Ironically, it was shaping up to be his best year. He was named to the American League All-Star team and had a 9-4 record with a 2.25 ERA at the time of the injury. Although he didn't officially retire until 1970, he never won another major league game.

In the 1967 regular season, he was a major contributor. He posted a 12-4 record for the Red Sox and boasted a 3.59 ERA. He started 11 games but was equally valuable as a reliever, going 8-3 and contributing five saves.

Game Two: Fenway Park, Boston / October 5, 1967

Boston 5, St. Louis 0

St. Louis	000	000	000	—	0	1	1
Boston	000	101	30x	—	5	9	0

WP: Lonborg (1-0)   LP: Hughes (0-1)
HR: Yastrzemski 2 (2)

In Game Two of the '67 World Series, Red Sox ace Jim Lonborg went the distance, allowing a single hit and no runs in a 5-0 win over the Cardinals at Fenway. George Scott looks on from first base. (Associated Press)

This time it was Boston's turn to play their ace. Jim Lonborg, the thoughtful Stanford graduate, had been anxiously waiting in the wings for a chance to see what he could do against the National League's best. The contrast between Gibson and Lonborg was almost laughable. Gibson was so focused that he wouldn't talk to opposing players and scarcely acknowledged his own. Lonborg, the 6'5", 210-pound Californian known as Gentleman Jim, appeared laid back and mild-mannered but Red Sox pitching coach Sal "The Barber" Maglie had been tutoring him in the art of intimidation. The future dentist had proven to be a good student. He led the American League in hit batsmen in '67 with 19, and possessed of a blazing fastball, hitters were reluctant to dig in against him.

The Cardinals starter on this soggy New England day was Dick Hughes, a promising 6'3", 195-pound right-hander who had contributed 16 wins to the Cardinals' successful pennant run.

Lonborg and Carl Yastrzemski, respectively the heart and soul of the Red Sox all season long, would have to excel if the team was to win. Yaz had gone 0-for-4 in the opener and

The swing: In Game Two of the World Series, MVP Carl Yastrzemski continued to power the Red Sox offense as he had done all season long, homering twice and driving in four of the five Red Sox runs in the 5-0 win. Here he connects with a Joe Hoerner pitch. (Associated Press)

after the game took batting practice as hard-bitten members of the Boston press looked on in shock. Such dedication was unheard of and would have seemed phony had it been show-cased by anyone but the author of the Impossible Dream season they had just witnessed. Inspired by Yaz, both Harrelson and Petrocelli joined him in the most discussed BP in World Series history.

Gentleman Jim almost had his nickname revoked on the very first pitch of the game. The term "purpose pitch" may be overused but never was it more apt. His first offering to Lou Brock was high and tight and sent the star of Game One reeling from the plate.

The other half of the heart-soul one-two punch, one Mr. Yastrzemski, was also back in full force. He homered in the bottom of the fourth to stake the Sox to a 1-0 lead and later told reporters, "I told Lonnie, 'You have enough, big guy. Go get 'em. (*The Picture History of the*

Boston Red Sox) Lonborg must have listened because he retired the first 19 men he faced and was spinning a perfect game until he walked Curt Flood in the seventh.

Just to add insurance in case Lonborg might falter, Yaz struck again in the seventh, this time launching a three-run homer off reliever Joe Hoerner to bring the score to 5-0. Yaz had now driven in four of the five Sox runs.

Going into the eighth, Lonborg had still not allowed a Cardinal base hit. Finally, with two out in the eighth, Julian Javier doubled to break up the no-hitter. It was the only hit the Cardinals would manage in the game, making Gentleman Jim only the fourth pitcher to throw a one-hitter in World Series history. The efficient Red Sox starter had used just 93 pitches in the complete game gem.

The Series was knotted at a game apiece and both teams had won with their best pitcher.

PLAYER PROFILE: JIM LONBORG

For one glorious season, Jim Lonborg was one of the great pitchers in Red Sox history. In 1967 he compiled a 22-9 record, leading the American League in starts with 39 and strikeouts with 246. His ERA was 3.16.

Although Lonborg played 15 major league seasons, he never returned to his '67 level of performance. After an infamous off-season skiing accident in which he broke his leg, he never returned to form, although his career record of 157-137 is still impressive. He left Boston in 1972 for a one year stint in Milwaukee before playing the final seven years of his career for the Philadelphia Phillies.

A graduate of Stanford University, Lonborg seemed to have unlimited potential when he came to the Red Sox in 1965. After two seasons of adapting to major league hitters, he hit his stride in '67 and, along with Yastrzemski, was the catalyst for the Red Sox Impossible Dream pennant. He was rewarded with the Cy Young Award, the first pitcher in Sox history to capture the coveted award. He was also named to the AL All-Star team.

Lonborg was on the mound when the Red Sox clinched the '67 pennant after two decades of team mediocrity. Given the context of the time, the impact in Boston of that triumph rivals even the celebrations following the 2004 World Series win. His World Series performance in Game Two was the perfect answer to Bob Gibson's brilliance in Game One. Lonborg pitched a one-hit masterpiece, only the fourth one-hitter in World Series history. He followed with another gem in Game Five before finally tiring in the seventh game loss to the Cards when he was pitching on two days' rest.

Lonborg returned to postseason play in 1976 and 1977 with Philadelphia. In '76 he lost his only NLCS start despite pitching well and went 0-1 again in the '77 NLCS.

Game Three: Busch Stadium, St. Louis / October 7, 1967

St. Louis 5, Boston 2

Boston	000	001	100	— 2	7	1
St. Louis	120	001	01x	— 5	10	0

WP: Briles (1-0)   LP: Bell (0-1)   HR: Smith (1), Shannon (1)

After a travel day the two pennant winners reconvened in St. Louis to resume their battle for baseball supremacy. With the two aces temporarily removed from the deck, the supporting staff took over the pitching duties.

Nelson Briles, 14-5 with a 2.43 ERA '67, was the starting pitcher for St. Louis while Gary Bell, 12-8 during the season (though 1-5 for the Indians before being acquired in early June), toed the rubber for Boston. The Cardinals had not forgotten the brush back pitch thrown toward Lou Brock in the previous game. The Red Sox had not forgotten the beaning of Tony Conigliaro in the middle of the stretch drive. Briles quickly retired Jose Tartabull on a ground-out and struck out Dalton Jones, bringing Yaz to the plate. Yaz later claimed that he knew he had a bulls-eye on him. Sure enough, Briles' offering bore in on the left-handed hitting slugger, striking him on the left leg. Williams charged from the Sox dugout and Schoendienst wasn't long joining the home plate discussion. Accusations and threats were exchanged but umpire Frank Umont quickly restored order and the game continued. Yaz was thrown out trying to reach second on a ball that eluded Cardinal catcher Tim McCarver. Seeking revenge and trying too hard throughout the game, Yaz had been essentially neutralized by the pitch that struck him. He failed to get a hit in his next three at-bats.

Lou Brock, the subject of the Game Two purpose pitch, seemed unaffected by all the fuss, leading off the bottom of the first with a ringing triple off Bell. Curt Flood then singled him in and just like that St. Louis had a 1-0 lead. In the second the assault continued. McCarver reached on a single to center and Mike Shannon followed with a two-run homer to left field to make the score 3-1. Rookie Gary Waslewski came on in relief of Bell at the start of the third and pitched perfect baseball, shutting down the Cardinal hitters for the next three frames. In the top of the sixth, pinch-hitter Mike Andrews singled up the middle and made it to second on a sacrifice by Tartabull. He scored the Red Sox first run when Dalton Jones singled to right.

St. Louis came right back in the bottom of the sixth when Brock bunted his way on base and Lee Stange, on in relief of Waslewski and clearly shaken by Lou's presence at first, allowed his pickoff throw to sail out of the reach of first baseman George Scott. When the dust settled Brock was perched on third. Following the proven formula, he scored on a Maris single to right-center field and the score was 4-1.

Reggie Smith slammed a solo home run in the top of the seventh to revive the Red Sox dugout, but that completed the Sox scoring against Briles who went the distance for the home team. The aging Maris hustled down the line to beat out an infield single in the home half of the eighth, bringing the slumping Orlando Cepeda to the plate. Cha Cha, as he was known to his teammates, doubled off the right-field wall scoring Maris to make it 5-2. The Red Sox went quietly in the ninth and they were down two games to one with Bob Gibson scheduled to pitch game four the next day.

PLAYER PROFILE: REGGIE SMITH

Reggie Smith was once part of one of the most promising young outfields in Red Sox history, playing center field between Carl Yastrzemski in left and Tony Conigliaro in right. The fiery Smith came to the Red Sox for a brief cup of coffee in 1966 just in time to be part of one of the greatest Red Sox seasons of all time the following year.

Smith was a seven-time All-Star, twice with the Red Sox, twice with the National League Cardinals and three times as a member of the LA Dodgers. He finished his 17-year career with 314 homers and a .287 batting average. He led the AL in doubles in 1968 with 37 and again in '71 with 33.

In 1967, the switch-hitting Smith was the starting second baseman when the season opened but switched to center after the first six games. He hit 15 homers and 24 doubles to add to Boston's offensive punch. In the World Series he batted .250 with two homers, including one in a losing cause in Game Three.

In the outfield Smith covered center field like a blanket, using his speed to track down countless long drives. When he fielded the ball, runners were reluctant to challenge his rifle arm.

A native of Los Angeles, Smith played in a total of four World Series, the other three with the Dodgers in '77, '78, and '81. In '81, in the twilight of his career, he was finally on the winning side as the Dodgers bested the NY Yankees four games to two. He came through with three homers in the '77 Series.

Game Four: Busch Stadium, St. Louis / October 8, 1967

St. Louis 6, Boston 0

Boston	000	000	000	—	0	5	0
St. Louis	402	000	00x	—	6	9	0

WP: Gibson (2-0)   LP: Santiago (0-2)

The 54,575 good citizens of St. Louis had scarcely made their way into cold, damp Busch Stadium and settled into their seats before Bob Gibson was pitching with a 4-0 lead.

In the top of the inning, a Carl Yastrzemski single had been wasted. The Cardinal half of the first inning started with—you guessed it—Lou Brock beating out a hit on a slow grounder toward third baseman Dalton Jones. Brock was now officially the greatest table setter of his time, holding the title until Martha Stewart took over the honor years later. Flood followed with a single to left and Maris scored them both with a double bagger to the deep recesses of left field. Cepeda sacrificed Maris to third and McCarver scored him with a single to right. Mike Shannon was retired but Julian Javier came through with a two-out seeing-eye single between third and short. Light-hitting Dal Maxvill singled to left field to plate the fourth Cardinal run of the inning. Having given up four runs on six hits, Red Sox starter Jose Santiago failed to make it out of the inning and was replaced by Gary Bell who had suffered a similar fate in the previous game and was presumably fresh. Bell finished the carnage by retiring Bob Gibson on a fly ball to left field.

As it turned out, one run would have been plenty but the Cardinals added two more in the third. Cepeda lashed a double into left field and advanced to third on a wild pitch. McCarver drove in his second run of the game with a sacrifice fly. Shannon drew a walk and Javier doubled him home, slicing the ball down the third-base line.

If there was a ray of sunshine for the Red Sox on this gloomy day it was the fact that the Cardinals were held scoreless after the third inning. In fact, Dave Morehead and 19-year-old rookie Ken Brett allowed just one hit in the last four innings of the game.

But the pitcher everyone was talking about was Bob Gibson, who had produced another classic. Gibson pitched brilliantly, allowing just five hits and a lone walk in his second complete game masterpiece of the series. In the top of the ninth, Yaz led off the inning with a double, the first man to reach second base in the game. Gibson bore down and the threat died on the vine. The final score was 6-0.

The Cardinals were now in the catbird seat and held a stranglehold on the Series, leading three games to one.

PLAYER PROFILE: JOSE TARTABULL

The Cuban-born utility man managed only two hits in the entire '67 Series and scored only one run in 13 at-bats. Both hits came in Game Four, a 6-0 loss to Bob Gibson and the Cardinals. Both times he was stranded on base.

His biggest claim to fame while with the Red Sox was a throw he made to nail White Sox runner Ken Berry at home plate during the frantic pennant race. His son Danny played 14 seasons in the majors, for a variety of clubs, and banged out 262 homers.

Game Five: Busch Stadium, St. Louis / October 9, 1967

Boston 3, St. Louis 1

Boston	001	000	002	—	3	6	1
St. Louis	000	000	001	—	1	3	2

WP: Lonborg (2-0)   LP: Carlton (0-1)   HR: Maris (1)

With the Red Sox teetering on the brink of elimination, Jim Lonborg took the mound for Boston. Starting for St. Louis was the man who would one day be a legend, third-year right-hander Steve Carlton. Lefty had won 14 regular-season games and had compiled an impressive 2.98 ERA.

With their best pitcher behind them the Red Sox hitters could relax a bit and concentrate on scoring runs. The Red Sox drew first blood in the third inning. With one away Joe Foy singled. Playing for one run, Mike Andrews attempted to move him to second on a sacrifice. Mike Shannon was unable to come up cleanly with the ball and both men were safe. Yastrzemski was caught looking on a called third strike from Carlton and it looked like the Cardinals might escape unscathed but Ken Harrelson came through with a timely single to give Boston a 1-0 lead. Carlton pitched well through the sixth when he was lifted in favor of reliever Ray Washburn.

Staked to the meager 1-0 lead, Lonborg pitched with the combination of poise and power that had made him the AL's best pitcher. Roger Maris managed a fourth inning single and then the Cardinals' bats went silent until the eighth when Javier reached on a Petrocelli error. The score remained 1-0 going into the top of the ninth as Ron Willis replaced Washburn on the mound. George Scott worked a walk, Reggie Smith doubled him to third and Petrocelli was given an intentional pass. The bases were loaded with no one out. The count was 1-0 on Elston Howard when

Schoendienst had seen enough and made the trek to the mound to replace Willis with Jack Lamabe. Howard didn't seem to mind the interruption, calmly dropping an RBI single in front of Maris in right field. Maris's throw to the plate was high and Smith slid in with the third Red Sox run.

The Cardinals' comeback attempt was snuffed out as Brock and Flood both grounded out. When Roger Maris showed a little of the old power stroke, hitting a ball over the fence in right, but Cepeda grounded out to end any threat. The Red Sox were back in contention, albeit down three games to two. They felt good that they were heading back to Boston.

PLAYER PROFILE: KEN HARRELSON

Fans who now know Ken Harrelson as the very one-sided voice of the Chicago White Sox should remember that he was once a key member of the 1967 Red Sox. When right-fielder Tony Conigliaro was struck by a Jack Hamilton fastball that ended his season (and almost his life), the Red Sox acquired Harrelson from the Washington Senators. He had gone to the Senators to escape owner Charlie Finley of the Kansas City Athletics, where Harrelson was unhappily employed from 1963–66. Known for his outrageous flair for style and for life, Harrelson not only *could* hit but he *was* an immediate hit with the hip youth of New England.

In Game Five of the '67 World Series he staked the Red Sox to a one-run lead with an RBI single and the Sox went on to win 3-1.

Known as "Hawk" due to his generous proboscis, the smooth-talking, snappy-dressing Southerner from Woodruff, South Carolina, remained with the Red Sox until 1969 when he was dealt to Cleveland. In 1968 he had his career year, leading the American League in RBIs with 109 while swatting 35 homers and earning a berth on the AL All-Star team.

Harrelson finished his career with 131 homers and a modest .239 average.

Game Six: Fenway Park, Boston / October 11, 1967

Boston 8, St. Louis 4

St. Louis	002	000	200	—	4	8	0
Boston	010	300	40x	—	8	12	1

WP: Wyatt (1-0)   LP: Lamabe (0-1)   SV: Bell (1)   HR: Brock (1), Yastrzemski (3), Smith (2), Petrocelli 2 (2)

This was a game the Red Sox had to win and the Fenway faithful didn't know what to expect. Game One had been a Gibson gem, Game Two a Lonborg one hitter. Game Three had seen the Cardinal bats come alive to pummel Sox pitching for ten hits. Game Four was another Gibson classic in the form of a 6-0 shutout. Game Five was another Lonborg beauty.

Gary Waslewski, who had pitched so brilliantly in relief in Game Three, earned the Boston starting assignment. Manager Dick Williams had once compared him to Thomas Edison because he experimented too much. He was hoping that the 26-year-old finally had the winning formula. In a piece of journalistic insensitivity that would never get past today's political correctness police, columnist Red Smith pointed out that Waslewski's grandmother was a full-blooded Cherokee and added, "the Indians never win."

St. Louis countered with Dick Hughes (16-6, 2.67 ERA). Within a year Hughes's career would be over, cut short by recurring arm problems. Meanwhile, anyone who doubted Williams' judgment in starting Waslewski was silenced forever.

Again the Red Sox struck first. In the second inning, Rico Petrocelli, whose swing seemed tailor-made for Fenway, lifted a Hughes offering over the Green Monster to give the Sox a 1-0 advantage.

In the top of the next inning, St. Louis decided to play a little wall ball of their own. Leading off, Javier pounded a double off the imposing structure. With two out, Brock struck again, singling in Javier with the tying run. Brock then swiped second and scored the go-ahead run on a Curt Flood base hit to left.

The Sox and Cards failed to score in their next times up but in the bottom of the fourth lightning struck not once, not twice, but thrice. The three home run bolts came off the bats of Carl Yastrzemski, Reggie Smith, and Rico Petrocelli and drove starter Hughes to the showers. Ron Willis came on to retire Elston Howard and escape further damage in the inning.

In the sixth, reliever John Wyatt relieved Waslewski who had walked two men and showed signs of tiring. Waslewski had done his job well, allowing only two runs in 5 ⅓ innings of work. Wyatt, the Red Sox fireman, came on and doused the potential Cardinal conflagration.

In the seventh, however, the Cardinals got to the Red Sox top reliever. Pinch-hitting, Bobby Tolan drew a walk, bringing Brock to the plate. At this point the name Brock was about as infamous in New England as Benedict Arnold—and he was about as popular. So far he had done everything except drive the team bus and hit a home run. After the at-bat the only thing missing from his resume was the bus job. He planted a long drive into the bleachers in distant right-center field and suddenly the score was knotted at 4-4.

The Boston fans were on the edges of their seats. If they lost, their Cinderella season was over; if they won, the grand ball known as Game Seven would be played the very next day. All this was intoxicating for fans who hadn't seen a winning season since 1958, let alone a shot at the world championship of baseball.

In the bottom of the seventh inning, the Red Sox responded to the pressure and the challenge. Before the inning was over, ten Red Sox batters would go to the plate and four of them would cross it with a Red Sox run. Schoendienst tried everything to quell the uprising, sending four pitchers to the mound to no avail. (In total the Cardinals used a World Series record-tying eight hurlers in the game.)

The Red Sox had tied the Series, with the clincher set to go in less than 24 hours. The stage was set.

PLAYER PROFILE: RICO PETROCELLI

A member of the Red Sox Hall of Fame (inducted in 1997), Rico Petrocelli is one of the core of young players who helped the Sox emerge from years of mediocrity to become perennial challengers for postseason play. After playing a single game in '63, Rico became a permanent fixture at Fenway two seasons later in 1965 and remained with the Red Sox throughout his 13-year career.

With a swing custom-made for Fenway, the right-handed native of Brooklyn, New York, hit 210 homers, primarily as a shortstop and third baseman. His best power seasons were from '69–'71 when he hit 40, 29, and 28 homers respectively. He was an All-Star in both 1967 and 1969.

In the 1967 World Series, Petrocelli hit two homers, both in the pressure-cooker Game Six 8-4 victory. In 1969, his 40 homers established a new record for home runs by a shortstop. In 1971, with the arrival of veteran Luis Aparicio, Rico was asked to vacate shortstop and move to third base. He responded like a pro and made only 11 miscues in 463 chances at the hot corner.

In 1975, Petrocelli and the Red Sox returned to the World Series. Although he was at the end of his career (he would retire at the end of the following season), he batted .308 and drove in four runs against Cincinnati pitching.

Game Seven: Fenway Park, Boston / October 12, 1967

St. Louis 7, Boston 2

St. Louis	002	023	000	—	7	10	1
Boston	000	010	010	—	2	3	1

WP: Gibson (3-0)   LP: Lonborg (2-1)   HR: Javier (1), Bob Gibson (1)

For the third time, Bob Gibson (2-0) got the starting assignment for St. Louis while Jim Lonborg (2-0) got the nod for the Red Sox. On the surface it looked like a classic battle of two aces, but in fact it was not. Gibson had an extra day of rest since his last start while Lonborg was pitching on just two days' rest. Gentleman Jim had attained godlike status in New England but even God rested on the seventh day. Nevertheless, the banner in the morning's Boston *Record American* promised "Lonborg and Champagne." The headline was inspired by a comment by Dick Williams, who said, "My rotation today is Lonborg and champagne." It was quickly obvious that while the champagne might have been vintage, Lonborg was definitely flat.

With a mixture of moxie and finesse, Lonborg managed to hold the Cardinals off the scoreboard until Dal Maxvill tripled off the center-field fence to begin the third inning. Lonborg retired Bob Gibson and Brock but Curt Flood cashed in Maxvill with a single and reached third on a Maris base hit. He then scored on a wild pitch. Suddenly it's 2-0 Cardinals and the Fenway crowd is deathly quiet.

With one out in the fifth frame, Gibson, a great all-round athlete, hit a majestic solo homer to stake his Cardinals to a 3-0 lead. Brock then singled to left field, stole second and third and scored on a sac fly by Roger Maris. It was a microcosm of the Series. The Cardinals now had a 4-0 lead and with Bob Gibson on the mound that was like money in the bank.

After an initial walk of Joe Foy, Gibson had been virtually perfect, recording 12 straight hitters. George Boomer Scott finally made some noise in the home half of the fifth with a booming triple off the wall in center. He scored on an errant throw by Julian Javier. And then the Red Sox bats fell silent again.

Cardinal catcher and future broadcaster Tim McCarver led off the sixth with a double. Shannon followed with a grounder to third that Joe Foy was unable to handle. With runners on first and second, Javier came to the plate. Williams tried to lift Lonborg but the warrior convinced him that he could escape the jam. Everyone in the ballpark—including the Red Sox—expected the bunt, but Javier crossed them all up by sending a fly ball over the Green Monster to break the game wide open. The scoreboard displayed three more St. Louis runs to make it 7-1 and the writing was literally on the wall for all to see. When Lonborg left the field at the end of the inning, the fans gave him a spine-tingling ovation. It was an ovation that left no doubt that Red Sox fans knew there would have been no Impossible Dream, no World Series, without Gentleman Jim.

The valiant Red Sox would not give up. They had been a team of naïve Don Quixotes all season long and wouldn't go home until one final tilt at the windmill. Rico Petrocelli started the eighth by legging out a two-base hit and eventually came around to score the last Red Sox run.

Gibson and Brock also received rousing ovations when they came to the plate in the top of the ninth. They were the architects of the Cardinals victory.

Leading off in the bottom of the ninth, Yaz was greeted by enthusiastic applause and responded with a booming single to right field as the applause grew. Harrelson, the man who

had replaced Tony C, grounded into a double play and George Scott struck out to end the dream. The final score was 7-2.

Gibson's World Series stats are incredible by any standards and superhuman by today's standards. Not only did he strike out ten Boston batters in Game Seven, he also powered a home run to lead St. Louis to the win and a World Series championship. In the Series, he started and completed three games and compiled an ERA of 1.00 while fanning 26 Boston batters in 27 innings. For the Red Sox, Yaz hit an even .400 with three homers and five RBIs.

Those with the common gift of hindsight have criticized Dick Williams for starting Lonborg on only two days' rest, but in fact he had little choice. "I'll be damned if I lose Game Seven with anybody but my ace," he reasoned. Lonborg had given up seven runs on ten hits in just six innings of work but there would be no criticism of the man who had taken the Red Sox to the seventh game of the World Series.

Carl Yastrzemski was heroic in defeat. The Long Island, New York, native went 10-for-25 in the Series for a .400 batting average, added three home runs and drove in five.

Many people said that the '67 World Series was anticlimactic after the season that Boston had put together. They were right, of course. The entire season at Fenway had possessed a World Series atmosphere. The 1967 season had seen the Boston Red Sox rise, phoenix-like, from the ashes of baseball history. Once again they were a team to be reckoned with and forty years later their fans would still be riding the Red Sox roller coaster that this Impossible Dream team put on the tracks. The Red Sox had lost the battle but they had won the hearts of fans everywhere and had planted their flag on the burgeoning new country that would eventually be known as Red Sox Nation.

PLAYER PROFILE: CARL YASTRZEMSKI

There would not have been a Red Sox pennant in 1967 if not for Carl Yastrzemski. He put together one of the most incredible seasons in major league history. Every day brought new heroics from Yaz and every day he found a way to turn those heroics into another Boston win.

The offense was one very tangible contribution he made. Yaz is the last player to capture a Triple Crown until 2012, with 44 homers (tied with Harmon Killebrew), 121 RBIs, and a .326 average. He also scored a league-best 112 runs and 189 hits and he led all AL hitters in on-base percentage (.421) and slugging (.622). In short, he was a one man wrecking crew.

In the field, Yaz treated left field as his own personal fiefdom and no one ever played it better than he did. His knowledge of the physics regarding caroms off the Green Monster was complete. His throws to the infield always hit the cutoff man. On the base paths he performed flawlessly. He was as important for his inspirational impact as for his exploits. He was a complete team player and a leader by example.

In the final six games of the '67 regular season, he took the team on his shoulders and refused to lose. As the Red Sox, Twins, White Sox, and Tigers battled down to the wire, Yaz responded to the pressure like a true champion. In his final 21 at-bats, he came through with 13 hits (a .619 clip) and the season concluded with the Red Sox a game in front of the pack.

In the World Series, Yaz hardly broke stride. He batted an even .400 with three homers, and drove in five runs. So consistent was he that it is difficult to identify his best performance, but he is selected here because this game represents the culmination of an extraordinary yearlong performance. In Game Seven, he singled in his last at-bat of his epic season and was accorded a standing ovation. Even though he was erased on a Harrelson double play ball, after which Scott struck out to end the season, every person at Fenway knew that Yaz had fought down to the last gasp. It was his season, beginning to end.

Yaz, or Captain Carl as he was sometimes known, was an 18-time All-Star. He led the AL in doubles three times, and in batting average three times. Three times he had 40 or more homers, and eight times he had 20 or more. He collected seven Gold Gloves and was the first person in American League history to hit 400 homers and total 3000 hits.

He was voted into the Baseball Hall of Fame in his first year of eligibility.

IN BETWEEN SERIES

It looked like 1967 would be the beginning of a veritable feast of Red Sox postseason appearances. Instead, the years from 1968 through 1974 were lean ones at best for Boston fans. The waiting period between the '67 appetizer and the much anticipated entrée would prove to be a long one.

Although the Sox never again plumbed the depths of the American League standings, they were still far from a winning franchise. In fact some cynics may have reasonably called the '67 team a flash in the pan, a million-to-one shot. In '68 they stumbled to fourth place, 17 games behind the pennant winning Detroit Tigers. This represented the last year before the advent of divisional play, guaranteeing that the Red Sox would never finish ninth or tenth again.

As he hits his second home run in Game Two, Carl Yastrzemski shows the classic swing that lifted the Red Sox to the Impossible Dream pennant of 1967 and offered fans hopes for future World Series glory. (Associated Press)

In '69 they finished third in the new six-team American League East, 22 games behind the Baltimore Orioles. In 1970, they remained in third, 21 games behind those same O's. And in 1971 they finished third again, 18 games behind mighty Baltimore.

In 1972, with rookie-of-the-year catcher Carlton Fisk (22 homers, .293 BA) calling the pitches and Luis Tiant (15-6, league-best 1.91 ERA) added to the rotation, the Red Sox surged to second place, a mere half-game behind the Tigers. The AL East race went down to the last head-to-head series of the season before the Tigers emerged victorious. Tiant had come to the Red Sox from Minnesota the previous year and, as unlikely as it seemed, the grizzled veteran was to become one of the exciting new faces on a youthful team.

1973 saw another second-place finish to Baltimore, eight games back, and in 1974 Brooks Robinson and company captured the AL East once again, with Boston completing the schedule in third place, seven games out. The Sox had actually stood atop the standings for most of the '74 season before collapsing.

And then came 1975.

1975 WORLD SERIES CINCINNATI REDS 4, BOSTON RED SOX 3

Every once in a while in sports the stars align just so, and the gods smile down upon a particular team. In 1975, the Red Sox were that lucky team. The gifts from above came to manager Darrell Johnson in the form of freshman outfielders Jim Ed Rice and Freddie Lynn, aptly dubbed "the Gold Dust Twins." The odds of landing two electrifying players of this caliber in one year are roughly equivalent to being struck twice by lightning on the same sunny day.

Lynn, a 23-year-old center fielder, was nothing short of outstanding. He batted .331, led the league in doubles with 47, hit 21 homers, and drove in 105 runs,

winning not only the Rookie-of-the-Year Award but also capturing the AL MVP Award, the first time in Major League history that anyone had achieved such dual honors. In the field, he was seen as another Dom DiMaggio; at the plate, his flawless swing harkened back to Joltin' Joe. On one memorable day—June 18—Lynn showed a Tiger Stadium crowd that he was, indeed, a force to be reckoned with. When the (gold) dust had settled, Lynn had gone 5-for-6 with three homers, a triple, and an infield single. He had hit for 16 total bases and driven home ten runs! In addition to his hitting skills, Lynn patrolled center field with the grace and savvy of a seasoned veteran. His speed and flair for the dramatic captured the imagination of all of New England.

Meanwhile, finishing second in rookie balloting was the Boston Strongman, 22-year-old Jim Rice. Rice batted .309, hit 22 home runs, and had 102 RBIs in his freshman year. After a term in the DH slot, he also played a decent left field although less than favorable comparisons with Williams and Yaz were inevitable.

The Red Sox lineup was now formidable, with team leader Carlton Fisk behind the plate, and Lynn, Rice, and Gold Glove right-fielder Dwight Evans in the outfield. The supporting cast included future Hall of Famer Carl Yastrzemski at first, fiery Rick "Rooster" Burleson at shortstop, and dependable Denny Doyle—acquired at midseason—at second. When Rice moved to left field, Cecil Cooper took over the DH role and excelled. Also in the mix were veteran Rico Petrocelli at the hot corner and a utility man by the name of Bernie Carbo filling in where needed in the outfield.

The pitching staff featured starters Bill "Spaceman" Lee, Roger Moret, Rick Wise, Luis Tiant, and Reggie Cleveland. Available from the bullpen were Dick Drago, Diego Segui, and Jim Burton. Midway through the season, in a key move, the Red Sox acquired reliever Jim Willoughby.

The Red Sox season began on a sad note as hometown hero Tony Conigliaro, attempting a second courageous comeback from a near-fatal beaning in 1967, was forced to hang up his spikes for good. Also of concern was the health of Carlton Fisk after a 1974 knee injury followed by a fractured arm suffered in spring training.

The Red Sox lost Jim Rice to a broken wrist on September 21 when he was hit by a pitch by Vernon Ruhle of the Tigers. Nevertheless, the Red Sox were able to avoid the late season collapse of 1974 and finally won the AL East by 4 ½ games over their nemesis, the Baltimore Orioles.

Starting in 1969, Major League Baseball introduced a new element to postseason play. Each of the two leagues was broken into divisions—the AL East and the AL West, the NL East and the NL West. To win the pennant, a team now had to not only win its division but then beat the other division winner in a best of five League Championship Series. The first time the Red Sox won the AL East came this year, 1975.

The 1975 AL West champion Oakland Athletics had just captured their fifth straight division title, and the Red Sox had earned the right to play them for the pennant. With the loss of Catfish Hunter to arbitration, the A's had to reload if not rebuild. They still had Vida Blue and Ken Holtzman to anchor their rotation but needed to go shopping. Early in the season they brought in Sonny Siebert and then made a deal to acquire Jim Perry and Dick Bosman. Stan Bahnsen was also brought aboard. The bullpen needed no help, not with the likes of Rollie Fingers, Paul Lindblad, and Jim Todd to call upon.

With the off-season addition of designated hitter Billy Williams, the A's offense was set. Reggie Jackson was a fearsome presence at the plate. Sal Bando was a veteran slugger who had helped the A's to three World Series championships in '72, '73, and '74. Gene Tenace was installed as catcher. Billy North offered speed as did speedster Claudell Washington who anchored the outfield. Joe Rudi was moved to first base where he teamed with rookie second baseman Phil Garner and shortstop Campy Campaneris. Other notables include Cesar Tovar, Jim Holt, Dal Maxvill, and future Red Sox Tommy Harper.

League Championship Series Game One: Fenway Park, Boston / October 4, 1975

Boston 7, Oakland 1

Oakland	000	000	010	—	1	3	4
Boston	200	000	50x	—	7	8	3

WP: Tiant (1-0)   LP: Holtzman (0-1)

The Red Sox defeated the A's 7-1 in Game One of the ALCS. Luis Tiant was his usual spinning, twisting, whirling self as he bamboozled the impressive A's hitters, holding them to one run and three hits in a complete game victory. Boston scored twice in the first, with the help of three Oakland errors, and added five more for good measure in the bottom of the seventh—and three of those runs were unearned as well. Just the two earned runs would have been sufficient, but the other five didn't hurt. Leadoff batter Juan Beniquez was the star on offense, going 2-for-4 with a double and stealing two bases as well.

League Championship Series Game Two; Fenway Park, Boston / October 5, 1975

Boston 6, Oakland 3

Oakland	200	100	000	—	3	10	0
Boston	000	301	11x	—	6	12	0

WP: Moret (1-0)   LP: Fingers (0-1)   SV: Drago (1)   HR: Jackson (1), Yastrzemski (1), Petrocelli (1)

In Game Two of the three-out-of-five playoff, Reggie Jackson homered in the first to give the A's a 2-0 lead, and they added a third run in the fourth on back-to-back doubles off starting pitcher Reggie Cleveland. But Boston relied on the man who had done so much for them for 15 great seasons—the man they call Yaz. Captain Carl chipped in with a two-run home run in the fourth, then doubled and scored the go-ahead run in the sixth. Rico Petrocelli contributed a homer for an insurance run in the seventh and Fred Lynn drove in a pair of runs as the Sox won over Charley Finley's green-clad squad, 6-3. Roger Moret took the win for Boston and Dick Drago threw three scoreless innings for the save.

League Championship Series Game Three: Oakland-Alameda County Coliseum / October 7, 1975

Boston 5, Oakland 3

Boston	000	130	010	—	5	11	1
Oakland	000	001	020	—	3	6	1

BOX+PBP   WP: Wise (1-0)   LP: Holtzman (0-2)   SV: Drago (2)

Yaz, who had been playing at first base all season, was installed in left in place of Rice when they got to the West Coast. He showed that he still knew a little about playing that position. Boston scored one unearned run in the top of the fourth, and three more times in the fifth on a double, three singles, and a wild pitch. They added another in the eighth. The only extra hit of the game was Burleson's two-base hit. Wise pitched well through 7 ⅓, but left with the tying runs on base. Drago came in, got a double play, and ended the threat, beating the A's 5-3. The Sox swept their way into the World Series.

Game One: Fenway Park, Boston / October 11, 1975

Boston 6, Cincinnati 0

Cincinnati	000	000	000	—	0	5	0
Boston	000	000	60x	—	6	12	0

WP: Tiant (1-0)   LP: Gullett (0-1)

It was the Luis Tiant show at Fenway Park on October 11 as the World Series against the NL champion Cincinnati Reds got under way. His "official" age was thirty-four but in the interest of journalistic integrity, most announcers referred to him as "ageless." They also called him El Tiante Elegante and the 18-game winner certainly earned the title on this day. Even before the game started, the fervent cry of "Loo-ie, Loo-ie" emanated from the Fenway Park crowd like a chorus of hallelujahs for Brother Luis's traveling salvation show. Pack up the babies and grab the old ladies. Their spiritual leader responded with a display of hypnosis and presti-digitation that would have made Mandrake the Magician jealous. The cigar-chomping Cuban mesmerized Reds hitters with an array of gyrations, pirouettes, and machinations from which the ball ultimately emerged, only to materialize a split second later in Fisk's catcher's mitt. It was the old shell game and Luis was the con man. Peter Gammons described it thusly: "Eleven head bobs, five bows, two cha-chas, and an ole."

Fireballer Don Gullett was 24 and no magician, but he was a 15-game winner with a 2.42 ERA.

Tiant retired the first three Reds—Rose, Morgan, and Bench—in the top of the first inning. In the bottom of the first, leadoff man Dwight Evans singled and Denny Doyle sacrificed him to second. Gullett walked Yaz but Fisk popped out. With two down, Lynn hit a ground ball to Morgan that deflected off his glove into center field. Morgan loudly protested that Yaz had blocked his view en route to second. Conception alertly backed up the play and nailed Evans at the plate.

Reunited after fifteen long years, Cuban pitching legends Luis Tiant Jr. and his father, Luis Tiant Sr., compare notes before Game One of the World Series. His father's advice obviously worked as Luis twirled a 5-hit, 6-0 masterpiece. (Associated Press)

The two aces battled into the seventh inning without allowing a run. After the fans had settled back in their seats from the seventh-inning stretch, Luis knocked a Gullett curveball to left field for a single to lead things off. The unexpected show of offense did nothing to diminish his folk hero stature. The crowd went berserk and the now familiar cry rent the air once more. Dwight Evans tried to bunt him to second and Gullett fielded the ball and promptly threw it into the outfield. Tiant eventually scored on a Yastrzemski single. With their black-bearded Moses leading the way, the more skilled Red Sox hitters soon followed. Clay Carroll, on in relief of Gullett, walked Fisk with the bases loaded to force in a run. Petrocelli singled to plate two more Sox. Burleson contributed a run-scoring single and Cecil Cooper hit a sac fly to make it a half dozen. After the parade, the left-field scoreboard showed a lone "6" marring the symmetry of a double string of "0's".

Unable to hit his pitches, the best the Reds could muster was excuses. What American League hitters had long since accepted as sleight of hand, the disgruntled Reds claimed was chicanery. Once, in the fourth inning, umpire Nick Colosi agreed, but otherwise Luis was left to spin his magic unimpeded. It was the first complete World Series game pitched in four years. Tiant had allowed just five hits.

Before the game, Luis Tiant's father Luis Sr. had been reunited with his son in a moving scene at Fenway Park. Luis Sr., a star of Cuban baseball, had been given special permission by Fidel Castro to come to Boston to watch his son pitch. Luis came through in style.

PLAYER PROFILE: LUIS TIANT

Luis Tiant was, quite simply, a force of nature. His windup was like a mini tornado and when the ball finally emerged from the funnel-shaped twister, the batter was as befuddled as Dorothy on her way to Oz.

Tiant won 229 games in his 19-year major league career (229-172), struck out 2,416 batters, and retired with an ERA of 3.30. The three-time All Star of indeterminate age came to the Red Sox in 1971 after six seasons in Cleveland and one in Minnesota.

Born in Marianao, Cuba, possibly in 1940, the man they called El Tiante threw four consecutive shutouts in 1966, tying a major league record (since broken). In 1968 he bamboozled hitters into a collective .168 batting average.

Tiant was a 20-game winner on four occasions, three as a Red Sox starter. As a member of the Indians, he led the American League in ERA in 1968 with a 1.60 ERA, the best AL mark since Walter Johnson's 1.49 in 1919. He led the AL again in 1972 as a member of the Red Sox. This time his ERA was 1.91.

In 1975, Tiant won 18 regular-season games while losing 14. He started 35 games and completed 18 of them, despite a bad back. His postseason performance was vintage Tiant. He spun a complete game three-hitter against Oakland in the ALCS and continued his dominance into the World Series. His five-hitter in Game One set the tone for a classic World Series.

In 1979 Tiant went to the New York Yankees as a free agent. He was one of the few to do so and still maintain his popularity with Boston fandom (how could you fail to smile when, in tortured English, he uttered his endorsement of Ballpark Franks: "It's great to finally be with a wiener.")

Tiant is in the Red Sox Hall of Fame (inducted in 1997) but many baseball fans believe that Luis should be in Baseball's Hall of Fame as well. His record certainly makes a solid case for his induction. But El Tiante's stats didn't tell the whole story. He was one of those forces of nature that had to be experienced first-hand to be fully appreciated.

Game Two: Fenway Park, Boston / October 12, 1975

Cincinnati 3, Boston 2

Cincinnati	000	100	002	—	3	7	1
Boston	100	001	000	—	2	7	0

WP: Eastwick (1-0)   LP: Drago (0-1)

Game Two proved to be a nail-biter. The weather was downright nasty with rain and a bitter wind combining to make conditions treacherous.

Bill "Spaceman" Lee took the mound for the Red Sox and Jack Billingham for the Reds. Lee served up an assortment of changeups, curveballs, and other slow-moving fare and retired the first nine Reds batters with relative ease.

Meanwhile the Red Sox had struck for three hits but just one run in the bottom of the first inning, the run coming on a single from the bat of Fisk. The Reds manufactured a run in the fourth when Morgan walked and reached third on a base hit by Bench. He scored when Tony Perez hit into a force play. The two teams matched zeros until the Red Sox struck again in the home half of the sixth. Yaz, the hero of the '67 season and World Series, singled and Petrocelli drove him in with the go-ahead run.

Billingham was sent to the showers by manager Sparky Anderson and Pedro Borbon took the mound for Cincinnati. There followed a 27-minute rain delay that left the 2-1 scoreboard

One of the smoothest Red Sox center fielders since Dom DiMaggio, Fred Lynn makes a great diving catch of a sinking Johnny Bench liner in Game Two of the '75 World Series. (Associated Press)

lead intact for the Red Sox. After the downpour, Lee returned to the mound and moved through the eighth smoothly with the exception of a harmless Pete Rose single.

The Red Sox failed to score in the bottom of the eighth and Lee took the mound in the top of the ninth with the Sox still clinging to a 2-1 lead. Johnny Bench greeted the Spaceman with a double to right field and manager Darrell Johnson decided to send in Dick Drago to close out the game. It looked like a great managerial ploy when Drago dispatched Perez and Foster. The Red Sox were one out away from a two-game Series lead. Davey Concepcion came to the plate and singled in the tying run. Concepcion then stole second base and scored the go-ahead run on a double by Ken Griffey. The Red Sox failed to score in the bottom of the ninth and the Reds were victorious.

Asked by a reporter after the game to "characterize the World Series so far," Bill Lee responded, "Tied." And so it was.

PLAYER PROFILE: BILL LEE

Bill "Spaceman" Lee is sometimes the victim of his own colorful off-field persona. Some fans forget that he was a very good pitcher for the Boston Red Sox and the Montreal Expos. The southpaw from Sonoma, California, won 119 games and lost 90 during his 14-year major league career. His lifetime ERA was 3.62.

For three consecutive years—1973–75—Lee won 17 games for the Red Sox, no small feat for a lefty pitching half his games with the Green Monster looming just over his right shoulder.

Lee was named to the American League All-Star squad in 1973 when he went 17-11 with a 2.75 ERA.

On the field Lee was a fierce competitor and fiercely loyal to teammates. Off the field his antics and outspokenness ruffled the baseball establishment and irritated his managers in Boston and Montreal. He severely criticized the Red Sox for trading his friend Bernie Carbo to Cleveland. He was eventually sent to Montreal in a trade for utility man Stan Papi, a trade that is still ridiculed in Red Sox Nation. When he boycotted the Expos for their perceived poor treatment of his friend Rodney Scott, he was soon shown the gate. His relentless energy and love of the game serve him well, many years after retiring from baseball.

Game Three: Riverfront Stadium, Cincinnati / October 14, 1975

Cincinnati 6, Boston 5

Boston	010	001	102	0	—	5	10	2
Cincinnati	000	230	000	1	—	6	7	0

WP: Eastwick (2-0)   LP: Willoughby (0-1)   HR: Fisk (1), Evans (1), Carbo (1), Bench (1), Concepcion (1), Geronimo (1)

If Game One was the Tiant game and Game Two was arguably the Concepcion game, then Game Three was definitely the Armbrister game. "Who," you may well ask, "is Armbrister?" During the 1975 season, Ed Armbrister appeared in 59 games and came to the plate 65 times for the Cincinnati Reds. He had no home runs, two RBIs and batted .185. Off year, you say? Actually, no. It was pretty typical of a five-year major league career in which he batted .245 and drove in 19 runs with four homers. With the surplus of talent on the field that day, including several future Hall of Famers, a 5'11", 160-pound native of Nassau, Bahamas, stole the show, and the game.

It was a tight, hard-fought contest from the first pitch and should have been a classic. Instead it was a classic of another kind. Rick Wise was on the mound for the Red Sox and the bespectacled right-hander brought his best stuff. The Reds countered with another righty in the person of Gary Nolan.

In the top of the second, Fisk hit a solo shot off Nolan to stake the Sox to a 1-0 lead.

For three innings, Wise was the story of the game. He pitched no-hit ball until the fourth, when Perez worked a walk and Johnny Bench hit a two-run homer to give the Reds their first lead of the day. The Red Sox failed to score in the top of the fifth and the Reds came storming back in the bottom of the frame. Dave Concepcion and Cesar Geronimo drove Wise from the mound with back-to-back homers followed by Pete Rose's triple. After Jim Burton replaced Wise, Rose scored on a sac fly by Joe Morgan. The Reds were up 5-1.

The Red Sox fought back against shaky Reds reliever Pat Darcy in the sixth inning. Darcy walked Yaz and then Fisk and unleashed a wild pitch that allowed both runners to move up. Yaz scored on a sacrifice fly off Lynn's bat to make it 5-2.

In the top of the seventh, the Red Sox once again got to Darcy. Evans sent a hot grounder up the middle for a single. Sparky Anderson brought on right-handed reliever Clay Carroll. The move paid off as Carroll induced Burleson to hit into a double play. The Red Sox sent left-handed hitting Bernie Carbo in to pinch hit for Reggie Cleveland but Anderson stuck with Carroll despite having lefty Will McEnaney waiting in the wings. Carbo fueled the second-guessers of Ohio by hitting an opposite field homer off the top of the fence. McEnaney came on to stop the bleeding, retiring the struggling Cecil Cooper on an infield pop-up.

Jim Willoughby came on in relief to preserve the status quo through the eighth inning. The Red Sox faced a 5-3 deficit heading into the top of the ninth. Fred Lynn was first up and failed to offer at a called third strike from McEnaney. Petrocelli didn't take any pitches at all, lining the first offering to left field for a single. Dewey Evans was next up and the Reds brain trust decided to make a pitching change. If Boston were to come back, it would have to be against the Reds' best bullpen resource, right-hander Rawly Eastwick. The right-handed Evans dug in at the plate. Evans took the first pitch, just out of his strike zone. Eastwick came back with a fastball and Evans jumped on it, driving it over the left-field barrier to tie the game. Riverfront Stadium suddenly became deathly quiet as Burleson came to the plate hoping to extend the rally. After falling behind on the count, Burleson fisted a fly ball into no-man's-land between second base and center field.

Faced with a decision whether to pinch-hit for Willoughby, Red Sox manager Darrell Johnson opted to stick with the man who had thus far neutralized the potent Reds offense. Willoughby bunted the ball toward first base and Perez made the easy out as Burleson glided into second. Cooper came to the plate with a chance to redeem himself for a poor hitting Series. After two amateurish swings he flied harmlessly to center for the final out. Extra innings would be needed to decide this one.

It was in the bottom of the 10th that Ed Armbrister became a household name among fans across America. Here's how it happened. Cesar Geronimo reached first on a single off Willoughby. Armbrister, a right-handed hitter, came to the plate to bat for Eastwick. His job was to lay down a sacrifice bunt and everyone in the ballpark and watching at home knew it. Sure enough, he bunted the ball straight down and it landed just in front of home plate. Thinking of the play at second base, Fisk attempted to pounce on the ball and collided with Armbrister, who was on his way to first. Then Armbrister collided with Fisk from behind and the catcher shoved him aside. His throw sailed above Burleson's outstretched glove and into center field.

The Red Sox screamed bloody murder but embattled umpire Larry Barnett was unmoved. What many saw as a clear case of interference was dismissed by Barnett as unintentional contact. He argued that the batter has as much right to leave the batter's box as the catcher does to pursue the ball. There was no intent to impede Fisk, the ump ruled.

When order was restored, Geronimo was on third and Armbrister on second. Roger Moret was brought in to face Pete Rose. The Red Sox opted for the intentional walk to set up the force play. Moret fanned Merv Rettenmund who had come on to bat for Griffey. The Red Sox were still only a double play from escaping the inning. But it was not to be. Regular season NL MVP Joe Morgan singled over a drawn-in outfield to drive in the winning run in a 6-5 Reds victory.

Sadly, despite home run heroics by Boston's Fisk, Carbo, and Evans and Cincinnati's Bench, Concepcion, and Geronimo, Game Three will forever be remembered for a five-foot bunt and the "Armbrister controversy."

The winning pitcher was Eastwick, while Willoughby absorbed the loss for the Red Sox.

PLAYER PROFILE: BERNIE CARBO

Bernie Carbo entered the majors as Cincinnati's top draft pick of 1965; he was selected in front of future Hall of Famer Johnny Bench. In his official rookie year of 1970, he justified such confidence by hitting 21 homers with 63 RBIs, and batting .310 to finish second in the NL Rookie of the Year voting. *The Sporting News* selected him as their top rookie of the year. The following year his numbers came back to earth and so did the expectations for this Detroit native. After two mediocre seasons, in 1973, the Reds shipped him to St. Louis where he batted .286 but showed no power.

In 1974 the left-hitting right-hander came to the Red Sox and showed some of his original punch, hitting a modest 12 homers and driving in 61 runs. As a utility man, DH, and sometime right-fielder he played an important role in the 1975 Red Sox pennant run. In 319 at-bats he hit 15 homers and drove in 50 runs.

Playing against his old team in the '75 Series, Carbo's bat came alive. In Game Three he hit a pinch-hit homer in the seventh inning of the controversial loss, offering Sox fans a preview of the drama yet to come. It was his pinch-hit eighth-inning homer in Game Six that unexpectedly tied a game that appeared to be a lost cause and set the stage for Carlton Fisk's legendary game-winner in extra innings.

Carbo retired with a .264 average, 96 homers, and 358 RBIs. He is in the Red Sox Hall of Fame and will forever be associated with one of the most dramatic moments in World Series history.

Game Four: Riverfront Stadium, Cincinnati / October 15, 1975

Boston 5, Cincinnati 4

Boston	000	500	000	—	5	11	1
Cincinnati	200	200	000	—	4	9	1

WP: Tiant (2-0)   LP: Norman (0-1)

It was Act Two of the Luis Tiant Show. This time the Red Sox pitcher gave up his magician's hat and became a kind of Houdini—escaping time and again from tight situations. Working on just three days' rest, Tiant didn't have his best stuff but was still able to compete on a combination of smarts, persistence, and sheer guts. When the game was over, his pitch count had reached an astronomic 163.

The Red Sox decided to bench the struggling Cooper and replace him at first base with Yastrzemski. Utility man Juan Beniquez took over in left field.

Reds starter Fred Norman made short work of the Red Sox in the first inning, allowing only a single by Yaz that Fisk failed to cash in. Tiant's odyssey began in the first as Rose fought off several pitches before singling up the middle. Ken Griffey hit a ball into the deepest recesses of left-center to score Rose. Griffey was thrown out on a textbook Lynn to Burleson to Petrocelli relay while trying to stretch a double into a triple and the marathon was on. Tiant walked the pesky Morgan and Perez grounded out, allowing Morgan to move to second on the play. Bench came to the plate and drove the ball on a line toward right field for a double that scored Morgan.

With the score now 2-0, Tiant settled down and retired George Foster for the final out of a long first inning.

In the third, Norman walked Tiant, who was rapidly becoming an offensive weapon for the Red Sox. Tiant then moved to second as Beniquez followed with a single. With runners on first and second, Doyle faked a bunt and then swung away, lofting the ball to center field for the first out. Yaz then grounded into a double play to end the inning.

Tiant survived the third, albeit with a couple of very loud outs, and the Red Sox struck back in the fourth off Norman. Evans drove in two runs with a triple and scored on a Burleson double. Tiant, Ruthian in build if not in fact, then singled off reliever Pedro Borbon to advance the Rooster to third where he scored on a fielding error by Tony Perez on a Juan Beniquez grounder. Tiant scrambled to second on the play and scored the Red Sox' fifth run on a single by Yastrzemski.

The Reds fought back in the bottom half of the fourth on a Concepcion double and a triple by Geronimo that scored two runs.

Having allowed nine hits, Luis was still on the mound in the bottom of the ninth as the Reds mounted yet another threat. With one out and two men on base, Griffey walloped a pitch toward the deepest part of Riverfront's left-field real estate. Fred Lynn dove for the ball and brought it down preventing two runs from scoring. Tiant retired Joe Morgan on a harmless pop-up and the Red Sox had again tied the Series.

PLAYER PROFILE: FRED LYNN

After a brief cup of coffee in 1974, Fred Lynn didn't just break into the majors in 1975, he crashed through the front door and ransacked the American League. In his rookie year, he not only captured the Rookie of the Year nod (beating out fellow "Gold Dust Twin" Jim Ed Rice) but was also named AL MVP. And no wonder. All he did was bat .331 (second in the AL), hit 21 homers, and drive in 105 runs in leading the Red Sox to the '75 pennant. He also topped the junior circuit in runs scored with 105 and doubles with 47 while slugging at a league-best .566 clip. Oh yes, and he also won a Gold Glove.

The odds of two players of the caliber of Lynn and Rice arriving in the same season are roughly equivalent to Halley's Comet shooting past twice in a week.

Lynn could do it all. The left-handed hitter had a smooth swing that produced prodigious drives to the deepest part of Fenway. In center field, his graceful, apparently effortless style reminded many of the DiMaggio brothers, Dom and Joe. He won four Gold Gloves in all.

Lynn won an American League batting title in 1979 with a .333 mark while hitting 39 home runs and driving in 122 runs. His slugging percentage was a league and personal high of .637.

Lynn's final career statistics fall short of the Hall of Fame level but not by much. He batted .283 with 306 homers and 1,111 RBIs in a 17-year career that also included stops in California, Baltimore, and San Diego. Some observers suggest that if he had remained with the Red Sox where he would have played half his games at friendly Fenway, he might have made it to the HOF. As it is, his stats are impressive. He hit 20 or more homers ten times, including a string of seven consecutive seasons.

He was named to nine AL All-Star teams and invariably excelled in them. In the '83 Midseason Classic he hit a grand slam, the only player to do so. He struck for four All-Star homers, putting him second to Stan the Man Musial in that department. Lynn was also MVP of the 1982 ALCS.

Game Five: Riverfront Stadium, Cincinnati / October 16, 1975

Cincinnati 6, Boston 2

| Boston | 100 | 000 | 001 | — | 2 | 5 | 0 |
| Cincinnati | 000 | 113 | 01x | — | 6 | 8 | 0 |

WP: Gullett (1-1)   LP: Cleveland (0-1)   SV: Eastwick (1)   HR: Perez 2 (2)

With the Series knotted at two wins apiece, the Reds finally showed why they were known as the Big Red Machine. Tony Perez broke out of a 0-for-15 hitting slump to hit two Green Monster home runs and drive in four runs against veteran Red Sox starter Reggie Cleveland. The right-handed Cleveland had won the starting assignment over promising southpaw Roger Moret.

Pete Rose chipped in with a double and an RBI for Cincinnati and Concepcion accounted for the other Reds score with a sacrifice fly.

The game began on a positive note for the Red Sox. With one out in the first inning, Denny Doyle tripled and scored on Yaz's sac fly to make it 1-0. Unfortunately the next 15 Red Sox batters failed to reach base. The next Red Sox batter to make it to first was Juan Beniquez who walked with two out in the sixth. The hitting drought lasted until Dwight Evans managed an eighth-inning single. Gullett was overpowering, masterful.

Cleveland wasn't pitching a bad game. He held the Reds scoreless for three innings before Perez's fourth-inning solo shot tied the game. In the fifth he gave up a single to Gullett, who scored on a two-bagger by Rose. At the end of the fifth frame, the score was 2-1 and the Red Sox were still very much in the game—if only they could buy a hit off Gullett.

The sixth inning did them in. Joe Morgan worked a walk and Cleveland showed his displeasure with the questionable calls of the home plate umpire. Morgan did his best to capitalize on Reggie's distress, dancing off first and trying to distract him. Cleveland became obsessed with his presence and threw repeatedly to first base. When Reggie finally turned his attention to the batter, one John Bench, the future Hall of Famer lined a single. Tony Perez then launched his three-run homer. Exit Cleveland and enter Willoughby with the score now 5-1. The way Gullett was pitching, the lead seemed insurmountable, and it was.

Willoughby pitched well for two innings before giving way to Dick Pole and then Diego Segui.

With two out in the ninth, the Red Sox finally staged a rally as Yaz, Fisk, and Lynn all reached base. Sparky Anderson sent the call out for Eastwick who struck out Petrocelli to quell the uprising.

Cincinnati had cruised to a 6-2 victory. They were now only one win away from a World Series title.

PLAYER PROFILE: REGGIE CLEVELAND

Reggie Cleveland hailed from Swift Current, Saskatchewan, a Canadian province better known for producing hockey players than baseball players.

Cleveland began his career with the National League St. Louis Cardinals. Following brief appearances in '69 and '70, he was in the majors to stay. By 1971 he was pitching in a rotation with Bob Gibson, Steve Carlton, and Jerry Reuss. Mixing his sliders, curves, and fastballs, he went 12-12 that season with a 4.01 ERA and won NL Rookie Pitcher of the Year honors from *The Sporting News*.

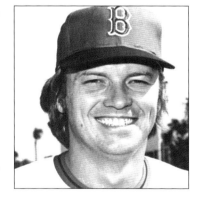

Cleveland came to Boston in 1973, along with Cardinal teammates Terry Hughes and Diego Segui, in a trade for Lynn McGlothen, Mike Garman, and John Curtis. The right-hander soon became an integral part of the Red Sox staff and remained with the team through the 1978 season.

When you have earned the nickname "Double Cheeseburger," you just might have a weight problem and that, along with other major league temptations, was part of Cleveland's undoing. He arrived in Boston in bad shape, overweight, and with a gimpy knee. His first year in Boston, he was a disappointing 12-14 with a 4.31 ERA.

Despite his troubles, he was in the starting rotation in 1975, along with Bill Lee, Luis Tiant, and Rick Wise. He started poorly and was banished to the bullpen until late July. That season, he was involved in a car crash that may have involved DUI.

Cleveland recovered to help lead the Red Sox' September charge to the pennant. His season mark was 13-9 and a 4.43 ERA, but his September record was 4-0 with a 2.21 ERA.

When he took the mound in the ACLS against Oakland, he became the first Canadian to start a postseason game. In Game Five of the World Series, he became the first Canadian pitcher to start a game in the Fall Classic. He kept the powerful Reds off the scoreboard until the fourth inning when he gave up a two-out homer to Tony Perez. The Red Sox came undone in the sixth and Cleveland gave up a second homer to Perez en route to a 6-2 loss.

Cleveland also pitched in a relief role in the ninth inning of Game Seven. With runners on second and third and the Red Sox trailing 4-3, he walked Johnny Bench to load the bases. Tony Perez, who had touched him up for two homers in Game Five came to the plate. Cleveland ended the threat by getting Perez to fly out. But it was too late; the game and the Series were lost.

Game Six: Fenway Park, Boston / October 21, 1975

Boston 7, Cincinnati 6

Cincinnati	000	030	210	000	—	6	14	0
Boston	300	000	030	001	—	7	10	1

WP: Wise (1-0)   LP: Darcy (0-1)   HR: Geronimo (2), Fisk (2), Lynn (1), Carbo (2)

The Reds weren't the only force of nature descending on Boston for Game Six. Mother Nature came calling as well, bringing with her a full roster of rain. It was a deluge and before it ended, the city was sodden. The rain washed out the scheduled game for October 18 and prevented play on the 19th and 20th. as well. It drenched Fenway Park and brought baseball to a screeching halt.

It seeped into the very strategy of the game. The World Series is designed to test the strategic abilities of the managers. Teams no longer have the luxury of time—time to heal from injuries, time to adjust lineups to allow for slumps and other unforeseen occurrences. In a best-of-seven Series decisions have to be made that would never be made during the regular season. Tired pitchers are forced back into action on two or three days' rest. Utility players are forced into action in key situations.

In the 1975 World Series, Mother Nature intervened to give everyone a much needed rest. The Red Sox had intended to start Bill Lee in Game Six. Lee hadn't pitched since Game Two and was well rested and ready. Suddenly every pitcher on both teams was rested and ready.

The shot heard 'round the world. Carlton Fisk wills the ball fair in Game Six of the 1975 World Series. The iconic home run set off wild celebrations throughout New England. (Associated Press)

Sparky Anderson decided to go with Gary Nolan and keep Gullett in reserve for a possible Game Seven. Johnson's decision was more complex.

Many baseball followers wondered if the Series could ever regain the public interest after such an extended layoff. Aside from the players becoming rusty, would the fans lose their interest?

After a three-day downpour, the Sox and the Reds finally got back to baseball. It was well worth the wait.

If you ever want to convince someone that baseball is the greatest sport, show them a video of Game Six of the 1975 World Series. If they still aren't convinced, they are probably beyond help.

Luis Tiant was the Red Sox starter and in the bottom half of the first Luis was staked to a three-run lead when Fred Lynn hit a three-run home run. He threw everything at the Reds but the kitchen sink and hung in there until the eighth inning when he was replaced by Moret.

The Reds got to Tiant in the fifth. After Geronimo struck out, the much-despised (in Boston at least) Armbrister worked a walk. Rose singled him to third. Ken Griffey then drove a ball to the deepest part of straightaway center field, Fred Lynn's personal fiefdom. Lynn raced for the ball and the two converged at the 379-foot sign. Lynn struck the wall with a sickening crunch and lay motionless. Fenway Park was suddenly as silent as the grave. And fans scarcely noticed that two Reds had crossed home plate and Griffey was on third. A seeming eternity later, Lynn rose from the ground to the relief of fans. Griffey scored from third, before the inning was brought to a close. The Reds had tied the game, 3-3.

In the top of the seventh, the Big Red Machine scored two more runs to take a 5-3 lead. Griffey and Morgan singled, and George Foster doubled them both in. And then Geronimo homered to lead off the eighth, and Roger Moret was called on to relieve Tiant. Moret got three quick outs, but the scoreboard read 6-3 in favor of the Reds. It looked like they had the World Series sewn up. There was a pall over Fenway Park.

But then Fred Lynn beat out an infield hit in the bottom of the eighth. And Rico walked. Bernie Carbo, pinch-hitting for Moret, came to the plate. Carbo worked the count to 3-and-2. On the next pitch, which was well inside, Carbo was fooled badly. Somehow he was able to make feeble contact and hit the ball foul. "The worst swing in World Series history," Pete Rose later called it. No doubt believing that the befuddled batter was set up for a fastball, Eastwick threw a heater down the center of the plate. Carbo unloaded on it, sending it deep to center field where it cleared the wall some 400 feet from home plate. The score was suddenly tied 6-6 and Fenway Park went nuts with new life!

The Sox held off the Reds in the top of the ninth and almost won it in the bottom. Doyle walked and made it to third on a single by Yaz. Will McEnaney replaced Eastwick and walked Fisk to load the bases and create a possible force at home. Lynn hit a fly ball down the left field line which George Foster caught and made a peg to home plate to nail Doyle who was trying to score. Third-base coach Don Zimmer had frantically been yelling "No, no, no," but the more optimistic Doyle heard "Go, go, go." It would take extra innings to decide this one.

In the 11th inning, the Reds threatened. There was a man on first and Joe Morgan drove the ball hard and deep to right field. Dewey Evans pursued the ball and made an incredible leaping catch at the wall, robbing Morgan of a home run. Not satisfied with grand larceny, Evans wheeled and threw a bullet to first to complete a double killing. It was another brilliant play in a series of memorable moments that the crowd was almost coming to expect. "Can you top this?" seemed to be the theme of the contest and in almost every case, someone took up the challenge. In the top of the 12th, Fisk made a brilliant catch of a pop foul off the bat of Johnny Bench, robbing a second row fan of an excellent souvenir in the process. Pat Darcy had pitched a perfect 10th and 11th for Cincinnati. Dick Drago and Rick Wise had stifled Cincinnati. When Carlton Fisk came to the plate in the bottom of the 12th, the game was already a classic among classics. Fans were drained and so were the players. The human mind and body can only take so much and the Fenway Park multitude had been through a season's worth of thrills in one game. Cincinnati's eighth pitcher of the game, Pat Darcy, toed the rubber and delivered a pitch high to Carlton Fisk for ball one. The next pitch was down and in and Fisk swung and pulled it violently to left field. From the time bat met ball the only question was on which side of the foul pole the ball would land. Lacking faith in his psychic power to will the ball fair, he mimed the act of pushing it fair as well, employing every ounce of body English he possessed as he leaped sideways down the first baseline. Did it work? Who knows? But something guided the ball fair and the crowd erupted as one in a cry of triumph that still sends chills up the backs of Red Sox fans almost 35 years later. The rest was pandemonium. As AP correspondent Will Grimsley put it: "It was like V-J day. Men went berserk. Women cried. Tykes bolted from the hands of their parents and got lost in the yelling, stampeding crowd."

Wise picked up the win in a rare relief role and Darcy was tagged with the loss.

PLAYER PROFILE: CARLTON FISK

Despite a Hall of Fame career that produced 376 homers, 1,330 RBIs, and 11 All-Star selections, Carlton Fisk is best known for a home run that came mere inches from being a long foul ball.

Fisk was a fiery leader and a man of great toughness and durability. He was a student of hitters and a teacher of pitchers, capable of making everyone on his staff better. But that 1975 home run is what raised him from a local hero to iconic status within Red Sox Nation.

Fisk, a "hometown" hero from Bellows Falls, New Hampshire, was the backbone of the Red Sox for 11 seasons before changing his socks and departing for Chicago. Fisk epitomized the blue collar work ethic of the Red Sox just as his nemesis Thurman Munson did with the Yankees.

Game Seven: Fenway Park, Boston / October 22, 1975

Cincinnati 4, Boston 3

Cincinnati	000	002	101	—	4	9	0
Boston	003	000	000	—	3	5	2

WP: Carroll (1-0)   LP: Burton (0-1)   SV: McEnaney (1)   HR: Perez (3)

When you've just witnessed a masterpiece, a game in which one writer correctly pointed out, "numbers didn't seem to mean much," everything else looks like paint-by-numbers and that was the case with Game Seven of the '75 Series. Some commentators even suggested, half seriously, that the game shouldn't be played at all, that the perfection of the previous game should not be sullied by comparison with another.

Such talk was futile and silly of course. The game was played and a World Series winner was declared. Bill Lee took the ball to the mound for the Red Sox and Don Gullett for the Reds. The Cincinnati manager declared that win or lose, his pitcher would someday go to the Hall of Fame. Spaceman responded that win or lose, he would definitely go to the Eliot Lounge, his favorite watering hole.

It was a good game, a close game, a game that saw the Red Sox build a third inning 3-0 lead behind the pitching of Lee. The left-hander kept the Reds off the scoreboard through five full innings.

The Sox runs came in on a one-out walk to Carbo, a Doyle single, and an RBI single by Captain Carl. Fisk was walked intentionally, and Lynn struck out. But then Gullett made the Fenway fans giddy with glee by walking Petrocelli to force one run in and then walking Evans to force in another.

In the top half of the sixth, Rose singled and after Morgan flied out to right field, Bench hit a grounder to shortstop. Burleson made the play and underhanded the ball to Doyle at second. With Charlie Hustle bearing down on him, Doyle threw wildly to first and the ball landed in the Red Sox dugout. Tony Perez was next up and with first base open, most observers thought that an intentional walk was in order.

But this was Bill Lee and Bill Lee marched to a different drummer. Any National League pitcher could have told Lee that you don't throw curveballs to Tony Perez because he feasted on them. In fact Red Sox scouting reports were there for him to see, in black and white. Lee claims today that the botched double play upset him. "I lost it and threw the blooper," he admits. "Someone should have come out and calmed me down." Not only did Lee throw a curveball, he threw the granddaddy of curveballs. The pitch was one you might see thrown in a Little League game on the moon. It rose to a high rainbow arc reaching its zenith midway to the plate and descended toward Fisk's waiting glove. It was a moment frozen in time and it seemed everyone at Fenway had time for a beer and ham sandwich before it arrived. Lee's Leephus pitch never did make it to Fisk's glove; there was no pot of gold at the end of this rainbow, only Tony Perez. Legend has it that Perez's eyes became as big as saucers as he hit a moon shot over the Green Monster.

Lee popped a blister on his pitching hand in the top of the seventh. After getting the first batter out, he walked Griffey and was lifted in favor of Roger Moret. He got another out, but Griffey stole second and Armbrister walked. Rose tied the game with a single to center, driving in Griffey from second base. After Moret walked Morgan, Darrell Johnson waved in Jim Willoughby who stopped the bleeding by getting Bench to pop up to Fisk. Willoughby kept the ball in the infield, pitching a perfect eighth.

The bottom of the eighth featured one of those moments that leave Red Sox fans shaking their heads. Evans drew a walk and Burleson failed in his first attempt to move him to second. Compounding his crime, Burleson then grounded into a 6-4-3 double play. And then in a move that is still second-guessed today, Johnson sent Cecil Cooper in to bat for Willoughby, the man who had effectively thrown a wrench into the Big Red Machine. Cooper struck out and the Fenway crowd buzzed its discontent.

Jim Burton took the mound for the Red Sox in the top of the ninth and promptly walked Ken Griffey. Griffey reached second on a well-executed sacrifice by Geronimo. Dan Driessen grounded out but Griffey moved to third on the play. And then 5'7", 155-pound super-pest Joe Morgan deposited a ninth-inning dying quail single into right field to score Griffey with the go-ahead run. Reds reliever Will McEnaney retired the first two Sox in order in the bottom of the inning and Yastrzemski, so often the hero, came to the plate. There would be no repeat of the Game Six lightning this time. Yaz flied out to left-center field and the Cincinnati Reds were the world champions of baseball.

Stars of the Series included Morgan, MVP Pete Rose who batted .370 for the Reds, Tony Perez with three home runs, Tiant with two complete game victories, and Yaz with his .310 average. But this was one of those rare occasions when the game itself transcended any of its component parts. And the first time in baseball history that Game Six was more historically significant than Game Seven.

Bill "Spaceman" Lee delivers his first pitch to leadoff batter Pete Rose in Game Seven of the 1975 World Series. Lee pitched five shutout innings and then threw a "Leephus" lob that Reds slugger Tony Perez hit over the Green Monster. The Red Sox went on to lose the game and the World Series on a ninth inning bloop single by Joe Morgan. (Associated Press)

PLAYER PROFILE: JIM WILLOUGHBY

Jim Willoughby is a member, in good standing, of the Red Sox "What If? Society." His colleagues in this exclusive group include Bill "What if they'd replaced Buckner with Stapleton for defensive purposes in Game Six?" Buckner, Babe "What if they'd never sold him to the Yankees?" Ruth, and Mel "What if they'd started him instead of Galehouse in the 1948 playoff vs. Cleveland?" Parnell—to name just a few.

Willoughby, a 6'2" right-hander from Salinas, California, played eight seasons for three different clubs: the Giants, the Red Sox, and the White Sox. His career numbers are modest. He won 26 games and lost 36 and sported a 3.79 ERA. With the Giants from 1971–74 he was almost always used as a starter.

With Boston, he was used exclusively as a reliever. Although he was new to the relief role, he embraced it and excelled at it. In 24 games, he went 5-2 with eight saves and a 3.54 ERA. He went on to make appearances in three World Series games and was the pitcher victimized in the infamous Armbrister fiasco in the 10th inning of Game Three. But he is best remembered for what might have been in Game Seven.

Willoughby had kept the powerful Reds bats at bay since entering Game Seven in the seventh inning. He had retired Johnny Bench with the bases full in the seventh and had recorded three straight outs in the eighth. In the bottom of the eighth, manager Darrell Johnson pinch-hit for Willoughby and the Reds scored what proved to be the winning run against his replacement Jim Burton in the ninth.

IN BETWEEN SERIES

After 1975, there was no dramatic collapse for Boston. The Red Sox remained competitive throughout the remainder of the 1970s. In 1976, they finished third behind the pennant winning Yankees and the Baltimore Orioles. In '77, with the American League East now expanded to seven teams, they tied with Baltimore for second on the strength of 97 wins, as the Yankees again captured the pennant. In 1978, it took 163 games before a winner in the AL East could be declared. The Red Sox and Yankees hooked up in a sudden death playoff game that was decided on a three-run homer by light-hitting Yankee shortstop Bucky Dent.

In 1979 the Red Sox once again missed postseason play as the Baltimore Orioles captured the flag and Milwaukee finished second in front of the Sox. The 1980s did not start well for Boston. They dropped to fifth place in 1980, and remained there in the strike-shortened 1981 season before rallying to a third-place finish in 1982 with a 89-73 record. They plummeted to seventh in 1983, dropping below the .500 mark with an ugly 78-84 mark. The following year they rose to fourth place, although still 18 games behind the winning Detroit Tigers. In 1985, they showed little sign that they were on the verge of a breakthrough. Wade Boggs led the league in batting with a .368 mark and in on-base percentage with an impressive .452, but the Red Sox finished fifth, winning 81 and losing 81. In other words, .500 baseball—the definition of mediocrity.

1986 WORLD SERIES NEW YORK METS 4, BOSTON RED SOX 3

The Boston Red Sox had become the Wile E. Coyote of baseball teams. Repeatedly, stubbornly, they had pursued their goal and had it within their grasp, only to have it slip through their fingers while they plummeted silently off a cliff.

The '86 Red Sox were to become the epitome of this phenomenon. They encompassed the star-crossed history of the team. If you want to know what it was to be a Red Sox fan prior to 2004, all you have to do is watch video from this Series. The '86 World Series is a microcosm of the 86 years of hope, frustration, and ultimate futility between the 1918 and 2004 World

Bruce Hurst leads the Red Sox to a 1-0 win over the NY Mets in Game One of the 1986 World Series. (Associated Press)

Championships. It was the curse of the Bambino writ large. The '86 Sox were to become the poster boys for "the agony of defeat."

Before the season began, expectations were not high. The Sox had finished 81-81 the previous season and none of the experts picked them to finish higher than fifth. Nevertheless, this was an interesting team with a ton of talent. Expectations rose a notch when leadoff man Dwight Evans homered off Jack Morris on the first pitch of 1986 season. Alas, the Sox went on to lose the game anyway. Was this some sort of sign of things to come?

To say that the '86 Red Sox exceeded expectations would be a gross understatement. There was Rocket Roger Clemens, the best pitcher in baseball. On April 29, Clemens struck out 20 Seattle Mariners in nine innings at Fenway, en route to a three-hit, 3-1 victory. Two of his victims were Spike Owen and Dave Henderson, who would be on his team before the season was over. Clemens went on to capture the Cy Young Award *and* the AL MVP on the strength of 24 victories and a 2.48 ERA.

Don Baylor, acquired from the hated Yankees in a trade for Mike Easler on March 28, brought leadership and experience in one imposing package. Baylor won the immediate respect of his teammates. He also contributed at the plate, with 31 homers and 94 RBIs.

Wade Boggs was once again a veritable hitting machine, leading the league in batting with a .357 mark and on-base percentage with a robust .453. There was Jim Rice, who batted .324 with 110 RBIs while accumulating 200 hits on the nose.

There was Oil Can Boyd, who some saw as the reincarnation of Satchel Paige. Unfortunately, the Can came unhinged at midseason when told that he had been passed over for selection to the American League All-Star team. Boyd threw a major league tantrum and was suspended by the Red Sox. At the time he was 11-6, second only to teammate Clemens in wins. There were persistent rumors of drug use and financial problems. Boyd admitted to being "overly emotional," and even suggested that he acted "like I'm from another planet." He finally returned to the Red Sox fold and finished the season with a 16-10 record and a 3.78 ERA.

There was Bruce Hurst, who battled a groin injury but still won 13 games and finished strong, going 5-0 in September with a 1.09 ERA. There was Bill Buckner, the hobbled but courageous veteran who chipped in 102 RBIs. There was Gold Glove man Dwight Evans, who had seasoned considerably since his appearance in the '75 Series. He slammed 26 homers and drove in 97 despite a mediocre .259 average.

The Red Sox finished the season with a 95-66 record, edging out the Yankees by 5 ½ games in the American League East.

AMERICAN LEAGUE CHAMPIONSHIP SERIES

The ALCS (as of 1985, a best of seven series) pitted the Red Sox against the AL West champion California Angels. The Angels featured a stellar pitching staff and a decent hitting lineup. The Angels had yet to reach the World Series in their 26 years of existence, despite large amounts of money invested by owner Gene Autry.

League Championship Series Game One: Fenway Park, Boston / October 7, 1986

California 8, Boston 1

| California | 041 | 000 | 030 | — | 8 | 11 | 0 |
| Boston | 000 | 001 | 000 | — | 1 | 5 | 1 |

WP: Witt (1-0)   LP: Clemens (0-1)

The ALCS got under way on a sour note in Boston as the Red Sox were steamrollered 8-1. Roger Clemens (24-4 in the regular season) gave up all eight runs in one of the worst performances of his career, though only two of the ten hits were for extra bases (both by Wally Joyner). Meanwhile Mike Witt allowed only five hits and a single run in his complete game victory. Brian Downing was the key to the Angels offense, driving in two of the four second-inning runs and two more in the eighth for half the California runs. Marty Barrett was almost the entire Red Sox offense, with two hits and the lone run batted in. It was a dismal night in Boston.

League Championship Series Game Two: Fenway Park, Boston / October 8, 1986

Boston 9, California 2

| California | 000 | 110 | 000 | — | 2 | 11 | 3 |
| Boston | 110 | 010 | 33x | — | 9 | 13 | 2 |

WP: Hurst (1-0)   LP: McCaskill (0-1)   HR: Joyner (1), Rice (1)

The second game was the mirror image of Game One as the Red Sox evened the series in a lopsided 9-2 win. It was far from classic baseball with the teams committing a total of five errors (three by California and two by the Red Sox). Bruce Hurst was the winning pitcher, despite allowing 11 hits—including a solo homer to Joyner. Kirk McCaskill started for the Angels and hung in until the eighth when he was relieved by Gary Lucas. The seventh inning proved disastrous for the Angels as they committed their three errors in one cluster, resulting in three Red Sox insurance runs. The Sox added three more tallies in the bottom of the eighth and cruised the rest of the way. Barrett again led the way, with two more RBIs during a 3-for-5 game, though Rice and Evans each drove in a pair, Rice's on a homer in the eighth.

League Championship Series Game Three: Anaheim Stadium, Anaheim / October 10, 1986

California 5, Boston 3

Boston	010	000	020	—	3	9	1
California	000	001	31x	—	5	8	0

WP: Candelaria (1-0)   LP: Boyd (0-1)   SV: Moore (1)   HR: Pettis (1), Schofield (1)

With the ALCS knotted at a game apiece, the two teams journeyed west to continue the showdown in Game Three. Angels starter John Candelaria (10-2 with a 2.55 ERA on the season) allowed only a single run (on three singles in the second) during a full seven innings of work before Donnie Moore took over. He gave up a pair of runs in the eighth but the Sox were still two runs short. Oil Can Boyd was the starter and loser for Boston. Dick Schofield and Gary Pettis both homered with two outs in the bottom of the seventh and the Red Sox never recovered. Rich Gedman drove in two of Boston's three runs.

League Championship Series Game Four: Anaheim Stadium, Anaheim / October 11, 1986

California 4, Boston 3

Boston	000	001	020	00	—	3	6	1
California	000	000	003	01	—	4	11	2

WP: Corbett (1-0)   LP: Schiraldi (0-1)   HR: DeCinces (1)

The Angels were on a roll and were playing with confidence going into Game Four. Working on just three days' rest, Clemens once again toed the rubber for Boston and threw shutout ball for eight innings. Doug DeCinces homered in the ninth and the Angels posted three runs to tie the score at 3-3. In the bottom of the 11th, Jerry Narron singled and reached second on a sacrifice bunt. Ruppert Jones was given a free pass and Bobby Grich lined a walkoff single to left field. Angels starter Don Sutton was removed in the seventh and the fifth Angels pitcher of the day, Doug Corbett, hung in to earn the win.

League Championship Series Game Five: Anaheim Stadium, Anaheim / October 12, 1986

Boston 7, California 6 (11 innings)

WP: Crawford (1-0)   LP: Moore (0-1)   SV: Schiraldi (1)   HR: Baylor (1), Gedman (1),

Boston	020	000	004	01	—	7	12	0
California	001	002	201	00	—	6	13	0

Henderson (1), Grich (1), Boone (1)

The Angels now had a stranglehold on the Series, up three games to one with one more game at home before having to worry about a possible return to the East Coast. Game Five starters were Bruce Hurst for Boston and Mike Witt for California. The game turned out to be a thriller. The Red Sox jumped on top in the second on a two-run homer by Rich Gedman. Bob Boone hit a solo shot in the third to keep pace. In the bottom of the sixth, the Angels took the lead. Doug DeCinces doubled off Hurst and Grich drove a pitch deep to left-center field. Dave "Hendu" Henderson leaped for the ball and appeared to have it, only to have it drop from his glove on impact with the wall. It landed over the fence for a two-run homer, giving the Angels a 3-2 lead.

With Bob Stanley on the mound in the seventh, the Angels scored twice more to increase their lead to 5-2. It looked like the season was over for Boston, but the Red Sox hitters weren't ready to trade their Louisville Sluggers for golf clubs just yet. In the top of the ninth, Buckner singled off Witt and Baylor cracked a home run to narrow the gap to 5-4. With two out and left-handed hitter Rich Gedman up, Angels manager Gene Mauch opted to play the percentages. He brought on southpaw Gary Lucas to retire Gedman and punch their ticket to the World Series. The move backfired as Lucas hit Gedman with the first pitch he threw. Mauch brought on Donnie Moore to get the final out. Dave Henderson achieved immortality in Red

Sox Nation by smacking a 2-2 offering over the left-field barrier, giving the Red Sox a 6-5 lead. The Angels came right back in the bottom of the ninth to force extra innings.

Both teams failed to score in the 10th but in the top of the 11th, Baylor—infamous for crowding the plate—was hit by a pitch. Evans moved him to second on a single and Gedman advanced him to third on a base-hit bunt by Gedman. Henderson, who had alternated between goat and hero all game long, decided the affair for good by hitting a sacrifice fly that scored Baylor with what turned out to be the winning run in the 7-6 slugfest.

League Championship Series Game Six: Fenway Park, Boston / October 14, 1986

Boston 10, California 4

California	200	000	110	—	4	11	1
Boston	205	010	20x	—	10	16	1

WP: Boyd (1-1)   LP: McCaskill (0-2)   HR: Downing (1)

The Angels had been marching to victory but were now back on their heels after a heartbreaking loss. Although the Angels jumped out to a quick 2-0 lead in the top of the first, Game Six was never really close. The Red Sox answered with two runs of their own in the bottom of the first and lit up the scoreboard with five more in the third en route to a 10-4 rout. The Can got his chance to even his record at 1-0; Boyd was the starter and winner for Boston, allowing three runs in seven innings while McCaskill absorbed the loss, tagged with the first seven of Boston's runs before he was banged out of the box in the bottom of the third. The ALCS was now tied at three games each.

League Championship Series Game Seven: Fenway Park, Boston / October 15, 1986

Boston 8, California 1

California	000	000	010	—	1	6	2
Boston	030	400	10x	—	8	8	1

WP: Clemens (1-1)   LP: Candelaria (1-1)   HR: Rice (2), Evans (1)

Game Seven was no contest. Roger Clemens took advantage of the opportunity for redemption to bring his playoff record to 1-1 as well. The Rocket allowed only four hits in his seven innings on the mound and by then the Red Sox were up 7-0. The three unearned runs the Red Sox scored in the second were sufficient (two came on a Wade Boggs single) but Rice and Evans powered the offense with home runs, Rice's a three-run blast in the fourth. Candelaria was the loser for the Angels, and manager Gene Mauch, who once again had been denied a trip to the Fall Classic.

THE WORLD SERIES

The first World Series between New York and Boston since 1912 was about to begin. The last Series game had featured Smoky Joe Wood for the Red Sox and Christy Mathewson for the New York Giants. In that classic contest, the Red Sox had emerged victorious to become world champs.

Much was made in the media about this return matchup between teams representing "the Athens and Sparta of baseball," as *Sports Illustrated* called them.

For Red Sox fans used to the pinstriped Bronx team and not their poor cousins from Flushing, it took about a minute to switch gears. It may not have been the Yankees but it wasn't hard for Boston fans to get a hate on for this other New York team. The Mets were definitely cocky. Before the season had even started, manager Davey Johnson promised that his team would dominate the league. Even Mets first baseman Keith Hernandez admitted that the Mets were not beloved among their National League rivals. "Who cares?" he shrugged. Other players were equally lacking in humility. Led by Gary Carter who never passed a camera or a mirror without smiling into it, the high-fiving Mets were brash, obnoxious, and very aware of their talents. Add to that the New York fans' inherent attitude of superiority, and you had a team that was easy to hate. *SI* writer Curry Kirkpatrick labeled them the "Letsgoes," and offered up 12 reasons to despise them, among them the aforementioned Carter, Hernandez, Davey Johnson, and the fans. Of the fans, Astros pitcher Charlie Kerfeld said, "People in New York have black teeth, and their breath smells of beer." Pausing for effect, he added, "And the men are even worse."

There were other clear contrasts between the teams. Mets manager Johnson was part of a new breed of pseudo-intellectual managers while Boston skipper John McNamara was a seat-of-his-pants kind of skip who would talk baseball for hours. The Red Sox were certainly the worse for wear physically. Buckner had a strained Achilles tendon that reduced his mobility defensively at first base as well as on the base paths. Veteran Tom Seaver, acquired as a fifth starter in a late June trade for Steve Lyons ("Cy Young for Psycho," quipped Baltimore reporter Kurkjian) had suffered a tear in the ligament of his right knee and was not available for the postseason.

Game One: Shea Stadium, New York / October 18, 1986

Boston 1, New York 0

Boston	000	000	100	—	1	5	0
New York	000	000	000	—	0	4	1

WP: Hurst (1-0)   LP: Darling (0-1)   SV: Schiraldi (1)

The Mets were still reeling from the ALCS series they had just completed against Houston. They had to battle Nolan Ryan in a 12-inning epic and then play comeback ball against the Astros in a 16-inning affair the next day to earn their ticket to the Fall Classic. The latter game went four hours and 42 minutes and left the Mets drained emotionally and physically.

Despite cruising in their last two ALCS contests, the Red Sox didn't have any cakewalk to the World Series either. Both league champions could be excused if they were a bit weary of mind and spirit. The Mets were the heavy favorites, and they deserved to be based on their 108-54 regular-season record alone. They finished an astonishing 21 ½ games ahead of Cincinnati in the NL East.

Most prognosticators felt that the Series would be an arms race. Both teams had great young pitchers. Game One was a matchup between Red Sox southpaw Bruce Hurst and the Mets' Ron Darling, a right-hander with 15 regular-season wins.

The first six innings were scoreless for both the Sox and the Mets. Despite his masterful pitching, Darling, opened the door just wide enough for the Red Sox to stick a foot in. In the top of the seventh, he walked Jim Rice. A wild pitch to Dwight Evans could not be corralled by catcher Gary Carter and Rice went to second on the play. With a man on second and nobody out, Evans grounded out to Darling who looked to hold Rice on second, then threw to first for the out. Rich Gedman hit a routine ground ball toward second baseman Tim Teufel that inexplicably went through his legs into the outfield. Jim Rice scored on the misplay, crossing home plate with his trademark pop-up slide well before Darryl Strawberry's throw. The score was 1-0 Boston (after the game, Teufel blamed the loss on his error and Mets fans were quick to agree).

In the ninth inning, Dwight Evans tried to score from second base on a line single over third by Dave Henderson. He was dead on arrival at home plate thanks to an accurate peg from left-fielder Kevin Mitchell. Evans cried foul, claiming that third baseman Ray Knight, still sprawled on the turf after his dive for the line drive, had tripped him as he rounded the bag. The score remained 1-0 going into the last of the ninth.

If Darling was good, Hurst was even better. The soft-spoken Mormon from a large Utah family had his courage questioned more than once in his Red Sox career, but beneath the timid exterior beat the heart of a competitor. Over eight innings, Hurst allowed just four hits and fanned eight Mets, many with his devastating split finger fastball after setting them up with a roundhouse curve. He was lifted for a pinch hitter, rookie Mike Greenwell, with the bases loaded in the top of the ninth but the decision was a sound one despite the fact that Greenwell flied out to end the threat. Hurst had thrown 133 pitches and a fresh Calvin Schiraldi was ready in the bullpen. Schiraldi, who had come to the Red Sox the previous winter from the Mets in a trade for Bob Ojeda, walked Strawberry who was then forced on a brilliant play at first by defensive specialist Dave Stapleton.

Schiraldi had preserved the razor-slim 1-0 lead, the same Schiraldi who had struck out five in the final two innings of Game Seven against the Angels. He finished four of the seven ALCS games and had an ERA of 1.50. It's not surprising that McNamara would call on Calvin later in the Series. Both Schiraldi, and Stapleton, had proven strong on defense.

Bill Buckner, Rich Gedman, Calvin Schiraldi, Bruce Hurst, Dave Stapleton, Marty Barrett, and Wade Boggs celebrate the Game One victory. (Associated Press)

PLAYER PROFILE: BRUCE HURST

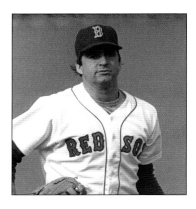

But for the infamous misplay by Bill Buckner, a passed ball, or a wild pitch, Bruce Hurst would have been the 1986 World Series MVP. When the NY Mets graciously but prematurely flashed their congratulations on the Shea Stadium scoreboard in Game Six, it seemed to be a done deal. The Red Sox were World Series champs and Bruce Hurst was the MVP. And what better choice could there be? During the Series, Darryl Strawberry famously said, with a straight face, "Roger Clemens is good, but he's no Bruce Hurst."

Alas, it was not to be. The Mets rallied to win the game and Series and Ray Knight was the MVP. But that takes nothing away from Hurst who, with some ninth-inning assistance from Calvin Schiraldi, blanked the Mets in Game One 1-0. He also won Game Five by a 4-2 score and pitched shutout baseball into the sixth inning of Game Seven before allowing three runs on four hits and a walk.

Game Two: Shea Stadium, New York / October 19, 1986

Boston 9, New York 3

Boston	003	120	201	—	9	18	0
New York	002	010	000	—	3	8	1

WP: Crawford (1-0)   LP: Gooden (0-1)   SV: Stanley (1)   HR: Evans (1), Henderson (1)

Game Two featured the two aces of the lineup in 24-game winner "Rocket" Roger Clemens and Dwight "Dr. K" Gooden. Gooden had been the National League Rookie of the Year in 1984, the Cy Young winner in 1985, and posted a record of 17-6 (2.84) in 1986. Fans reasonably anticipated another pitching duel but it was not to be. The Red Sox touched up the five Mets pitchers for 18 hits and 9 runs.

In the third inning, Spike Owen walked to lead off the inning for the Red Sox. In his first major league at-bat, Clemens bunted the ball up the first-base line. Smooth fielding Keith Hernandez fielded the ball but short-hopped it off second baseman Rafael Santana's leg. The Red Sox took full advantage of the miscue as Boggs followed with a double down the left-field line. The next two batters, Barrett and Buckner, each singled and the Red Sox were up 3-0.

The Mets came right back in the bottom half of the third, scoring two runs to make it 3-2. Santana singled and so did Gooden. Wade Boggs, who had taken countless ground balls from coach Johnny Pesky in an effort to discard the good-hit, no-field label, made a great play on a bunt by Dykstra, but the runners advanced. Backman singled in a run. Boggs made another exceptional play, retiring Hernandez by smoothly handling a ball defected off Clemens's leg and firing to first. Gooden scored on the play. The third out robbed Carter of a base hit between third and short.

In the top of the fourth inning, Hendu Henderson picked up where he left off in the ALCS. Henderson, he of the gap-tooth smile and flair for the dramatic, hit a solo shot to make it 4-2. Henderson's hop step toward first was becoming almost as famous as Carlton Fisk's less elevated version in Game Six of the '75 classic.

In the top of the fifth, Rice singled. Dwight Evans launched a mammoth two-run home run to make the score 6-2. In the bottom of the fifth, Evans flashed some leather, making a spectacular diving grab of a Lenny Dykstra liner.

By the sixth inning, Gooden had been shelled for six runs and eight hits, and was banished to the showers. Clemens had proved mortal, too, and was gone before the fifth inning was in the books. The former Texas Longhorn allowed three runs on five hits and an uncharacteristic four walks.

The much-maligned Red Sox middle relievers came on and shut down the Mets for the remainder of the game. Steve Crawford picked up the win and Maine's Bob Stanley finished the job. Stanley in particular had been a target of Boston boo birds all season long. Stanley was 6-6 with a 4.37 ERA and only 16 saves.

PLAYER PROFILE: DAVE "HENDU" HENDERSON

In the age of Manny and Papi, it is easy to forget the excitement generated by Dave Henderson in the fall of '86. For "Hendu," it seemed the bigger the game, the bigger the drama.

In 1986, he was in the spotlight throughout the Red Sox post-season and in the process added his name to an exclusive list of clutch Boston performers. The image that endures for many Red Sox fans is of his dramatic home run in Game Five of the '86 ALCS. The California Angels held a three-games-to-one stranglehold on the series and were playing in front of their fans in Anaheim. With the Angels in front 5-2 in the top of the ninth, it looked like the
end of the Sox season. Veteran Don Baylor provided a glimmer of hope with a two-run homer, making it 5-4. With two out, Henderson came to the plate with catcher Rich Gedman on first.

Hendu worked the count to 2-2 on Angels reliever Donnie Moore and then unloaded on a pitch that disappeared over the fence. Henderson did his version of the famous Carlton Fisk home run skip down the first baseline and the Red Sox led 6-5. The Angels came back to tie in the bottom of the inning but the Red Sox prevailed in the 11th when Henderson sacrificed home what proved to be the winning run. The sudden disastrous loss in Game Five seemed to drain the spirit from the Angels, and they lost the next two games at Fenway 10-4 and 8-1 to give the Red Sox the series.

Ironically Hendu could have been the goat of Game Five as he had Bobby Grich's long drive deflect off his glove over the fence for a sixth-inning home run that had given the Angels a 3-2 lead.

Henderson was only a member of the Red Sox for parts of two seasons, the latter part of 1986 and the first part of 1987. He came to Boston from the Seattle Mariners in 1986. During the '87 season, he went to San Francisco and in 1988 crossed the bay to Oakland, where he played for six more seasons. He was named to the AL All-Star team in 1991, and finished that year with 25 homers and 85 RBIs. He ended his career in 1994 as a member of the Kansas City Royals. In all he powered 197 baseballs over major league fences while batting .258 and collecting 708 RBIs.

In the 1986 Series, he batted an even .400 and contributed two homers in the losing cause, including one in the Game Two 9-3 victory. He contributed three hits in the game, scored two runs and drove in two. He finally won a World Series title with the Oakland A's in 1989 as they defeated San Francisco.

Game Three: Fenway Park, Boston / October 21, 1986

New York 7, Boston 1

| New York | 400 | 000 | 210 | — | 7 | 13 | 0 |
| Boston | 001 | 000 | 000 | — | 1 | 5 | 0 |

WP: Ojeda (1-0)   LP: Boyd (0-1)   HR: Dykstra (1)

The Red Sox were up two games to nothing, coming back to Fenway—and, naturally, Boston fans were nervous. Being a Sox fan does that to you. Students of World Series history could have told them that teams that won the first two games on the road almost always won it all (the exception being the previous year when the Cardinals had overcome such a deficit). The Red Sox had no intention of letting the Mets up off the mat.

The Mets starter for Game Three was Bobby Ojeda who had worn a Red Sox uniform in '85. By the time he reached the mound to pitch, he was presented with an unexpected homecoming gift.

Dennis "Oil Can" Boyd, the 6'1", 144-pound native of Meridian, Mississippi, was handed the ball for the Red Sox. The Fenway faithful were scarcely in their seats before leadoff man Lenny Dykstra had knocked Boyd's third offering into the right-field cheap seats. Rattled, the emotional one gave up back-to-back singles to Wally Backman and Keith Hernandez. Gary Carter then doubled home Backman and Hernandez took third. Darryl Strawberry struck out and Ray Knight hit a ground ball toward third baseman Wade Boggs. Boggs fielded the ball and threw home, trapping Hernandez in no-man's-land. Red Sox catcher Gedman ignored baseball fundamentals and failed to chase Hernandez back toward third, where Carter had now taken up residence.

Instead Gedman threw towards third base, now covered by Owen, but Boggs, playing down the line in anticipation of a rundown, intercepted the ball, allowing Hernandez to scramble to third. Meanwhile, Carter retreated to second and unbelievably made it ahead of the throw to Marty Barrett. Both runners were safe.

It was a nightmarish beginning for the Red Sox and their fans. Mets DH Danny Heep took full advantage and drove the ball into center field to score the two gift runs. Going into the bottom of the first, the Red Sox were already down 4-0.

Bobby Ojeda had all the run support he would need. He pitched seven strong innings and gave up only one run, before handing the ball to reliever Roger McDowell. The Red Sox tally came in the third inning as Henderson singled, Boggs walked, and Barrett singled home the lead runner.

The Mets padded their lead in the seventh inning. Santana reached on a base hit and Dykstra followed suit. Hernandez drew a walk and Carter singled to score two more. They scored their final run in the eighth as Strawberry singled off reliever Joe Sambito. A wild pitch followed, then a passed ball, and then a double off the bat of Ray Knight.

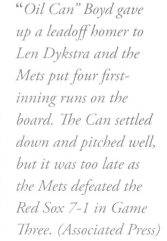

"Oil Can" Boyd gave up a leadoff homer to Len Dykstra and the Mets put four first-inning runs on the board. The Can settled down and pitched well, but it was too late as the Mets defeated the Red Sox 7-1 in Game Three. (Associated Press)

PLAYER PROFILE: MARTY BARRETT

Second baseman Marty Barrett played ten years in the majors, all but his last with the Red Sox. A product of the Red Sox farm system, arguably his most notable achievement came in the minors with the Pawtucket Red Sox. In 1981 he was part of baseball history as his Pawsox played a 33-inning contest against the Rochester Red Wings. Barrett scored the winning run in the bottom of the 33rd.

In 1986, Barrett put together a fine season, batting .286 and driving in 60 runs. The durable native of Arcadia, California, also swiped 15 bases and hit 39 doubles. In the play-offs, he was even better, establishing a record with 24 hits (14 games). He was named MVP of the ALCS.

In the World Series, he continued to excel, batting a lusty team-leading .433 with a .514 on-base percentage. In Game Three, he was one of the few offensive bright spots in the 7-1 Red Sox loss, managing two hits and driving in the lone Red Sox tally. Many observers felt that he deserved to be the MVP of the World Series, as well as the ALCS, if the Red Sox had been able to prevail.

Game Four: Fenway Park, Boston / October 22, 1986

New York 6, Boston 2

New York	000	300	210	—	6	12	0
Boston	000	000	020	—	2	7	1

WP: Darling (1-1)   LP: Nipper (0-1)   SV: Orosco (1)   HR: Dykstra (2), Carter 2 (2)

The Red Sox still held a 2-1 lead in the '86 World Series but somehow it didn't seem that way to Red Sox fans. The perpetual underdogs were waiting for the other shoe to drop.

Ron Darling, hard-luck loser of Game One, ascended the mound for the Mets.

The only thing going for Red Sox starter Al Nipper was that he was well rested. Nipper hadn't pitched in 18 days, in actual fact, since the last game of the season. His regular season had been disastrous. He received a four-inch-deep cut near his right kneecap on May 18 in a collision at home plate and was on the DL until late June. His record was an unimpressive 10-12 with a 5.38 ERA. Not surprisingly, Red Sox fans and media howled at manager John McNamara's decision to start the star-crossed right-hander. It was a decision based in reality. With Seaver on the sidelines, the remainder of the rotation was overworked and tired. Nipper was, depending on who you asked, the stop-gap, the finger in the dyke, or the cannon fodder.

For the first three innings, Nipper seemed to vindicate McNamara's gamble as the mighty Mets failed to score. Unfortunately, key Red Sox bats remained unsullied throughout the game. Boggs went 0-for-5, as did Bill Buckner.

In the top of the fourth inning, Wally Backman hit a liner that deflected off Nipper's glove for a single. After Hernandez grounded out, Gary Carter drove a fat delivery over the Green

Monster to stake the New Yorkers to a 2-0 lead. Darryl Strawberry then shot the ball to left field for a double and Ray Knight drove him home with a single up the middle to make it 3-0.

Nipper fought valiantly for six innings before being replaced by reliever Steve Crawford in the seventh. Crawford could not contain the Mets bats as Mookie Wilson stroked a one-out single to center field. After Rafael Santana struck out, Dykstra hit a long drive to right center. Evans tracked it down and it looked as if he was about to make another of his trademark brilliant catches but it was not to be. The ball was dislodged from his glove as he hit the wall, landing beyond the barrier for a two-run homer. The score was now 5-0 for the Mets and the Fenway Park crowd was growing restless. The Red Sox were still unable to get to Darling in the bottom of the inning.

In the top of the eighth, Carter crushed his second homer of the game, this one a solo shot over the Wall, to give the Mets a 6-0 lead. Only after the Mets lifted Darling in the seventh and brought on Roger McDowell did the Red Sox bats show signs of life. A Jim Rice double, singles by Evans and Gedman, and a sac fly off the bat of Dave Henderson plated two runs and drove McDowell from the mound after just two-thirds of an inning. Jesse Orosco came on to mop up and the Red Sox and Mets were tied at two games apiece. So much for home field advantage.

PLAYER PROFILE: AL NIPPER

Al Nipper came to the Red Sox in the same freshman class that brought Roger Clemens to Boston. In spite of the fact that they were named 1984 co-rookie pitchers of the year for the Red Sox, about the only thing they have in common is that they are both bipeds.

Nipper was well named. He was the prototypical junk ball pitcher who relied on locating his pitches and nipping the corners. His best season was his rookie year when he went 11-6. After that, injuries hampered his development and his career ended after seven seasons. His final statistics are mediocre. He won 46 games, lost 50 and posted an ERA of 4.52.

His World Series performance was equally mediocre. He lost Game Four, giving up seven hits and three runs in six innings of work. He walked one batter and gave up a two-run home run to Gary Carter in the fourth inning.

Brought on in relief in the eighth inning of Game Seven, Nipper was spectacularly ineffective. In one-third of an inning, he gave up three hits, including a homer by Darryl Strawberry, two earned runs, and a walk.

Game Five: Fenway Park, Boston / October 23, 1986

Boston 4, New York 2

New York	000	000	011	—	2	10	1
Boston	011	020	00x	—	4	12	0

WP: Hurst (2-0)   LP: Gooden (0-2)   HR: Teufel (1)

Hendu Henderson did everything with flair. Here he scores from third on a sac fly, sliding headfirst across the plate as the Red Sox win Game Five 4-2. (Associated Press)

The Red Sox were right back where they started, on even terms—only now the World Series was reduced to a best two out of three affair.

Bruce Hurst had his extra day of rest, courtesy of manager McNamara and now all of New England waited to see if it would pay off. This time his mound opposite would be Gooden, looking to make amends for his ineffective performance in Game Two. The fastball pitcher seemed to have lost confidence in good ol' Number One and resorted to an assortment of off-speed pitches throughout the game.

The Red Sox capitalized on a Mets fielding gaffe to score their first run of the game. With one out in the second inning, Dave Henderson hit a ball to right-center field for an apparent double. It was a hustle play: Strawberry didn't and Henderson did. Hendu motored to third for a triple while Darryl idled before retrieving the ball. Spike Owen then hit a sacrifice fly to score the go-ahead run.

The Mets were generous to the Red Sox again in the third inning as Santana misplayed a ground ball off the bat of Buckner. Evans then singled to add another run. Both teams blanked the fourth inning, but Boston quickly went back on the offensive in the fifth. Rice tripled to right-center field and Don Baylor sent him home with a seeing-eye single to right. With Baylor on first and Evans at the plate, McNamara called for the hit and run. Evans slapped a single and Baylor made it to third. Mets skipper Davey Johnson pulled Gooden and replaced him with Sid Fernandez who fanned Gedman for the first out. Henderson doubled to score Baylor and the Red Sox lead was 4-0.

While the Red Sox were gathering nine hits and four runs in less than five innings against Gooden, Hurst was pitching shutout ball. His pitching menu was much more varied than Gooden's and he kept Mets hitters off balance throughout the game, despite scattering ten hits. Only in the eighth inning did New York finally break through as Tim Teufel selected an appetizing menu item and ate it up, sending the ball over the fence to make it 4-1.

The Mets scored again in the top of the ninth when Wilson doubled and scored on a Santana single. It was Hurst's second complete game win of the Series; until the eighth-inning homer by Teufel, he had held New York scoreless for 15 ⅓ innings.

PLAYER PROFILE: DON BAYLOR

Don Baylor brought leadership and a steadying influence to the 1986 Red Sox. He was the epitome of the seasoned veteran and won the instant respect of his teammates. Baylor came to Boston in '86 after stops in Baltimore, Oakland, California (he was MVP in 1979), and New York.

Aside from his valuable clubhouse presence, Baylor brought some very tangible assets to Beantown. Despite a low batting average of .238, he hit 31 homers, drove in 94 runs, and drew 62 walks. Baylor was fearless, crowding the plate and defying pitchers to throw inside. He worked 805 walks in his career and was hit by pitches on a regular basis—leading the league in that category eight times, including the 35 times he was hit in 1986.

In the '86 Series, he batted a disappointing .182 in limited action. In Game Five, Baylor singled to drive in a run and later scored in the 4-2 victory.

The Austin, Texas, native played two seasons in Boston before going to Minnesota in late '87 and then closing out his impressive career in 1988 back in Oakland. His career numbers tell the story. In 19 seasons, he hit 338 homers and collected 1,276 RBIs. Nine times, he hit over 20 homers and three times topped the 30 mark. In 1979, with California, he led the American League in runs with 120 and in RBIs with 139, as he was named to the AL All-Star team. In 1995, Baylor was named NL Manager of the Year for his leadership of the Colorado Rockies.

Game Six: Shea Stadium, New York / October 25, 1986

New York 6, Boston 5

Boston	110	000	100	2	—	5	13	3
New York	000	020	010	3	—	6	8	2

WP: Aguilera (1-0)   LP: Schiraldi (0-1)   HR: Henderson (2)

Red Sox starter Rocket Roger Clemens deals in Game Six. The game would become a symbol of Red Sox failures in the big game. (Associated Press)

If the '86 World Series was a microcosm of Red Sox history, Game Six was a microcosm of the microcosm, because this one game was the distilled essence of generations of frustration. If you wanted to further split the atom, there was poor Bill Buckner who fairly or unfairly bore the brunt of fan frustration.

The Red Sox returned to New York up three games to two, but having failed to take full advantage of the home team edge. The starters were Clemens for the Red Sox and Bob Ojeda for the Metropolitans. Things started well for Boston. Boggs beat out an infield hit. After the next two batters were retired on routine fly balls, Jim Rice drew a base on balls. Evans unloaded on a pitch and lined the ball off the left-field wall to score Boggs. Oh yeah, since this was New York a man dropped from the skies and parachuted onto the field of play just before the walk to Rice.

Playing a little National League style small ball, the Sox scored again in the second inning as Owen singled to center and went to third on a well-executed hit and run with bat control freak Wade Boggs. Owen scored on a base hit by Marty Barrett.

Clemens was in control for the Red Sox, allowing just one walk (to Strawberry) over the first four innings. It was a different story in the fifth, as Strawberry drew another walk and then swiped second. He cashed in the Mets first run on a single by Ray Knight. Wilson followed with another single that Evans failed to field cleanly, allowing Knight to scurry to third. Pinch-hitter Danny Heep grounded into a double play but Knight scored on the twin killing. The score was tied at 2-2. The sixth inning was scoreless, but in the top of the seventh, the Red Sox went back on top. With McDowell on in relief of Ojeda, Barrett walked and reached second when Buckner grounded out.

In the Sox seventh, what should have been a routine out off the bat of Rice turned into a first and third situation when Knight committed an error on his throw to first. Barrett scored the Red Sox third run on a ground ball out by Evans. The slow-footed Rice barely avoided being doubled up on the play, sliding into second just ahead of the tag. The relay to first base just nipped the charging Evans. Rice almost made it a two-run cushion when Gedman singled to left field. Unfortunately, Rice was unable to beat a strong throw from Mookie Wilson in left and the one-run margin remained intact.

The Red Sox brain trust left itself open to much second-guessing in the top of the eighth. The Sox had a man on second base with one out when McNamara opted to pinch-hit rookie Mike Greenwell for Clemens, instead of sending in veteran Don Baylor. While Baylor fumed and cooled his heels, Greenwell pursued three balls outside of the strike zone and there were two out. The Red Sox proceeded to load the bases with two walks off McDowell. Expecting left-hander Jesse Orosco to enter the game, McNamara told Baylor to be prepared to hit for Buckner. The signal was sent to the Mets bullpen and in came Orosco. While the reliever warmed up, Baylor retired to the clubhouse to take practice swings, in the belief that he would be called upon to hit. When he returned to the dugout, Buckner was already hobbling to the plate. He swung at the first pitch and lofted a fly ball to center to end the inning. In his autobiography, Don Baylor writes: "I never asked Mac what happened. I know he had a change of heart. I know he cares about his veteran players, had seen Buck play on two bad legs, two bad feet, drive in 102 runs for the team. I don't know if Buck asked to stay in. I don't know if Mac wanted him on the field for the final celebration. All I know is the situation at-bat we had all talked about had come and gone. We had a chance to break the game open. … Mac was one horrid hour away

In Game Six, Calvin Schiraldi came in for starter Roger Clemens in the bottom of the eighth after Clemens was pinch-hit for in the top of the inning due to a blister on his pitching hand. Bill Buckner is in the background. (Associated Press)

from joining Gene Mauch in the most uncomfortable position of all—a manager being second-guessed by millions."

Indeed, all through the last half of the 1975 season it had been McNamara's practice to install Dave Stapleton at first base for defensive purposes in late innings. That practice was now being ignored in the most important game of the postseason. The decision to leave Buckner in had just wounded the Red Sox; it was now about to deliver the fatal blow.

The Mets had six outs left to stave off elimination. Conversely, the Red Sox had to shut the Mets down for six more outs and they would become the world champs for the first time

Hendu Henderson is congratulated after his home run gave the Red Sox the lead in the 10th inning of Game Six. It would not last. (Associated Press)

since 1918. Schiraldi began to pitch in relief of Clemens, who had struck out eight and allowed just four hits before developing a blister on his pitching hand. Pinch-hitter Lee Mazzilli singled to right field off his former Mets teammate. Super-gnat Len Dykstra laid down a bunt and Schiraldi fielded it in front of the mound and went to second for the force play. Mazzilli, running on the pitch, beat out the throw and the relay was too late to erase Dykstra at first. Backman efficiently sacrificed the two runners to second and third. With first base open, the Red Sox walked Hernandez intentionally bringing the always dangerous Gary Carter to the plate. Carter hit a sacrifice line drive to left field enabling Mazzilli to scamper home with the tying run. Strawberry flied out, but the damage had been done. The score was tied.

The Red Sox went relatively quietly in the top of the ninth but the Mets almost won it in the bottom half. Knight walked and Wilson moved him to second via a bunt, and reached first base safely himself thanks to an error by Gedman. Howard Johnson pinch-hit for Easler but struck out. Mazzilli flied out and Dykstra did likewise to push the game into extra innings.

What followed was grueling and excruciating for fans of both teams. In the top of the 10th, Dave Henderson, the hero of the ALCS donned his cape and giant "S" and once again homered in the clutch, this time off Rick Aguilera, to give the Red Sox the lead. After Aguilera settled down and struck out Owen and Schiraldi, Boggs slashed a double to left-center and Barrett brought him home on a single. The Sox were exhilarated, sitting on a 5-3 lead now, with just three outs between them and the Promised Land. The Red Sox were on the verge of exorcising the curse of the Bambino once and for all.

In the last of the 10th, Schiraldi looked strong, inducing Backman to fly out to left. Two outs to go. Schiraldi faced Keith Hernandez. The big first baseman also flied out, this time to center field. One out from victory. The Mets, in a gracious if not heartfelt gesture that will haunt Red Sox fans forever (hadn't Anthony Perkins been equally gracious to Janet Leigh just before the shower scene in *Psycho*?), flashed their surrender on the message board above left field: "The NY Mets Congratulate the Boston Red Sox, 1986 World Series Champions."

Gary Carter came to the plate and promptly singled to left. Pinch-hitter Kevin Mitchell followed with another single, to center field. Knight came to the plate and Schiraldi got two quick strikes on him. The Red Sox were one out away, no, one pitch away, from the elusive prize. Knight singled up the middle to drive in the fourth Mets run. The score was now 5-4 for the Red Sox with the tying run on third in the person of Mitchell. McNamara put the call out for the much-maligned Bob Stanley, the 6'4", 215-pound nice guy from Portland, Maine. All of Red Sox Nation said a silent prayer. With the count at 2-2, Stanley unleashed a wild pitch that allowed Mitchell to score the tying run while Knight moved to second.

The next play is burned into the souls of Boston fans. Mookie Wilson hit an innocent looking ground ball toward Bill Buckner at first base. The ball went through Buckner's legs and Ray Knight jumped onto home plate with the winning run and was immediately swallowed up in a throng of his Mets teammates.

Game Seven would be needed to decide the winner of the 1986 World Series.

PLAYER PROFILE: BILL BUCKNER

Bill Buckner batted .188 in the 1986 World Series with six hits in 32 at-bats. He will forever be remembered as the goat of Game Six, as Mookie Wilson's ground ball to first base eluded his grasp and the Mets rallied to win the game and eventually the Series.

Sadly forgotten by many are the contributions Buckner made to the Red Sox in 1986. Also forgotten is an exceptional career of 22 years duration. He retired with a .289 batting average and two 200-hit seasons. In total, he played 2,517 games and had 1,715 hits. In his younger days he was a speedster who was always a threat to steal. In 1974 he swiped 31 bases for the Dodgers. Even in 1985, despite having suffered a serious ankle injury years earlier, he still managed to steal 18 bases.

A great ballplayer who deserved a better fate, Bill Buckner leaves the field in Game Six after a miscue that was to become a metaphor for Red Sox ineptitude. (Associated Press)

Buckner began his career as a member of the LA Dodgers in 1969 and played for the Bums until 1977 when he moved to the Windy City to toil for the Cubbies. During the 1984 season he came to Boston where he would stay until midway through the '87 season. He then moved to the California Angels and the Kansas City Royals before ending his career back in Boston in 1990.

As a member of the Chicago Cubs, Buckner led the National League in 1980 with a .324 average. The following year he led the NL in doubles with 35 and repeated the feat for the '83 Cubs with 38. Buckner was one of the game's great contact hitters, striking out only 453 times.

In the 1986 campaign, "Billy Buck" was heroic. Playing on gimpy knees, he still managed to hit a career-best 18 homers and drive in 102 runs. He somehow legged out 39 doubles and batted .267. Down the stretch his eight September homers and 22 RBIs powered the Red Sox.

In short, Bill Buckner should not be defined by a single miscue in a single game. Being dubbed a goat haunted Buckner for years. Television editors played and re-played the moment incessantly; Red Sox fans were sick of seeing it, too. Winning a couple of world championships helped reduce it to something more of a curiosity, and then the Red Sox had a stroke of brilliance, bringing Buckner back to Boston for Opening Day 2008, where a full house stood and applauded him for several moments in a cathartic welcome home.

Game Seven: Shea Stadium, New York / October 27, 1986

New York 8, Boston 5

Boston	030	000	020	—	5	9	0
New York	000	003	32x	—	8	10	0

WP: McDowell (1-0)   LP: Schiraldi (0-2)   SV: Orosco (2)   HR: Evans (2), Gedman (1), Strawberry (1), Knight (1)

Fittingly, rain postponed Game Seven for another day, giving the cities of Boston and New York and the entire nation the opportunity to reflect on what had happened. The Red Sox were still alive and in theory they stood just as good a chance of winning the World Series as the NY Mets. In theory, that is. In reality, they were in shock.

With the extra day's rest provided by the rain the Red Sox decided to send Bruce Hurst to the mound once again. Oil Can Boyd was devastated by the decision. The good news was that Hurst had already won two games and his calm demeanor was greatly needed right now. The

bad news was that Hurst was still working on only three days' rest and that was a lot to ask of anyone in this New York pressure cooker.

 With panic or desertion the only other options, the Red Sox took to the field and tried to erase the events of the two prior games from their minds. At first it seemed to be working. With Ron Darling on the mound for the very motivated Mets, the Red Sox struck first. Leading off the second inning, Evans homered to left-center field. Gedman came to the plate and hit a ball to the deepest part of right-center where Strawberry was in hot pursuit. The ball and Strawberry arrived at the fence at the same time. Darryl leaped for the sphere and momentarily had it in his webbing, only to come down empty-handed. Back-to-back homers and suddenly the memory of Game Six began to fade. Henderson walked and was sacrificed to second by Hurst. Boggs singled him home for the third Boston run.

 The Mets lifted Darling in the fourth in favor of Sid Fernandez and the reliever effectively shut down the Red Sox attack for the next two innings. With one man gone, the Mets finally got to Hurst in the home half of the sixth inning. Pinch-hitting for Fernandez, Mazzilli hit a

Dwight Evans homers as the Red Sox put three early runs on the board in Game Seven. It was not enough as the Mets prevailed 8-5 and the Red Sox World Series drought continued unabated. (Associated Press)

single into left field. Mookie Wilson followed with another single. Teufel walked and the bases were loaded. Keith Hernandez singled to center field and drove in two runs. Carter hit a fly ball to shallow right that Evans trapped and threw to second to force Hernandez for out number two, but Teufel scored the tying run.

With Schiraldi pitching for the Red Sox in the seventh, Knight homered to give the Mets a 4-3 lead. Sensing they had the Sox unraveling, the Mets continued their assault. Dykstra singled, then reached second on a wild pitch. Santana singled him home. McDowell sacrificed.

Schiraldi was taken out and Sambito came on but fared no better, walking Wilson and Backman before surrendering a sac fly to Hernandez to make it Mets 6, Red Sox 3. Stanley, the much despised one, successfully closed out the inning.

The Red Sox showed a ton of heart fighting back for two runs in the top of the eighth to bring them within one. Buckner and Rice singled and Evans doubled them both home. Orosco came on for the Mets and finished the inning.

Any hopes of a dramatic comeback were crushed when the Mets added to their lead in the bottom of the inning. Strawberry homered off Nipper and Knight singled. He went to second on a ground ball out and the Sox walked Santana to set up the DP. Knight scored the final run when Orosco singled. The final score was 8-5. There would be no comeback for the 1986 Red Sox.

When Red Sox fans are tempted to take their recent success for granted, they should cast their memories back to the 1986 World Series, when it looked like the sun would never shine on Red Sox Nation again.

PLAYER PROFILE: DWIGHT EVANS

Few Red Sox fans will ever forget Dwight Evans's magnificent throw in Game Six of the '75 World Series. It was part of the incredible tableau that made up the "greatest game ever played."

Evans was blessed with a rifle arm that few base runners were foolhardy enough to challenge. He patrolled right field as well as anyone in the history of the Red Sox franchise and stole countless extra base hits from countless hitters. In spite of playing half his games in Fenway's notorious sun field, his defensive prowess was rewarded with nine Gold Gloves.

Evans's career began in 1972 with the Red Sox and he played 19 summers for Boston before going to Baltimore in 1990 to play one final season. The native of Santa Monica, California, retired with 385 homers, 1,384 RBIs, and a .272 batting average. The three-time

All-Star led the American League in homers (22) and walks (85) in the strike-shortened 1981 season.

In '81 he posted a league-best .403 on-base percentage. He also led the AL in runs in 1984 with 121 and was tops in walks two more times, in '85 (114) and '87 (106). His best statistical performance was in 1987 as he batted .305, hit 34 homers, and collected 123 RBIs. Evans was the American League home run king of the 1980s, hitting 256 round trippers from 1980-89. Eleven times in his career he hit 20 home runs or more.

In the 1986 World Series, Evans batted .308 with two home runs and nine RBIs. In Game Seven, Dewey scored one run on three hits and drove in three in the 8-5 loss to the Mets. His homer in the second inning put the Red Sox in front temporarily and he doubled in the eighth to score two more and bring the Sox within a run.

Evans was named to the Boston Red Sox Hall of Fame in 2000 and remains a fan favorite in the Boston area.

IN BETWEEN SERIES

Maybe it was the result of the 1986 World Series loss, a kind of postseason stress disorder yet to be recognized by medical science. Whatever the reason, the 1987 Red Sox fell to fifth place and a 78-84 record. By 1988, they had obviously found an antidote and/or good counselor and finished first in the AL East. Unfortunately, they were swept by the Oakland A's four games to none in the ALCS.

In 1989, the Red Sox finished third with an 83-79 record but in 1990 they once again captured the AL East. Once again they were swept 4-0 by the Oakland A's in the ALCS. In '91 they finished second to the Toronto Blue Jays and in 1992 free-fell to seventh and last place, 23 games behind the Blue Jays. The Jays went on to win the World Series. In '93 the Blue Jays made it two World Championships in a row while the Red Sox made a modest climb to fifth position in the eastern division.

In 1994, a new division, the Central, was added to the American League, reducing the number of teams in the AL East to five. The Red Sox finished fourth. They could take some kind of warped solace in the fact that if they didn't win the World Series, neither did anyone else as a players' strike wiped out postseason play.

In 1995, the Red Sox finished first and met the Cleveland Indians in the first American League Division Series, another hurdle that now had to be faced before reaching the World Series. The Indians eliminated them in three straight games. In '96, they finished the season in third place, seven games behind the Yankees and in 1997 the Red Sox slipped to a fourth place finish. The following year, however, they rose to second, albeit 22 games behind New York.

As the AL Wild Card team, they won the right to once again face the Indians in the ALDS. This time the Tribe defeated them three games to one.

In 1999, the Red Sox again finished second to the Yanks and again they captured the AL wild card. And, yes, again they faced the Cleveland Indians in the ALDS. The Red Sox prevailed three games to two and the Red Sox earned the right to face the mighty Yankees in the ALCS. The New Yorkers came out on top four games to one and went on to win the World Series against the Atlanta Braves.

The much anticipated Year 2000 saw the Red Sox finish second to the Yankees for the third consecutive time. This time there was no consolation prize in the form of a wild card and the Red Sox went directly to the golf course. In 2001, the Yankees made it four consecutive times they had finished one peg above the Sox, in first place in the AL East. It was becoming very predictable. Once again there would be no postseason play in Beantown.

Guess what? In 2002, the Red Sox finished second to the Yankees in the AL East. This time they managed 93 wins and still finished 10 ½ games back. And ditto: in 2003, the Red Sox were second-best yet again, the sixth time they had played Avis to New York's Hertz. This time however, there was a difference. The Red Sox didn't just go away. In fact, playing as the AL wild card team, they defeated the Oakland A's in the ALDS and got another shot at their Big Apple nemesis.

The ALCS had just about everything, even the grotesque spectacle of Pedro Martinez brawling with Don Zimmer, Sadly, the story had an unhappy ending as the Red Sox lost to the Bombers four games to three. Many people blame manager Grady Little's decision to leave an obviously spent Martinez in Game Seven for the loss. Somehow, though, Red Sox fans felt good about the storybook year they had just witnessed. If only the script writer could have changed the ending! They were looking for a sequel.

2004 WORLD SERIES
BOSTON RED SOX 4, ST. LOUIS CARDINALS 0

In the spring of 2004, the Boston Red Sox remained a team of great expectations. They had come close just often enough to keep their fans ravenous without actually starving them. The fans had bounced back from disappointments in '46, '67, '72, '75, '78, '86, and now 2003. Was there a limit to the fans' patience? Would the disastrous loss to the Yankees in the 2003 ALCS represent that limit?

When the Red Sox convened at spring training in Fort Myers, Florida, there were a lot of unanswered questions. One had already been answered. A-Rod, ardently pursued by both the Yankees and Red Sox, would be

wearing pinstripes when the season began. How long would Nomar Garciaparra, unhappy with the unseemly pursuit of fellow shortstop A-Rod (among other things), remain a part of this team? Was newcomer Curt Schilling the missing piece of the rotation puzzle? Would newly acquired Keith Foulke prove to be the answer to Boston's bullpen woes? Would Manny Ramirez sulk after being put on irrevocable waivers only to have no takers? Could rookie manager Terry Francona mold these diverse personalities, oversized egos, and enormous talents into a cohesive unit?

But perhaps the biggest question was how (and if) the Red Sox would ever recover from the 2003 ALCS debacle against NY. Once again the Red Sox had seemed to have victory within their grasp, only to let it get away. This time it had been the highly questionable Game Seven decision by manager Grady Little to leave Pedro Martinez in the game when everyone else in the known universe knew that he had no more gas in the tank. The result was a comeback by the Yankees, culminating in a soul-destroying Aaron Boone homer off Tim Wakefield to win the game and the series. The big question hung darkly over their heads for the entire summer of 2004 and into the postseason. Did this team have the talent and character to finish the job this time around?

In late April, the Red Sox swept the Yankees at the Stadium but anyone who thought that this was any kind of real payback was delusional. Nomar didn't play until June 9, missing the first 57 games due to injury. When he did return he pouted and made it very obvious he wanted to be traded. On July 1 at Yankee Stadium, the difference between the Yankees' Derek Jeter and Nomar came into sharp relief/focus and even for diehard Nomar supporters, the argument was settled once and for all. While Nomar sulked in the Red Sox dugout, Jeter sacrificed his body by diving into the crowd in successful pursuit of a foul ball. It was one of the most dramatic games of the year.

If there was a turning point in the 2004 season, it came on July 24 in the third inning of yet another Red Sox-Yankee epic at Fenway. It was not a classic for baseball purists to savor. The final score was 11-10 and the game featured four errors by the victorious Red Sox. Sometimes desire is all that separates two elite teams and it was desire that gave the Red Sox an edge in this game and a spark for the rest of the season. The Red Sox faced a 3-0 deficit when starter and part-time rock star Bronson Arroyo hit A-Rod with a pitch. The Yankee star took exception and expressed his feelings to Jason Varitek. Varitek responded by giving Rodriguez a vigorous glove massage to the face. Yankee starter Tanyon Sturtze joined the fray and was manhandled by Gabe Kapler.

The game resumed and both teams battled to the final bell like heavyweight boxers. The Yankees led 10-8 going into the home half of the ninth. The Red Sox pushed one across, and then Bill Mueller struck the knockout blow with a walk-off two-run homer to win the game.

On July 31, the Red Sox finally pulled the trigger on a four-team trade that sent Nomar to the Chicago Cubs. The Red Sox got Doug Mientkiewicz from Minnesota and Orlando Cabrera from Montreal. The Sox also picked up Dave Roberts from the Dodgers. All three would prove to be keys to the Red Sox fortunes.

ALDS

There had been yet another refinement in postseason play in 1995. Each league was broken into three divisions. The Red Sox won the AL East that first year, but were swept in three games in the new best-of-five Division Series by the Cleveland Indians. They'd lost three games to one to the Indians in 1998, and lost in five to the Indians in 1999. Remember that sequence of annual events, when we get to the 2007 ALCS.

In 2003, the Sox dropped the first two but beat Oakland three games in a row to win the ALDS, but then gave away the deciding game of the ALCS to the dreaded Yankees.

It was a new year now, though, and this time the Red Sox had to get past the Anaheim Angels in the American League Division Series. The Angels had tied for the AL lead in batting with a .282 mark and boasted such impressive offensive assets as Vladimir Guerrero, Bengie Molina, Garrett Anderson, and Steve Finley. The pitching was fourth best in the AL and featured Bartolo Colon, Kelvim Escobar, Jarrod Washburn, and John Lackey.

Division Series Game One: Angel Stadium of Anaheim, Anaheim / October 5, 2004

Boston 9, Anaheim 3

Boston	100	700	010	—	9	11	1
Anaheim	000	100	200	—	3	9	1

WP: Schilling (1-0)   LP: Washburn (0-1)   HR: Ramirez (1), Millar (1), Erstad (1), Glaus (1)

The Boston Red Sox were back in the postseason, this time facing the Anaheim Angels in the American League Division series. The winner would earn the right to play the winner of the New York Yankees–Minnesota Twins series.

In Game One, the Red Sox sent Curt Schilling to the mound against Angels starter Jarrod Washburn. Angel fans were set to unleash their Rally Monkeys on the unsuspecting Sox, but didn't get a chance.

In the top of the first Manny Ramirez shot a line-hugging drive to left field and coasted in to second with a double. David Ortiz singled to score Manny and the Sox led 1-0. In the fourth frame the Red Sox exploded for seven runs. It started when Ortiz drew a walk and Kevin Millar homered to pad the Red Sox lead to 3-0, but the Red Sox assault had only just begun.

They loaded the bases and scored two unearned runs on an innocent-looking Johnny Damon bounder to third. Chone Figgins fielded the ball and threw homeward, trying to prevent further scoring with a force at home, but Figgins threw the ball away and the score was 5-0. With two out, Manny added an exclamation point with a three-run homer to dead center field, making it 8-0. The Angels scratched out three runs, but it was too little, too late. Schilling gave up three runs on nine hits in 6 ⅔ innings of work.

Division Series Game Two: Angel Stadium of Anaheim, Anaheim / October 6, 2004

Boston 8, Anaheim 3

| Boston | 010 | 002 | 104 | — | 8 | 12 | 0 |
| Anaheim | 010 | 020 | 000 | — | 3 | 7 | 0 |

WP: Martinez (1-0)   LP: Rodriguez (0-1)   SV: Foulke (1)   HR: Varitek (1)

Game Two featured Boston's Pedro Martinez against Bartolo Colon. Pedro had struggled at the end of the regular season, losing his final four games while posting an ugly 7.72 ERA. The last time he had taken the mound in the postseason was as part of the infamous Game Seven meltdown against the Yankees in the 2003 ALCS. Anyone who doubted Pedro's state of mind was soon reassured. He pitched seven strong innings, giving up six hits and three runs while striking out six.

The Red Sox came out swinging. Leadoff man Johnny Damon singled and went to second on a base hit by Mark Bellhorn. Ortiz walked to load the bases but the threat died on the vine.

In the second, the Angels continued to flirt with disaster. Once again the Red Sox drew first blood as Colon walked Manny with the bases loaded, scoring Bill Mueller who had hit the first of three straight singles. Bellhorn was picked off second base to end the inning. The Angels responded in the bottom of the second as Martinez walked Troy Glaus who scored after Jeff DaVanon and then Dallas McPherson singled to tie the game.

In the bottom of the fifth, the Angels rallied. Jose Molina dropped a single in between Ramirez and Cabrera on a ball that could have been caught. Eckstein followed with another single and Pedro plunked Darin Erstad to load the bases. Vladimir Guerrero drove in Molina and Eckstein with a line single to right-center field to give the Angels their first lead in the series. It didn't last long. With two out in the top of the sixth, Jason Varitek struck back with a two-run homer off Colon that tied the game at 3-3. In the seventh stanza, with Francisco Rodriguez on in relief of Colon, the Red Sox scored on a Manny sac fly to give the Red Sox the lead for good.

In the ninth, the Red Sox added four insurance tallies against Brendan Donnelly, including three runs courtesy of Orlando Cabrera's bases-loaded double. The final score was 8-3 for Boston. Once again the Rally Monkey failed to come through. In fact with the Red Sox holding a 2-0 stranglehold in the series, the only monkey was the one on the Angels' back.

Division Series Game Three: Fenway Park, Boston / October 8, 2004

Boston 8, Anaheim 9 (10 innings)

Anaheim	000	100	500	0	—	6	8	2
Boston	002	310	000	2	—	8	12	0

WP: Lowe (1-0)   LP: Rodriguez (0-2)   HR: Guerrero (1), Glaus (2), Ortiz (1)

Back in Boston for Game Three, the Red Sox had to battle into the 10th inning before finally subduing the Angels by an 8-6 margin. Red Sox starter and part-time rocker Bronson Arroyo took the hill for Boston, while the Halos countered with talented but inconsistent Kelvim Escobar. David Ortiz, not yet "officially" owner of the title "The Greatest Clutch Hitter in the History of the Boston Red Sox" (that plaque would not be presented him until a ceremony the following September at Fenway), took a giant step towards the "Mr. Clutch" designation in the 10th inning of this game. For the third straight time the Red Sox got on the scoreboard first, scoring a pair in the bottom of the third and driving Escobar to the showers. Bellhorn drew a walk and after Ramirez flied out to center, Ortiz doubled to move him to third. Trot Nixon singled Bellhorn home and Ortiz ambled to third. Big Papi scored on a Kevin Millar groundout to the right side of the infield as Nixon took second.

Arroyo pitched a great game for six innings, allowing only three hits and two earned runs while striking out seven. The Red Sox coughed up the 6-1 lead in the seventh. Arroyo walked Jeff DaVanon to open the inning and Sox manager Francona brought on Mike Myers who promptly issued a walk to Jose Molina. Myers was replaced with workhorse Mike Timlin. Timlin induced a pop-up to shortstop from Pride but Eckstein singled to load the bases. Timlin then walked Darin Erstad to force in a run. With the bases still juiced, free-swinging Vladimir Guerrero struck for a grand slam off Timlin and the Angels had scored five runs to tie the game at 6-6. Alan Embree came on and stopped the bleeding.

The score remained knotted after nine and the game entered extra innings. Derek Lowe was brought on to keep the Angels off the scoreboard in the 10th, and despite a walk, a sacrifice bunt, and a single, Lowe held up his part of the bargain.

Batting against Francisco Rodriguez in the home half of the 10th inning, Johnny Damon slashed a line drive single to left. Mark Bellhorn tried to sacrifice him to second but his bunt attempt was hit too hard, allowing time for the force of Damon at second. Manny whiffed for the second out of the inning. Angels manager Mike Scioscia went to the bullpen and brought on southpaw and Game One loser Jarrod Washburn to face lefty Ortiz. Sometimes playing the percentages backfires and this was one of those times. Ortiz hit a two-run homer off Washburn to win the game and the series for Boston.

The Red Sox reward for beating up on the Angels? The New York Yankees.

ALCS

It doesn't happen often, but every once in a while the color cartoon is better than the main feature. Sometimes the warm-up act overshadows the main attraction. It's almost blasphemy to call a World Series anticlimactic but in 2004 a darn good case could be made for that line of thinking. The Red Sox faced off against the NY Yankees in the American League Championship Series and there were few who didn't believe that this was the meeting of baseball's best teams. Since the structure of Major League baseball ensures that these two teams will never meet in a World Series, let's call the 2004 ALCS the de facto Fall Classic.

League Championship Series Game One: Yankee Stadium, New York / October 12, 2004

New York 10, Boston 7

Boston	000	000	520	—	7	10	0
New York	204	002	02x	—	10	14	0

WP: Mussina (1-0)   LP: Schilling (0-1)   SV: Rivera (1)   HR: Varitek (1), Lofton (1)

In terms of Red Sox frustration, Game One of the ALCS was an extension of Game Seven of the 2003 ALCS against these same Yankees. Mike Mussina was on the mound for the Yankees while the Sox answered with Curt Schilling. Schilling had put himself on the line before the game by saying, "I'm not sure I can think of any scenario more enjoyable than making 55,000 people from New York shut up."

Mussina was practically unhittable, retiring the first 19 batters he faced and making many look foolish as they waved at his knuckle curve. After six innings of play, the New Yorkers were up 8-0, five of the runs courtesy of left fielder Hideki Matsui's three hits and five RBIs.

Schilling was struggling. His fastball was subpar and he didn't have command of his usually devastating splitter. His ankle seemed to be giving him trouble. He lasted only three innings before being replaced by Leskanic, followed by a veritable parade of other relievers (Leskanic, Mendoza, Wakefield, Embree, Tomlin, and Foulke).

The Red Sox unexpectedly came storming back in the seventh inning to score five runs on just five hits. With one out, Bellhorn ended any thoughts Mussina may have had of a perfect game by doubling deep to left center. Then Ramirez grounded out. Ortiz kicked off a rally with a single that sent Bellhorn to third. Millar doubled to score both runs. Trot Nixon singled home Millar. Jason Varitek then homered off reliever Tanyon Sturtze to add two more. The score was now 8-5 and the Yankee fans were slightly less self-satisfied. After the Yankees failed to score in the bottom of the seventh the Red Sox offense went back to work. Big Papi knocked a triple off reliever (and former Red Sox) Tom Gordon to score two more runs and bring the Red Sox within a single run, 8-7.

At this point, the Yankees' brilliant closer Mariano Rivera made a dramatic return from Panama where he had been attending a funeral earlier the same day. No doubt energized by his return, the Yankees scored two more insurance runs in the bottom of the eighth. Alex Rodriguez and Gary Sheffield both singled and Bernie Williams hit a double over Manny's head to score both.

Rivera retired the Red Sox in the top of the ninth and the Yankees led the ALCS one game to none.

League Championship Series Game Two: Yankee Stadium, New York / October 13, 2004

New York 3, Boston 1

| Boston | 000 | 000 | 010 | — | 1 | 5 | 0 |
| New York | 100 | 002 | 00x | — | 3 | 7 | 0 |

WP: Lieber (1-0)   LP: Martinez (0-1)   SV: Rivera (2)   HR: Olerud (1)

Jon Lieber got the start for the Yankees in Game Two and Pedro Martinez for Boston. Lieber was a control pitcher and he dominated the Red Sox throughout the seven innings he pitched. When he exited after the seventh, he had done his job, allowing just a single run on three hits.

Martinez had not pitched badly. He coughed up a first-inning run after walking Jeter and giving up an RBI single to Sheffield but had otherwise kept the Yankee hitters in check until the bottom of the sixth. In the sixth, though, John Olerud hit a two-run homer off Pedro to give the Yankees a 3-0 lead and cause the chant of "Who's your daddy?" to echo throughout the Bronx. The chant was actually Pedro's own words—uttered when the Yankees hit him hard in September—coming back to haunt him.

The Red Sox scored a single run in the top of the eighth but for the second time it was a case of too little too late. Trot Nixon hit a leadoff single to drive Lieber from the mound. Varitek doubled off reliever Tom Gordon, scoring Nixon. After Gordon got two more outs, Mariano Rivera recorded the final four outs just as he had done the previous night.

To add to the Red Sox misery, Curt Schilling had been diagnosed with a tear of the tendon in his right ankle and his ability to pitch again in the postseason was highly questionable.

League Championship Series Game Three: Fenway Park, Boston / October 16, 2004

New York 19, Boston 8

New York	303	520	402	—	19	22	1
Boston	042	000	200	—	8	15	0

WP: Vazquez (1-0)   LP: Mendoza (0-1)   HR: Rodriguez (1), Sheffield (1), Matsui 2 (2), Varitek (2), Nixon (1)

The Red Sox returned to Fenway where they were expected to have a big advantage. Not this time. Starter Bronson Arroyo was just one of many victims of the onslaught. Arroyo gave up six runs and six hits and left the game before recording an out in the third.

The Yankees scored 19 runs on 22 hits, including four home runs and eight doubles, to crush the Red Sox 19-8. The fans began to drift out of the ballpark as the excruciating inning wore on, in a state of shock. Few thought that any team, let alone this one, could recover from such a humiliating loss. The Red Sox scored runs too, just not enough of them. Yankee starter Kevin Brown was also chased from the mound in the second inning. The Sox actually held a 4-3 lead at the end of the second, but in the fourth the Yankees took what amounted to batting practice off three different Red Sox pitchers. Most of the fifth inning offense came from Sheffield's three-run homer and Ruben Sierra's two-run triple. It was now 11-6 New York.

In the fifth the batting blitz continued with A-Rod and Sheffield hitting doubles to score two more runs and make it 13-6. In the top of the seventh, the Yankees added four more and in the ninth Matsui added an exclamation point in the form of a two-run home run.

League Championship Series Game Four: Fenway Park, Boston / October 17, 2004

Boston 6, New York 4 (12 innings)

New York	002	002	000	000	—	4	12	1
Boston	000	030	001	002	—	6	8	0

WP: Leskanic (1-0)   LP: Quantrill (0-1)   HR: Rodriguez (2), Ortiz (1)

David Ortiz strikes a walk-off homer in Game Four of the ALCS. It would prove to be the first of many such dramatic game-winners for the greatest clutch hitter in Red Sox history. (Boston Red Sox)

To the surprise of many, the sun actually rose on the morning of Sunday, October 17, 2004. The Red Sox were now battling for respect and their fans were looking at some vestige of respectability to hang on to when they were confronted by Yankee friends over the next 12 months. Just one win was all they asked for, or at least a decent loss. Don't let the bitter 19-8 taste remain over the winter.

Derek Lowe was asked to step into the gap left by the absence of Schilling due to his ankle injury. The Yankees struck first on a two-run homer by Alex Rodriguez in the top of the third. With Orlando Hernandez on the mound for the Yankees, the lead lasted until the fifth when Red Sox bats finally came alive. Actually Hernandez helped to resuscitate them by issuing three walks followed by a run-scoring single to Orlando Cabrera. Ortiz followed with a single that scored two more runs and the Red Sox had a 3-2 lead. The Yankees answered back immediately and went back ahead 4-3 in the top of the sixth.

The one-run Yankees margin held up until the bottom of the ninth. With the seemingly untouchable Mariano Rivera on the mound, Kevin Millar resisted the temptation to swing at some tempting pitches and drew a walk. Dave Roberts was inserted to run for the slow-footed Millar and stole second, almost certainly the biggest steal in Red Sox history. A Bill Mueller scorched single sent him home with the tying run. There was still nobody out. Rivera worked through it, but it was his first blown save in 36 postseason appearances.

The two teams battled through two and a half scoreless frames until the bottom of the twelfth. The Yankees had loaded the bases in the top of the 11th but reliever Curtis Leskanic

Dave Roberts and the biggest steal in Boston Red Sox history. (Boston Red Sox)

was able to get Bernie Williams to fly to center for the final out. With Paul Quantrill on the mound for the Yankees, early in the morning of the 18th, David Ortiz sent a drive into the bleak Boston night sky. The ball landed in the right-field bullpen and Fenway Park went a little bit crazy. "We'll see you later tonight!" exclaimed Joe Buck on the Fox TV broadcast. The Red Sox had battled back from the brink and after five hours and two minutes had kept a flicker of hope alive in Red Sox Nation. If it's true that there are no moral victories, this was as close as you can get. Red Sox fans could at least show their faces in public again.

League Championship Series Game Five: Fenway Park, Boston / October 18, 2004

Boston 5, New York 4 (14 innings)

New York	010	003	000	000	00	—	4	12	1
Boston	200	000	020	000	01	—	5	13	1

WP: Wakefield (1-0)   LP: Loaiza (0-1)   HR: Williams (1), Ortiz (2)

The Red Sox and Yankees got under way again at Fenway Park that same evening with Red Sox hopes riding on the arm of Pedro Martinez. The Yankees hitched their wagon to Mike Mussina, the man who had approached perfection in Game One. This time the Red Sox charged from the gate with two runs in the bottom of the first inning. After Damon grounded out, Cabrera reached on a single and moved to third on another single, this time by Ramirez. Ortiz drove in the first run with the third straight single as Ramirez moved to second. Millar walked, loading the bases. Mussina walked Varitek with the bases jammed for the second Red Sox run. Mueller then struck out to end the inning.

In the second inning the Yankees got on the board on a solo blast by Bernie Williams. The two teams blanked the next three innings until the New Yorkers struck again in the sixth. With one out, Jorge Posada and Ruben Sierra each singled. After Tony Clark whiffed, Martinez then hit Miguel Cairo and the bases were loaded. Jeter doubled in all three runs and the Yankees led 4-2.

The Red Sox opened their half of the eighth with a homer off Tom Gordon to make it 4-3. Millar worked a walk and once again Dave Roberts entered the game as a pinch runner.

David Ortiz is mobbed after his walk-off homer in Game Four of the ALCS allows the Red Sox to play another day. (Boston Red Sox)

A Trot Nixon single sent the speedy Roberts to third. Mariano Rivera was brought on but for the second straight time couldn't seal the deal. Jason Varitek's sac fly tied the game and the two teams were locked in another extra inning affair.

Arroyo came in to pitch for Foulke and got three outs. In the bottom of the 10th Doug Mientkiewicz doubled and made it as far as third but the Red Sox were unable to get him home. In the 11th the first two Red Sox reached but Esteban Loaiza took over from Quantrill and pitched out of the crisis. Again the Sox came up empty.

In the top of the 12th, the Red Sox put the ball into the hands of knuckle-ball specialist Tim Wakefield. Wakefield is much loved in Boston but anyone who says he isn't nervous when Wakefield is on the mound is probably a liar. Cairo reached him for a single and took second on an error by Manny Ramirez. Wakefield pitched himself out of the minefield and the game continued. In the top of the unlucky 13th, Jason Varitek showed why he sits down when Wakefield pitches. Varitek was guilty of three passed balls in the inning but still the Yankees failed to score.

Finally, in the bottom of the 14th inning with two out, Loaiza alternated strikeouts and walks to the first four batters, leaving two on and two out. Big Papi ambled to the plate and concluded a 10-pitch at-bat with a walk-off single to center field.

The game surpassed the previous night's record-setting marathon at 5 hours and 49 minutes.

League Championship Series Game Six: Yankee Stadium, New York: October 19, 2004

Boston 4, New York 2

Boston	000	400	000	—	4	11	0
New York	000	000	110	—	2	6	0

WP: Schilling (1-1)   LP: Lieber (1-1)   SV: Foulke (1)   HR: Bellhorn (1), Williams (2)

The Red Sox were definitely back in contention, but the Yankees still held a one-game lead and they were back in Yankee Stadium where history—long past and recent past—was their ally. And in the whole history of baseball, no team had ever come back from a deficit of 0-3 to win a four-game postseason series—but the Red Sox had the Yankees feeling just a little jumpy.

The starters were Curt Schilling for the Red Sox and Jon Lieber for the Yankees. The game began as a pitching duel, as the two moundsmen threw shutout ball for the first three innings. With two down in the fourth inning and nobody on, Millar doubled and then Jason Varitek broke the string with a two-out base hit that scored him. Cabrera singled and then the slumping Mark Bellhorn deposited a home run into the left-field stands. He'd had a couple of hits in Game Five, but even those two only brought Bellhorn to being 4-for-34 at the time. Bellhorn's blast struck a fan and fell back on the field. Umpire Jim Joyce initially ruled that the ball was still in play but Terry Francona charged from the dugout to loudly dispute the call. To their credit the umpiring crew huddled and the call was reversed. Bellhorn was waved around the bases with a three-run homer and the Red Sox led 4-0.

Pitching in obvious pain, Schilling nonetheless hung in for seven effective innings, allowing only one run on a Bernie Williams solo shot in the seventh. As the innings mounted, Schilling's sock had become increasingly stained with blood. Reporters later revealed that he was pitching with a dislocated tendon in his right ankle. Doctors had sutured skin from his leg to deep connective tissue near the bone. The purpose was to prevent the tendon from sliding out of place and impacting his pitching mechanics. The surgeons had practiced the technique on a cadaver—an unknown hero in Red Sox history. It was a kind of Dr. Frankenstein creation that captured the attention of the whole country.

Bronson Arroyo took over in the eighth and gave up a one-out double to Miguel Cairo. Jeter followed with a single to drive in Cairo and make it 4-2. Then came controversy. Alex Rodriguez hit a grounder to Arroyo who fielded it smoothly and ran to apply the tag on the Yankee star. When he reached out to make the play, A-Rod slapped Arroyo's arm and he dropped the ball. Jeter scored on the play and A-Rod was at second. Once again the umpires convened a meeting. Once again the verdict was in favor of the Red Sox. Jeter was banished back to first and A-Rod was out. The Red Sox escaped the inning with no further damage done.

Yankee fans were irate and Boston manager Francona had to pull his team from the field to protect them from flying objects hurled from the stands. Finally the New York Police Department, outfitted in riot gear and circling the perimeter of the infield, restored order, although for the rest of the game, Yankee Stadium took on the look of an unstable South American banana republic.

In the bottom of the ninth, with the score still 4-2, Keith Foulke came on to protect the lead. He walked Matsui and Sierra and Tony Clark came to the plate with two outs, representing the winning run. Foulke struck out Clark to end the game.

As improbable as it seemed, the ALCS was tied at three games apiece.

Red Sox ace Curt Schilling offered up his blood, sweat, and tears to win Game Six of the ALCS. (Boston Red Sox)

League Championship Series Game Seven: Yankee Stadium, New York / October 20, 2004

Boston 10, New York 3

Boston	240	200	011	—	10	13	0
New York	001	000	200	—	3	5	1

WP: Lowe (1-0)   LP: Brown (0-1)   HR: Damon 2 (2), Bellhorn (2), Ortiz (3)

It had all come down to this. The Red Sox had come back from the three games to none deficit to tie the ALCS. They had come back from a 19-8 shellacking in Game Three to within one game of advancing to the World Series. The starting pitcher for the Red Sox was Derek Lowe, and Kevin Brown would toe the rubber for the Yankees. All of a sudden the Yankees were the team on the run. The Yankees were the team with the pressure. The Yankees were the team with something to prove. David Ortiz got things going in the top of the first with a two-run homer off Brown. In the second, the Red Sox were relentless, loading the bases. With everything riding on this game, manager Joe Torre removed Brown and Javier Vazquez came on in relief. Johnny Damon hit Vazquez's first pitch into the crowd in right field for a grand slam and Boston had a 6-0 lead. In the fourth, Damon hit another home run, this time a two-run shot to ensure his place in Red Sox history.

Johnny Damon homers to doom the Yankees in Game Seven of the ALCS, sealing the greatest comeback in playoff history. (Boston Red Sox)

Lowe allowed the Yankees only one run and one hit in six innings. Pedro Martinez entered the game in the seventh to the usual chants of "Who's Your Daddy?" He gave up two runs before Mike Timlin and Alan Embree closed out the game and the series. The final score was 10-3 and the Red Sox had made history, becoming the only major league team to come back from an 0-3 hole to win four straight games.

David Ortiz was selected as the MVP of the ALCS.

WORLD SERIES

Game One: Fenway Park, Boston / October 23, 2004

Boston 11, St. Louis 9

St. Louis	011	302	020	—	9 11 1
Boston	403	000	22x	—	11 13 4

WP: Foulke (1-0)   LP: Tavarez (0-1)   HR: Walker (1), Ortiz (1), Bellhorn (1)

It was the 100th World Series and 86 years had passed since Boston had last won one.

The Red Sox had slain the dragon in New York, but the castle still had to be stormed and the Holy Grail still had to be captured. Standing in their way were the St. Louis Cardinals, the same knaves who had thwarted their quest in both 1946 and 1975. The Cardinals lineup was certainly not to be taken lightly. They had won more games—105—than any team in major league baseball in 2004. They had possibly the best player in the game at first in Albert Pujols. Scott Rolen, with his .598 slugging percentage, played third, and Gold Glove center fielder Jim "Hollywood" Edmonds, he of the 111 RBIs and .643 slugging percentage, batted fifth. It was no accident that they boasted the highest scoring offense in the National League.

Anchored by Woody Williams (11-8) and Jason Marquis (15-7), their pitching staff had the second-best ERA in the NL. The Cardinals, whose own quest had included a seven-game ordeal against the Houston Astros, were missing only dominant right-hander Chris Carpenter, who had a 15-5 season mark and club-best 3.46 ERA before being sidelined with a bruised nerve on the biceps of his pitching arm.

One thing is certain. No matter how loosely you define the term, Game One was no fall classic. It was the kind of game during which Little Leaguers should be sent to their rooms, or at least told to avert their eyes. "That was not an instructional video," Francona later told reporters. The Red Sox committed four errors and there was one glaring Cardinal sin. The Red Sox also coughed up leads of 4-0 and 7-2 and seemed determined not to hold the lead.

The great Carl Yastrzemski throws out the first World Series pitch. (Boston Red Sox)

The Red Sox charged from the gate in the bottom of the first inning, scoring four runs against St. Louis starter Woody Williams. ALCS hero Johnny Damon doubled to lead off the game. Williams then hit shortstop Orlando Cabrera to put runners on first and second. After Manny Ramirez flied out, David Ortiz bent a three-run homer around the right-field foul pole. A Bill Mueller single scored Kevin Millar with the fourth tally.

The Cardinals fought back in the top of the second inning as Edmonds bunted his way aboard and scored on Mike Matheny's sac fly. The Cards continued to peck away in the third inning when Canadian Larry Walker hit a solo shot to narrow the lead to 4-2. The Red Sox continued their assault in the bottom of the third. Bill Mueller reached on a walk, Doug Mirabelli singled, and Bellhorn walked. Damon singled Mueller in. With only 2 ⅓ innings under his belt, Williams was lifted in favor of reliever Dan Haren but the Red Sox scarcely noticed. Cabrera singled to score plodding Doug Mirabelli and Bellhorn plated the seventh run on a fielder's choice. It was now 7-2 and had all the earmarks of a runaway, but the Red Sox pitching wasn't much better.

Boston starter Tim Wakefield issued five walks in his 3 ⅔ innings of work, four in the top of the fourth alone. St. Louis took advantage of the knuckleball when Edmonds scored on a sac fly off the bat of Matheny. Reggie Sanders crossed home plate on a throwing error by Millar. Tony Womack scored the third run on a ground ball out to Mueller at third.

The teams were like two slightly punch-drunk fighters, landing blows at will with neither willing to fall down.

The Cardinals tied the game again with two more runs in the top of the sixth. With Bronson Arroyo on the mound for Boston, So Taguchi beat out an infield hit and took second when Arroyo made a wild throw to first. Edgar Renteria lined to center field for a double and Taguchi scored. Walker, playing in his first World Series, and making the most of his opportunity, doubled Renteria home and the score was suddenly 7-7.

In the bottom of the seventh, Cardinals reliever Kiko Calero couldn't locate the plate and issued free passes to Bellhorn and Cabrera. Ramirez eased in Bellhorn with a hard single up the middle. The Cardinals brought on Ray King to face Ortiz and Papi hit a blue darter to second where Womack played it off his collarbone. Cabrera scored on the play and Womack had to leave the game. The Red Sox had regained the lead, 9-7, but not for long.

In the top of the eighth, Mike Matheny singled with one out and Jason Marquis was brought in to run for him. Roger Cedeno, pinch-hitting for Taguchi, also singled, putting runners on first and second. Renteria reached Red Sox closer Keith Foulke for another single and Ramirez momentarily bobbled the ball, allowing Marquis to score the eighth Cardinals run. Walker then hit a fly ball toward Ramirez and Manny caught his spikes while attempting his (not quite so) patented sliding catch ("Snipers got me," Manny suggested to teammate Dave Roberts). Cedeno crossed home plate with the tying run. The Cardinals almost took the lead when Pujols drew an intentional walk but Foulke dug deep to retire Rolen and strike out Edmonds to keep it at 9-9.

In the bottom of the eighth, with Julian Tavarez now on the mound for St. Louis, errors continued to mar the game. This time it was Cardinals shortstop Renteria who opened the door, allowing Jason Varitek to reach first on his botched backhand attempt at a grounder. It was a game-breaker, as it turned out, because Mark Bellhorn pulled a pitch deep to right field. The only question was whether it would be fair or foul. The ball hit Pesky's Pole for a home run and caused an impromptu celebration as Bellhorn arrived at home plate.

With the gift of second life, the Red Sox faltered but did not fall. With one out, Marlon Anderson doubled but Foulke retired the next two batters to close out the free-for-all. It may have been winning ugly—but it was still a win.

PLAYER PROFILE: MARK BELLHORN

Signed by the Red Sox as a utility infielder, Mark Bellhorn was thrust into the spotlight as the Red Sox starting second baseman following injuries to Pokey Reese. Bellhorn seized the opportunity and finished the season with a .264 batting average, 17 homers, and 82 RBIs. A statistical aberration, he was third in the league in walks and first in strikeouts.

Bellhorn struggled in the ALDS and ALCS but finally recovered to defeat the Yankees with a homer in Game Six of the League Championship Series. He also homered in Game Seven to help put the Yankees on ice.

His two-run eighth inning poke off Tavarez in the World Series Game One slugfest set the tone for the Red Sox in the 2004 World Series.

Initially a minor folk hero in his native Boston, Bellhorn's popularity faded along with his offensive statistics in 2005. He was released by the Red Sox and quickly signed with the Yankees where he continued to under-perform. In 2006, he joined the San Diego Padres and most recently played for the Cincinnati Reds with just one hit in 14 at-bats in 2007.

Regardless of his shortcomings as a hitter, Bellhorn's name will endure forever as a key cog in the Red Sox first World Series championship in 86 years. For many, the disheveled utility man symbolizes the never-say-die spirit of the '04 Sox.

Game Two: Fenway Park, Boston / October 24, 2004

Boston 6, St. Louis 2

| St. Louis | 000 | 100 | 010 | — | 2 | 5 | 0 |
| Boston | 200 | 202 | 00x | — | 6 | 8 | 4 |

WP: Schilling (1-0)   LP: Morris (0-1)

Matt Morris drew the starting assignment for the Cardinals and New England's newest folk hero, Curt Schilling, took the mound for the Red Sox. Since the bloody sock incident in the ALCS, Schilling's folkloric fame was at least on a par with Paul Bunyan. Schilling still had a ligament in his right ankle surgically attached to the outside of his ankle. For the Red Sox, it had been the symbolic opposite of an Achilles heel, and served as a red badge of courage representing the Red Sox' will to win. If there were ever a leader that a team could rally around, it was General Schilling.

Schilling pitched six innings, allowing only one run on four hits but there have been no-hitters that deserve less praise. Schilling gave up a double to Albert Pujols in the first inning but stranded him thanks to a great play by Bill Mueller on a Scott Rolen line drive to third. With two down in the bottom of the first, those illustrious icons of intimidation, Manny and Papi, both reached via walks. Jason Varitek then tripled to the farthest reaches of Fenway's outfield triangle to score both runners and stake the Red Sox to a 2-0 lead.

In the top of the second, usually sure-handed third baseman Mueller somehow dropped a Jim Edmonds pop foul. Schilling retired Edmonds but in his condition, every extra pitch had physical repercussions. Schilling walked Reggie Sanders and Tony Womack followed with a single but the threat was ended when Mueller initiated a slick double play on a liner by Mike Metheny.

Schilling kept the Cardinals off the scoreboard until the top of the fourth when errors once again threatened to undermine his valiant efforts. Pujols scored from third when Mueller muffed a Sanders grounder. In the bottom half of the inning, Kevin Millar was hit by a pitch and Mueller struck a double to right field. With runners at first and third, the suddenly powerful Bellhorn put a charge in a Morris offering for a long two-run double to the center-field fence. He was making up for lost time, bringing his bat to bear in the World Series.

In the top of the sixth, Mueller tied a World Series record with his third error of the game, this one putting Scott Rolen on first with two out. Bellhorn then misplayed an Edmonds grounder and suddenly there were runners on first and second. Mueller redeemed himself, registering the third out on an unassisted force play at third on a ball hit right at him by Sanders. The Red Sox had escaped the threat.

With Cal Eldred on the mound for the Cards in the sixth, Trot Nixon singled to lead off the inning. After retiring the next two batters, Eldred gave up a single to Damon and Cabrera clanged a Fenway single off the Green Monster to score two more Boston runs and make it 6-1. With Mike Timlin on in relief in the eighth inning, Renteria drew a walk and went to third on a Walker groundout and a Pujols single. Scott Rolen sacrificed him home with a fly ball to center. Foulke was brought in to quell the uprising and the Red Sox won the game, 6-2. The winning pitcher was Schilling, despite the Red Sox' four errors, a total of eight in the first two games of the Series.

A determined Curt Schilling pitches in Game Two of the World Series. Schilling wrote a dramatic chapter in baseball history that will be difficult to top. (Boston Red Sox)

PLAYER PROFILE: CURT SCHILLING

Like hobbled Kirk Gibson's inspirational homer in Game One of the 1988 World Series, Curt Schilling's courageous effort in Game Two gave the entire Red Sox team a lift.

Schilling embodies the will to win and the off-season trade that brought him from the Arizona Diamondbacks to the Red Sox proved to be a stroke of genius. Schilling went on to record a 21-6 mark and led the Red Sox to the postseason. He is, quite simply, a winner. His statistics, as impressive as they are, do not begin to tell the whole story.

Ironically, the Schilling saga began in Boston where the right-hander was a Red Sox farm hand. He was dealt to Baltimore and subsequently to Houston before becoming a household name in 1993 as a member of the NL pennant-winning Phillies. He came into his own with a 16-7 record and 186 strikeouts. Significantly, he excelled under the pressure of the playoffs, he posted a 1.69 ERA in the NLCS, winning the series MVP. He followed up with a five-hit, 2-0 shutout of the Blue Jays in the World Series.

In 1997 he struck out 319 with a 2.97 ERA and fanned an even 300 the following year. In 2000, he was traded to Arizona and in '01 went 22-6 with a 2.98 ERA as the Diamondbacks won the NL pennant. Again he excelled in the limelight of the playoffs, racking up four wins, no losses, and a 1.12 ERA. He and mound mate Randy Johnson were named co-winners of the World Series MVP Award. In the '02 campaign, he was 23-7 and his strikeout total again topped the magic 300 mark (316). For the second year in a row he finished second in the Cy Young balloting.

Game Three: Busch Stadium, St. Louis / October 26, 2004

Boston 4, St. Louis 1

Boston	100	120	000	—	4	9	0
St. Louis	000	000	001	—	1	4	0

WP: Martinez (1-0)   LP: Suppan (0-1)   HR: Ramirez (1), Walker (2)

The Red Sox and Cardinals moved to St. Louis for Game Three and the National League champions were hoping that some home cooking and a friendly crowd might change things. It didn't. With Pedro Martinez on the mound for the Red Sox, the Red Sox played errorless ball and came through with timely hits to bring the Red Sox to the brink of a world championship.

With two down in the top of the first, Manny Ramirez blasted a Jeff Suppan fastball over the left-center field wall to make it 1-0.

Pedro loaded the bases in the bottom half of the inning with one out and it looked as if the game might become another slugfest, but Ramirez made an accurate throw home on an Edmonds fly ball to double up slow-running Larry Walker at the plate.

In the bottom of the third, Suppan legged out an infield single and Renteria followed with a double to right-center. Walker hit a grounder to Bellhorn that should have scored Suppan, but the pitcher hesitated in running home and first baseman David Ortiz fired across the diamond, catching him off the third-base bag and recording a double play to end the inning.

With two out in the fourth, Bill Mueller doubled to left-center field. Trot Nixon stroked a single to right field for the second Red Sox run. In the fifth frame, leadoff man Johnny Damon doubled to right field and Cabrera moved him to third with a single. Ramirez pulled a pitch to left for another single, scoring Damon with the third run. Ortiz flied out and Varitek made out on a fielder's choice. Mueller, still atoning for the previous day's trio of errors, hit a frozen rope single through the right side of the infield and Cabrera trotted home with run number four. Al Reyes came on to record the final out but the damage had been done.

Martinez pitched seven innings and was replaced by Timlin to start the eighth inning. Timlin retired the Cardinals with no further damage and gave way to closer Foulke in the ninth. After getting the first batter he faced, Foulke gave up a home run to Larry Walker, the only run he would allow in the 2004 post-season, but the Cardinals could do no more. The Red Sox had a commanding lead in the 2004 World Series, but then they had been in a similar situation just a week or so earlier—staring at the yawning deficit that saw the Yankees up three games to none.

PLAYER PROFILE: PEDRO MARTINEZ

Pedro Martinez will go down in history as one of the greatest Red Sox pitchers—perhaps the greatest. He came to the Red Sox from the Montreal Expos in 1997 and in 1999 set the baseball world on its ear with a 23-4 mark, 313 Ks, and a 2.07 ERA. He captured that year's Cy Young Award, giving him one in both leagues, and finished second in MVP voting.

In 2000, Martinez was virtually unhittable. Despite a pedestrian 18-6 record, his ERA was a microscopic 1.74. The next lowest that year—ironically compiled by Roger Clemens—was 3.70. Almost daily, he had statisticians rushing to the record books to determine the historic nature of his pitching feats. Among other things, they discovered that American League hitters batted a combined .167 against him and that he had broken new ground as the only starter in major league history with twice as many strikeouts as hits allowed (284 whiffs vs. 128 hits).

Pedro Martinez looks skyward after a stellar performance in Game Three of the World Series. It would be his last appearance in a Red Sox uniform. (Boston Red Sox)

Following an injury plagued 2001, Pedro again led the AL in ERA in 2002 with a 2.26 mark to go with his 239 strikeouts. His season record was 20-4. In 2003 he once again posted a league-best ERA (2.22).

When Martinez left the Red Sox after the 2004 season, he left behind a sterling record of 117-37, while wearing the Bosox colors.

Game Four: Busch Stadium, St. Louis / October 27, 2004

Boston 3, St. Louis 0

Boston	102	000	000	—	3	9	0
St. Louis	000	000	000	—	0	4	0

WP: Lowe (1-0)   LP: Marquis (0-1)   SV: Foulke (1)   HR: Damon (1)

A total lunar eclipse served as partial background to this historic game.

Leadoff man extraordinaire Johnny Damon got things started with a home run on the fourth delivery from Card starter Jason Marquis in the top of the first inning. The ball disappeared over the right-field wall and Red Sox fans everywhere rejoiced. The Red Sox scored in the first inning of every World Series game and the Cardinals hadn't enjoyed a lead against the Sox in any of the games.

Derek Lowe was on the mound for the Red Sox with a chance to end the Curse once and for all.

Manny Ramirez singled with one down in the third and Ortiz doubled to right. Varitek hit a hot grounder to Albert Pujols and the first baseman fired home to nail Ramirez for the second out of the inning. Mueller walked to load the bases and Trot Nixon unloaded on a 3-0 pitch in a bid for a grand slam. He had to settle for a double off the right-center field wall, driving in Ortiz and Varitek to make it 3-0.

Facing reliever Danny Haren in the top of the eighth, Bill Mueller came through with a single. Nixon doubled, his third two-bagger of the game. Gabe Kapler came on to run for Nixon. Jason Isringhausen was brought in to face Bellhorn. Bellhorn struck out, as did the next batter, and Pujols made a nice play on a Damon grounder, throwing home to force Mueller and end the inning.

Lowe was lifted for a pinch hitter in the eighth after striking out four and allowing just four hits over seven innings. He was the third Red Sox starter in a row to not give up an earned run. Arroyo took over in the bottom of the inning and walked Reggie Sanders with one out but Alan Embree took over and got the last two outs.

The bottom of the ninth saw Keith Foulke on the mound for the Red Sox. Pujols, the $100 million man for St. Louis lined a defiant single through the pitcher's legs. Hopeful Cardinals fans were silenced by a Rolen fly ball out to Kapler in right. Foulke then struck out Jim Edmonds on three pitches to set the stage for the finale.

The Red Sox were one out away from their first World Series championship since 1918. Edgar Renteria, who would become the regular Boston shortstop the following year, was the only thing standing between the Red Sox and victory. Renteria hit a comeback grounder that Foulke fielded cleanly and tossed underhanded to Doug Mientkiewicz for the final out. Thus did the Curse of the Bambino end, not with a roar but with a whimper.

But the roars weren't long in coming and can still be heard reverberating throughout Red Sox Nation on clear summer nights. The impacts of the win were many and varied. Champaign corks popped and tears were shed. Grandfathers, grandmothers, fathers, daughters, and grandchildren embraced unashamedly.

Disbelief was rampant. No statistics are available regarding the number of self-inflicted pinch wounds incurred over the ensuing weeks and months, but anecdotal evidence suggests they were at epidemic levels.

Some tried to make the lunar eclipse significant in some way. Writer Thomas Boswell disagreed: "The victory that arrived on this evening for the Red Sox and their true believers was

Lowe, and behold. Derek Lowe pitches seven strong, scoreless innings in Game Four, allowing only three hits as the Red Sox win their first World Series in 86 years. After going winless in his last five season starts, the sinkerball specialist ended up pitching all three postseason clinchers. (Boston Red Sox)

The duckboat parade. (Boston Red Sox)

far too rare and precious, too long overdue and spectacular in its consummation, to be upstaged by something so commonplace as the earth, moon and stars." ("From Woebegone to Champions," *Washington Post*, October 28, 2004)

Statistics show that many elderly New Englanders died shortly after the World Series win—significantly more than the normal number. The theory is that they had clung to life long enough to see their dream come true and they could now die in peace.

The Red Sox had been dominant in the Series, holding the Cardinals' three best players, Rolen, Edmonds, and Pujols to a combined .133 batting average (4-for-45), no homers, and one RBI.

Manny Ramirez was named Series MVP.

PLAYER PROFILE: DEREK LOWE

Derek Lowe came to the Red Sox from Seattle as part of the most one-sided transaction since Jack bartered his bovine for a handful of beans. Lowe and battery-mate Jason Varitek were swapped to the Red Sox in exchange for Heathcliff Slocumb.

With the Red Sox, the sinkerball specialist started slow, going 5-15 in his first two campaigns before finding his niche as a closer in 1999. In 2000, he solidified his position as one of baseball's elite closers, leading the AL with 42 saves.

After being shuttled from closer to other bullpen assignments in 2001, Lowe returned again to a starting role in 2002 and responded with a 21-8 record and a sparkling 2.58 ERA. On April 27, he tossed a no-hitter against the Tampa Bay Devil Rays at Fenway. In 2003 his ERA ballooned to 4.47 despite a very respectable 17-7 record.

In 2004, he was once again asked to rotate between bullpen and starting assignments. His 14-12 record as a starter—with a 5.42 ERA—shook the confidence of the Red Sox brain trust. But this was all forgotten when the postseason arrived and Lowe became an integral part of the Red Sox glorious postseason run. As events unfolded, it was Derek Lowe who earned the win in the deciding game of the ALCS, the final seventh game of the hard-fought League Championship Series against the Yankees, and the final game of the World Series.

IN BETWEEN CHAMPIONSHIPS

The Red Sox reigned as World Champions until October 26, 2005. When the Sox of another color won the World Series, the reality befell Boston fans. It wasn't as bad as it could have been; there was at least some appreciation for the fact that the White Sox had waited 88 years for their own time on top.

But since Boston had won on October 27, 2004, Red Sox Nation was even denied a full year on top: their reign lasted just 364 days.

And the fact remained: the Red Sox were no longer champions of the baseball world. There had been a fleeting dream of repeating, but as the season came to an end, the Red Sox had found themselves tied with New York in the standings—and the Yankees had the slightest edge: they'd won ten of the 19 head-to-head matchups during the season. They'd wanted to win the division, and had a four game lead as late as September 10. But Boston was 12-9 in the last three weeks, and the Yankees put on a push and finished 16-5. The last of the 19 games between the two teams saw Tim Wakefield pitch a brilliant game against Randy Johnson. Wake went the distance. Johnson was relieved by Tom Gordon and Mariano Rivera. The Red Sox only got three hits and failed to score. The Yankees only got three hits, too, but the first one was a solo homer by Jason Giambi in the first inning. The lead in the division was this 1-0 Yankees win in New York.

Even though they'd let Pedro Martinez go, and Derek Lowe, and even though Curt Schilling had not regained the form he'd had before his ankle injury and the resultant bloody sock, the Red Sox still made the postseason. There was hope. But the White Sox swept them in the Division Series and that hope died quickly. The Yankees lost in the first round, too, though they took it to the full five games before bowing to the Angels.

Bosox fans knew they still had a good team. Then there was 2006. Again, the season opened with

Every Red Sox fan has a story about the 2004 playoffs. The authors recounted several in the book *Blood Feud: The Red Sox, the Yankees, and the Struggle of Good versus Evil.* It is, in our humble view, without a doubt the best of the 38 books on the Ultimate Triumph that flooded the market over the following 12 months. The US Census Bureau's population estimate for the City of Boston in 2003 was 581,616. The estimated number of people who poured into the city for the "rolling rally" parade that celebrated the world championship was 3,200,000—in other words, well over five times the population of the city itself.

One guy got caught in the unexpected limelight: first baseman Doug Mientkiewicz, who caught and kept the ball flipped by Foulke. The catch sealed the victory and estimates of its worth in the immediate aftermath ranged as high as $1,000,000. Too bad Mientkiewicz didn't accept the suggestion (made by a humble author) to get it appraised quickly and donate it to the Red Sox Foundation for the tax break it could give him. The team challenged his right to keep the ball for himself. It provided some hot stove controversy and even prompted a staged debate in the pages of the *Boston Globe Magazine* between author Bill Nowlin and one Alan Dershowitz. Attorney Dershowitz made the point that "Of all the people on this incredible team that gave us all so much joy, Mientkiewicz seems to be the least deserving. He didn't play a central role in getting us into the World Series or winning the World Series." He was in the right place at the right time, though. Would a future Foulke hold on to the ball and try to run to first, securing the souvenir for himself rather than making the safe play? Both debaters agreed that if the Red Sox kept winning World Series, the ball's value would diminish. In the end, the first baseman loaned the ball to the Red Sox and then donated it to the Hall of Fame.

hope, hope that—among other things—the Red Sox could finally finish above the Yankees in the standings. That would be a point of pride. Even though the Yankees hadn't won a World Series since the last year of the previous century, it was still galling that they kept winning the AL East. Eight years in a row, since 1998, the Yankees took first place. But a rash of injuries and a calamitous home series against the Yankees in late August when the Red Sox lost five games in a row to the visitors did them in. On August 16, the Red Sox had been two games behind the Yankees. On August 21, they were 6 ½ games back. The Red Sox finished in third place, 11 games out of first place—one behind the second-place Toronto Blue Jays.

By the time the 2007 season began, it had been 732 long days since the Red Sox were last world champions. This time, the Red Sox took no mercy. They took first place for good on April 14 and never once let go. They were 16-8 in April and 20-8 in May, and held a full ten-game lead over the second-place Orioles as June dawned. It's a good thing they built up such a large lead since they were just 13-14 in June and, indeed, 60-50 over the final four months of the season.

The Yankees surged near the end and there were some tense moments, particularly after the Sox lost four in a row and found themselves just a game and a half ahead of the Yankees with just nine games to play. But the Red Sox rallied and won six of the last nine, holding off the New Yorkers, finishing two games ahead. For much of the season, it was thought the Yankees might end up in third place. Not only did they put a scare into the Red Sox, they won the Wild Card and earned themselves yet another trip to postseason play.

2007 WORLD SERIES BOSTON RED SOX 4, COLORADO ROCKIES 0

The Colorado Rockies rode into their first World Series on one of the most incredible winning streaks in baseball history. They'd won 14 of their last 15 regular-season games, and then swept both the NLDS and NLCS in the minimum seven games for the double sweep. That made it 21 of their last 22 ballgames. Couldn't a team this hot win at least four of the next seven and win a World Championship, even if they were facing the best team in the American League?

Winning all those games at the end of the season certainly wasn't easy, and even when they did, they still didn't win the NL West. They finished a half-game behind the Arizona Diamondbacks, and that only because they defeated the San Diego Padres in a one-game playoff to determine the Wild Card. And beating the Padres wasn't easy, either. The two teams battled and battled and were tied 6-6 after nine innings. Three innings later, they were still tied 6-6. In the 13th, the Padres scored twice—but the Rockies scored three times and won the right to compete in the playoffs. Whereupon they swept the NL East champion Phillies and then swept the Diamondbacks. They secured the National League pennant on October 15 and then had to wait until the Red Sox beat the Indians on the 21st, just to find out which team they'd be playing.

There can be a couple of downsides to winning so many games in a row. No streak lasts forever. Talent will usually win out, but over the course of a season only a handful of teams have ever won more than 60 percent of their games. Even the best teams lose about 40 percent of their games and, by the time the World Series began, the Rockies had only lost one game since September 15. One loss in 38 days. The law of averages might say they were due for at least a couple of losses. Momentum counts, but had the Rockies ridden momentum as long as can reasonably be expected?

Too much time off can cancel out momentum. After all the exhilaration they'd experienced, the Rockies then sat idle for eight full days—the 16th through the 23rd. It's not easy to keep one's skills up, or keep an edge, with so many days off, no matter how many drills or practices are planned. The Red Sox themselves faced a shorter version of the same in 1946. After wrapping up the AL pennant, they had to wait six days to find out who would win the NL flag as the Cardinals played the Dodgers in a best-of-three playoff (St. Louis winning it in two). Trying to keep sharp, Boston played a number of big leaguers but even that backfired when Ted Williams was hit on the elbow by a practice pitch and was almost unable to play in the World Series. Manager Clint Hurdle tried to keep the Rockies sharp, but one has to wonder if they found maintaining that focus and that momentum too difficult a task.

2007 AMERICAN LEAGUE DIVISION SERIES

It was a postseason of sweeps. In the National League Division Series, the Diamondbacks swept the Cubs and the Rockies swept the Phillies. The Red Sox swept the Angels. Only the Yankees won a game—one game (Game Three) before Cleveland took Game Four. The Rockies swept the Diamondbacks in the NLCS, and—ultimately—the Red Sox in turn swept the Rockies in the World Series. But we're getting ahead of ourselves here.

Game One: Fenway Park, Boston / October 3, 2007

Boston 4, Anaheim 0

| Anaheim | 000 | 000 | 000 | — | 0 | 4 | 0 |
| Boston | 103 | 000 | 00x | — | 4 | 9 | 0 |

WP: Beckett (1-0)   LP: Lackey (0-1)   HR: Youkilis (1), Ortiz (1)

The Red Sox went into the Division Series facing a powerful Anaheim Angels team, though one that was diminished by the loss of center fielder Gary Matthews, Jr. for the postseason due to a late September knee injury and by the conjunctivitis suffered by Garret Anderson in his right eye that hampered him and forced him to leave the third game after two innings. But Boston's ace Josh Beckett (20-7, 3.27 ERA) shut them down in Game One with a 4-0 four-hit shutout at Fenway Park. The last time a Red Sox pitcher had shut out an opponent in the postseason was when Luis Tiant blanked the Cincinnati Reds 6-0 in the first game of the 1975 World Series—and he himself kicked off the six-run Red Sox rally with a single in the bottom of the seventh that was all the scoring in the ballgame. It was Beckett's third shutout in six postseason starts. During regular-season play, he had only two shutouts in 166 starts.

On the evening of October 3, 2007, the first-inning solo home run by Kevin Youkilis into the seats atop the Green Monster was all the Sox would need. Not knowing that at the time, it was good that Youk doubled his next time up, in the bottom of the third, and that David Ortiz followed him with a two-run homer into the right-field grandstand. The third run of the inning, and the last of the game, came when Manny Ramirez followed Ortiz with a walk, took second on John Lackey's wild pitch, and scored when Mike Lowell singled into center field. 4-0, Red Sox.

That was all the scoring in the game. And there wasn't all that much hitting from that point on, either. In fact, the Red Sox only had one more hit in the game, an infield hit by Drew that glanced off Lackey's glove in the sixth. Lackey was no slouch; he'd led the AL in ERA with a 3.01 record and was 19-9 in the matter of wins and losses. Against the Red Sox, though, he had an ERA of 8.38.

Beckett, whose 20 wins led the American League, had allowed Chone Figgins an infield single to second base in the first inning, but then retired the next 19 batters in a row—enough to tie for the third-longest such streak in baseball postseason history. For Beckett, who had won the final game of the 2003 World Series with a shutout of the Yankees, it was back-to-back postseason shutouts. He never did walk a batter. There were no Red Sox errors and Beckett hit no one. The Angels got one hit in the seventh (Vladimir Guerrero), one hit in the eighth (Howie Kendrick), and one hit in the top of the ninth (Guerrero again). They were all singles. No other runner reached base. Beckett threw a rarity these days: a complete game (the Sox had five complete games in 2007, no pitcher throwing more than one). He struck out eight. He couldn't have pitched a much better ballgame. After the game, Angels manager Mike Scioscia said, "Really, the story tonight is Josh Beckett."

Game Two: Fenway Park, Boston / October 5, 2007

Boston 6, Anaheim 3

Anaheim	030	000	000	—	3	7	0
Boston	200	010	003	—	6	6	1

WP: Papelbon (1-0)   LP: Speier (0-1)   HR: Ramirez (1)

Where the first game was a masterpiece from the mound, the second game provided drama on offense. Once again, the Red Sox took a lead in the bottom of the first. It was Red Sox rookie Daisuke Matsuzaka pitching against the Angels' Kelvim Escobar (18-7, 3.40 ERA in the regular season). Dice-K had started well but seemed to become fatigued as the season progressed; he finished with a mark of 15-12, 4.40 ERA. Matsuzaka had struggled in the first, walking Orlando Cabrera and getting tagged for a single by Garret Anderson, but he escaped without allowing a run. The Sox scored twice in the bottom of the first, with Youkilis once more kicking things off. This time, Youk worked a walk. Ortiz singled and he moved up a base. After Manny lined out to center field for the second out, Mike Lowell walked to load the bases, and the biggest disappointment of the season—right-fielder J. D. Drew—singled to drive in the first two runs.

Dice-K let the lead get away from him in the top of the second. He walked Kotchman and Morales singled. Kendrick struck out, but Kotchman scored from third on the second out and with back-to-back doubles Figgins drove in Morales and Cabrera drove in Figgins. The Angels had a 3-2 lead.

The Angels played aggressively, and Anderson doubled to lead off the third, but even though he kept putting men on base, Matsuzaka pitched out of trouble in the third and fourth and was finally relieved in the fifth after allowing a two-out single, a stolen base, and a wild pitch. Javier Lopez doused the fire.

The Red Sox tied the game in the bottom of the inning when Rookie of the Year Dustin Pedroia doubled to left field to lead off, ultimately scoring on Mike Lowell's bases-loaded sacrifice fly. Three more Red Sox pitchers came on in succession, each recording four outs without any one of them allowing a hit, a walk, or a run: Manny Delcarmen, Hideki Okajima, and Jonathan Papelbon.

That brought the Red Sox to the bottom of the ninth in a 3-3 tie. The Angels had received strong relief from Scot Shields (two hitless innings) and Justin Speier, who only gave up a leadoff single in the ninth to Julio Lugo, another disappointment on offense for the Red Sox.

With one productive out, Pedroia moved Lugo to second. Francisco Rodriguez came in to pitch to Youkilis and struck him out for the second out of the inning. Mike Scioscia didn't want him to face David Ortiz, though, so Rodriguez walked him intentionally to pitch to the right-handed Manny Ramirez. It was the sixth intentional walk of the game, setting a record. Right move, probably. Wrong result, definitely. On a 1-0 count, Manny homered over the Coke bottles atop the Green Monster, over everything in left field, a majestic three-run walkoff homer that traveled clear across Lansdowne Street into the night. It was the first walkoff home run of Manny's Red Sox career.

It was the ninth time the Red Sox had won a postseason game in a walkoff, and the fifth time in just the last five years. It's seemed to have become a Red Sox specialty. The list:

2003, ALDS Game Three: Boston 3, Oakland 1 (11 innings)

2004, ALDS Game Three: Boston 8, Anaheim 6 (10 innings)

2004, ALCS Game Four: Boston 6, New York Yankees 4 (12 innings)

2004, ALCS Game Five: Boston 5, New York Yankees 4 (14 innings)

2007, ALDS Game Two: Boston 6, Anaheim 3

For the first time all year, Manny talked to the press. "He's one of the greatest closers in the game and I am one of the best hitters in the game. You know, he missed his spot, and I got good timing on the ball and that's it. It feels great, man." He explained he hadn't been feeling right all year. "But I guess, you know, when you don't feel good and you still get hits, that's when you know you are a bad man."

Game Three: Angel Stadium, Anaheim / October 7, 2007

Boston 9, Anaheim 1

Boston	000	200	070	—	9	10	0
Anaheim	000	000	001	—	1	8	0

WP: Schilling (1-0)   LP: Weaver (0-1)   HR: Ortiz (2), Ramirez (2)

Curt Schilling came into the playoffs with one of the best records of any postseason pitcher in baseball history. He pitched seven full innings, allowing six hits and one walk, but only found himself in trouble one time—the bottom of the third, when the bases were loaded with two outs. He got Reggie Willits to pop up foul to Jason Varitek. Schilling had struggled in 2007, winning only nine games and losing eight, with a 3.87 ERA. Jared Weaver was pitching for the Angels; he'd just completed his sophomore season with a 13-7 (3.91) mark. With a 6.97 ERA against Boston, he'd not been a hard problem to solve for the Red Sox. He got through the first three frames well enough, but David Ortiz hit a home run to lead off the fourth and Manny Ramirez went back-to-back with a homer of his own. 2-0, Red Sox. After a cautious Weaver walked Ortiz to lead off the sixth, Scioscia brought in Scot Shields and he got them through the sixth and seventh. Curt Schilling was pitching a good game, scattering a hit here or there, but not letting in any runs. After seven innings, the score remained 2-0 for the Red Sox. If they could get through two more innings, they'd complete the sweep and advance to the League Championship Series.

Lugo walked to lead off the top of the eighth. Scioscia brought in Speier to pitch to Pedroia. Pedroia doubled and drove in Lugo, taking third base on the throw and scoring on Youk's sacrifice fly to center field. 4-0, Red Sox—the bases clear and one out. Ortiz singled, Ramirez walked, and Mike Lowell doubled. Darren Oliver relieved Speier. Drew reached on a fielder's choice, scoring Ellsbury (running for Ramirez). Varitek doubled and drove in Lowell, then Coco Crisp singled and drove in both Drew and Varitek. By the time the inning was over, it was 9-0 for the Red Sox.

Schilling could safely call it a game. Hideki Okajima pitched a scoreless eighth. Dustin Moseley threw the top of the ninth, and the Red Sox brought in Eric Gagne to close it out. The arrival of Gagne on the field prompted fear in Red Sox fans in late 2007. The former ace reliever hadn't recorded even one save for the Red Sox, and had blown several opportunities. Even with a 9-0 lead, fans were antsy. The first batter he faced, Maicer Izturis, doubled. Then Gagne threw a wild pitch and Izturis took third base. Kendrick drove him in with a sacrifice fly to right field, and the Angels had a run. When you're down to your last three outs and have to score nine runs to tie the score, though, you don't want to give away outs. Gagne struck out Haynes and retired pinch-hitter Quinlan on a fly ball to right field. Game over. It seemed all too easy.

Having been swept in 2004 and now again in 2007, the Red Sox now held a 9-0 winning streak against the Angels dating back to Game Five of the 1986 League Championship Series.

Of the eight Red Sox pitchers who faced the Angels in the three games, six of them had ERAs of 0.00. Only Matsuzaka (three) and Gagne (one) were charged an earned run. Angels pitchers weren't so fortunate. Every Red Sox starting position player had at least two hits, and Ortiz had five (batting .714). Manny had four RBIs, and Drew, Lowell, and Ortiz each had three. The Red Sox earned 16 walks; only seven Angels walked. Sox hitters hit five homers; Sox pitchers didn't give up one.

2007 AMERICAN LEAGUE CHAMPIONSHIP SERIES

Game One: Fenway Park, Boston / October 12, 2007

Boston 10, Cleveland 3

Cleveland	100	001	010	—	3	8	0
Boston	104	032	00x	—	10	12	0

WP: Beckett (1-0)   LP: Sabathia (0-1)   HR: Hafner (1)

Josh Beckett got the game ball to pitch Game One of the ALCS. He was up against Cleveland's C. C. Sabathia, who had an excellent 19-7, 3.21 record in 2007. Balloting for the Cy Young Award was done prior to the playoffs; in November, we learned that Sabathia won the 2007 award. He had the best strikeout-to-walks ratio on the league, was second in wins (to Beckett), third in won-loss percentage (also behind Beckett), and fifth in ERA. He threw more innings and faced more batters than anyone in the league and, with Fausto Carmona, provided a 1-2 pitching duo that propelled the Indians to the playoffs. He'd never been that impressive against the Red Sox, though, with a career 2-4 record and a 3.91 ERA. But this was expected to be a real pitcher's duel.

Twenty-game winner Josh Beckett out-duels Cleveland's C. C. Sabathia in Game One of the 2007 ALCS. The Red Sox won 10-3. (Boston Red Sox)

Beckett was going to be facing a strong Indians lineup who'd handled the Yankees in the Division Series with relative ease. He had suffered from the gopher ball in 2006, giving up 36 homers, but had cut that back to 17 in 2007. After striking out the first two Indians, Travis Hafner guessed right and hit a 96-mph fastball into the Cleveland bullpen to give Cleveland a quick 1-0 lead. Beckett then struck out Victor Martinez to close out the top of the first. Red Sox leadoff batter Dustin Pedroia lined out right to Sabathia, but then Youkilis, Ortiz, and Ramirez all singled and tied the score. Lowell grounded into a double play to end the inning.

Beckett retired the side in order in the second, third, and fourth. Sabathia did in the second, but in the third he was hammered for four runs. Lugo led off with a double. Playing for one run, Pedroia sacrificed him to third. Youk walked and Big Papi was hit by a pitch. The bases were loaded and Sabathia was looking shaky. He got ahead 0-2 on Manny Ramirez, but walked him on four consecutive pitches—all sliders, and a couple of them that bounced on their way to the plate, granting Manny an easy RBI. Mike Lowell doubled to right field, driving in two more. Bobby Kielty was walked intentionally to re-load the bases. Varitek grounded softly to third base, but there was no chance at the double play and Ramirez scored. Crisp grounded out. With a 5-1 lead, the Sox were sitting pretty.

The first batter up in the fifth, Ortiz reached base for the third time in the game. Manny singled and Lowell walked. With the bases loaded and nobody out, Kielty singled to right field driving in two runs. He took second on the throw in. Kielty was in the game because Terry Francona saw his 9-for-29 history hitting against Sabathia. It paid off; Kielty drove C. C. from the mound. Manager Eric Wedge decided he'd seen enough of his starter and asked rookie Jensen Lewis to close out the inning. He did, but not before Jason Varitek doubled to right-center field to drive in Kielty. 8-1, Red Sox. Sabathia had pitched 4 ⅓ innings, walked five, hit a batter, and given up eight earned runs on seven hits.

Beckett gave up two hits and one run in the top of the sixth, Casey Blake doubling into the left-field corner and scoring on Asdrubal Cabrera's single. With Lewis back on the mound for Cleveland, Pedroia and Youkilis both singled to right field. Wedge turned to Aaron Fultz, who walked Ortiz and then (with the bases loaded) walked Ramirez. It was the second time in the game that Manny had picked up an RBI by walking with the sacks full. Between him and Papi, the two reached base ten times in the game. It was the exact opposite of the 1995 Division Series, in which Mo Vaughn was 0-for-14 and Jose Canseco was 0-for-13. Wedge brought in his third pitcher of the inning, Tom Mastny. Lowell's sacrifice fly scored Youkilis, but Mastny did retire all three batters he faced. 10-2, Red Sox.

The Indians scored one more run, off Javier Lopez who pitched the eighth. Blake doubled again, and Cabrera brought him in, this time with a sacrifice fly. Beckett left after six, with the game well in hand, and Timlin, Lopez, and Gagne each pitched one inning. Gagne managed to both load the bases in the ninth, and strike out the side. A master of understatement, Eric Wedge talked about his starting pitcher: "C. C. didn't have it tonight." Sox fans were feeling great; they didn't know what was going to unfold over the next three games.

Game Two: Fenway Park, Boston / October 13, 2007

Cleveland 13, Boston 6

Cleveland	100	311	000	07	—	13	17	0
Boston	003	030	000	00	—	6	10	0

WP: Mastny (1-0)   LP: Gagne (0-1)   HR: Sizemore (1), Peralta (1), Gutierrez (1), Ramirez (1), Lowell (1)

The second game featured Curt Schilling against Fausto Carmona. Neither pitcher made it through five. In just his second year in the majors, Carmona registered a 19-8 record with a 3.06 ERA, second best in the League just as his 19 wins (tying him with Sabathia, Lackey, and Wang) placed him second behind Beckett. The Indians wasted little time putting a run on the board. Leadoff hitter Grady Sizemore hit the fifth pitch of the game to center field for a two-base hit. Schilling got the next two batters, but then Victor Martinez doubled in Sizemore. Ryan Garko grounded out.

Carmona walked two Sox in the bottom of the first, but escaped damage.

The mighty Dustin Pedroia swings for the fences in the 13-6 Game Two ALCS loss to Cleveland. (Boston Red Sox)

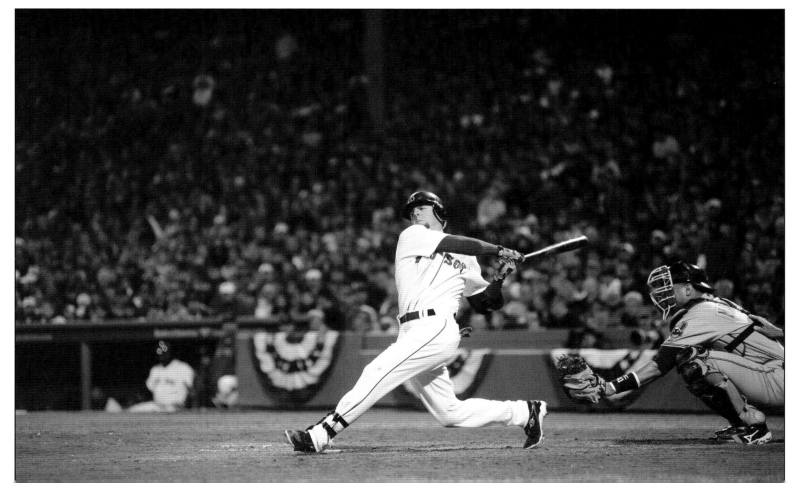

Schilling handled the Tribe in the second and third, and then saw the Sox take the lead in the bottom of the third. Crisp singled and stole second. Pedroia walked but his at-bat was flanked by strikeouts of Lugo and Youkilis. Ortiz singled, to the pitcher. It was the 10th plate appearance in a row that Ortiz had reached safely, tying Billy Hatcher (1990) for the postseason record. With the bases loaded, Manny Ramirez—for the third time in two games—walked to force in a run. And Mike Lowell singled, driving in both Pedroia and Ortiz. It was 3-1, Red Sox. At this point in the game, Ortiz now sported an amazing .900 on-base percentage in the 2007 playoffs (18-for-20).

Schilling couldn't hold the lead. After getting Hafner to fly out, Martinez singled, Garko singled, and Jhonny Peralta hit a three-run homer. The Indians tagged on another run when Sizemore homered in the top of the fifth. After back-to-back singles, Sox manager Francona pulled Schilling. He'd given up five earned runs in 4 ⅔ innings. Manny Delcarmen got Garko to hit into a force play to end the inning. The Indians held a 5-3 lead, but the Red Sox leapfrogged over that in the bottom of the inning, taking Schill off the hook. After Youkilis singled, Wedge quickly replaced Carmona— the second of his two aces had failed to make it through the fifth. Rafael Perez ended Ortiz's streak by getting him to ground out; Cabrera fielded the ball at second and threw out Youk trying to take third on the play. But then Manny Ramirez hit a two-run homer into the Red Sox bullpen. It was the 23rd postseason home run for Ramirez, putting him in first place all-time. Bernie Williams had hit 22. Mike Lowell followed with a home run of his own, to give the Red Sox a 6-5 lead.

That's when the Red Sox stopped scoring. The Indians paraded Lewis, Betancourt, Mastny, and Borowski to the mound and they gave up just three hits in 6 ⅔ innings. The Red Sox pitchers didn't do as well. Delcarmen let Cleveland tie it in the top of the sixth on a walk to Peralta, a single by Lofton (Peralta took third), and a grounder that brought Peralta home. Okajima came in, got one out, but then loaded the bases before getting the third out.

Oki retired the side in the seventh, and Timlin retired the side in the eighth. It wasn't easy, but Papelbon got through the ninth. The game went into extra innings, though Pedroia's single and Ellsbury's stolen base (running for Pedroia) had the Sox set up for a win in the bottom of the ninth. It wasn't to be. After battling Betancourt for ten pitches, Youkilis flied out to center field on the 11th one and ended the inning. Nothing happened in the 10th, but a lot of things happened in the top of the 11th—the Indians blew the game wide open.

Given how poorly he'd pitched in his limited time with the Red Sox, there was a feeling the game was over when Eric Gagne took over for Papelbon. He lasted one-third of an inning, striking out Blake, the first man up. Sizemore singled and Cabrera walked, and when Trot Nixon came up to bat for Josh Barfield, Francona replaced Gagne with Javier Lopez. Nixon—who'd played for the Red Sox from 1996 through 2006—singled to right field, driving in Sizemore with the go-ahead run. A wild pitch let Cabrera score. The Sox walked Martinez on purpose, but Garko singled. Only one run came in. Jon Lester was asked to pitch for Lopez, but Peralta doubled off him and, after getting the second out, right-fielder Franklin Gutierrez hit a three-run home run. Blake struck out, his second strikeout in the inning, which might have been nice but for the fact that the Indians had scored seven runs, taken a 13-6 lead, and set a record for the most runs scored in an extra inning in the postseason.

As Michael Silverman pointed out in his *Boston Herald* column, the first trio of Red Sox relievers had performed well, allowing just one run in 5 ⅓ innings of work, while the second trio managed to "triple-handedly convert a 6-6 game into a 13-6 Indians victory." Schilling was down on himself, saying after the game, "This was all about me coming up small in a big game." But the Red Sox had plenty of chances to score in later innings and did not.

Though Drew and Crisp both singled in the bottom of the 11th, Varitek struck out in between them and Lugo hit into a game-ending double play. The Series was even and both teams decamped for Cleveland to play three games at Jacobs Field.

Game Three: Jacobs Field, Cleveland / October 15, 2007

Cleveland 4, Boston 2

Boston	000	000	200	—	2	7	0
Cleveland	020	020	00x	—	4	6	1

WP: Westbrook (1-0)   LP: Matsuzaka (0-1)   SV: Borowski (1)   HR: Varitek (1), Lofton (1)

Cleveland's Jake Westbrook had the unenviable task of trying to stop the Red Sox, where both aces (Sabathia and Carmona) had failed—but at least he wasn't being asked to bail the Tribe out of an 0-2 deficit. Westbrook hadn't pitched well in the regular season, with a losing record (6-9) and a decent but not spectacular ERA (4.32). He was an even 62-62 after 155 starts spread over eight seasons. The Red Sox gave Matsuzaka the ball again.

Westbrook got Pedroia, but then walked Youk. The Indians put on the Ortiz shift and it worked to perfection as Papi hit into a double play that was remarkable in that it was a 4-5-3 double play, with third baseman Blake being the pivot man at second base due to the extreme shift. Matsuzaka induced a groundout, and struck out two. Westbrook saw the bases full of Red Sox and nobody out, after a single, a walk, and an error, but a shallow fly to left field and a double play squelched the rally. The Indians then scored twice. Garko singled and—first-pitch hitting, Kenny Lofton banged a two-out, two-run homer off Dice-K, a ball that just reached the right-field seats over Drew's leap. "It really got us kick-started," enthused Eric Wedge after the game.

Again, in the top of the fourth, the Red Sox seemed poised to score when Ortiz doubled to left field. Manny Ramirez hit the ball sharply to left—but Ortiz was too far off the bag toward third, was hit by the ball, and was retired. Westbrook was often ahead in the count and that served him well, as did his ability to keep the ball down. Red Sox batters were by no means as patient as they had been in Game One. Two groundouts ended the inning, and three more groundouts comprised the Red Sox fifth. In his first trip to the postseason, Matsuzaka, for the second time, didn't make it through the bottom of the fifth. After striking out Nixon, Blake singled. A wild pitch allowed him to scamper to second, and contributed toward the walk served to Sizemore. Cabrera singled, scoring Blake and moving Sizemore to third. Hafner's groundout to second base brought in Sizemore. It was 4-0 for the Indians when Victor Martinez singled on Dice-K's 101st pitch, and Francona walked out to the mound. Mike Timlin took over.

Timlin struck out two and got two groundouts from the four Indians he faced. The Red Sox collected two runs when Varitek homered, driving in Drew ahead of him. Drew had singled. When Lugo singled, Wedge replaced Westbrook with Lewis. The score was 4-2 and held through the end of the game. Lewis, Betancourt, and Borowski retired the seven batters they faced in mopping up, and between Timlin, Okajima, and Delcarmen, the most they allowed was one eighth-inning walk. The bullpens had done the job. For the second postseason start in a row, Dice-K had not. This time he bore the loss.

With the Red Sox down two games to one in the Series, the *Boston Globe*'s Nick Cafardo wrote, "It's fair to say the Sox look shaky after last night's 4-2 loss. It's also fair to say the Indians seem to have them a little wobbly, not quite staggering, but wobbly."

In the meantime, the Colorado Rockies wrapped up the National League Championship Series, continuing their magical season by sweeping the NLCS from the Diamondbacks, just as they had swept the NLDS from the Phillies.

Game Four: Jacobs Field, Cleveland / October 16, 2007

Cleveland 7, Boston 3

Boston	000	003	000	—	3	8	1
Cleveland	000	070	00x	—	7	9	0

WP: Byrd (1-0)   LP: Wakefield (0-1)   HR: Youkilis (1), Ortiz (1), Ramirez (2), Peralta (2), Blake (1)

Paul Byrd was next up for the Indians. Their fourth starter had been in the majors since 1995 and had enjoyed his best year yet with the Indians in 2007. He was 15-8, with a 4.59 ERA. Several days after his Game Four start, the *San Francisco Chronicle* broke the story that he had spent $24,850 on more than 1,000 vials of HGH and hundreds of syringes from 2002 to 2005. The report had no bearing on the game. And he pitched well enough to add another win to his postseason record; he'd beaten the Yankees in Game Four of the Division Series. The Red Sox started veteran knuckleballer Tim Wakefield, second on the team in wins with a 17-12 record and a 4.76 ERA.

The first half of the game was scoreless. Byrd allowed four hits in the first five innings, but the Sox couldn't score. Wakefield only allowed one hit, a fourth-inning double by Peralta. He walked two, but he looked good to the halfway point. Then came the bottom of the fifth. Those seven-run innings'll kill you every time.

Wakefield was facing the bottom of the order. On the second pitch, Casey Blake launched a home run to left. Franklin Gutierrez singled, also to left, and then Wake hit Kelly Shoppach with this first pitch. After Sizemore's grounder forced Shoppach at second, Cabrera singled off Wakefield's glove to drive in the second run of the inning. Hafner struck out. Victor Martinez singled and drove in Sizemore. Francona pulled Wakefield. Manny Delcarmen, in relief, faced Jhonny Peralta, who hit a three-run homer to make it 6-0. "Just one bad pitch," said Delcarmen, "It was supposed to be low and away." Kenny Lofton added a seventh run with a single and a stolen base, scoring on Blake's single.

Indians fans were euphoric, waving thousands of towels reading "It's Tribe Time Now." And so it seemed. The inning was a disaster for the Red Sox. They were losing 7-0, with just 12 outs standing between them and being down three games to one in the Series. The Indians last won a World Series in 1948. Given the Red Sox win in 2004 and the White Sox win in 2005, only the Cubs had been waiting longer than the Indians.

The Sox struck back quickly and put a big dent in Cleveland's lead. Youkilis homered to left, Ortiz homered to right, and (after Lewis replaced Byrd) Ramirez homered to center. It was the first back-to-back-to-back in LCS history, and shaved three runs off the Indians' lead. But Lewis gave up just one more hit in two innings of work, and Betancourt gave up none. The game ended 7-3 and, indeed, the Red Sox were down three games to one.

It felt a bit like 2004 all over again—the Red Sox had swept the ALDS but now were facing elimination in the ALCS and would have to win three games in a row to advance to the World Series. Of course, they'd been there before—twice, both in 1986 and again in 2004—and come through both times. All told, though, only ten of the 65 teams who'd found themselves down three games to one had triumphed in a best-of-seven series.

And if anyone embodied looseness, it was Manny Ramirez. In the postseason, he suddenly started talking to the media for the first time all year. And he mystified diehard Red Sox fans after Game Four by saying, "We're just going to go have fun and play the game. That's it. If we play hard and the thing doesn't come like it's supposed to come, we'll move on. It doesn't happen, so who cares? There's always next year. It's not like the end of the world or something." For fans who live and die with the Red Sox, those were hard sentiments to grasp. But maybe it's all about keeping loose.

Game Five: Jacobs Field, Cleveland / October 18, 2007

Boston 7, Cleveland 1

Boston	101	000	230	—	7	12	1
Cleveland	100	000	000	—	1	6	1

WP: Beckett (2-0)   LP: Sabathia (0-2)   HR: Youkilis (2)

"You're dangerous when you have nothing to lose," philosophized Kevin Youkilis after the game. Reiterating the mantra from 2004, all the Red Sox had to do was win one game. And they had Josh Beckett on his regular rest. Schilling, Matsuzaka, and Wakefield combined for a 9.00 ERA in their three starts. The Sox needed a stopper.

They also needed some offense, but were facing Sabathia again. With one out in the top of the first, Youkilis homered over the left-field seats and onto the plaza. In each of the first four games, the Indians had scored first. Now the tables were turned. Sabathia struck out Ortiz, but Manny doubled and Mike Lowell singled. Unfortunately, third-base coach DeMarlo Hale sent Manny home and he was easily thrown out at the plate. Beckett was hit in the first inning, too, giving up a leadoff double to Sizemore, a bloop hit to the shortstop position, and Cabrera singled. Sizemore scored on Hafner's double play, but this early in the game, that was a good tradeoff. Martinez singled, and Sox fans were worried. It was 1-1, but Beckett had given up three hits in the first inning. If he couldn't stop the Indians, it really would be Tribe time.

Though he hit Varitek with a pitch during the inning, Sabathia struck out Kielty and Crisp and got Lugo to fly out. Beckett pitched in parallel, walking Gutierrez but striking out two and getting Lofton to ground back to the mound. Pedroia singled off Sabathia in the third, but was erased when Youk hit a ball back to the pitcher, who converted it into a double play. Ortiz walked, but then Manny hit a long drive that hit off the yellow line on the very top of the wall in right field. He thought it was a home run, admired it, and trotted to first—where he had to stay when the umpires (correctly) ruled it as not having left the park. Ortiz did run it out, and scored on the play. Manny didn't know it yet, but he had hit the game-winning drive. Beckett retired the top of the Indians order 1-2-3 with a K, a 4-3 grounder, and another K.

Both Kielty and Varitek singled to lead off the fourth, and Sabathia was looking vulnerable again but recovered by striking out Crisp for the second time and getting Lugo to hit into a DP. Three Indians grounded out.

The fifth inning was full of activity but devoid of runs. With two outs, Wedge moved to the Ortiz shift—and Papi hit the ball right between second and third for a single. Then Sabathia threw a wild pitch and walked Ramirez. He hit Lowell with a pitch to load the bases, but Kielty flied out to right field. It remained 2-1, Red Sox. When Lofton seemed to assume he'd walked on a 3-0 pitch that was called a strike, he'd flipped his bat and started to head to first. Beckett barked something and Lofton lifted a fly ball to left for the first out. He took offense at whatever Beckett had said, and decided to visit Beckett on the mound. The benches and bullpens emptied but nothing untoward occurred. Gutierrez struck out, but then Blake singled and Sizemore hit a high chopper that bounced over Beckett and ticked off Lugo's glove as Lugo ranged to the right-field side of second base. That moved Blake to third. Beckett struck out Asdrubal Cabrera on three pitches.

Both sides went down in order in the sixth. It had been a decent pitcher's battle, though neither were razor sharp. Starting off the seventh, Sabathia had evidently tired. Pedroia doubled and Youkilis tripled (off Sizemore's glove) to almost the precise same spot in right-center, and Betancourt replaced Sabathia, who saw the fourth Boston run come in thanks to an Ortiz sacrifice fly to left field. Betancourt retired the three men he faced. Beckett's error let Lofton reach base, but that was the action in the Indians' seventh.

The Red Sox put the game out of sight in the eighth. Rafael Perez came in to pitch. He walked Drew, got Tek to fly out to right, and then committed an error himself, allowing Crisp to reach safely. Julio Lugo bunted for a base hit, loading the bases. Wedge had Tom Mastny relieve. A passed ball charged to Victor Martinez made it 5-1 Red Sox, as Drew scored. The other two runners moved up so Mastny pitched around Pedroia and wound up walking him. But then he walked Youkilis, too, and everyone watched Crisp trot home as Youk collected his third RBI of the game. Ortiz hit another sacrifice fly, bringing the score to 7-1. Ramirez struck out.

Beckett retired the side in the bottom of the eighth. Drew, who'd taken over for Kielty in right after Sabathia left the game, doubled in the top of the ninth, and some fans began to notice that the major offensive disappointment of the season was coming through in the play-offs. Drew had driven in three runs in the ALDS and, while he still hadn't driven in a run in the ALCS, he was 5-for-16.

Jonathan Papelbon, who hadn't pitched for five days, needed a bit of work and Beckett had more than done his job. Pap threw the ninth and gave up a double to Garko and a walk to Lofton, but got out of it and Beckett got a win, his third of the postseason. He'd given up just two hits after the first inning, struck out 11 in the game while only walking one, and had indeed stopped the Indians.

The Tribe had a cushion. They were still up three games to two, but the Red Sox had new life. All they had to do was win one more game and the Series would be tied. They felt good as they took the flight back to Fenway. "There's no pressure here," Manny declared, "We've got confidence."

Game Six: Fenway Park, Boston / October 20, 2007

Boston 12, Cleveland 2

Cleveland	010	000	100	—	2	6	2
Boston	406	000	02x	—	12	13	0

WP: Schilling (1-0)   LP: Carmona (0-1)   HR: Martinez (1), Drew (1)

It was a rematch of Schilling vs. Carmona just as in Game Two, where neither of them made it through five. This time the two pitchers went in opposite directions, and the difference gave the Red Sox momentum. Schilling had been back in Boston and watched Beckett's masterful win on television. He sent out an email after the game, as he is wont to do, telling the *Globe*'s Gordon Edes, "It's very cut and dry. I either clutch up and do what they pay me to do or we go home, pretty simple really." On the offday, he admitted to an element of fear: "There's always fear. I'm scared to death to go out and fail tomorrow. I'm terrified of letting my teammates down and the fan base down and this organization down because they're counting on me to survive, and to get past another day. I'm scared to death to not do well tomorrow. But I'm also very cognizant of the fact that fear is something that had always driven me and always pushed me."

Five times the Red Sox had come into a playoff series down three games to two. Every one of the five times, the Sox evened the series with a win. Could they do it a sixth time?

Schill shut down Cleveland in the first with two grounders and a strikeout. Carmona, that was another story. The key to hitting Carmona, batting coach Dave Magadan told the Red Sox, was patience. Don't be fooled by his sinker. Often as not, it goes for a ball—unless you swing at it and miss or hit it on the ground. Sox batters made him throw 36 pitches in the first inning alone— one of them a very big pitch. Pedroia singled and Youkilis singled—both of them infield hits. Ortiz walked and the bases were loaded with nobody out, but there hadn't been a big hit yet. Ramirez struck out. Lowell flied to shallow right field, and Pedroia had to hold on third. The Fenway faithful were feeling deflated, but those who hadn't yet noticed the rebirth of J. D. Drew woke up with a start on the fifth pitch of his at-bat when he banged a line drive to straightaway center field that just barely cleared the wall into the television camera position. It was a grand slam. It was 4-0. Carmona walked Varitek, but Jacoby Ellsbury—making his first start in the postseason, in place of the punchless Coco Crisp—grounded out back to Carmona.

Drew's grand slam was only the third one hit by the Red Sox in postseason play. Troy O'Leary had hit one against these same Indians in October 1999 and Johnny Damon had hit one against the Yankees in 2004.

Victor Martinez hit a towering home run off Schilling right down the right-field line to start the second, and it was 4-1, but Schilling settled down. Pedroia doubled and Youkilis singled but the Ortiz shift paid off and he hit into an inning-ending double play. Nixon and Blake both singled, but the next three men went down in the top of the third. In the bottom of the inning, the Red Sox put the game away. Carmona walked Ramirez and walked Lowell and then Drew got his fifth RBI of the game, singling to center to score Manny. That was enough. Carmona was told to take the rest of the day off and Rafael Perez relieved. He got Tek to fly out to center, but deep enough that Lowell tagged at second and took third base. Ellsbury singled and drove in Lowell. Then Lugo—the other offensive disappointment during the season—doubled over third base and into the left-field corner and drove in two more. Youkilis singled off the Wall and two more runs scored, the second one coming in on a bizarre play. Youk had been too aggressive and was caught in between first and second. Cabrera, the second baseman, threw to Garko at first—while keeping his eye on Pedroia ranging off third base. The ball hit Youk in the helmet and went astray, and Pedroia easily scored, though Youkilis stayed on first. It was time to give another pitcher a try; Aaron Laffey got the call.

Ortiz grounded out to first base and Garko stepped on the bag for the out, then threw to second to get Youkilis but he bounced the ball and it went out into center field. Nothing came of it, though. Manny walked (for the second time in the inning), but Lowell flied out. The score, however, was 10-1.

Things settled down in the middle innings. Two Indians singled off Schilling. Laffey retired nine in a row, gave up a single to Lowell in the sixth, but then struck out Drew.

Garko hit a three-bagger to lead off the seventh inning, and scored on Peralta's sacrifice fly. Laffey put down all three Sox in the seventh.

Javier Lopez came in from the bullpen and got his three guys in the top of the eighth. The Red Sox scored two more times after Joe Borowski took over from Laffey. It started with a walk to Youk and a double by Papi. The first run scored on a Ramirez sacrifice fly. Lowell singled and drove in the pinch-running Eric Hinske. Drew singled and Varitek walked, and Ellsbury was up with the bases loaded. He hit a shot, but right to Peralta at short.

Eric Gagne was asked to close out the game, pitching the ninth. And, unusual for him in 2007, he did. A fly ball and a couple of grounders and the Series was tied, three games apiece.

Schilling got the win. He was now 4-0 in elimination games. Carmona joined Sabathia wondering what had gone wrong. The two Indians aces had started four games in the ALCS, Sabathia with 12 earned runs in 10 ⅓ innings (10.45 ERA) and Carmona with 11 earned runs in six innings of work for a 16.50 ERA.

The Red Sox, for the third time in five years, had pushed the League Championship Series to a seventh game. It was the third time the Sox had come back from being down three games to one in the postseason. Boston was abuzz, knowing the first pitches of Game Seven were to be thrown by the $103 million man, Daisuke Matsuzaka, the Japanese pitcher who'd excelled in pressure situations in his homeland but had seemed to lose his spark as the year wore on in 2007.

Game Seven: Fenway Park, Boston / October 21, 2007

Boston 11, Cleveland 2

Cleveland	000 110 000	—	2	10	1
Boston	111 000 26x	—	11	15	1

WP: Matsuzaka (1-1)   LP: Westbrook (1-1)   SV: Papelbon (1)   HR: Pedroia (1), Youkilis (3)

The Red Sox had paid $51 million as a "posting fee" just for the exclusive right to negotiate with Matsuzaka. The negotiations resulted in a long-term contract, but one that cost them another $52 million in guaranteed money. Despite two tough losses in April, he pitched well early and was 7-2 after beating the Rangers on May 25. His ERA went up, then down, then up again. He'd lost five of his last eight decisions and seemed to be struggling as the longer American season wore on, and as he typically pitched with one less day of rest throughout. He hadn't made it through the fifth in either of his two postseason starts, and was 0-1, only because he'd been rescued in Game Two of the ALDS when the Sox came from behind to tie. He was facing Jake Westbrook, who'd handled the Red Sox well in Game Three of the LCS, and earned the 4-2 win. The Indians had won three in a row. Now could the Red Sox do the same, and take it to the next level?

A bit bizarrely, a member of the Baltimore Orioles threw out the first pitch and there was no question which AL team he was rooting for: it was Kevin Millar, from the 2004 Red Sox. Bill Mueller of the '04 Sox had thrown out the first pitch before Game Six, but at least Mueller was in the other league and no longer a player.

Dice-K set down the Indians in order in the first with a pop-up to second, a groundout to second, and a strikeout. Westbrook let Pedroia single to left and let Youkilis single to left. He struck out Ortiz, though. A hard-hit but seemingly tailor-made double play ball took a freak bounce and shot over the shortstop's head. Ramirez was safe on first and Pedroia scored from second. Lowell singled, and loaded the bases, but Drew couldn't cash in as he had the night before. He hit into a double play. Nonetheless, all was forgiven after Game Six.

Matsuzaka continued in the second and third, allowing just a single (and subsequent wild pitch) in the third. Varitek doubled to lead off the Red Sox second. Ellsbury singled him to third.

Lugo hit into a double play, but Tek came in the back door. 2-0, Red Sox. Youkilis doubled to lead off the Red Sox third, took third on a grounder, and (after Ramirez was walked intentionally) scored on Lowell's sacrifice fly. Three innings, one run in each, and the Red Sox led 3-0.

Alternating outs and doubles resulted in the Indians getting one run in the top of the fourth; Hafner hit the first one and Garko's drove him in. The Red Sox singled twice but couldn't score. The Indians added their second run in the top of the fifth, even though Kenny Lofton was thrown out at second trying to stretch his leadoff single into two bases. Gutierrez singled, Blake singled (Gutierrez taking third), and Sizemore's sacrifice fly narrowed the score to 3-2. The three singles in a row left Sox fans worried whether Dice-K was going to blow the lead. The 2-3-4 batters for the Red Sox were up, but Westbrook struck out Youk and Manny, with Ortiz grounding out in between the K's.

Pitching coach John Farrell and manager Francona were also unsure about Matsuzaka, so they brought in Hideki Okajima to pitch. The sixth was easy for Oki. Westbrook mowed down three more Red Sox.

In the seventh, Peralta flied out, but Lofton reached on an error. Franklin Gutierrez singled, over the third-base bag; the ball caromed off the short wall into left. Taking no chances, Indians

Battery-mates Jason Varitek and Jonathan Papelbon celebrate after the final out in Game Seven of the ALCS. The Red Sox blew out the Indians 11-2. (Boston Red Sox)

third-base coach Joel Skinner held up Lofton at third, though it seemed he might have scored the tying run. Blake grounded into a 5-4-3 double play.

Hoping to keep it a one-run game, Rafael Betancourt came in. He'd already appeared in six postseason games for the Indians and could boast a 0.00 ERA. Blake committed an error on Ellsbury's ball, allowing him to reach second base. Lugo sacrificed, bunting Ellsbury over to third, but the Red Sox got two runs out of the inning when Pedroia homered into the Green Monster seats—making the score 5-2 and allowing the Fenway faithful to breathe a little more freely.

Okajima gave up back-to-back singles to Sizemore and Cabrera in the top of the eighth. Even with the extra insurance runs, a Travis Hafner homer would tie the game. Jonathan Papelbon was well-rested. Since the Division Series began back on October 3, he'd only appeared in three games for a total of 4 ⅓ innings. To ask him to get the Red Sox into the World Series by throwing two full innings was not to ask too much. He struck out Hafner, and induced Martinez to ground out to second base, forcing Cabrera when Pedroia threw to Lugo. And he got Garko to fly out to center field.

Then all the Red Sox did was take a little batting practice, teeing off on Betancourt and Lewis for six runs on five hits. Ramirez popped up to second base, but then Lowell doubled, Drew drove him in with a single, and Varitek doubled. Drew held at third. Ellsbury was walked. Bases loaded. One out. Lugo struck out. But Pedroia doubled, clearing the bases, and scored himself when Youkilis homered off the Coke bottles high above the left-field Wall. It was 11-2, Red Sox.

Though Peralta found Papelbon for a single, Lofton and Gutierrez both made outs. That brought up Blake, who drove a ball into the triangle in center. Even with a six-run lead, Coco Crisp—who'd taken over defensively in center while Ellsbury took Manny's place in left—went all out. He caught the ball, slammed into the bullpen wall, and held on. The game was over. Down three games to one, Boston had to win three in a row to survive—and scored 30 runs to Cleveland's five. The Red Sox were headed to the World Series, and while the Red Sox celebrated in the infield, Crisp picked himself up and limped in to join the celebration.

THE WORLD SERIES

Game One: Fenway Park, Boston / October 24, 2007

Boston 13, Colorado 1

Colorado	010	000	000	—	1	6	0
Boston	310	270	00x	—	13	17	0

WP: Beckett (1-0)   LP: Francis (0-1)   HR: Pedroia (1)

Despite fighting through seven games, the Red Sox had their rotation lined up the way they wanted it. Josh Beckett was the man the Red Sox asked to tame the heretofore rampaging but now well-rested Rockies. The MVP of the ALCS was already 3-0 in the postseason with a cumulative 1.17 ERA. The Rockies had more than enough time to lead with their ace, too. Jeff Francis was in his fourth year in baseball, a 2002 first-round draft pick for the Rockies. He was coming off a 17-9, 4.22 season and was 2-0 with an ERA of 2.13 in postseason play.

Beckett was loaded for bear, maybe wanting a little payback after being hammered by the Rockies in June for six runs in just five innings. Beckett struck out the side in the top of the first in 15 pitches. Francis threw one pitch to Dustin Pedroia, then another—and the Red Sox rookie hit a home run in his first World Series at-bat, just over the Wall in left-center field and into the Monster seats. Next up, Kevin Youkilis, who hit a solid double to right field. David Ortiz grounded out, but advanced Youk to third. Manny Ramirez singled into left field and Youk scored. 2-0, Red Sox. After Lowell flied out, Varitek singled and Manny took second. He scored when Drew doubled to right field. The Red Sox led 3-0.

Using a blazing fastball and an assortment of curves and changeups, Beckett went six strong innings in Game One of the ALCS, allowing four hits and two runs, including a first-inning homer to Travis Hafner. He didn't allow another hit until the fifth inning. (Boston Red Sox)

The Rockies laid down a marker, getting a quick run of their own in the top of the second. Beckett struck out his fourth in a row in Todd Helton, but then third baseman Garrett Atkins doubled. Atkins had hit a grand slam off Beckett in that June ballgame. Beckett rebounded, getting his fifth strikeout victim in Brad Hawpe. But Colorado's star rookie, Troy Tulowitzki doubled to center and drove in Atkins. The Rockies' sixth out was a grounder, Lugo to Youkilis. And the Red Sox took back the run right away; after two out, Youkilis walked and Ortiz doubled him in. After two innings, it was 4-1 in Boston's favor.

Neither party scored in the third, though Helton doubled in the top of the fourth. The Sox added two more runs, again after two outs. Ortiz singled and Ramirez doubled, Ortiz holding at third. Mike Lowell was walked intentionally so Francis could take his chances with Varitek. Tek hit a ground-rule double that bounced into the left-field stands, scoring Ortiz and Ramirez.

And then the Red Sox went nuts, scoring seven more runs in the bottom of the fifth. Francis was gone by now, replaced after four full by fellow left-hander Franklin Morales. Julio Lugo singled to lead off, but was forced at second when Ellsbury's bunt was fielded cleanly and quickly. Pedroia popped up to second base. Once again it didn't look like anything was happening. Two outs and a man on first. Ellsbury strolled to second, though, on a balk. Then Youkilis lined a double into left and Ellsbury scored. Ortiz lined a double to center and Youkilis scored. Ramirez lined a single to left and Ortiz scored. Lowell doubled, too, but Manny had to stop at third. Varitek walked on five pitches. With the bases loaded, Drew hit an infield single and everyone moved up one base. Clint Hurdle had seen enough of Morales, and waved in Ryan Speier.

With the bases loaded, Speier didn't give up a hit. What he did, though, is throw 16 pitches, 12 of which missed the strike zone. He walked Lugo, driving in Lowell. He walked Ellsbury, driving in Varitek. He walked Pedroia, driving in Drew. And he walked off the mound and into the visitors dugout after Hurdle came out to get him. All three inherited runs had scored; Morales had faced nine batters in two-thirds of an inning and was charged with seven earned runs. Speier had faced just three batters—all with the bases loaded—and walked every one of them. Patient Red Sox batters had now walked in seven runs in the '07 postseason.

It was 13-1, Red Sox, and still just the fifth inning. Eleven runs had scored after there were two outs. Matt Herges came on and got Youkilis to fly out to right. Unsurprisingly, walking in three runs in a row was a first in World Series play.

Beckett gave up two singles in the sixth, but the first one was erased by a double play and the second one was followed by a fly ball to Drew in right. Herges retired the Red Sox in order in the sixth. Jeremy Affeldt and LaTroy Hawkins both got in an inning of work for the Rockies, with just a single by Lugo. Beckett pitched through the seventh; Tulowitzki doubled but didn't get past third base. Timlin pitched a perfect eighth and Eric Gagne—as he'd done in Game Six against Cleveland—again threw a perfect inning in the ninth.

They couldn't all be this easy, could they? Colorado's winning streak had ended. "That's not the way we drew it up," Hurdle admitted.

Beckett had come through once more, and he was now 4-0 in the 2007 playoffs—and sure to be rested for Game Five, should the Series run that long. Beckett was now 7-2 lifetime in postseason play, with an ERA of 1.75 and a 35-2 strikeout to walks ratio.

The eight doubles the Red Sox hit tied the record for the most doubles in any World Series game, a record that had stood since 1925. The 12-run margin was the largest in any World Series opener. "We definitely had a lot of momentum going," said Kevin Youkilis. "I think those last three games against the Indians, we were rolling on all cylinders." Youk hit .500 with seven RBIs in the ALCS. In the first game of the World Series, he hit two doubles and walked once and scored all three times. Scoring 13 times on 17 hits was all fine and well, but as Mike Lowell observed, looking ahead to Game Two, "It'll be 0-0 in the first inning."

PLAYER PROFILE: JOSH BECKETT

Beckett was the second pick overall in the June 1999 free-agent draft, selected by the Florida Marlins. In 2001, he was named Minor League Player of the Year by both *The Sporting News* and *Baseball America*. By September that year, he was in the majors and throwing well. Increasing his workload each year, he built up a record of 17-17 over his first three seasons but truly shone in the 2003 World Series against the Yankees. He was dealt a hardluck loss in Game Three, despite giving up just three hits and two runs in 7 ⅓ innings, but won the final Game Six with a five-hit complete game shutout in Yankee Stadium. That gave him a Series ERA of 1.10, and the Most Valuable Player Award.

The Marlins became a mediocre team right afterward and Beckett's next season was 9-9, but in 2005 he put together a 15-8 campaign, with a 3.38 ERA. The Red Sox came calling, swinging a big deal with the Marlins to send a package of four prospects that included Hanley Ramirez and Anibal Sanchez in a seven-player swap which also netted the Sox one Mike Lowell. Beckett pitched well for the Red Sox in 2006, though struggling with the gopher ball. In 2007, he put it all together and was the only 20-game winner in the league, 20-7 with a 3.27 ERA. He was also named the MVP in the crucial League Championship Series, winning two games while only allowing nine hits and three runs in the two games combined. In Game One, Beckett held the Rockies to one run while the Red Sox rolled up 13. It wasn't even close; Rockies pitchers walked eight Red Sox, while Beckett struck out nine and only permitted one walk.

Game Two: Fenway Park, Boston / October 25, 2007

Boston 2, Colorado 1

Colorado	100	000	000	— 1	5	0
Boston	000	110	00x	— 2	6	1

WP: Schilling (1-0)   LP: Jimenez (0-1)   SV: Papelbon (1)

Hail the conquering hero. Fenway fans rise as one to salute Curt Schilling as he leaves the mound in the sixth inning of Game Two of the World Series against Colorado. Schilling gave up one earned run and struck out four as the Red Sox went on to win 2-1. (Boston Red Sox)

The Red Sox had now scored 11 or more runs in three consecutive postseason games. In stark contrast to the lopsided 13-1 laugher, though, Game Two was more of a pitchers' duel. As Bob Ryan put it, "Man cannot live on double-digit victories alone. He needs to pull out one of those 2-1 games every now and then, too."

The starters were the veteran Curt Schilling for the home team and 23-year-old right-hander Ubaldo Jimenez for the Rockies. Jimenez started 15 games and was an even 4-4, with a 4.28 ERA. But he had a fastball that could reach 100 mph, and Hurdle said, "He's shown some special pose for a young pitcher. He's got good stuff." As it would turn out, he had the best stuff of any of Colorado's four starters. It just wasn't quite good enough.

The game started poorly for the Red Sox: Schilling hit leadoff batter Willy Taveras. After Kaz Matsui flied out to center, NL batting champion Matt Holliday (.340) hit hard to third base, a difficult play scored a single but which wound up with runners on second and third as the ball hit off Lowell's glove and got away from him. Lowell fired to second base to try to cut down Holliday at second, but the ball glanced off Lugo's glove. Todd Helton grounded out to first base, with both runners moving up and Taveras scoring through the back door. Atkins grounded out. Colorado had an early 1-0 lead.

Even though he hit a batter in the second and walked two in the third, Jimenez didn't allow a hit through the first third of the game. Schilling gave up a couple of singles, but there were no more runs scored until the bottom of the fourth when the Red Sox tied it on a one-out walk to Lowell, a single to Drew on which Lowell raced from first to third, and a deep sacrifice fly to center by Varitek. 1-1.

The Red Sox took the lead in the bottom of the fifth. With two outs and nobody on, Ortiz walked. Manny singled him to second, and Lowell doubled down into the left-field corner to drive in the go-ahead run. Affeldt came in to relieve and walked Drew to load the bases. Even though the switch-hitting Varitek was due up, Herges came on to relieve Affeldt. He got Tek to fly out to left field.

Even though he didn't have a high pitch count (81), and Boston had but a one-run lead, Francona took out Schilling in the top of the sixth after Holliday singled with one out and Schilling walked Helton. Left-handed reliever Hideki Okajima was beckoned in. Francona knew he was well-rested; he'd been given a lighter load over the last few weeks to rest him for the postseason and he hadn't pitched for four days. The first Japanese-born pitcher ever to appear in World Series play got Atkins to ground out to Youkilis at first (both runners moved up), and struck out Brad Hawpe with the minimum three pitches. Okajima retired all seven batters he faced, striking out four of them. With two out in the top of the eighth, and the Sox still clinging to a one-run lead, Jonathan Papelbon was asked to close out the game. The first batter he faced was Matt Holliday, who completed a 4-for-4 day with an infield single that glanced off Papelbon and was fielded by Pedroia—but was then picked off first base.

Remarkably, for a man pitching in his 143rd game, it was the first runner Papelbon had ever picked off in a big league game. Holliday dove for the bag but never made it back. The inning was over and Papelbon was spared pitching to Todd Helton with a man on base. Holliday readily admitted that he'd planned to try and steal second on that pitch. "I knew he was slow to the plate and I was just trying to be aggressive and get in scoring position." Holliday had stolen 11 of the 15 bases he'd attempted in 2007, and bench coach Brad Mills knew that when Holliday was on first with two outs, he liked to try to steal on the first pitch. He had a color-coded chart with the data right there with him on the bench. That's good game preparation. Mills signaled for the pickoff. Perfect execution. Inning over.

In the ninth, Papelbon struck out Helton, got Atkins to line out to center, and struck out Hawpe to end the game. The three Boston pitchers had allowed one run on five hits and won a squeaker of a game, 2-1, both Red Sox runs scored by batters who'd reached first thanks to a Jimenez base on balls. The Rockies had scored just two runs in 18 innings (only getting one hit in 11 times they had runners in scoring position) and had to feel a bit demoralized at their inability to win a game in which their pitchers had held the Sox to two. Schilling typically gave the credit to others: "That was the Papa-jima Show. That was great to watch."

For Curt Schilling, the win further cemented his stature in the postseason. For pitchers with ten or more decisions, Schilling holds the record for the highest winning percentage in the postseason. He is 11-2, an .846 winning percentage. He's 4-0 (.093 ERA) in Division Series play, 3-1 in LLCS play (3.47 ERA), and 4-1 in the World Series (2.06), the one Series loss dating back to 1993 with the Phillies.

A quiet star, Mike Lowell always gave 100 percent. Here the World Series MVP slides into third ahead of the tag in the fourth inning of Game Two of the World Series. He later scored to give the Red Sox their first run in the 2-1 victory. (Boston Red Sox)

PLAYER PROFILE: MIKE LOWELL

Mike Lowell came to the Red Sox in the "Josh Beckett" trade of November 2005, talked about at the time as a "throw-in" during the deal—a high-salaried player on a team that was trying to slash payroll. For the Red Sox, it couldn't have worked out better. His first year, he set an all-time record defensively playing third base with a .987 fielding percentage around only six errors, easily eclipsing Rico Petrocelli's .976 mark, set when Rico only made 11 errors in 1971. Mike hit .284 and drove in 80 runs with the help of 20 homers. He instantly became a well-respected quiet leader in the clubhouse.

And he upped the ante in 2007, batting .324 (seventh in the league) and driving in 120 runs (placing him fifth). Mike played in his fourth All-Star Game and came in fifth in league MVP voting. But some would say there's no higher honor than to be named the Most Valuable Player in the World Series, as was Mike Lowell for his contributions in 2007. In Game Two, the Rockies held a 1-0 lead through three innings, but in the bottom of the fourth Lowell walked and later scored, to tie the game. And in the fifth inning, he doubled to left field to drive in David Ortiz with the go-ahead run.

Game Three: Coors Field, Denver / October 27, 2007

Boston 10, Colorado 5

Boston	006	000	031	—	10	15	1
Colorado	000	002	300	—	5	11	0

WP: Matsuzaka (1-0)   LP: Fogg (0-1)   SV: Papelbon (2)   HR: Holliday (1)

The third game of the Series presented a number of challenges to the Red Sox. They'd be playing at altitude, playing without the designated hitter, and starting Daisuke Matsuzaka. Since Independence Day, Matsuzaka was 5-7 and had given up nine earned runs in 14 ⅓ innings in the postseason. His start in the crucial Game Seven against the Indians had shown improvement, though, providing his longest outing (albeit only five innings) combined with the fewest number of earned runs (two). The Red Sox resolved the no-DH issue by giving

Kevin Youkilis a respite and starting David Ortiz at first base. It wasn't a total stretch; Ortiz had played 239 games at first through the years, and played it well—a .989 lifetime fielding percentage.

Jacoby Ellsbury started his fifth game in a row in place of Coco Crisp, who'd hit just .161 in postseason play (5-for-31), with two RBIs. Ellsbury singled, and Pedroia singled after him—both of them infield hits. The table setters were on base, but Josh Fogg struck out Ortiz, and got Ramirez and Lowell on fly balls to the outfield. Fogg was a native of Lynn, Massachusetts, and posted a 60-60 record through the 2007 season; he was 10-9 (4.94) in 2007 itself. He'd been brilliant in the postseason, 2-0, only allowing one earned run in eight full innings—two in relief in the NLDS and a six-inning win in Game Three of the NLCS against Arizona. He'd escaped the first and, though Lugo doubled in the top of the second, thrown two good innings in his first World Series appearance.

For the Rockies, staring down big odds stacked against them was nothing new this year. They'd been down, one strike from elimination, and here they were in the World Series and in their home park.

Colorado's Kaz Matsui singled to lead off the bottom of the first, reaching second on Drew's error. He was cut down trying to take third when Holliday hit back to Matsuzaka, who threw to Lowell for the fielder's choice. In the second, Dice-K again put on the leadoff batter, hitting Atkins, but the game was scoreless after two innings.

Ellsbury collected his second hit with a double to left field. Pedroia put down a beauty of a bunt, and reached safely while Ellsbury easily reached third base. Ortiz doubled, too, scoring Ellsbury. With first base open and still nobody out, Hurdle called for Fogg to walk Ramirez. Why Fogg was still in the game at this point is a good question. Mike Lowell drove in two more with a bases-loaded single to center field. Manny stopped at second. Drew popped up. Manny tried to score on Varitek's single to left field, but was thrown out at the plate. Lugo walked and the Sox had the bases loaded again, but there were two outs and—with no DH—Matsuzaka was up for the first time. He was 0-for-4 with two strikeouts in regular-season interleague play. Likely figuring Fogg was going to try to get ahead of him, he swung at the first pitch and punched it between third base and shortstop for a two-run single. The last pitcher to get a hit in a World Series game for the Red Sox was Bill Lee, back in 1975.

Ellsbury doubled for the second time in the inning, driving in Lugo. Six runs were in, and Josh Fogg was finally taken out. Franklin Morales came in and got Pedroia to ground out.

Matsuzaka left the base paths and took to the mound, striking out Morales and Matsui and getting Tulowitzki to ground out to Lugo. After three innings, it was 6-0 Red Sox. Rockies fans were glum indeed. They were no longer riding the high that took the team all the way from fourth place in the NL West on September 1 to the World Series.

Morales threw the fourth and fifth with just a Drew double, and Affeldt retired the side in the sixth. The Rockies got a walk in the fourth and two singles in the fifth.

With a six-run lead, and the confidence they weren't giving up much in the way of offense, Francona had Youkilis take over at first base. After Matsuzaka got Holliday on a ground ball to Lowell leading off the sixth, he walked Helton on eight pitches and then walked Atkins on just four. Francona walked to the mound, signaling for the left handed Lopez. It didn't work out the way he'd hoped. Hawpe singled and Helton scored. Yorvit Torrealba singled and Atkins scored. Time for Timlin. Ryan Spilborghs hit the ball deep to center field where Ellsbury made the catch against the wall. Jeff Baker batted for Affeldt and scorched the ball to shortstop. Lugo leaped and just barely caught the ball. The inning was over. It was 6-2, Rockies.

Matt Herges struck out the side in the Red Sox seventh: Ramirez, Lowell, and Drew. And the Rockies closed the gap, with three more runs in the bottom of the seventh. Matsui laid down a bunt single, then stole second on Timlin. Tulowitzki singled, and Matsui was on third. With two on and nobody out, the call went out to Okajima who'd pitched 9 ⅔ scoreless innings in postseason play.

On the first pitch Okajima threw, Matt Holliday hit a three-run home run, bringing the Rockies to one run down. Then Helton singled and the Rockies had the tying run on first, with still no outs. Okajima buckled down and struck out Atkins and Hawpe, and got Torrealba to ground out back to the mound.

Hurdle replaced Herges with Brian Fuentes. He induced Varitek to ground out, but then walked Lugo. Crisp singled and Ellsbury hit his third double of the game, scoring Lugo. Pedroia followed with a double of his own, driving in both Crisp and Ellsbury. Neither Youk nor Manny could get anything done but the Red Sox had just restored their four-run lead and this time there were only six outs remaining for the Rockies.

Manny Delcarmen took over for Okajima. He got the first two men, but then Matsui singled and Tulowitzki walked, so Francona summoned in Papelbon for the last four outs. Holliday flied out to left field. Inning over.

The Red Sox then added one more run. LaTroy Hawkins was pitching, the ninth player in the nine hole in the Colorado lineup. Lowell hit a leadoff single, moved to second base on Alex Cora's bunt. Lowell then stole third base. He scored on Varitek's sacrifice fly.

With a 10-5 lead, Papelbon got Helton and Atkins, but Hawpe hammered a triple to right field. It was but a blip, though. Torrealba grounded out to Lugo at short.

PLAYER PROFILE: DAISUKE MATSUZAKA

The signing of Daisuke Matsuzaka created a level of expectation that might have been difficult for almost anyone to fulfill. To have committed over $100,000,000 between the posting fee to the Seibu Lions and the guaranteed six years of salary to a ballplayer who'd never pitched an inning in the American major (or minor) leagues was a brave and bold statement by the Red Sox. Matsuzaka had been exhaustively scouted, though, by Boston's Craig Shipley and Jon Deeble. He was certainly an established veteran of the Japanese major leagues. From his initial splash at the fabled high school Koshien tournament—throwing a complete game shutout one day, 17 innings the very next day, and then a no-hitter in the final, through his years with the Lions, to his being crowned the MVP of the 2003 World Baseball Classic, it was clear he was a very special pitcher.

Adjusting to a different culture, with more travel, a five instead of six-day rotation, and even a slightly different baseball, Matsuzaka still won 15 games for the Red Sox in his "rookie year" and then held Colorado to two runs on three hits through the 5 ⅓ innings he threw in Game Three. He contributed at the plate as well, his third-inning single driving in the fourth and fifth runs of the six the Sox pushed across in the inning that made all the difference.

Game Four: Coors Field, Denver / October 28, 2007

Boston 4, Colorado 3

Boston	100	010	110	—	4	9	0
Colorado	000	000	120	—	3	7	0

WP: Lester (1-0)   LP: Cook (0-1)   SV: Papelbon (3)   HR: Lowell (1), Kielty (1), Atkins (1), Hawpe (1)

The Rockies faced a formidable challenge. In the history of major league baseball, only one team had come back from being down three-games-to-none in a seven-game playoff and won the series. That was the team the Rockies were playing.

It was quite a story line, the two starting pitchers presented. Aaron Cook had suffered a spate of blood clots in 2004 that began in his shoulder but spread to his lungs. He overcame that and fought his way back into big league ball, but almost missed his chance to pitch in the postseason due to an oblique injury that saw his season end on August 10 and kept him off both the NLDS and NLCS rosters.

Jon Lester had been diagnosed with cancer late in the 2006 season and left the team for treatment. Chemotherapy worked its wonders and here he was, warming up in the bullpen to throw what could prove to be the deciding game in the World Series.

Cook took the mound first, to face the visiting Red Sox. Mr. Two-Bagger Jacoby Ellsbury hit yet another double to lead off the game, slapping it to the opposite field, to left field. He'd now doubled in four of his last five at-bats. Pedroia grounded out, but Ellsbury was safe on third. And scored on Ortiz's single to right field. Ramirez grounded into a double play. The Sox were on top, 1-0.

Lester retired the first three batters, the ball never leaving the infield. In the second inning, Lester was tagged for a double by Todd Helton to lead off but died on third. Cook had settled down and retired the Red Sox in order in the second, third, and fourth. Lester walked Hawpe in the fourth, but the score still stood 1-0. Both starters were pitching good games.

Mike Lowell doubled to left field in the top of the fifth. He scored on Varitek's single to right field. 2-0, Red Sox. Cook was the only Colorado batter to hit safely in the Rockies' fifth, with a bunt to Pedroia. And Cook got Boston's 2-3-4 hitters in order in the sixth. Lester got his first two batters, but when he walked Atkins, Francona called on Delcarmen to pitch to Spilborghs. He struck him out. Lester had pitched 5 ⅔ innings of shutout ball in the World Series.

Lowell was first up in the seventh. This time he homered, and it was 3-0 for the Red Sox. Affeldt took over on the mound. He struck out Drew, saw Varitek reach on an infield single to third, but then got Lugo to hit into a double play.

The Rockies started the seventh with a home run, too: Brad Hawpe hit one out. Cory Sullivan pinch-hit for Affeldt and singled to center field. The tying run was at the plate, and Mike Timlin took over from Delcarmen. Working toward his fourth World Championship ring, Timlin struck out Matsui and struck out Tulowitzki.

For the third half-inning in a row, the leadoff batter homered. This time it was Bobby Kielty, batting for Timlin, off Fuentes, who was pitching for Affeldt. Kielty saw one pitch in the World Series, and he hit it into the left-field seats for a home run. It turned out to be the deciding run in the ballgame.

Ellsbury singled, but Pedroia hit into a double play. Ortiz walked, and Crisp ran for him. Manny Corpas came in to pitch. He struck out Manny Ramirez.

The fourth home run of the two innings came in the bottom of the eighth, a two-run homer hit off the new Red Sox reliever, Okajima. With one out, Helton singled and then Atkins homered. It was 4-3, but the Red Sox still had the lead. Jonathan Papelbon was asked to get the final five outs. He got Spilborghs to ground out and Hawpe to fly out.

One inning to go, with a one-run lead for the Red Sox. Corpas retired the three Red Sox batters he faced in the ninth. Papelbon retired all three Rockies, too, but there was one heart-stopping moment when Jamey Carroll hit a one-out drive to the seats in left field only to see Jacoby Ellsbury—who'd been shifted to left defensively in the eighth inning—leap up and make the catch. Papelbon then fired a fastball past pinch-hitter Seth Smith for the final out.

That the Red Sox outscored the Rockies in the Series 29-10 was a bit misleading, in that two of the games were one-run games and Colorado had closed to within one run as late as the seventh inning in Game Three. Nevertheless, a win is a win and a sweep is a sweep.

The Red Sox had swept the World Series again, just as they had against the Cardinals in 2004. Both times they'd swept the Division Series, fought to overcome a serious deficit in a seven-game League Championship Series, then swept the World Series.

"Words cannot describe how good this feels," declared a jubilant Jon Lester after the game as the celebration swirled around him. "It's been a whirlwind year for me." Red Sox fans didn't know what to make of it all. It was disorienting enough to have won a World Series in 2004 after 86 years of waiting. How would fans handle winning two in four years? It didn't take long before some began to search their souls and hope and pray they wouldn't become spoiled by success, that they wouldn't become … like Yankees fans.

PLAYER PROFILE—JONATHAN PAPELBON

A fourth-round 2003 draft pick, Jonathan Papelbon rose rapidly through the Red Sox system and debuted on July 31, 2005. His first three appearances were as a starter; he went five or more innings each time but wound up with three no-decisions. Since that time, and despite some thought of becoming a starter once more prior to the 2007 season, he's pitched exclusively in relief. And very effectively at that. In fact, through the 2007 season, Papelbon's 1.62 career ERA is the lowest earned run average in major league history for any pitcher who's thrown over 150 innings.

He broke through in a big way in 2006, facing 257 batters in 68 ⅓ innings of stellar relief work. He set a club record for the most saves in a row to start a season: 20, and the most saves in his rookie season, 35. His ERA of 0.92 beat out Dutch Leonard's 0.96 ERA for the best earned run average ever posted by a Red Sox pitcher who'd thrown 50 or more innings in a season. Leonard was a starter and set his mark in 1914, during the "dead ball" era).

In both of his first two full seasons, he was named to the All-Star team. In 2007, his ERA was 1.85 with 37 saves. In the postseason, he was 1-0, with four saves (including three of the four World Series games). With postseason appearances in both 2005 and 2007, he has faced 55 batters over 14 ⅔ innings in nine games. His combined postseason earned run average? 0.00.

GAME FIVE?

Rockies fans holding tickets for Game Five received a refund for their tickets. Those who bought incredibly expensive tickets through ticket agencies or from scalpers—well, they just ate the difference between face value and the premium they paid. Game Six, scheduled for Fenway Park on Halloween, never needed to be played. And the first baseball game ever scheduled for November—Game Seven at Fenway—was not to be. Sox fans in New England were glad to bask in the glow of their second World Championship in four years.

MIKE LOWELL—WORLD SERIES MVP

The "throw-in" in the Josh Beckett deal, the player whose large contract the Red Sox had to assume before the Marlins would trigger the trade that brought Beckett to the Red Sox—that was Mike Lowell, the man named MVP of the 2007 World Series.

"You can take that term 'throw-in' and throw it away," said John Henry, who'd known Lowell since Henry was owner of the Marlins and Lowell had played there. Sox fans didn't want to lose Lowell, but his contract was up. Right then and there, at Coors Field as the celebration on the field picked up steam, the chant went up: "Re-sign Lowell." When the parade was held back in Boston, Jason Varitek was carrying a sign on board one of the duckboats: RE-SIGN LOWELL. Unprecedented as it was for the captain of the Red Sox to be lobbying ownership to ink a new contract with the third baseman, that didn't stop Tek. Nor did it stop Curt Schilling from posting the same sentiment, in the same words, on his postgame blog. And ownership did work things out to hold on to Mike Lowell.

Lowell had hit .400 in the Series, with an on-base percentage of .500, and he'd scored six runs in the four games. He led the team by a good margin in slugging percentage, with .800 thanks to his home run and three doubles. He'd scored the first run and driven in the second in the 2-1 win in Game Two. He'd driven in the second and third runs in Game Three as the rout began in Boston's six-run third inning. In Game Four, he doubled to lead off the fifth and homered to lead off the seventh, scoring both times in the 4-3 victory.

2013 WORLD SERIES BOSTON RED SOX 4, ST. LOUIS CARDINALS 2

There are many examples of Red Sox teams that probably should have won the World Series but didn't. The 2013 Boston Red Sox were the exact opposite—a team of low expectations. Perhaps that's what made their championship run so shockingly delicious, like being fed castor oil by your mother and discovering that it tastes like chocolate pudding. It seemed to come out of nowhere. The win in 2004 was a magical one, coming as it did after the Yankees had beat up on the Sox and had them down three games to none in the ALCS. But given how close the Sox had come in 2003, it was really no surprise that they challenged again.

The drama of that season came first from the fact that they'd been ten or more games out of first place for a good portion of August and, second, because they overcame the 0-3 deficit in the LCS. Comebacks always make for high drama and beleaguered Sox fans were giddy with the joy that comes with answered prayers.

It hadn't really taken anyone by surprise when they won in 2007. We all knew they had the talent. It was still remarkable and satisfying that they were the first team in the twenty-first to win more than one world championship, in "modern times" (the new century) now holding a 2-0 edge in World Series wins over the New York Yankees. (New York finally won one in 2009).

But in 2011, the Sox had totally fallen apart. It was a team that began the season famously dubbed "BEST TEAM *EVER!*" by the *Boston Herald* on its March 31 front page. Then they lost their first six games. It took them until May 15 to reach .500 (20-20), a quarter of the way into the season.

Only 11 days later, they reached first place and they were in first place more games than not through September 1. They even had a nine-game lead in the Wild Card standings. Three weeks later to the day, they were eight games behind the first-place Yankees. They finished third, seven games out. Their record in September 2011 was a dismal 7-20.

Ownership may have over-reacted. Within two weeks, GM Theo Epstein was gone. And rather than retain two-time World Series–winning manager Terry Francona, it was felt—and perhaps was true—that he'd lost control of the clubhouse. He was replaced by Bobby Valentine.

In 2012, the Sox under Valentine lost 93 games and won only 69. It was the worst record for a Red Sox team in almost 50 years—since 1965. They finished in last place, 26 games out of first and appeared totally demoralized and even disinterested. Future historians may call this benighted year the Valentine's Decay Massacre. Had the Red Sox re-entered the Dark Ages?

Could they really be that bad? It didn't seem so on paper, but the most optimistic prognosticators seemed to pick the Sox to maybe win 88 games in 2013, maybe finish third, and just possibly have a chance to dip a toe into the playoffs.

On April 15, a couple of hours after Mike Napoli's walkoff double won a 3-2 game over the Rays, two bombs exploded near the finish line of the Boston Marathon, killing an 8-year-old boy and two young women. The team was on its way out of town, but they immediately adopted the "Boston Strong" motto and throughout the season the Red Sox would honor victims of the bombings in ceremonies at Fenway Park.

Against all odds—or at least all Las Vegas odds—the 2013 team won, and won again, and kept on winning. They were in third place for all of three days, May 12-14. They were in first place most of the time, except for 12 other game days in May and four at the end of July. The rest of the time, the other 147 game days, they were looking down at the rest of the pack. And yet it seemed that no one really believed it, or at least believed it would last. For the first time in franchise history, the team had gone from worst to first. The Unthinkable Dream had truly become the Improbable Dream.

The Sox had sold out Fenway for every game from May 15, 2003, through the end of the 2011 season. There was some grumbling about empty seats near the tail end of 2011, but compared to 2012, attendance had only declined 10,998 for the whole season—a negligible .0036 percent. By 2013, however, attendance dropped by 209,670, below 3 million after five years above. Ticket sales were soft all season long—even into the first round of the playoffs!

Fans just didn't trust the team any more. Something was going to go wrong. This was all a mirage that would crumble as it had in 2011—blowing that nine-game lead. Basically, most people didn't believe in the 2013 team until they could no longer disbelieve—until they made the World Series.

The team itself was a different matter. They believed in themselves and they believed in each other. There was a unifying theme that grew early—and grew literally—and that was the beards. During spring training, many began to grow them, and they kept it going until it became a "thing." The various styles became a metaphor for this tight-knit yet very individual band of bearded brothers. Soon you could glance into the stands and see entire families—men, women, and small children—sporting a variety of eye-catching facial hair. As with Samson's flowing locks, the hair seemed to become part of the Red Sox strength, and not even Delilah herself would even dare suggest they shave.

AMERICAN LEAGUE DIVISION SERIES

Perhaps surprised to be there, and with home field advantage throughout to boot, the Red Sox welcomed the Wild Card–winning Tampa Bay Rays to Fenway for the Division Series. The Rays had finished 5 ½ games behind Boston in the AL East, and had shut out the Indians, 4-0, at Progressive Field in the "play-in" game.

In head-to-head battles with Tampa Bay, the Sox had taken the regular-season series, 12 games to 7 (they were 6-4 at home and 6-3 on the road).

The Sox were idle for four days while they waited for the Wild Card sudden death winner to emerge. They even played an intrasquad "tune-up" scrimmage at Fenway, the "Blue" team against the "Red" team. It was a mixed-up sort of game; you couldn't keep the players straight without a scorecard—and there was no scorecard designed to follow this game. In the first inning, Quintin Berry played the outfield for *both* teams—center field for the red team and right field for the blue team. And that was just the start. When the game was over, the scoreboard flashed the sign RED SOX WIN! and the p.a. system played "Dirty Water."

The Sox now knew their first round foe. They also knew that they had two tough lefties to face in Matt Moore and David Price.

Game One: Fenway Park, Boston / October 4, 2013

Boston 12, Tampa Bay 2

Tampa Bay	010	100	000	—	2	4	0
Boston	000	530	04x	—	12	14	0

WP: Jon Lester (1-0)   LP: Matt Moore (0-1)   HR: Rodriguez (1), Zobrist (1)

Jon Lester struck out the side in the first, and the first man in the second, pleasing the home crowd. The Rays, however, scored first, on a Sean Rodriguez solo home run off Jon Lester in the top of the second. The Rays scored second, too, adding one more run in the top of the fourth on another homer off Lester, this one off the bat of Ben Zobrist. The Red Sox didn't have a hit through three. Tampa Bay rookie lefty Matt Moore (17-4 during the season) had held the Red Sox to a collective .109 batting average in the regular season. He had thrown 17 scoreless innings in a row against the Red Sox including nine innings of two-hit ball on July 22.

Dustin Pedroia ignited the home town offense with a single right up the middle to lead off the bottom of the fourth, and David Ortiz hit a ground-rule double to right-center on a 2-0 pitch—a ball that Rays right-fielder Wil Myers should have caught with ease. He was camped under the ball, but then suddenly stepped in and turned to watch the ball simply bounce off the warning track and into the Red Sox bullpen. He'd apparently seen center-fielder Desmond Jennings out of the corner of his eye. But Jennings wasn't even within range, assuming that Myers would easily make the play. Or not.

Mike Napoli popped up to second base, but Jonny Gomes came through with a Wall ball double off the Covidien sign to tie the game (for Gomes, it was the first he'd had in postseason play, coming into the game 0-for-7). After Jerrod Saltalamacchia struck out, Stephen Drew hustled and beat out an infield single when Moore took a split second too long to get to the bag, and drove in what proved to be the game-winning hit, driving in Gomes, who hustled just as hard, scoring all the way from second base on what could have been a fairly routine play. Will Middlebrooks doubled to left field, driving in Drew when Rodriguez misplayed the carom. Rays starter Matt Moore might have seen the inning end right there, with Boston up 4-2, but after he fanned Jacoby Ellsbury for the third out of the inning, catcher Jose Lobaton let the ball get away from him—a passed ball and Ells took first while Middlebrooks took third. Shane Victorino made it a five-run inning with a single between first and second.

Lester stopped giving up hits after the fourth, cruising with an 8-2 lead after Boston scored three more runs in the fifth. Two doubles, two intentional walks, and two singles saw Salty drive in two and Ellsbury one.

Maybe it was overkill but the Red Sox added four more runs in the eighth. Ellsbury singled and stole second, then came home on Victorino's single. The bases got loaded and Napoli walked in another run. There was still nobody out. Gomes hit into a double play, but Pedroia scored from third. Salty singled and drove in the 12th run of the game. By the end of the game, everyone in the Red Sox lineup had a hit and everyone scored at least one run. Everyone had an RBI except, oddly, Pedroia and Ortiz. Junichi Tazawa and Ryan Dempster closed it out.

No official errors were assessed the Rays, but there were mental errors galore—Myers, a poorly played left-field by Rodriguez, the passed ball. …

Rays manager Joe Maddon understated, "We didn't play our best game tonight."

Game Two: Fenway Park, Boston / October 5, 2013

Boston 7, Tampa Bay 4

Tampa Bay	010	021	000	—	4	8	2
Boston	202	110	01x	—	7	11	0

WP: John Lackey (1-0)   LP: David Price (0-1)   SV: Koji Uehara (1)   HR: Ortiz 2 (2)

The Red Sox scored first and more often in Game Two. David Price (2012 Cy Young Award winner) seemed to always be tough against Boston. He was 2-2 in 2013, but with a 2.48 ERA. The Red Sox game plan was, contrary to their usual practice of working the count, to be aggressive against Price. It worked. Ellsbury singled to lead off the first, then stole second—taking third on a throwing error by catcher Jose Molina. He came home easily on Pedroia's sacrifice fly to right-center. David Ortiz gave the Sox another run with a homer into the Red Sox bullpen, caught by Franklin Morales. It was 2-0, Red Sox.

A walk, a deep single, and a sacrifice fly gave the Rays a run in the top of the second, but the Sox put up two more in the bottom of the third on back-to-back doubles by David Ross and Ellsbury, a Victorino single, and a run-producing groundout by Pedroia. In the fourth, Drew tripled off the wall (this time it was DeJesus who misplayed the carom and Drew had really run hard) to drive in Gomes and make it 4-1.

Tampa Bay closed to within a run when James Loney doubled in two off Red Sox starter John Lackey. The two teams traded another run each, Pedroia doubling in Ellsbury in the bottom of the fifth and Yunel Escobar singling in Jennings in the top of the sixth. Price was so concerned with holding Ellsbury on first base that Pedroia got better pitches to hit. Pedroia said, "I got in a 2-0 count because [Price] was throwing balls away in case Ells was going to run—to try to throw him out. And I got a 2-0 pitch to hit, hit it, and drove him in." It was Ellsbury's fourth run scored in the two games; he was 5-for-9 at the plate.

Ortiz led off the bottom of the eighth with another home run, this one inside the Pesky Pole. It was the first time he'd homered twice in a postseason game. Price had only allowed two homers to left-handed hitters all year long. Now he'd given up two in one game to Big Papi, the first homers Ortiz ever hit off him in 42 prior at-bats.

Craig Breslow got five outs, Tazawa got three, and closer Koji Uehara struck out two batters and got Myers to end the game on an infield grounder.

The Red Sox had scored 19 runs in 16 innings, with 25 hits. And they held a two-games-to-none lead.

Game Three: Tropicana Field, St. Petersburg / October 7, 2013

Tampa Bay 5, Boston 4

Boston	100	020	001	—	4	7	0
Tampa Bay	000	030	011	—	5	11	1

WP: Fernando Rodney (1-0)   LP: Koji Uehara (0-1)   HR: Lobaton (1), Longoria (1)

Game Three was a bit of a seesaw affair. The Sox scored first, in the top of the first, but they should have come up with more than the lone run they did off Alex Cobb, with one run in, the bases loaded and just one out.

The bottom of the fourth provided a scare for the Sox when Clay Buchholz almost alternated walks and strikeouts, loading the bases but striking out the side without giving up a run. In the fifth, a double, a single, and a wild pitch brought in one, and Ortiz singled in another. For a moment, it was 3-0 Red Sox. Only four innings stood between them and a Sox sweep of the Division Series.

A single for the Rays, and a double, and two outs … and the always dangerous Evan Longoria tied the game with a three-run homer into Tropicana's left-field seats. Buchholz worked his way out of the inning despite a walk and another single. The Rays had been on the ropes, but now they were counter-punching. Buchholz pitched a solid sixth. Craig Breslow and Taz split the seventh. It still stood 3-3 after seven.

In the bottom of the eighth, Franklin Morales didn't see a ball hit out of the infield, but he left with two runners on base and just one out. Escobar singled off Brandon Workman, loading the bases, and then an infield roller by Delmon Young resulted in him being thrown out at first, but the go-ahead run coming in the back door from third.

Tampa Bay's closer Fernando Rodney came in to shut down the Red Sox, but Will Middle-brooks walked. Xander Bogaerts pinch-ran for him. Ellsbury dropped one in behind third baseman Longoria for a single. Victorino bunted for a base hit and settled for a sacrifice. Pedroia grounded out, short to first, but Bogaerts scored to tie the game, 4-4.

Koji Uehara, Boston's surprise closer of the season (after injuries sidelined Joel Hanrahan and then Andrew Bailey), pitched the ninth. The first two batters up were dangerous ones—Zobrist and Longoria. He got the first out on one pitch, and the second out on two more pitches, but then on pitch #5, the previously hitless Jose Lobaton hit a game-winning walkoff home run to deep right-center—bouncing off a fan's glove and splashing right into the fish tank that houses the actual rays.

The sudden turn of events stunned Red Sox fans because they had come to see Koji as a machine. He'd recorded a regular-season 1.09 earned run average, and was enjoying a scoreless inning streak of 30 ⅓ innings. At one point he had retired a club-record 37 consecutive batters, a perfect game and then some—working under the ever-changing conditions of a reliever. The last time he'd allowed a home run was back in June. He'd recorded a WHIP (walks plus hits per inning pitched) of 0.565 in the regular season—it was the lowest in major league history for a pitcher working 50 or more innings. In the 2013 postseason, he went one better—despite the homer to Lobaton (unexpected though it was, it was still a home run), his postseason WHIP was 0.512.

Game Four: / Tropicana Field, St. Petersburg / October 8, 2013

Boston 3, Tampa Bay 1

Boston	000	000	201	—	3	6	0
Tampa Bay	000	001	000	—	1	6	0

WP: Craig Breslow (1-0)   LP: Jake McGee (0-1)   SV: Koji Uehara (2)

In a 5 p.m. game, the Detroit Tigers pulled even with Oakland, two wins apiece, setting up a deciding Game Five in Oakland on the 10th. The Red Sox game at Tropicana started at 8:30, moments after the game in Detroit ended. The starters were Jeremy Hellickson for Tampa Bay and Jake Peavy for Boston. Joe Maddon pulled Hellickson quickly, when he loaded the bases with nobody out but Jamey Wright struck out Salty and got Drew to line into a 3-6 double play, Mike Napoli being caught off second. Peavy was bailed out by a double play in the fourth. Neither team scored through the first five innings—though the Rays were on their fourth pitcher by then.

Escobar doubled to lead off the fifth inning and advanced to third on an infield groundout. David DeJesus singled him in, and the Rays had a 1-0 lead. Peavy was pulled after 5 ⅔. Craig Breslow struck out James Loney.

Jake McGee took over for Tampa Bay to pitch the top of the seventh. After one out, Bogaerts pinch-hit for Drew, who was only 1-for-32 against left-handed relievers in the regular season. Bogaerts walked, and, following a strikeout of Will Middlebrooks, Ellsbury singled, sending Bogaerts to third. The Red Sox had runners on the corners. Joel Peralta came in to pitch (the sixth Rays pitcher of the game). On his very first pitch to Victorino, Ellsbury stole second and Peralta threw a wild pitch. Bogaerts scored the tying run and Ellsbury ended up on third base. Then Victorino singled him in, running hard to beat out a weak infield roller to shortstop, and giving Boston a 2-1 lead.

Breslow struck out the side in the bottom of the seventh and retired the first batter in the eighth. After he gave up a single, Taz took over. He struck out Matt Joyce and then manager John Farrell called for Koji, who struck out DeJesus.

Fernando Rodney was shaky in the top of the ninth. He walked Bogaerts and struck out Middlebrooks, then threw a wild pitch and walked Ellsbury. His erratic outing continued as he hit Victorino on a 3-2 count, loading the bases with one out and giving the Red Sox an excellent shot at an insurance run.

Pedroia hit a ball (off Chris Archer) far enough to right that Bogaerts could tag and score. 2-1, Red Sox, on the sacrifice fly. Maddon brought in his ninth pitcher of the game to get the final out. After the game, Bogaerts, who'd only turned 21 on October 1, didn't seem to be fazed by being in the postseason and scoring the winning run of the game: "I tried to stay calm and stay with my approach. Walks are fine."

Uehara retired the Rays 1-2-3.

The Red Sox had won the Division Series. Celebrations were in order.

AMERICAN LEAGUE CHAMPIONSHIP SERIES

The Tigers disposed of the A's on October 10, so the battle for the pennant—the American League Championship Series—was to be joined starting two days later. The Tigers had one day off; the Red Sox had three, and had earned home-field advantage throughout the playoffs. The two teams had played seven games against each other in the regular season, with the Tigers winning four, despite being outscored by the Red Sox, 43-35. Detroit's record had been 93-69. Boston had been 97-65. The Tigers had hit for a .283 average (.347 OBP) and had a team ERA of 3.61. The Sox had hit .277 (.349 OBP) with a team ERA of 3.79. The Red Sox had scored more runs, 853-796. The Tigers had the nearly unbeatable Max Scherzer (21-3, 2.90 ERA), a shoo-in for the Cy Young Award.

Game One: Fenway Park, Boston / October 12, 2013

Detroit 1, Boston 0

Detroit	000	001	000	—	1	9	0
Boston	000	000	000	—	0	1	1

WP: Anibal Sanchez (1-0)   LP: Jon Lester (0-1)   SV: Joaquin Benoit (1)

The Tigers had Scherzer, and Justin Verlander, and Doug Fister—and Anibal Sanchez, who no-hit them for six innings in Game One. In fact, four Tigers pitchers kept a no-hitter going into the bottom of the ninth. It was a tough-luck loss for Jon Lester, who gave up just one run—in the top of the sixth.

Sanchez even managed to strike out four batters in the first inning. (Victorino swung at strike three, but the ball got away from the catcher—a wild pitch, and Vic took first base). He walked two in the second inning, but he settled down nicely for the third, fourth, and fifth. He'd once been a member of the Red Sox, but left in the trade that brought Josh Beckett and Mike Lowell to Boston.

The Tigers scored the one and only run of the game in the sixth, after a walk and a hit-by-pitch, when Jhonny Peralta singled—a little blooper, really—to short-center field.

Sanchez played with fire once more, walking the bases loaded in the bottom of the sixth, with a wild pitch mixed in early on—but escaped without damage. Manager Jim Leyland decided it was time to make a change. It was nice that his pitcher had a no-hitter going, but this was the ALCS and

Sanchez had thrown 116 pitches. No time for individual glory. Leyland wanted to win the game. Indeed, the Sox failed to get a hit in the seventh or the eighth, off three different relievers. It was only in the bottom of the ninth that the Red Sox got a hit. Mike Napoli struck out, but Daniel Nava hung tough, fouling off three pitches after there were two strikes, and then lined a single to center field. Quintin Berry ran for him, and stole second putting him in scoring position with just one out.

The Sox were spared the embarrassment of being no-hit, but the next two batters made outs (Drew drove a long fly ball to right-center, and Bogaerts popped up). Drew's drive was one of only four to reach the outfield in the entire game.

The game was over. And Scherzer was on tap.

It was the first playoff game ever between two charter members of the American League, and it was as close as a game could be.

Game Two: Fenway Park, Boston / October 13, 2013

Boston 6, Detroit 5

Detroit	010	004	000	—	5	8	1
Boston	000	001	041	—	6	7	1

WP: Koji Uehara (1-0)   LP: Rick Porcello (0-1)   HR: Avila (1), Cabrera (1), Ortiz (1)

Game Two looked like it might be a repeat of Game One. Scherzer didn't allow the Red Sox batters a hit for the first five innings (making Boston's total all of one hit through the first 14 innings against Detroit pitching). He hit a batter (Victorino) and walked two, but he didn't allow even one base hit.

The score was 1-0 after five. Victor Martinez had doubled off Clay Buchholz in the bottom of the second, taken third on Peralta's single, and scored on another single by Alex Avila. Clay buckled down then, and Omar Infante grounded into an inning-ending double play. That burst of three hits was the only offense the Tigers had mustered against Buchholz. It was one run and three hits for the Tigers, and no runs and no hits for the Red Sox.

Miguel Cabrera hit a home run deep to left in the top of the sixth, and suddenly Buchholz imploded. On the very next pitch, Prince Fielder doubled to left. Four pitches later, Victor Martinez doubled again, to right-center. It was 3-0, and then quickly 5-0 when Avila jumped on the first pitch he saw and homered deep to right. John Farrell still stuck with Clay, but when Infante singled, he made the move and brought in Brandon Workman.

It wasn't just that the Red Sox weren't hitting. One of the reasons they weren't hitting was that they were striking out. Through the first 16 innings, the Sox were 3-for-51, with 30—count 'em, 30—K's. Scherzer struck out ten of the first 18 batters he faced. The Sox bats had produced one hit in the first 14 innings and were in danger of losing their classification as offensive weapons.

The Red Sox finally broke the ice when Victorino singled and Pedroia hit a deep double that scored him. The score was now 5-1, but there was still little hope among Red Sox fans. It looked as though they were going to lose the two home games that kicked off the series. So much for home field advantage. They'd scored just the one run in those first two games. And that's where it stood after seven. Things were not looking good at all.

Workman and then Felix Doubront kept the Tigers from adding to their lead in the seventh and the eighth. Scherzer had done his job; he'd thrown 108 pitches allowing only two hits through seven. Now it was time for Leyland to turn to the bullpen. Jose Veras came on to pitch the bottom of the eighth. Veras got the first out, but then Middlebrooks doubled. Leyland called for Drew Smyly, who walked Ellsbury. Leyland made another move and brought in Al Alburquerque, who struck out Victorino. Pedroia then singled into shallow right field and the Red Sox had the bases loaded, with two outs, and David Ortiz—yes, Mr. Clutch himself—at the plate.

This really couldn't happen, could it? Ortiz had come through too many times in the past. Joaquin Benoit was summoned to get Ortiz out—even though he was a right-hander being asked to get out a left-handed hitter. And Ortiz was ready for him; he'd been studying Benoit on video during the day—just as he studied all possible pitchers he might face. "I watch everybody," Ortiz said. "I watch every single pitcher so when it comes time to go against me I know how he's going to approach me."

On the first pitch he saw, Big Papi hit a grand slam into the Red Sox bullpen, with one swing of the bat tying the game at 5-5. Tigers right-fielder Torii Hunter made a valiant effort and slammed hard into the bullpen wall, tumbling into the pitchers' sanctuary. It had been a valiant effort by a real warrior. An instantly iconic photograph showed Hunter's upended two legs pointing skyward in a "V" just as the elated Boston policeman stationed in the bullpen, Steve Horgan, raised his two arms in a similar "V"—like a referee signaling "touchdown."

Dan Shaughnessy wrote in the *Globe*: "Incredible? Unbelievable? Cosmic? Epic? Go ahead. Choose your word. This was right up there with any of the thrills we've seen at the ancient yard over the last century."

Dave O'Brien's call on Red Sox radio: "The Red Sox have tied it! The Red Sox have tied it! David Ortiz! David Ortiz! David Ortiz!"

The Red Sox were back in it, and they had the momentum. Mike Napoli struck out, but it took seven pitches to get him. He'd set a Red Sox franchise record for strikeouts in the regular season (with 187) but seen a major league best 4.59 pitches per plate appearance.

That was Napoli's modus operandi, his Jekyll and Hyde hitting record. Like July 21 when he hit a third-inning three-run homer against the Yankees at Fenway to give the Sox a 4-3 lead, struck out three times, grounded into a double play and then won the game in the bottom of the ninth with another home run.

Ortiz's home run was the 15th he'd hit in postseason play for the Red Sox.

Uehara pitched the top of the ninth and kept the score 5-5 with a pop-up to second and a pop-up to short sandwiched around a strikeout.

Leading off the bottom of the ninth, against Rick Porcello, Jonny Gomes singled to short-stop—former Red Sox Jose Iglesias had come into the game—and took second base on Iglesias's throwing error—which was also misplayed by Prince Fielder at first. On a 2-1 count, Porcello threw a wild pitch to Saltalamacchia and Gomes took third. With no one out, things were looking good. It didn't take long. Leyland could have walked the bases loaded but instead kept pitching to Salty. The infield was in, and Salty hit the very next pitch through the shortstop hole, under the diving Iglesias, and into left field and the Red Sox had grabbed a win. A walkoff at Fenway. It seemed like it had been a year of walkoffs at Fenway. Of their 53 wins at home in the regular season, 11 of them had been walkoffs.

The ALCS was even now, one win apiece.

Game Three: Comerica Park, Detroit / October 15, 2013

Boston 1, Detroit 0

Boston	000	000	100	—	1	4	0
Detroit	000	000	000	—	0	6	1

WP: John Lackey (1-0)   LP: Justin Verlander (0-1)   SV: Koji Uehara (1)   HR: Napoli (1)

With the exception of the explosion in the eighth inning of Game Two—arguably just one bad pitch—the Red Sox still hadn't hit much, and the drought continued against Justin Verlander in Game Three. It was a 4 p.m. start, delayed a little bit due to a power outage of another sort during the second inning. Verlander held the Red Sox hitless through 4 ⅔ and then gave up nothing more than an inoffensive infield single to Gomes. The Red Sox got another hit in the sixth, but nothing came of that, either.

Meanwhile, John Lackey was pitching shutout ball for the Red Sox, too. There were a lot of K's in this game. Verlander struck out the side in the second and in the third and Lackey struck out four in a row during the same two frames.

Verlander hadn't allowed a run for the last 33 innings, going back into the regular season.

He threw one bad pitch—on a 3-2 count to Mike Napoli in the top of the seventh. After two sliders, Verlander came in with a fastball and Napoli connected. He homered over the wall and off the back wall of the Red Sox bullpen in left-center field. The Sox had a 1-0 lead. Verlander had already struck out Napoli twice in the game. Of some interest: in Napoli's first major league plate appearance, back in 2006, he'd also homered off Verlander.

Lackey had held the Tigers scoreless through 6 ⅔ and struck out eight without walking a batter.

With two outs in the bottom of the seventh, Breslow relieved Lackey. The bottom of the eighth saw something unusual—three Red Sox pitchers combined to strike out the side (Breslow, Tazawa, and Uehara). There was a walk and a single in there, too, with runners on first and third with just one out. But the K's did the trick and no one scored. Tazawa got Cabrera and Uehara got Fielder. Tazawa's strikeout of Cabrera was probably the biggest out of the game; the thought might have been to bring in Koji, but Cabrera had had some success against Uehara in the past and both Farrell and pitching coach Juan Nieves agreed to stick with the harder-throwing Tazawa, who got Cabrera on a pitch a few inches outside. Uehara finished off Fielder on three pitches.

It was a 1-0 game, the same score as Game One but with the Red Sox on top. Tigers DH Victor Martinez singled to lead off the bottom of the ninth. But Uehara got Peralta to hit into a 6-4-3 double play and then struck out Avila to end the game, the 23rd strikeout of the game (12 Sox struck out and 11 Tigers).

One-time Fenway pariah John Lackey was now a heroic 2-0 in the 2013 postseason.

Game Four: Comerica Park, Detroit / October 16, 2013

Boston 4, Detroit 3

Boston	000	001	101	—	3	12	0
Detroit	050	200	00x	—	7	9	0

WP: Doug Fister (1-0)   LP: Jake Peavy (0-1)

Jake Peavy, the 2007 Cy Young Award winner when he was with the San Diego Padres, had not done well the two times he'd made the postseason, 0-1 for San Diego in 2005 and 0-1 in 2006.

He'd pitched very well indeed in Game Four of the 2013 ALDS, however, holding the Rays to one run in 5 ⅔ innings. He hadn't factored in the final decision.

Peavy came up short again in this fourth game, though. He got through the first frame OK, but in the bottom of the second gave up a single to Victor Martinez, and then two walks. One out came on a fly ball too shallow in center to serve as a sac fly—but he walked Austin Jackson (on four pitches) and gave the Tigers a gift run. Jose Iglesias grounded into a force play at second and Detroit got another run—though it was really a tailor-made double play ball that would have—and should have—ended the inning—except for the fact that Pedroia got uncharacteristically handcuffed and could only get the one out.

The Tigers took advantage. Torii Hunter doubled in two more and Cabrera followed that with a single, and the Tigers led, 5-0. It was enough to give them the game—even though the Red Sox out-hit them, 12-9. It was one thing to collect hits, but they needed timely hits, and these ones came at the least opportune times: the Sox were 2-for-16 with runners in scoring position. And some of the Sox hitters weren't hitting at all—Drew was 1-for-13 and Middlebrooks was 1-for-10.

Peavy finished out the second and breezed through the third, but when the Tigers opened the fourth with a ground-rule double and then an RBI single, John Farrell had seen enough. Peavy was charged with seven runs in three innings plus. By the time the inning was over, the Tigers led, 7-0. Workman, Dempster, Morales, and Doubront worked five innings without giving up a run.

The Red Sox chipped away with one run each in the sixth, seventh, and ninth, with Salty, Victorino, and Ellsbury each driving in one. But the hole they'd dug was too deep, and Boston lost the game. This was the first game in the series that wasn't a one-run contest. Detroit had evened the series, two wins apiece.

It was said that Peavy had just gotten too hyped up for the game and hadn't controlled his emotions well enough. He took the loss, and—looking ahead—the ALCS became a best-of-three series, with the last two games (if necessary) in Boston. All well and good, perhaps, but the trio of starters the Tigers had on board had been the three who had allowed the Red Sox just six hits in their first three efforts, and struck out 35 Boston batters. They'd recorded a combined 0.86 ERA.

Game Five: Comerica Park, Detroit / October 17, 2013

Boston 4, Detroit 3

Boston	031	000	000	—	4	10	0
Detroit	000	011	100	—	3	10	1

WP: Jon Lester (1-1)   LP: Anibal Sanchez (1-1)   SV: Koji Uehara (2)   HR: Napoli (2)

Anibal Sanchez and Jon Lester matched up again. This time Sanchez proved a lot more hittable. He'd not given up a hit in Game One, but had to leave after six innings because he'd thrown 116 pitches. In Game Five, he gave up a hit to Dustin Pedroia in the first inning, but it was the second and third innings that cost him the game. Leading off the second was Mike Napoli; on a 3-1 count, he hit a titanic home run 460 feet to straightaway center field and into the plant growth placed there as a backdrop, in the "batter's eye."

Gomes reached on a single, and then reached third base on Xander Bogaerts's double off the wall near the "B Strong" logo that had been added after the Boston Marathon bombings. David Ross doubled off the base of the left-field fence, scoring Gomes (while Bogaerts held up at third base). Ellsbury singled to drive in another run. Ross was cut down at the plate on a fielder's choice, and Pedroia grounded out. It was 3-0, on four hits. For Bogaerts, who had just turned 21 on October 1, it was his first start. He was the youngest player to start a playoff game for the Red Sox since a guy named Babe Ruth.

The Red Sox added one more run in the third when Napoli doubled, took third on a ball hit back to pitcher Sanchez, and then scored on a wild pitch. Far from the fastest runner in the game, he scored nonetheless, in part—he said after the game—because it was just one of those things he keeps in mind when on base: be ready to take advantage if there were a wild pitch. Even though his run made it 4-0 at the time, it turned out to be the winning run.

In the end, Sanchez lost the game because Jon Lester pitched just a little bit better than he did. He gave up just two runs, one in the fifth and one in the sixth. Junichi Tazawa allowed a third run in the bottom of the seventh. It was now 4-3, Red Sox, after seven.

The run-an-inning scoring stopped with the eighth as Breslow and Uehara retired all six batters they faced, Koji getting the final five. Iglesias popped up to Pedroia. Both teams had ten hits. It was the fourth one-run game in the League Championship Series, and the Red Sox held a three-games-to-two lead. They needed only to win either of the two games scheduled for the friendly confines of Fenway.

Game Six: Fenway Park, Boston / October 19, 2013

Boston 5, Detroit 2

Detroit	000	002	000	—	2	8	1
Boston	000	010	40x	—	5	5	1

WP: Junichi Tazawa (1-0)   LP: Max Scherzer (0-1)   SV: Koji Uehara (3)   HR: Victorino (1)

Shane Victorino and Tigers catcher Alex Avila have a front row seat as they watch Victorino's grand slam blast off Jose Veras in the seventh inning of Game Six of the ALCS vs. Detroit. (Boston Red Sox)

"Let's just get it over with tonight. I don't want to have to come back again tomorrow night." That was the sentiment among seasoned Red Sox ticketholders. If the Red Sox could win, they'd be headed to the World Series again—truly it was what would have seemed the Improbable Dream back in April. Many could still remember years like 1986, when all the Red Sox needed to do was win one of the last two games—but did not.

Still, this was a game the Red Sox could afford to lose. Even if they lost this one, to Max Scherzer, they'd still have another shot in Game Seven. It was a Buchholz vs. Scherzer matchup. In Game Two, Scherzer had given up just two hits (one run) in seven innings of work. Buchholz had given up five runs and had a 6.17 postseason ERA coming into Game Six.

This time, they both pitched well—and each gave up four hits. As tightly as almost every one of the games in this series had been played, one hit could make all the difference. That was very much the case in Game Six.

Buchholz gave up a leadoff single to Hunter, but got out of the first inning with 22 pitches thrown (all but four of them for strikes)—plus a lot of throws to first base holding Hunter close.

The two teams weren't in the same class in base stealing; the Tigers had only swiped 35 bases in the regular season while the Red Sox had stolen 123. The Tigers had pushed their power hitters toward the top of the order, but Cabrera had been subpar since the beginning of September and Prince Fielder came into Game Six without a run batted in for his last 17 postseason games. Scherzer struck out Ellsbury on three pitches, all three strikes taken. He allowed a single to Pedroia, and walked Ortiz, but escaped unscathed. He'd thrown 21 pitches. Scherzer struck out the side in the second.

Xander Bogaerts was in the game; he'd been given preference over Will Middlebrooks, who'd been mired in a 1-for-10 slump in the ALCS. For a rookie, Bogaerts showed extraordinary plate discipline. He'd had nine plate appearances in the ALCS and drawn three bases on balls. Both he and Ellsbury walked to lead off the third, but Victorino's bunt was popped up to a sliding Scherzer. Then Pedroia hit a long ball that just missed being a home run, very high and over everything but foul as it passed the "Fisk Pole" by maybe four inches. Then he hit into a 5-3 double play.

The game remained scoreless to the midpoint as the Red Sox managed only one hit. Scherzer got the first two batters in the bottom of the fifth, but Bogaerts ran the count full and then doubled high off the wall in left-center, a scant five feet to the left of the painted yellow line on the wall; to the right, it would have been a home run. Ellsbury swung at the first pitch and lined a single in front of Hunter in right, giving the Red Sox a 1-0 lead.

Buchholz had fallen apart in the sixth inning of Game Two, giving up four runs so when Hunter walked and Cabrera grounded a single into left field, the manager brought in Franklin Morales to pitch to Prince Fielder. At that point Buchholz had thrown 85 pitches. Morales walked Fielder on four pitches. Victor Martinez, the offensive star of the series for the Tigers, singled high off the wall in left and drove in two, giving the Tigers a 2-1 lead. Morales was replaced by Brandon Workman, who induced a 4-2 double play with Pedroia tagging Martinez heading to second and throwing home to the plate. Fielder was caught off base at third, and fell down as he retreated to the bag. Salty fell on top of him, making the tag. Workman then struck out Avila, looking.

Scherzer hit Victorino, walked Pedroia, and there were two on with nobody out and David Ortiz at the plate. Ortiz lunged at a pitch and flied out to the warning track in left; he was 1-for-9 with runners in scoring position in the ALCS. Scherzer unleashed a wild pitch and both runners advanced, but he managed to strike out Napoli and get Salty to pop up to short. The lead remained Tigers 1, Red Sox 0.

Workman gave up a hit to Austin Jackson in the top of the seventh, but picked him off. Then Iglesias singled off Workman, and Workman couldn't quite pick up Hunter's bunt and was charged with an error. There were now two on, two out. Tazawa vs. Cabrera, Taz won the battle when Stephen Drew cut off what looked like a base hit up the middle, throwing out the soon to be back-to-back MVP winner.

After the seventh-inning stretch, Jonny Gomes missed a home run by less than a foot, the ball bouncing high off the Green Monster. He was on second base representing the tying run. Stephen Drew was 1-for-19 in the ALCS. He struck out for the tenth time in 20 at-bats. Bogaerts walked again, on six pitches. The left-hander Drew Smyly relieved Scherzer to pitch to Ellsbury. Iglesias bobbled the groundball ball behind second base—conceivably a double-play ball, even with Ellsbury running—and everyone was safe. The bases were loaded. Shane Victorino was up, facing Jose Veras, and the crowd sang along with his walkup music: "Every little thing's gonna be alright!" An 0-2 curveball. Second row of the Monster seats in left. Grand slam. The Red Sox had a 5-2 lead. Every little thing was, indeed, alright.

Harkening back to Game Two, it was the second time Scherzer had left the game with a lead and the second time a grand slam off a reliever had propelled the Sox into the lead.

It was the third game in the ALCS in which one hit made all the difference for the Red Sox.

Breslow put down the Tigers 1-2-3 in the eighth. And, for what it was worth, Al Alburquerque struck out the side in Boston's bottom of the eighth. The Red Sox had struck out a record 73 times in the six games of the ALCS.

Nothing but strikes. Uehara threw 12 pitches in the top of the ninth. Every one of them was a strike. He struck out Avila in the bottom of the ninth on three pitches, got an assist on the second batter, fielding Infante's bunt and throwing him out, and after a single by Jackson, struck out Iglesias.

The Red Sox were headed to the World Series for the third time in ten years.

The MVP of the series was Koji Uehara, who won Game Two and earned saves in three games. He'd appeared in five of the six games and allowed just four hits, striking out nine of the 21 batters he faced and walking none. He didn't allow a run. When he was asked on the field, during the postgame presentation if he'd been nervous and felt the pressure facing Iglesias for the final out that would send his team to the World Series, he answered, "To tell you the truth, I almost threw up."

THE WORLD SERIES

Game One: Fenway Park, Boston / October 23, 2013

Boston 8, St. Louis 1

St. Louis	000	000	001	—	1	7	3
Boston	320	000	21x	—	8	8	1

WP: Jon Lester (1-0)   LP: Adam Wainwright (0-1)   HR: Holliday (1), Ortiz (1)

Jon Lester got the nod to start the 2013 World Series. He was 2-1 (2.33) so far in the 2013 postseason, with opponents hitting .229 off him. The Series itself was the fourth time the Red Sox and Cardinals had squared off. St. Louis won both the 1946 and 1967 World Series, both times taking seven games to do so. In 2004, Boston won, sweeping St. Louis. Naturally, Red Sox fans liked the idea of drawing even with the Cardinals, two World Series wins apiece.

Game One Red Sox starter Jon Lester doffs his hat to the fans as he leaves the game in the eighth inning at Fenway Park. Lester did not allow a run as the Red Sox cruised to an 8-1 win.

Game One Red Sox starter Jon Lester doffs his hat to the fans as he leaves the game in the eighth inning at Fenway Park. Lester did not allow a run as the Red Sox cruised to an 8-1 win. (Boston Red Sox)

Lester had started the regular season 6-0, and finished 15-8 (3.75). The team ERA was 3.79. Lester's 15 wins were the most of any Red Sox pitcher. Clay Buchholz came second with 12 wins. Lester led the team in innings pitched and in strikeouts. The Cards got a Matt Holliday single off him in the top of the first, but no more than that.

The Red Sox drew first blood, off Adam Wainwright. He'd had a better season than any Red Sox pitcher (19-9, with a 2.94 ERA), and he'd been 2-1 with a 1.57 ERA in the post-season. Opponents were only hitting .207 against him. He'd struck out 20 and only walked one. This wasn't his best night. The first thing he did was to walk Ellsbury, never a good idea. Victorino lined one to left. Pedroia singled to shallow center. Ellsbury had to hold at second. Ortiz grounded the ball toward second and reached on a Pete Kozma's error on Carpenter's flipped feed to the bag. The bases were loaded. Or at least that was the end result because initially second base umpire Dana DeMuth called it an out and the Red Sox bench erupted. The umpires conferred and agreed that Kozma had never had possession of the ball. It was the first time in the 2013 postseason that the umpires had had to overrule one of their fellows; clearly, after consulting each other, they got it right.

When play resumed, Mike Napoli took two balls, then hit a gapper to left-center that took two bounces and then struck the wall. Ortiz saw where the ball was headed and scored all the way from first base, waved in all the way by third-base coach Brian Butterfield. After two outs, Wainwright ended the 31-pitch inning. Red Sox, 3-0.

Strikeout, strikeout, groundout, and Lester sat down in the second. The Red Sox added two more runs on two singles. Drew's wasn't a legitimate single; it was the easiest-possible pop-up for the pitcher to catch, but Wainwright just gazed at the ball as it came down about one foot in front of him. David Ross hit a single just barely over the second baseman's glove. Ellsbury flied out. Victorino hit a ball between short and third, and Kozma got a glove on it but again couldn't squeeze the glove shut to actually catch the ball. It was his second error. This was sloppy St. Louis baseball. Pedroia poked an RBI single through the same hole, and Ortiz followed with a sacrifice fly deep to right field. (Carlos Beltran reached into the Cardinals bullpen and pulled the ball back in. Otherwise, it was a grand slam). The Red Sox held a 5-0 lead.

No one scored again until the seventh. Lester gave up two singles in the fourth (getting out of a bases-loaded situation with a 1-2-6 double play) and two in the fifth, but no one scored. The team that scored next was … the Red Sox.

Wainwright had left after five innings and 95 pitches. John Axford pitched the sixth and struck out the side.

In the bottom of the seventh, Randy Choate got Ellsbury to ground out. Then Seth Maness got Victorino. Pedroia reached on the third error assessed to St. Louis, when David Freese bounced a routine throw to first base into the dirt. Kevin Siegrest was brought in to pitch to Big Papi. His first pitch was sent high in the air, coming down just barely into the first row of bleacher seats behind the Boston bullpen. 7-0, Red Sox. Ortiz had been batting .216, but now had his 16th career postseason home run.

St. Louis Cardinals shortstop Pete Kozma bobbles the double play ball as Dustin Pedroia slides into second. After initially calling Pedroia out on the force, the umpires conferred and changed the decision: Safe!

Lester retired the first two batters in the top of the eighth, and then he was retired—given the rest of the night off, and leaving to a huge ovation. He'd thrown 112 pitches, allowed five hits and a walk, and struck out eight. He

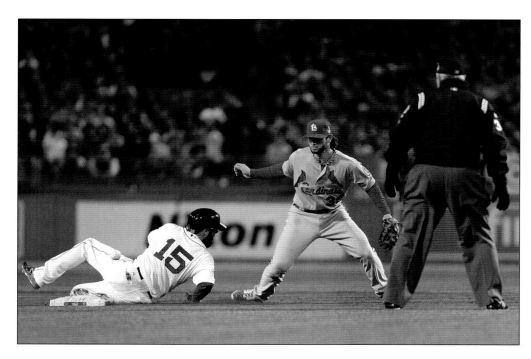

Dustin Pedroia slides safely into second base during Game One. (Boston Red Sox)

hadn't given up a run. Tazawa struck out the third man. And "Sweet Caroline" played.

In the bottom of the eighth, Daniel Nava pinch-hit for Gomes. In his first full season, Nava played in 134 games and hit for a .303 average—eighth in the American League. He doubled into the left-field corner. He jogged to third on a wild pitch, then scored run #8 when Bogaerts lined a sacrifice fly to left.

With the score 8-0, Ryan Dempster had only to get three outs and the game would be over. First up was Matt Holliday. On the fourth pitch, he homered into the light tower atop the wall in left center. St. Louis was on the board, but that was the only run they got.

After the sweeps in 2004 and 2007, this Game One win was Boston's ninth consecutive World Series victory. And the Cardinals looked like they were totally overmatched.

As a side note, Cardinals manager Mike Metheny had been the starting catcher on the 2004 Cardinals team that was swept by the Red Sox in that year's World Series.

PLAYER PROFILE: DAVID "BIG PAPI" ORTIZ

Since arriving in 2003, David Ortiz has been integral in bringing three World Series championships to Boston in a ten-year span. In the process, the amiable native of the Dominican Republic has become one of the most popular sports stars in a city that has been blessed with a galaxy of them.

Red Sox fans can thank their lucky stars that another of those stars, Pedro Martinez, convinced the Red Sox front office to take a long hard look at acquiring his fellow countryman after Ortiz's release by the Minnesota Twins. In fact he wasn't so much released as unleashed to wreck havoc on American League pitchers.

Ortiz took to Boston like a duck boat to water. In his first season, he struck for 31 homers and 101 RBIs and even got some MVP support in sparking the Red Sox to a postseason spot. Once in the playoffs, he showed some of the flair for drama we would soon come to expect, homering twice against the Yankees in a losing effort in the ALCS. In 2004 he batted .301, slugged 41 homers and drove in 139 runs while slugging another-worldly .603 (his OPS was .983) as he helped power the Red Sox to a World Series championship. In the playoffs his assault on pitchers continued as he batted .409 with 23 RBIs and five homers. His uncanny ability to come up big in the clutch was now in the spotlight for all to see. The walk-off homer became his trademark. He did it in the tenth inning of Game Three of the ALDS off Jarrod Washburn of the Anaheim Angels to advance the Red Sox to the ALCS against the Yankees.

He did it against New York's Paul Quantrill in the 12th frame of Game Four to cue the greatest comeback in postseason history. In the next game he used a walk-off single to beat the Yankees in the 14th inning. In the World Series, he introduced himself to National League pitchers by hitting a three-run shot off St. Louis Cardinals starter Woody Williams in the first inning of Game One to set the tone for the four-game sweep and the Red Sox first championship in 86 years.

If he had been a flash in the pan and stopped right there he would still have been remembered forever in the land of the bean and the cod. After all, before the 2005 season started the Red Sox had presented him with a plaque calling him "the greatest clutch-hitter in the history of the Boston Red Sox." But he didn't stop, or even slow down. In 2006 he set the new team standard for regular-season home runs, hitting 54 to eclipse the 50 hit by Hall of Famer Jimmie Foxx in 1938. In 2007, he led the Red Sox to their second World Series championship of the new century. Two great offensive years followed and then in 2007 he hit 35 homers and added 52 doubles while batting .332 and driving in 117 runs to lead the Sox to yet another World Series. Once in the October Classic, he batted a lofty .370 and hit three homers as the Sox beat the Colorado Rockies in four straight games.

Injuries slowed him down in the next few seasons although his statistics were still impressive. In 2013 he was back in full force with 30 homers, 103 RBIs, and a .309 batting average as he once again helped carry the longshot Red Sox to the postseason. On the big stage of the playoffs he added five homers, 13 RBIs, and a lusty .353 batting mark. He struck for two long balls off Tampa Bay ace David Price in Game Two of the ALDS and a dramatic grand slam against the Detroit Tigers in eighth inning of Game Two of the ALCS. In the World Series against St. Louis, he more than earned the MVP Award as he homered twice and added six RBIs as the Red Sox won in six.

David Ortiz is, indeed, Senor Octubre.

He has single-handedly made the Designated Hitter a respected occupation and holds most significant DH hitting marks. Aside from his World Series heroics, Ortiz can boast nine All-Star Team selections.

Game Two: Fenway Park, Boston / October 24, 2013

St. Louis 4, Boston 2

St. Louis	000	100	300	—	4	7	1
Boston	000	002	000	—	2	4	2

WP: Michael Wacha (1-0)   LP: John Lackey (0-1)   SV: Trevor Rosenthal (1)   HR: Ortiz (2)

The Cardinals' 22-year-old right-hander, Michael Wacha, ran his record in the postseason to 4-0, with a strong Game Two effort against the Red Sox. In his first three games—against the Pirates in the NLDS and two against the Dodgers in the NLCS, he'd allowed all of one run, a solo home run to Pittsburgh's Pedro Alvarez. In effect, one bad pitch. It was the only hit of the game for the Pirates. None of the three games was a complete game, but he'd essentially thrown a one-hitter and two shutouts in 21 innings before facing the Red Sox. He had a 0.43 ERA in the playoffs.

Wacha had only pitched a partial season, 64 ⅔ innings in 15 appearances. He'd been 4-1 with a 2.78 earned run average.

He was matched against John Lackey of the Red Sox, having himself a comeback year. Lackey had suffered through an execrable 2011 season, going 12-12 with a 6.41 ERA, in fact leading the American League in earned runs allowed. It wasn't all his fault. He had Tommy John surgery on his right elbow not long after the season was over, and missed the whole of 2012. Lackey had also gone through a divorce, while his wife was fighting breast cancer, and was seen as one of the central figures in the "fried chicken and beer" collapse at the end of 2011 (if you don't remember it, consider yourself fortunate, but you could look it up).

In 2013, Lackey had a biceps strain in his very first start. Despite posting a losing record (10-13) for a winning team, he pitched well (3.52 ERA—and much better at home than on the road) and threw 189 ⅓ innings. (The team ERA was 3.79; in six of his starts, the Sox offense scored zero runs). He'd won the clinching Game Five against the Rays in the Division Series, and won Game Three against the Tigers with 6 ⅔ innings of shutout ball.

Neither team scored for the first three innings. Each team had two base runners and each had four strikeouts. Matt Holliday led off the fourth inning with a triple to deep right-center that bounced off the side of the Sox bullpen and bounded behind Ellsbury. Pedroia lunged and dove to his right and about six inches off the infield dirt, he snared a sinking liner from Matt Adams for one out. Yadier Molina chopped a high-bounding ball that hopped over Lackey and was fielding by Pedroia; his only play was to first, with Holliday—who'd read the hop—scoring on the throw.

The Red Sox tried to get one back, Pedroia doubling off the scoreboard to kick off the bottom of the fourth. Ortiz walked on five pitches, but Napoli grounded into a double play and Gomes popped up.

In the bottom of the sixth, after Wacha had completed 19 consecutive scoreless innings in the postseason (tying Bob Gibson for the Cardinals' franchise record), Boston took the lead with a one-out walk to Pedroia and, on a 3-2 pitch, Big Papi hit a high changeup and powered the pitch into the first row of the Monster Seats in left-center field. It was 2-1, Red Sox.

It seemed there had often been a tendency to leave Lackey in a little too long in regular-season games, but he had only thrown 80 pitches, so he started the seventh. He struck out Allen Craig on three pitches, but then David Freese (hitting .186 in the postseason) made him throw eight, and worked a walk. Jon Jay singled. Freese held at second, but after Craig Breslow came on in relief, the two runners executed a double steal, successful because Salty couldn't get a grip on the ball. Lefty against lefty, Breslow walked the #9 hitter, Daniel Descalso. Bases loaded. Matt

Carpenter flied out to left, a sacrifice fly to tie the game. If the play had ended there, it would have been OK, but now it was Boston's turn to look as clumsy as St. Louis had in Game One.

Gomes caught Carpenter's shallow fly, but his throw was six feet or so up the line toward first and Saltalamacchia stretched out like a first baseman but let the ball get by him. Breslow—backing up the play—threw wildly to third base, way over Drew's head, with the ball one-hopping all the way into the seats. There were two errors charged on the play that gave St. Louis the lead and put Descalso on third.

Carlos Beltran singled to right and scored Descalso. It was 4-2, Cardinals.

The Sox didn't get the ball out of the infield in the seventh. They had a chance to score in the eighth when Ellsbury reached on an error and, after two K's, Ortiz singled. But Napoli popped up to short. Trevor Rosenthal struck out the side in the bottom of the ninth.

The Red Sox streak, winning nine consecutive World Series games, had been snapped before it could reach ten. It was another hard-luck loss for Lackey. Lackey unlucky? "That's kind of obvious," he told writers after the game.

The Series was tied, one game apiece. Each team's fielding had helped the other to a win.

The Cardinals were happy to head home with a split. They'd play there at Busch with the Sox deprived of the DH and facing two Boston pitchers who had question marks next to their names.

PLAYER PROFILE: JOHN LACKEY

How do you go from being one of the most reviled athletes in Boston to a symbol of forgiveness worthy of *Shawshank Redemption?* Well, first you shed a few pounds, recover from surgery and you get your pitching mojo back. Then you help to lead the underdog Boston Red Sox to their third World Series championship in ten years.

Lackey had won Game Seven of the 2002 World Series for the Anaheim Angels and come to Boston from the Angels in 2010 with an $82 million, five-year contract and big expectations. His first season was less than stellar as he recorded a ho-hum 14-10 record and a worrisome 4.40 ERA. The 2011 campaign was even more distressing. After a disastrous start, an elbow strain forced him on the disabled list and when he returned he was terrible. When his season was mercifully over, his record was 12-12 and his ERA had ballooned to 6.41, the highest ever for a Red Sox starter with 150 innings of work. In fact he allowed more earned runs (114) than any AL pitcher. Even more disturbing to Red Sox Nation were reports that he and a coterie of fellow pitchers were using the clubhouse as their own Animal House, drinking beer and eating fried chicken between starts.

This did not go over well with Red Sox fans who were outraged that a player with his astronomic salary would not put forth his best effort, or at least stay in shape. They also blamed Lackey and his fellow revelers for prompting the dismissal of Tito Francona, the manager who had brought two World Series titles to Beantown.

During the winter of discontent that was the off-season, Lackey underwent Tommy John surgery and was sidelined for the entire 2012 season, missing the one-year Bobby Valentine management experiment. Once again reports surfaced that part of his rehabbing routine included more beer in the clubhouse.

Red Sox fans can put up with many things, but lack of effort is not one of them. When Lackey returned to the mound in 2013, he was seen as a part of the problem, not the solution. They cursed the five-year contract that shackled them to this over-priced loser. When he strained his right bicep in his first season start, fans were prepared for another long season. And then things began to change. The man who had recently been as popular as dry rot was suddenly re-gaining the reputation he'd once had as a battler—a tough, emotional pitcher who the Red Sox had thought they were getting. At 10-13, his season record was not impressive but his ERA had dropped to 3.52 and he was a hard-luck loser on several occasions. Once in the postseason, he won games in the ALDS, the ALCS, and the World Series. His redemption was complete.

Game Three: Busch Stadium, St. Louis / October 26, 2013

St. Louis 5, Boston 4

Boston	000	011	020	—	4	6	2
St. Louis	200	000	201	—	5	12	0

WP: Trevor Rosenthal (1-0)   LP: Brandon Workman (0-1)

Game Three was a close one, which saw the Red Sox catch up twice but ultimately fall behind a third time, in the bottom of the ninth, on a play that left everyone but the umpires confused.

Cardinals pitcher Joe Kelly, 25, got the Sox in order in the top of the first. The righty had started in 15 games and relieved in 22 others; he'd been 10-5 in the regular season with a 2.69 ERA.

Jake Peavy was looking for a little redemption. He'd lost two National League Division Series games against St. Louis when he was with the Padres, once in 2005 and once in 2006, and he'd lost Game Four of the 2013 ALCS. The Cardinals beat on Peavy for four singles in their half of the first, but were held to only two runs. It was the first time they'd scored in the first inning in the 2013 postseason. The Red Sox had Felix Doubront start to loosen up even before the second out.

Boston didn't get the ball out of the infield in the first inning, the second inning, or the third. It was only in the top of the fourth—the score still 2-0, St. Louis—that they got a hit (an infield single Ellsbury beat out). Finally, a ball to the outfield, but it was just a fly ball off Pedroia's bat.

The Red Sox lost Game Three on a controversial interference call as third base ump Jim Joyce ruled that third baseman Will Middlebrooks had impeded Cardinals base runner Allen Craig, preventing him from scoring. The ruling ended the game 5-4 as Craig was allowed to cross home with the winning Cardinals run. (Boston Red Sox)

Peavy settled down through the second and third, but gave up a single, a base on balls, and another single in the top of the fourth. Nobody out, and Workman got up in the pen. A graphic on TV informed viewers that Reggie Sanders of the Cardinals had hit a grand slam off Peavy in the 2005 playoffs. But Farrell stuck with Peavy and he struck out Kozma and got the pitcher (Kelly), and Carpenter to pop up in the infield.

Xander Bogaerts finally put the Sox in position to score with a triple to lead off the fifth, hit to right-center between the outfielders and bouncing all the way to the bullpen wall. Salty walked but Drew (.093) stepped to the plate—and struck out, awkwardly. He couldn't have looked much worse at the plate than he had throughout most of the Series, but Farrell kept him in there for his defense (and his potential power—Drew had hit 13 homers in the regular season, and won two games with walkoffs— May 6 with a double and July 31 with a single in the bottom of the 15th).

Peavy was due up, but with an opportunity to put a run on the board, Mike Carp pinch-hit. He grounded out, second base to short, but Bogaerts scored on a ball that would have been a double play if Carp hadn't chopped the ball high enough that he was able to beat the relay to first. Ellsbury struck out.

Felix Doubront pitched two scoreless innings, during which the Red Sox tied the score with another run in the top of the sixth. Victorino walked and Kelly got Pedroia, who slashed a ball right over third base, grabbed by Freese. Randy Choate was brought in to pitch to Ortiz, who singled through the shift and Victorino ran all the way to third. Seth Maness came in to pitch to left-fielder Daniel Nava, and Nava singled to left and brought in the Flyin' Hawaiian to tie the score. Bogaerts hit into a double play.

In the bottom of the seventh, St. Louis got two more runs, taking a 4-2 lead, when Carpenter beat out an infield single off Breslow and Beltran was barely grazed by a Breslow pitch. Tazawa relieved Breslow, but Holliday doubled just under a diving Middlebrooks and straight down the third-base line, scoring both base runners. Tazawa buckled down and got out of the inning without further damage.

Boston bounced right back, to re-tie the score, adding two runs in the top of the eighth after loading the bases with one out off Carlos Martinez. Cardinals ace Trevor Rosenthal took over. Nava grounded into a forceout at second base, scoring one run, and Bogaerts reached on a bouncer up the middle, scoring Shane Victorino. Nava now had two RBIs. It had been a bit of a mystery why John Farrell had used Jonny Gomes more often than Nava, particularly given that Nava ranked third in the league in OPS. Gomes had gone 5-for-32 in the postseason and only had one hit in his last 17 at-bats. At least in Drew's case (4-for-42 coming into the game, and one hit in his last 36 at-bats), there was the mitigating factor of his stellar defensive play at shortstop. Gomes had had two walkoff game-winners during the season, as had Drew. And Nava had had one.

Brandon Workman struggled a little in the bottom of the eighth, with a single, a stolen base, and an intentional walk, but St. Louis failed to score. Rosenthal tightened up and struck out two (Workman batted for himself) and got the third out on a grounder to third. After the game, Farrell admitted he'd messed up and not implemented a double switch, taking Workman out in favor of, say, Mike Napoli.

In the bottom of the ninth, Workman struck out Adams but Molina singled. Koji Uehara was summoned from the bullpen. Allen Craig pinch-hit for Rosenthal, swung at the first pitch, and slashed a double to the left of left-fielder Nava. Then came a very unusual play, robbed of some of its drama because many people—at the ballpark and at home—had no clear idea just what they had seen. Jon Jay hit the ball to Pedroia at second, who made a brilliant play and fired the ball to home plate and erased Molina for the second out of the inning. Salty didn't have his foot on the plate and had to wait a split-second to tag the incoming Molina, and then—rather than simply hold the ball—hurried a throw to third base hoping to force out the slow-footed Craig heading into the bag. His throw went wild, and Craig ran for home. The errant ball was corralled by Nava, who threw home where Salty blocked the plate. The throw seemed to get Craig out at the plate, but everyone was treated to the vision of the plate umpire calling Craig safe—then pointing to third base. There had been a collision at third base, Craig falling down on top of Will Middlebrooks who was diving to try and catch the ball, then scrambling to right himself to head for home plate.

Even before Nava fielded the throw, Middlebrooks was said to have obstructed Craig, who was therefore awarded the plate—and the winning run. It was a bizarre way for the game to end. There wasn't much else that Middlebrooks could have done; he had to go for the ball. Under the rule, intent didn't matter. His body was in Craig's way. No one could remember any game ending on an obstruction call. But it did end, with a Cardinals win, and now St. Louis had the advantage, up two games to one.

It was the second game in a row in which an errant Red Sox throw cost them the game. Add Game One, when it was the Cardinals who made multiple miscues, and this World Series was not impressing anyone with the defense shown by the two pennant-winners.

Carlos Beltran said, "At the time, I had no idea what happened. Maybe 75 percent of the guys on the field didn't know what had happened. All I knew was that we won." After the game, MLB's Joe Torre said the rule regarding obstruction would be reviewed over the winter.

PLAYER PROFILE: DUSTIN PEDROIA

Dustin Pedroia would have been right at home on the "Go Go" White Sox of 1959 or the 1950 Philadelphia Phillies "Whiz Kids." Heck, he would have looked right at home on the 1927 Yankees, God forbid. In short (sorry Dustin), he's a throwback to another time, a time when major league rosters contained names like Pee Wee and Minnie and Stubby and Wee Willie. It was a time when GMs didn't stop reading scouting reports if the height and weight weren't to their liking. They looked beyond such physical characteristics, at things like heart and ability and drive and desire. Luckily the Red Sox front office has some of that throwback attitude too, because they did just that when they signed Dustin Pedroia and stuck with him.

Pedroia has a major league resume that is hard to beat. In 2007 he was Rookie of the Year and a World Series champion. In 2008 he was AL MVP. He has won the Silver Slugger Award and has three Gold Gloves. All this from a 5'8", 165-pound tightly-wrapped package of baseball perfection. Pedroia lives and breathes the game. In his first year he batted .317 and drove in 50 runs in the regular season. He batted .395 in the ALCS against the Cleveland Indians and struck for a two-run homer in the seventh inning and a three-run double in the eighth to drive in five runs in the Game Seven clincher.

He continued to garner national attention in the World Series, hitting the second pitch he saw over the Green Monster to give the Red Sox the lead. It was only the second time in MLB history that a player had started the October Classic with a dinger, and the first time a rookie had done so.

In 2008 he batted .326 with a league-best 213 hits, 17 of them homers, a league-leading 54 of them doubles. He also added 20 swipes and topped the AL in runs scored with 118. This Silver Slugger offensive display coupled with his Gold Glove-caliber fielding earned him the MVP Award. His bat was cooled in the ALDS against the Angels but caught fire against the Tampa Bay Rays in the ALCS as he batted .346 with three homers and a .731 slugging average. Unfortunately it was in a losing cause.

Pedey had another great year in 2009, topping the junior circuit in runs scored (115) finishing with 48 doubles, third-best in the majors. He was hampered by a broken bone in his foot in 2010 although he insisted on keeping his defensive reflexes sharp by fielding grounders on his knees. The injury bug bit him again in 2012 as he tore a muscle in his right thumb and subsequently broke the ring finger of his left hand. He insisted on playing despite the injury.

In 1913, he tore a left-thumb ligament in his hand sliding into first base—on Opening Day, but eschewed surgery, played in 160 games, batted .301, drove in 84 runs, won his third Gold Glove, and got the Sox off to a solid start in the playoffs with five RBIs against the Rays. There aren't many 5'8" franchise players, but Pedroia is one of them and the Red Sox recognized the fact by signing him to an eight-year, $110 million contract midway through the 2013 season. Some players perform better with the confidence boost of such an enormous deal, some underperform. There was no discernable difference in Pedroia's approach to the game. When you consistently give 100 percent, there is little room for improvement.

Game Four: Busch Stadium, St. Louis / October 27, 2013

Boston 4, St. Louis 2

Boston	000	013	000	—	4	6	2
St. Louis	001	000	100	—	2	6	0

WP: Felix Doubront (1-0)   LP: Lance Lynn (0-1)   SV: Koji Uehara (1)   HR: Gomes (1)

This was meant to be Nava's game in left field, with Gomes having the day off. Gomes was 0-for-8 in the Series. As it worked out, they both got to play. About an hour and a half before the game, Victorino had to beg off due to a balky back, and Nava took his place in right, freeing up Gomes to play in left. David Ross took over for Saltalamacchia behind the plate.

Nava had hit a grand slam on the very first pitch he'd seen as a rookie, and had an .831 OPS in 2013, third in the league only to Mike Trout and Jose Bautista. He'd homered 12 times to Gomes's 13. Gomes had hit for a .247 average, Nava (in 170 more plate appearances) .303.

The game featured Lance Lynn (15-10, 3.97) pitching for the Cardinals and Clay Buchholz (12-1, 1.74) for the Red Sox. Buchholz clearly had a superior season—in fact, a truly spectacular season—when he was healthy. But from June 9 to September 9, he didn't pitch at all. After Buchholz used eight pitches to strike out Lynn, back-to-back singles by Carpenter and Beltran (and an error by Ellsbury on Carpenter that skidded past Pedroia and took a bad hop just as

For the second time in as many games, the final out of Game Four came suddenly. This one came courtesy of a nifty Koji Uehara pickoff move that caught Cardinals pinch-runner Kolten Wong napping and sent the Red Sox home victorious.
(Boston Red Sox)

Ellsbury went to glove it, enabling the batter to reach second) resulted in one run for St. Louis in the bottom of the third.

Lynn faced the minimum 12 batters, with one single erased on a double play, through the first four. In the top of the fifth, Ortiz hit a gap double to right-center (he was now 7-for-10 in the Series) and then Gomes walked—taking ten pitches to earn the base on balls, after starting the at-bat with two strikes. Bogaerts walked and the bases were loaded with nobody out. Stephen Drew hit a sac fly to left, which scored a run and tied the game (the ball hit Ortiz as he reached the plate). But that was all they got.

Carp had pinch-hit for Buchholz; Felix Doubront took over pitching duties for the Red Sox. The Cards went out in order, on nine pitches—two K's sandwiched around a lineout to left.

Before the top of the sixth, the television camera showed David Ortiz talking to the team in an impromptu dugout huddle, trying to fire them up.

Ellsbury and Nava made outs, though. Then, with the two outs and nobody on, Pedroia dropped a single into left and Ortiz walked on four pitches. Manager Mike Metheny replaced Lynn with Seth Maness. Jonny Gomes was up; he was 1-for-18 in the postseason and had nine at-bats and no hits in the World Series. On a 2-2 pitch, as the Busch fans obeyed the message board instructions ("LET'S GET LOUD") and started waving towels, Gomes swung and hit a three-run homer into the visitors bullpen in left field to give the Sox a 4-1 lead.

When Gomes reached the dugout, Napoli gave his beard a hard tug, as did Ross, and he was pummeled by most of the other players. It was the first extra-base hit by any Red Sox outfielder in the entire Series.

This was the same Maness who had come in and given up a game-tying hit to Nava in the sixth inning of Game Three. Bogaerts hit the next pitch for a single, but languished on first when Drew grounded out.

Doubront pitched a scoreless sixth and got the first two outs of the seventh, but Shane Robinson struck a pinch-hit double and Craig Breslow was brought in to pitch to Carpenter. He singled to right and Robinson scored. It was 4-2. Tazawa, with two runners on base, got Holliday to ground out.

John Lackey pitched the bottom of the eighth (his first relief appearance since 2004) and allowed neither a hit nor a run. He was the third starter to pitch in Game Four—Buchholz, Doubront, and now Lackey. He had just pitched in Game Two, but it was his side day and with the double switch he was able to come in and bat fourth, getting Mike Napoli into the game for his defense at first base. He would bat third in the top of the ninth. After a groundout, a throwing error by Bogaerts and a subsequent wild pitch got a runner to third base before a pop fly to shortstop and a ground ball to shortstop ended the inning.

The sixth Sox pitcher of the game, Koji Uehara, pitched the bottom of the ninth, hoping to preserve the 4-2 lead. Descalso grounded out. Allen Craig pinch-hit for the pitcher and drove the ball deep to right field, one-hopping the wall and taking a high bounce back to Nava. Craig's subpar ankle limited him to a single. Kolten Wong took Craig's place, as a pinch runner.

The tying run was now at the plate. The Fox announcers both agreed the Red Sox wouldn't try to hold Wong on first base. His run wasn't even the tying run, and holding him on the bag would leave a hole in the right side of the infield with two left-handed hitters coming to the plate. But hold him on they did. Carpenter hit a high pop-up to Pedroia who ranged into shallow right to collect the second out of the inning. Carlos Beltran came to the plate. A home run would tie the game. A single, a walk … anything to keep the hometown hopes alive. If he could get on, Matt Holliday was on deck. He took ball one, low, then took strike one.

And then Koji picked off Wong, to end the game! It was the second game in a row that ended with a very unusual play. It was so unexpected that the TV was focused on a Cardinals fan in the crowd and didn't catch the throw in real time, only picking up Napoli's catch and tag—and the game was over. Beltran never swung the bat. Imagine how Wong felt, taking the bat out of Beltran's hands, caught off the base, and ending a game on the biggest stage in baseball. The Fox announcers were forced to eat crow.

Uehara said he made the play on his own, not after any signal from Ross. No, there hadn't been anything he read about Wong in the scouting reports. "I don't read the scouting reports," he admitted with a laugh.

For his part, Ross said, "That was awesome. It was kind of like last night. I bet they're dumbfounded like, 'What just happened?'"

The Red Sox as a team were hitting .188 (not counting Ortiz, they were only hitting .147), but now the Series was tied again, and if the Series went seven games, two of the three games to come would be played in Boston, with the DH restored for the Red Sox.

The hirsute Red Sox pulled together all season long and sometimes it was painful. David Ross welcomes Jonny Gomes with a beard yank after Gomes's 3-run home run against the Cards in the sixth frame of Game Three of the 2013 Fall Classic. (Boston Red Sox)

PLAYER PROFILE: SHANE VICTORINO

Shane Victorino just plays the game right. He looks like he's having fun out there: talking with the ump, chatting with the opposing catcher or first baseman. Always wearing a smile. Victorino—Great baseball name. Great baseball player.

Known as "The Flyin' Hawaiian," Victorino came to the Red Sox in a three-year $39 million dollar deal in the off-season prior to the 2013 campaign. After a disastrous 2012 season, the Red Sox were looking for some character guys to right a ship that sometimes looked to be foundering. They couldn't have found a better one than the former World Series champion with the 2008 Philadelphia Phillies. Tangible proof of that character can be seen in his trophy room. He has earned both a Lou Gehrig Memorial Award (2008) given to the player who has contributed "exceptional community service" and the Branch Rickey Award (2011) presented to the player who best exhibits the legendary character and integrity of the Iron Horse on the field and off.

As a newcomer to Fenway and its various delights and eccentricities, he was placed in the toughest right field in baseball. From the beginning he played like he owned the real estate, often with reckless abandon, and at season's end was rewarded with his fourth Gold Glove. In the 2013 postseason (he's appeared in 60 postseason games in his career), he drove in 12 runs, most of them coming when he not one but two grand slams, one of only two players to do so in the history of the game. In Game Six of the ALCS, his come-from-behind four-bagger in the bottom of the seventh de-clawed the Detroit Tigers and punched the Red Sox ticket to the World Series. And, without a homer in the mix, he drove in four of Boston's six runs in their 6-1 Game Six win that gave the Red Sox their first World Series championship climax at home in 95 years.

Game Five: Busch Stadium, St. Louis / October 28, 2013

Boston 3, St. Louis 1

Boston	100	000	200	—	3	9	0
St. Louis	000	100	000	—	1	4	0

WP: Jon Lester (2-0)   LP: Adam Wainwright (0-2)   SV: Koji Uehara (2)   HR: Holliday (2)

What would this game hold? The first two games of the Series were comedies of errors, even the plays that weren't strictly scored as errors. It was only fair that one game went each way. The second pair of games ended abruptly and even bizarrely. Again, each team got one win.

The Red Sox had every reason to suspect that Adam Wainwright would be a lot tougher on them than he'd been in Game One. Two of those five runs had been unearned. He led the NL in wins; he was probably going to be tough. Indeed, he struck out the side in the top of the first (all three looking), and struck out the side in the second (all three swinging).

But … hold on a minute. Mixed in among the first-inning K's were back-to-back doubles by Dustin and David. Pedroia and Papi. Pedroia's came on a 2-2 count, bouncing to the left-field wall between the left fielder and the corner. Ortiz hit one just barely inside the bag at first, and continuing foul from there—a two-base hit, and one run resulted. Ortiz was now 9 for 12 in the World Series, with six RBIs. Over one-third of the 26 hits to this point in the five games of the Series had come off Ortiz's bat.

Jon Lester put together some strikeouts, too, though he gave up a single in the second and a single in the third. He was the leadoff batter in the third inning and 0-for-31 at the plate in his career. Yet he became the first Red Sox batter to hit into an out, rather than whiff. He grounded the ball 15-20 feet down the third-base line and Molina pounced and threw to first.

Ortiz singled again in the top of the fourth; with that hit into right field, he had reached base in nine consecutive plate appearances, tying a World Series record. He was now batting .769.

In the bottom of the fourth, Lester gave up a gopher ball to Matt Holliday, who hammered a homer that went off a fan's outstretched hands and dropped onto the grass in center field, a little to the left of dead center. The score was tied, 1-1. And so it stayed through the fifth and sixth. It was a good, old-fashioned pitchers' duel.

As it turned out, the celebratory fireworks after Holliday's homer marked the last true moment for Cardinals fans to cheer in 2013.

In the top of the seventh, after recording his 10th strikeout of the game (Nava), Wainwright was touched up for a couple of runs by the bottom of the Boston batting order. Bogaerts singled right over the mound and up the middle, and Stephen Drew (who'd struck out 17 times in the postseason) worked a walk, which turned out to be the only free pass of the whole game. David Ross hit a ground-rule double that landed a few inches fair and then bounced into the stands in left. Ross's two-bagger scored Bogaerts and gave the Red Sox the lead. Even though there were two runners in scoring position with just one out, Farrell wanted to keep Lester as his pitcher so let him bat. He just slapped the ball back on a hop to Wainwright, who threw him out. Ellsbury made it 3-1, dropping a line drive into straightaway shallow center. That scored Drew, but third-base coach Butterfield aggressively waved in Ross only to see him cut down by Robinson's throw to home plate. Inning over.

Lester held the lead, retiring the side in the seventh and getting the first out in the bottom of the eighth. After Freese doubled, he got Kozma to fly out, and then Farrell called on Koji to face Matt Adams and go for a four-out save. He struck out Adams on three pitches and put down without incident the three batters he faced in the ninth.

There were no errors in the game and no weird endings. It was the first "normal" game of the Series, a 3-1 Red Sox win that put them up three games to two, with the two ballclubs returning to Boston to finish out the Series.

Lester got the win. He was 4-1 in the 2013 postseason with an ERA of 1.56.

It was Uehara's seventh save of the postseason.

It was great fun watching David Ross in the postgame interviews on TV. It was his first appearance in the World Series, at age 36 and having missed much of the season with two concussions. And he'd driven in the winning run of the game. He was so visibly happy to be sitting taking questions ("I'm up here talking to you guys, this is pretty cool, right?") that he not only offered to stay all night, but asked if he could stay at the interview table while the other players got interviewed.

PLAYER PROFILE: JON LESTER

Every time he goes to the mound you wonder which Jon Lester you're going to get. Will it be the guy who in 2008 pitched a no-hitter against the Kansas City Royals, the guy who can make hitters look totally overmatched and befuddled, or will it be that other guy? The other guy doesn't seem to know what to throw or when. He looks hesitant and makes bad decisions and worse pitches. That guy appears once in awhile, most notably in the latter part of 2011 and throughout 2012.

The 2013 season was only weeks old before Lester sent a clear message that he was back as a dominant pitcher. He pitched a one-hitter without allowing a walk on May 10 against the Toronto Blue jays, a team with a potent lineup of hitters.

His season record rebounded to a more Lester-like 15-8 and his ERA shrunk to 3.75 as the underdog Red Sox made it to the postseason. In Game One of the ALDS against the Tampa Bay Rays he struck out the first four batters he faced and went 7 ⅔ strong innings, striking out seven as the Red Sox won, 12-2.

He was also tabbed to start Game One of the ALCS against the heavy hitting Detroit Tigers. This time he went 6 ⅓ frames and gave up a single run in a classic showdown with Anibal Sanchez. Sanchez and his relief corps allowed only a single hit and the Tigers won the game, 1-0 at Fenway. In Game Five, the two pitchers faced off again, this time in Detroit. Lester exacted a measure of revenge, giving up two earned runs while going five innings as the Red Sox won by a 4-3 margin.

In the World Series, he was again asked to get the Red Sox off to a strong start and he did so in a 8-1 laugher. He also won Game Five, allowing just four Cardinals hits in 7 ⅔ innings for a 3-1 victory which placed the Red Sox on the verge of their third World Series title in a decade.

His 2013 playoff record was 4-1 with a 1.56 ERA in six starts. His career ERA in post-season play is 2.11.

And so, the Sox have no choice but to open their wallet for Lester, who almost certainly will seek at least a five-year contract worth upwards of $20 million per season.

Game Six: Fenway Park, Boston / October 30, 2013

Boston 6, St. Louis 1

St. Louis	000	000	100 —	1	9	1
Boston	003	300	00x —	6	8	1

WP: John Lackey (1-1)   LP: Michael Wacha (1-1)   HR: Drew (1)

No Boston team had won a World Series in Boston since 1918. Yes, the Red Sox had won in 2004 and 2007 but both of those wins were in the camp of the opposition. It had been 95 years since Boston fans could celebrate a win of the World Series at home. Fans filing into Fenway didn't want it to go to seven games. They wanted to get it over with in Game Six, and not have to play a do-or-die contest on Halloween. Sure, the Curse was dead but bad things can happen in a seventh game—witness 1946, 1967, 1975, and 1986, for instance.

The Red Sox had a .654 winning percentage in games played at home.

Here was John Lackey back again, pitching for the third time in the 2013 World Series. He was 1-0 in the Division Series, 1-0 in the League Championship Series, and had an opportunity to win a game now in the World Series, a win that would be a Series-clincher if he could pull it off. He'd lost Game Two, by one run, and he'd pitched a hitless, runless inning of relief in Game Four. Lackey had won the deciding Game Seven for the Angels in the 2002 World Series. If he won this night's game, he'd be the first pitcher to ever win a clinching game for two different franchises.

Seen here pitching in the first inning of Game Six of the World Series, John Lackey morphed from goat to hero during the 2013 season and postseason. (Boston Red Sox)

In ten pitches, he retired the Cardinals in order in the top of the first—thanks to some good fielding by Gomes in left and to good positioning based on Red Sox scouting reports that enabled Pedroia to field Beltran's hard-hit ball.

In the second, Lackey ran into some difficulty, with the first two batters (Craig and Molina) both singling, Craig's a hard drive off the left-field wall. Adams then put a scare into Sox fans with a ball hit to the left-field warning track, but he was out, and so was Freese. Lackey threw a wild pitch that moved up both runners, but struck out Jon Jay to end the threat.

Michael Wacha started for St. Louis. He walked Ortiz (on nine pitches) in the first, and gave up a single and a walk in the second. It was the bottom of the third before either team scored. Jacoby Ellsbury singled through the hole between first and second. He moved to second on Pedroia's broken-bat groundout. Ortiz was walked intentionally. (no surprise there!) Mike Napoli—able to play first base again, now that Ortiz was the designated hitter—struck out. Gomes was hit by a pitch, and the bases were loaded.

Up came Shane Victorino. The crowd was singing at top volume: "Every little thing gonna be all right." His grand slam had won Game Six of the League Championship Series, the game that won the series, but he was 0-for-10 in the World Series. What happened next was only fitting. He slammed a ball that would have been a grand slam again, in pretty much any other ballpark. Here it hit the Green Monster no more than ten feet from the top of the wall. It cleared the bases, Gomes sliding under a tag at the plate and gave the Red Sox a precious 3-0 lead.

The roar of the crowd at Fenway was deafening. Thank you, Bob Marley.

Victorino took third on the throw to home. He was shouting and pounding his chest with both fists like a berserk gorilla. This was a demonstrative team, from Gomes flexing his muscles like a boxing champion at second base during the season to the chest-pounding and beard-tugging in the postseason. Bogaerts slashed a ball to third base for the final out.

In the fourth, the Sox doubled their 3-0 lead. Stephen Drew finally came through (he'd been 1-for-16 in the Series and .078—4-for-51—in the postseason), homering on the first pitch he saw and driving it into the Red Sox bullpen, caught by Franklin Morales (who had also caught Ortiz's home run in Game Two of the Division Series). Ellsbury doubled off the bottom of the fence in front of the Cardinals bullpen, framed by outs by Ross before him and Pedroia after him. With first base open, Ortiz was walked once more—his third base on balls of the game, second intentional. Lance Lynn relieved Wacha to pitch to Napoli.

Beards and champagne. Clubhouse celebration after the 2013 World Series win. (Boston Red Sox)

Napoli looped a single to center, driving in Ellsbury. Then Gomes walked, loading the bases. Victorino was up, welcomed by another huge ovation, and he drove in his fourth run of the game with a single in front of Holliday in left. Victorino had incredible postseason stats with the bases loaded in the World Series: 6-for-8, with two grand slams and 20 RBIs. The score was 6-1, Red Sox. This was looking good.

It really was astonishing how well the underperforming members of the Red Sox had come through. Drew's homer had provided an important insurance run. Mike Napoli's only hit before his fourth-inning single had been his three-run game-winning double in the first inning of Game One. Jonny Gomes was 0-for-9 when he hit his game-winning three-run homer in Game Four. David Ross had the game-winning hit in Game Five, his RBI double. And Victorino had been 0-for-10 in the World Series before his three-run double (which proved the game-winner) here in Game Six. He now had 12 RBIs in the 2013 postseason.

St. Louis kept slapping hits off Lackey—they wound up with nine of them, all off the Red Sox starter, one more than Boston managed in the entire game. But the only run the Cardinals ended up scoring came in the seventh. Lackey expended only four pitches to get the first two batters, but then Descalso singled and Carpenter doubled. Beltran singled to left, scoring Descalso. It was 6-1, Red Sox. After a wild pitch while walking Holliday to load the bases, Lackey was lifted (to raucous applause) and Tazawa got Craig to ground out to Napoli, who flipped the ball back to Taz covering the bag.

Workman worked the eighth. Nine pitches, three outs. The crowd was as hyped as a crowd can be. They tasted victory. The authors of this book have attended close to 1,000 ballgames at Fenway Park and never heard anything this loud and this sustained. Through the eighth and ninth innings, it was unceasing.

After the game, Gomes said, "I work in a museum. And this is the loudest the museum's been in a long time." Gomes had started 11 of the 16 postseason games in left field; the Red Sox were 10-1 in those 11 games.

Ortiz never did get a hit in Game Six; he was walked four times, for the third time intentionally in the bottom of the eighth.

The Red Sox didn't score. Could they get three outs before St. Louis scored five runs? Would they go from worst in 2012 to first in 2013? Would they win the World Series at home for the first time in 95 years? Would they win their third world championship in the last ten years?

It wasn't a save situation, but it was only appropriate that Koji Uehara be called on to pitch the ninth and close out the game. He did. Jay hit a routine fly ball fairly deep to left. Then Descalso hit another fly ball to left, not as deep. Only one out away. Matt Carpenter ran the count to 2-2. Only one pitch away. He fouled off the fifth pitch. Then he fouled off the sixth pitch. All he was doing was delaying the inevitable. Things were just *not* going to go bad for the Red Sox this time around. There was no curse, and only a dimming memory of the time when it seemed that if something *could* go wrong for the Red Sox, it *would* go wrong.

Not any more.

On his seventh pitch to Carpenter, Koji got him to strike out swinging.

The place exploded. Total redemption. The celebration began.

PLAYER PROFILE: KOJI UEHARA

Before he had thrown his first pitch in the majors, Koji Uehara was a respected veteran in his native Japan and internationally. Pitching for the Yomiuri Giants from 1999 to 2008, he compiled a 112-62 record and an impressive overall ERA of 3.01. Primarily a starter, he also saw time limited time as a reliever and even as a closer. The two-time Olympian helped his homeland capture an Olympic bronze in 2004, and at the 2006 World Baseball Classic in San Diego he and his teammates struck gold.

At the age of thirty-four, Uehara came to North America to play for the Baltimore Orioles in 2009. He was added to the O's starting rotation and started 12 games before he was demoted to the unglamorous role of set-up man the following year. He was dealt to the Texas Rangers midway through the 2011 season where he was used sparingly and with limited success.

The seasoned veteran signed a one-year deal with the Boston Red Sox in December of 2012. Only after projected closers Andrew Bailey and Joel Hanrahan suffered injuries was he given a shot at the closer role. The move to Koji made sense. The previously unappreciated right-hander had quietly compiled one of the best strikeout-to-walk ratios in the history of the game, for players with 100 innings pitched. He responded to the challenge with 21 saves in 24 opportunities and posted a 1.09 ERA. His WHIP (Walks and Hits per Innings Pitched) was 0.57, so low that it looked like a misprint but was in fact a new record for pitchers with at least 50 innings of work. At one point he retired 37 consecutive batters—effectively a perfect game plus the next ten batters.

The slightly built 6'2", 195-pound Uehara was a workhorse in 2013, pitching 88 innings. Thirteen of them were pressure-packed postseason outings where he posted one win and three saves. He captured the 2013 ALCS MVP for his outstanding performance in his five appearances against the Detroit Tigers to get the Red Sox into the World Series.

He continued to dominate in the World Series, equaling the postseason record for saves by notching his seventh. Appropriately he was on the mound and delivered the final pitch—a strikeout—in Game Six of the 2013 World Series for the champion Red Sox.

****

We are pleased to present this definitive history of the Boston Red Sox in World Series play. Like all history books it is inevitable that it will one day be rendered incomplete. We sincerely hope that date is not far off and that we are soon sent scurrying back to our keyboards to add additional chapters to the long and glorious record of the Boston Red Sox.

BIBLIOGRAPHY

Abrams, Roger, *The First World Series and the Baseball Fanatics of 1903* (Boston: Northeastern University Press, 2003)

Alexander, Charles C., *Spoke: A Biography of Tris Speaker* (Dallas: Southern Methodist University Press, 2007)

Bevis, Charlie, *Jimmy Collins: A Baseball Life* (Jefferson, NC: McFarland, 2012)

Boston Globe, *Believe It* (Chicago: Triumph Books, 2004)

Boston Globe, *For Boston: From Worst to First, The improbable Dream of the 2013 Red Sox* (Chicago: Triumph Books, 2013)

Boston Globe, *So Good! The Incredible Championship Season of the 2007 Red Sox* (Chicago: Triumph, 2007)

Boston Herald, *Boston Red Sox, 2004 World Champions* (Champaign, IL: Sports Publishing, 2004)

Boston Herald, *Boston Red Sox, 2007 World Series Champions* (Champaign, IL: Sports Publishing, 2007)

Bradlee, Ben Jr., *The Kid: The Immortal Life of Ted Williams* (New York: Little, Brown, 2013)

Browning, Reed, *Cy Young* (Amherst, MA: University of Massachusetts Press, 2000)

Burgess, Chuck and Bill Nowlin, *Love That Dirty Water: The Standells and the Improbable Boston Red Sox Anthem* (Burlington, MA: Rounder Books, 2007)

Castiglione, Joe with Douglas B. Lyons, *Can You Believe It? 50 Years of Insider Stories with the Boston Red Sox* (Chicago: Triumph Books, 2012)

Cataneo, David, *Tony C.* (Nashville: Rutledge Hill Press, 1997)

Coleman, Ken with Dan Valenti, *The Impossible Dream Remembered* (Lexington, MA: Stephen Greene Press, 1987)

Corbett, Bernard, *March to the World Series: The 1986 Boston Red Sox* (Boston: Quinlan Press, 1986)

Crehan, Herb and James W. Ryan, *Lightning in A Bottle* (Boston: Branden, 1992)

Editors of Major League Baseball, *2013 World Series Champions: Boston Red Sox* (Toronto: Fenn, M&S, 2013)

Femia, Vin, *The Possible Dream* (Worcester, MA: Chandler House Press, 2004)

Francona, Terry and Dan Shaughnessy, *Francona: The Red Sox Years* (Boston: Houghton Mifflin Harcourt, 2013)

Frommer, Harvey and Frederic J. Frommer, *Red Sox vs. Yankees: The Great Rivalry* (Champaign, IL: Sports Publishing LLC, 2004)

Frost, Mark, *Game Six: Cincinnati, Boston, and the 1975 World Series: The Triumph of America's Pastime* (New York: Hyperion, 2009)

Gammons, Peter, *Beyond the Sixth Game* (Lexington, MA: Stephen Greene, 1986)

Golenbock, Peter, *Red Sox Nation* (Chicago: Triumph, 2005)—an updated version of his book *Fenway*

Gorman, Lou, *One Pitch from Glory* (Champaign, IL: Sports Publishing, 2005)

Hafen, Lyman, *Flood Street to Fenway: The Bruce Hurst Story* (St. George, UT: Publisher's Place, 1987)

Hirshberg, Al, *What's the Matter with the Red Sox?* (New York: Dodd, Mead, 1973)

Holley, Michael, *Red Sox Rule* (New York: Harper Entertainment, 2008)

Hubbard, Donald J., *The Red Sox Before the Babe: Boston's Early Days in the American League, 1901-1914* (Jefferson, NC: McFarland, 2009)

Keene, Kerry, Raymond Sinabaldi and David Hickey, *The Babe in Red Stockings* (Champaign, IL: Sagamore, 1997)

Linn, Ed, *The Great Rivalry* (New York: Ticknor and Fields, 1991)

Massarotti, Tony, *Dynasty: The Inside Story of How the Red Sox Became a Baseball Powerhouse* (New York: St. Martin's, 2008)

Massarotti, Tony and John Harper, *A Tale of Two Cities: The 2004 Yankees-Red Sox Rivalry and the War for the Pennant* (Guilford, CT: Lyons Press, 2005)

Masur, Louis P., *Autumn Glory* (New York: Hill & Wang, 2003)

McSweeney, Bill, *The Impossible Dream* (New York: Coward-McCann, 1968)

Mnookin, Seth, *Feeding the Monster* (New York: Simon & Schuster, 2006)

Montville, Leigh, *Ted Williams* (New York: Doubleday, 2004)

Montville, Leigh, *Why Not Us?* (New York: Public Affairs, 2004)

Nash, Peter J., *Boston's Royal Rooters* (Charleston, SC: Arcadia, 2005)

Nowlin, Bill and Jim Prime, *Fenway Park at 100: Baseball's Hometown* (New York: Sports Publishing, 2012)

Nowlin, Bill, *Mr. Red Sox: The Johnny Pesky Story, 1919-2012* (Cambridge, MA: Rounder Books, 2004)

Nowlin, Bill, ed., *Opening Fenway Park in Style: The 1912 Boston Red Sox* (Phoenix, AZ: Society for American Baseball Research, 2012)

Nowlin, Bill., ed., with Mark Armour, Len Levin, and Allan Wood, *When Boston Still Had the Babe: The 1918 World Champion Red* Sox (Burlington, MA: Rounder Books, 2008)

Nowlin, Bill and Jim Prime, *Blood Feud: The Red Sox, The Yankees, and the Struggle of Good versus Evil* (Cambridge, MA: Rounder Books, 2005)

Nowlin, Bill and Dan Desrochers, *The 1967 Impossible Dream Red Sox* (Burlington, MA: Rounder Books, 2007)

Nowlin, Bill and Cecilia Tan, eds., *'75: The Red Sox Team that Saved Baseball* (Cambridge, MA: Rounder Books, 2005)

O'Nan, Stewart and Stephen King, *Faithful* (New York: Scribner, 2004)

Ortiz, David with Tony Massarotti, *Big Papi: My Story of Big Dreams and Big Hits* (New York: St. Martin's, 2007)

Pahigian, Joshua R., *The Red Sox in the Playoffs* (Jefferson, NC: McFarland & Co. Inc., 2006)

Pedroia, Dustin with Edward J. Delaney, *Born to Play: My Life in the Game* (New York: Simon Spotlight, 2009)

Petrocelli, Rico and Chaz Scoggins, *Tales from the Impossible Dream Red Sox* (Champaign, IL: Sports Publishing LLC, 2007)

Prime, Jim, *Amazing Tales from the 2004 Boston Red Sox Dugout* (New York: Sports Publishing, 2014)

Prime, Jim and Bill Nowlin, *Amazing Tales from the Red Sox Dugout* (New York: Sports Publishing, 2012)

Prime, Jim and Bill Nowlin, *Ted Williams: The Pursuit of Perfection* (Champaign, IL: Sports Publishing LLC, 2002)

Reynolds, Bill, *Lost Summer: The '67 Red Sox and the Impossible Dream* (New York: Warner Books, 1992)

Ryan, Bob, *When Boston Won the World Series* (Philadelphia: Running Press, 2003)

Shaughnessy, Dan, *The Curse of the Bambino* (New York: Penguin, 1991)

Shaughnessy, Dan, *One Strike Away* (New York: Beaufort, 1987)

Shaughnessy, Dan, *Reversing the Curse* (Boston: Houghton Mifflin, 2004)

Simmons, Bill, *Now I Can Die in Peace* (New York: ESPN Books, 2005)

The Sporting News, *Curse Reversed* (St. Louis: Sporting News Books, 2004)

Stout, Glenn, *Fenway 1912: The Birth of a Ballpark, a Championship Season, and Fenway's Remarkable First Year* (Boston and New York: Houghton Mifflin Harcourt, 2012)

Stout, Glenn and Richard Johnson, *Red Sox Century* (Boston: Houghton Mifflin, 2004)

Sullivan, George, *The Picture History of the Boston Red Sox* (Indianapolis: Bobbs-Merrill, 1979)

Sullivan, Robert, *Our Red Sox* (Cincinnati, OH: Emmis Books, 2005)

Tan, Cecilia, and Bill Nowlin, *The 50 Greatest Red Sox Games* (New York: John Wiley, 2006)

Whalen, Thomas J., *When the Red Sox Ruled: Baseball's First Dynasty, 1912-1918* (Chicago: Ivan R. Dee, 2011)

Williams, Dick and Bill Plaschke, *No More Mr. Nice Guy* (New York: Harcourt, Brace, Jovanovich, 1990)

Williams, Ted and Jim Prime, *Ted Williams' Hit List* (Indianapolis: Masters Press, 1996)

Williams, Ted with John Underwood, *My Turn At Bat* (New York: Fireside, 1988)

Wood, Allan and Bill Nowlin, *Don't Let Us Win Tonight—An Oral History of the 2004 Boston Red Sox's Impossible Playoff Run* (Chicago: Triumph Books, 2014)

Wood, Gerald C., *Smoky Joe Wood: The Biography of A Baseball Legend* (Lincoln, NE: University of Nebraska Press, 2013)

Yastrzemski, Carl, *Yastrzemski* (New York: Rugged Land, 2007)

Yastrzemski, Carl and Gerald Eskenazi, *Yaz: Baseball, The Wall and Me* (NY: Doubleday, 1990)

Yastrzemski, Carl and Al Hirshberg, *Yaz* (New York: Viking, 1968)

Zingg, Paul J., *Harry Hooper* (Urbana, IL: University of Illinois Press, 1993)